Praise fo

"Terrifically entertainin
—*The New York Times*

"Riveting cultural history."
—*Vanity Fair*

"Friedman . . . eschews easy laughs. Instead, he delivers substance and wit, ranging confidently over a huge amount of material with just the right tongue-in-cheek distance."
—Daniel Mendelsohn, *New York Magazine*

"Friedman's opus blends utterly enjoyable entertainment and commendable scholarship; the language is lucid and unpretentious; the topics are developed thoroughly without incurring pedantry; and the humor . . . is as welcome as it is restrained."
—F. Gonzalez-Crussi, M.D., *The Washington Post Book World*

"[F]requently sharp and funny."
—*Newsday*

"A model of its kind."
—*Kirkus Reviews*

"This is exactly the type of book I love . . . intelligent, literary, and fascinating."
—Lucy Grealy, author of *Autobiography of a Face*

"This is cultural and intellectual history at its engrossing, entertaining, and illuminating best."
—Ben Yagoda, author of *About Town*

"With equal parts candor and finesse, Friedman disassembles widely believed myths about the slithering sex snake."
—*Orange County Weekly*

## ABOUT THE AUTHOR

David M. Friedman has written for *Esquire*, *GQ*, *Rolling Stone*, *Vogue*, *The Village Voice*, and many other publications. He was a reporter for *Newsday* and the *Philadelphia Daily News*. He lives in New York City.

# A Mind
## of Its
# Own

A CULTURAL HISTORY OF THE PENIS

David M. Friedman

PENGUIN BOOKS

PENGUIN BOOKS

Published by the Penguin Group

Penguin Putnam Inc., 375 Hudson Street,
New York, New York 10014, U.S.A.
Penguin Books Ltd, 80 Strand, London WC2R 0RL, England
Penguin Books Australia Ltd, 250 Camberwell Road,
Camberwell, Victoria 3124, Australia
Penguin Books Canada Ltd, 10 Alcorn Avenue,
Toronto, Ontario, Canada M4V 3B2
Penguin Books India (P) Ltd, 11 Community Centre,
Panchsheel Park, New Delhi – 110 017, India
Penguin Books (N.Z.) Ltd, Cnr Rosedale and Airborne Roads,
Albany, Auckland, New Zealand
Penguin Books (South Africa) (Pty) Ltd, 24 Sturdee Avenue,
Rosebank, Johannesburg 2196, South Africa

Penguin Books Ltd, Registered Offices:
Harmondsworth, Middlesex, England

First published in the United States of America by The Free Press,
a division of Simon & Schuster, Inc. 2001
Published in Penguin Books 2003

1  3  5  7  9  10  8  6  4  2

THE LIBRARY OF CONGRESS HAS CATALOGED
THE HARDCOVER EDITION AS FOLLOWS:
Friedman, David M., 1949–
A mind of its own : a cultural history of the penis / David M. Friedman.
p.   cm.
Includes bibliographical references and index.
ISBN 0-684-85320-5 (hc.)
ISBN 0 14 20.0259 3 (pbk.)
1. Penis—Social aspects.   2. Penis—History.   I. Title.
GT498.P45 F75 2001      200104528
573.6'56—dc21

Printed in the United States of America
Designed by Jeanette Olender
Picture research by Natalie Goldstein

For Jack G. Friedman

# CONTENTS

# A Mind *of Its* Own

# I

## The Demon Rod

Unlike her life, Anna Pappenheimer's death was a public event. Residents of Munich by the thousands rubbed shoulders to witness it, forming a circle on a hill outside the city's main gate. Boys squeezed through the snorting horses that gave the chief magistrate and other dignitaries a perch above the bustling throng. Pickpockets worked their trade and more righteous entrepreneurs sold pamphlets citing the crimes and blasphemies that led this wife of an itinerant outhouse cleaner to be condemned to the fate that now awaited her. Pappenheimer probably welcomed her death: Minutes earlier the fifty-nine-year-old mother of three had been dragged from her jail cell, site of her confession, to the square in front of Town Hall, where a tub of burning coal was tended by two young men. An older man in a black hood and leather gloves stepped forward and grabbed tongs that had been thrust deep into that fiery mass. He tore open Pappenheimer's shirt. He used the glowing pincers to tear off her breasts. As the crowd gasped, the screaming woman was thrown into a cart normally used to haul manure. Heralded by pealing church bells, Pappenheimer's death procession set off for the hill beyond the city walls. There her limp, bloody body was tied to a chair and carried atop a large pyre. "Lord Jesus, for Thee I live," said a priest. *"Lord Jesus, for Thee I live,"* echoed the faithful. The hooded man threw lit torches into the woodpile. Smoke and cinders began to rise. Dogs, excited by the smells, began to bark and leap into the air. The crowd met Pappenheimer's screams with cheers. From a distance it looked like a carnival.

Anna Pappenheimer was one of thousands of women killed during the witch hunts that reached their grisly peak between the fourteenth and seventeenth centuries. Some of those killed were accused of causing crop failures, others of performing abortions. But there was one crime that virtually all the women confessed to after torture, beginning with the first "documented" witch to be executed in public, the Frenchwoman Angela de la Barthe, in 1275. That crime was knowledge of the Devil's penis.

Pappenheimer's education took place in a Bavarian barley field. A black-garbed stranger approached her there, doffed his hat, and treated the impoverished woman with courtesy. "What a fine day, madam," he said. "It will soon be spring, don't you think?" Pappenheimer looked away. "Don't pretend you do not know me," the man said. "I am Lucifer, sometimes called 'The Evil One.' Yet I can be a good friend to those who trust me." He gently stroked Pappenheimer's face; soon she was feeling lust unlike any she had ever known. Pappenheimer shuddered when his penis entered her. It felt, she later told the Inquisitor, "as cold as a piece of ice."

The Devil's penis was the obsession of every Inquisitor and the "star" of nearly every witch's confession. The women invariably said it was cold but there was disagreement on other details. Some located his penis at his rear. Some said he had two, others that it was forked. Most reported it was black and covered with scales. Several said "there was nothing where scrotum and testicles should be hanging." One likened the Devil's penis to that of a mule, which the Evil One constantly exposed, so proud was he of its massive size and shape. The Devil's ejaculate was said to exceed that of one thousand men. But others claimed his penis was smaller than a finger and not even as thick. This led a French Inquisitor to guess that Satan served some witches better than others.

These confessions say something about the fantasies of

women, but they reveal much more about the anxieties of men, especially those regarding their defining organ. Five centuries ago women were not merely thought sexually insatiable; it was believed they could make a man impotent, or even make his penis disappear. The *Malleus Maleficarum,* the definitive guide for witch hunters published in 1486, wrote of a woman who stole dozens of penises, then hid them in a tree where they lived like birds in a nest. So tentative was man's belief in his phallic integrity during this era that some men strutted about in a cod-piece, an often brightly colored cover for the crotch in men's breeches padded and molded in the shape of a permanent erec-tion. "The first piece in the arming of a warrior," Rabelais called it. The gap between what those soldiers in the battle of the sexes advertised—and what was actually there—speaks vol-umes about the defining issue of that conflict which, throughout history, has often been deadly for women. In 1536 King Henry VIII, owner of the largest cod in England, beheaded his second wife, Anne Boleyn, a former courtesan whom he denounced as a sorceress after he lost the interest—or was it the erectile abil-ity?—to continue their sexual relations.

What can explain the victimization of Anne Boleyn, Anna Pappenheimer, and the other women, of high and low station alike, who suffered as they did? Misogyny, in all its subtle and beastly expressions, likely provides the overall answer. But a more tightly focused lens enables us to see in their deaths the predominance of one of the driving forces—the ongoing cul-tural obsession with the penis, the insecurities it fostered, and the perceived harm it could do. We can see how it became, through the mix of fevered fantasy and obsessive insecurity, the very agent of the transfer of evil. In short, the demon rod.

How did the penis come to be so demonized? Today, when even married men of the cloth take erection-enhancing drugs prescribed by their physicians, the idea that man saw his defin-ing organ as a tool of the Devil seems hard to believe. No one was born believing that. But there is something in the mind of

Western man, an uneasiness about his link with his penis—a word defined here not merely as the penile shaft and glans, but encompassing the testes, sperm, and all the other parts and products of the male genitalia—that made Western man receptive to that distortion. To tell the story of how that relationship came to be seen as corrupting, we must have a conversation with the dead. A dialogue is possible only if we understand the world as they understood it.

The priests and politicians who persecuted Anna Pappenheimer did not see the body as a temple. For them it was a flimsy vessel for a churning stew of vile processes—sex, defecation, urination, and vomiting—which was constantly erupting. The most obscene of this effluvia was semen; the polluted spigot through which it emerged was the penis. These ideas, spread by the Fathers of the Church, were conceived more than a thousand years before scientists figured out the physiology of erections, more than a thousand years before a sperm cell was sighted under a microscope, more than a thousand years before there was *any* detailed grasp of the biology of sex. The same gulf also awaited a discussion of libido or the unconscious, penis envy or castration anxiety. All sexual behavior seemed a mystery. At the center of this enigma stood the penis and, like many mysteries, this one was deemed sinister.

The Christian idea of the polluted spigot was an effort to define the undefinable, to grasp the universal law behind man's relationship with his penis and the "control" issues it raised. A man can hold his manhood in his hand, but who is really gripping whom? Is the penis the best in man—or the beast? Is man in charge of his penis or is his penis in charge of him? How is he supposed to use it? And when does that use become abuse? Of all the bodily organs only the penis forces man to confront such contradictions: something insistent yet reluctant, occasionally poetic, other times pathetic, a tool that creates but also destroys, a part of the body that often seems *apart* from the body. This is the conundrum that makes the penis hero and villain both in a drama that shapes every man. And mankind along with it.

Augustine, the sainted Bishop of Hippo, found his answer sixteen centuries ago in man's lack of control. It was a proof of man's alienation from the sacred, and a punishment for Adam's insult of God in Eden that original sin passed from one generation to the next through semen. In a culture where the Virgin symbolized all that was pure, the penis stood for all that was evil. What defined Mary's sanctity was her lack of contact with a penis.

As vexing as the male organ clearly could be, it was not thought of as a demon rod by the pagan cultures that preceded Western Christendom. It was seen as many things, both noble and coarse. The penis was an icon of creativity; it was the link between the human and the sacred, an agent of bodily and spiritual ecstasy that hinted of communion with the eternal. Yet it was also a weapon against women, children, and weaker men. It was a force of nature, revered for its potency, yet just as amoral. It tied man to the cosmic energy that covered the fields each year with new herds and crops—and just as often destroyed them. The organ's "animal" urgency didn't trouble the ancients. Didn't the gods combine the human and the savage in their own *amours*? All these complexities and contradictions, the very unpredictability of life itself, were embodied by one body part above all in antiquity—the penis.

That's "penis," not "phallus." The latter is a perfectly apt word for the erect organ and all the symbolic meanings that attach to that state. Unfortunately, it has often been used to cloak or "clean up" the word "penis," something I believe to be unnecessary. Because of recent incidents involving Bill Clinton and John Bobbitt, to name but two, the word "penis" has appeared in more mainstream media outlets, and been said in conversations around more watercoolers, than ever before. This book hopes to further that trend in a less prosecutorial context, sharing the conviction of another writer who investigated the cultural aspects of the penis more than four centuries ago.

"Whoever could make Man grow out of an over-nice dread of words," wrote Michel de Montaigne, "would do no great harm to this world."

───────────

From the beginnings of Western civilization the penis was more than a body part. It was an idea, a conceptual but flesh-and-blood gauge of man's place in the world. That men have a penis is a scientific fact; how they think about it, feel about it, and use it is not. Ideas of the penis vary from culture to culture and from one era to the next. It is possible to identify the key moments in Western history when a new idea of the penis addressed the larger mystery of man's relationship with it and changed forever the way that organ was conceived of and put to use.

Evidence of one of the oldest of those ideas was found in the ruins of the Sumerian city of Eridu, in the south of modern Iraq, where archaeologists unearthed cuneiform tablets more than five thousand years old. The penis symbolized both irrational nature and divine intelligence in this ancient civilization. It was a mystery, the unknowable god within, and this idea was expressed in core religious beliefs. Much of the literature found in Eridu, composed in the world's first written language, celebrates the exploits of the god Enki. Typically drawn as a large bearded man wearing a cap with many horns, Enki was mankind's great benefactor, the "Determiner of Destinies" and "Organizer of the Universe," who, in the Gilgamesh epic, helps to save man from the flood sent by other gods. Because Sumer was (and Iraq still is) an arid region between the Tigris and Euphrates Rivers, two waterways prone to flooding, water was both a precious and, at times, dangerous substance in this "cradle of civilization." Without irrigation from those rivers, survival was impossible. Whoever gave life to those rivers was the very *idea* of life. Poetry from the third millennium B.C. identifies that creative force as Enki—more accurately, Enki's penis:

> After Father Enki lifted his eyes over the Euphrates,
> He stood up full of lust like an attacking bull,
> Lifted his penis, ejaculated,
> Filled the Euphrates with flowing water.

Six lines later Enki does the same for the Tigris:

> He lifted his penis, he brought the bridal gifts,
> Like a great wild bull he thrilled the heart of the Tigris,
> [And stood by] as it gave birth.

In other poem cycles, Enki uses his penis to dig the world's first irrigation ditches, invents human sexual reproduction, and fathers the first human baby, after which he exults, "Let now my penis be praised!"

This ecstatic, life-creating idea of the penis was shared by the Egyptians, whose gods made similar boasts. In hieroglyphs written four thousand years ago inside the pyramids, one Egyptian deity and his penis provide an intriguing alternative to the current Big Bang theory of the universe's origin. "I created on my own every being," says the god Atum. "My fist became my spouse. I copulated with my hand." Atum's penis creates all life, divine and mortal, through this act of sacred masturbation, starting with the god of air and the goddess of moisture, who emerge whole from his semen. These gods mate and give birth to Geb, god of the Earth, and Nut, goddess of the sky. The mating of this divine couple is seen on many ancient papyri. These drawings show a naked Nut arching over the Earth god, who is on his back, his erect penis pointing skyward. For Egyptians this was not pornography; it was a religious map of their universe.

Once a year Pharaoh, the Egyptian king, paid homage to another perpetually erect god—Min, god of procreation. "Hail to thee, Min, that made his mother to bear!" said Pharaoh, in a prayer marking the belief that this god was so potent he fathered himself. After Pharaoh praised Min at his Theban temple for granting him sons, the god's statue was placed on a platform carried by shaved-headed priests in white linen. Min was always sculpted standing so as to make his huge penis all the more visible. In solemn procession behind this statue walked Pharaoh and his queen, followed by a white bull, a beast thought to be Min incarnate, and more holy men carrying lettuce, a plant whose milky sap, symbolic of Min's semen, was deemed sacred.

The sacredness of the penis was the central idea in Egypt's most important myth, a story that established the Egyptian belief in the Afterlife and the divine bloodline of Pharaoh. This is the myth of Osiris and Isis, the brother and sister who ruled as king and queen of Egypt in the first age of the world. Osiris handed down a code of laws and taught his people to cultivate grain. Isis identified the medicinal properties of herbs and invented the loom. They were loved by their subjects but hated by their jealous brother Seth, who tricked Osiris into lying inside a chest, which Seth's henchmen then threw into the Nile. Isis found Osiris's corpse, but Seth recaptured it, tearing the body into fourteen pieces and scattering them throughout the kingdom. After a long search Isis located all but the king's penis.

In one version of the myth, the queen took what she found and fashioned it into a whole, making the first mummy. Then she made herself into a hawk and hovered over the crotch of her dead mate, using the flapping of her wings to bring forth a new penis. Isis lowered herself onto this magically reconstituted organ and received Osiris's seed. The child of this union was Horus, from whom all Pharaohs claimed descent. To avenge his father's death, Horus eventually killed and emasculated Osiris's murderer, Seth. According to Plutarch, the Greek who visited Egypt near the turn of the first century, a statue in Koptos showed Horus holding up his trophy—Seth's penis—in his hand. Later another resurrection story would be preached in nearby Judea, then throughout the entire Mediterranean basin, about a man born of God and a virgin who lived a life of chastity that offered a direct path to personal salvation, if one

believed the Son of God had risen from the dead. In Egypt a sacred myth preached the salvation of an entire culture through
the death and rebirth of a god's penis.

That magic organ, so potent it defeated death, dominated the
Egyptian Afterlife. The re-membered Osiris flaunted his virility
in the Underworld, where he ruled as king: "I am Osiris . . . stiff
of penis . . . . I am mightier than the Lord of Terror; I copulate
and I have power over myriads," he says in *The Egyptian Book
of the Dead*. By contrast, a spell against a serpent in the *Book*
says, "You shall not become erect. You shall not copulate." The
link between impotence and defeat had grim real-life consequences for Egypt's enemies on the battlefield. Proof was inscribed in the walls of Karnak, circa 1200 B.C., by Pharaoh
Merneptah, after a triumph over the Libyans:

Penises of Libyan generals: 6
Penises cut off Libyans: 6,359
Sicilians killed, penises cut off: 222
Etruscans killed, penises cut off: 542
Greeks killed, penises given to the king: 6,111

Three thousand years later, an American president would show
how powerful this linkage still could be in the mind of a leader.
Robert Dallek writes in *Flawed Giant: Lyndon Johnson and His
Times, 1961–1973* of an unforgettable off-the-record encounter
between President Johnson and skeptical reporters pressing him
to explain why the United States was still fighting in Vietnam.
Frustrated that his political reasoning was not convincing his
listeners, the president unzipped his pants, pulled out his penis,
and said, "*This* is why!"

A wall relief even older than Pharaoh Merneptah's shows
that Egyptians put the knife to their own penises. Found in
1889 at the Saqqara necropolis on the West Bank of the Nile,
across from the ancient site of Memphis, the sculpture shows a
man kneeling in front of a boy. The child's hands are restrained

by the man's assistant, who stands behind the boy. In his left hand the circumciser holds the child's penis, the foreskin extended. In his right hand he grips a small knife.

"Hold him, that he might not faint," the man says, in hieroglyphics. "Do your best," says the assistant.

This terse exchange, dated circa 2400 B.C., proves that circumcision has a long history in Egypt. Herodotus, the Greek "Father of History," who visited Egypt around 450 B.C., thought his hosts invented the rite. In the early twentieth century, anthropologist Grafton Elliot Smith concurred, writing that circumcision was part of a sun-worshiping cult that began in the Nile Valley fifteen thousand years ago and was then copied by neighboring peoples. The Old Testament's Book of Jeremiah mentions that Edomites, Moabites, and Ammonites—neighbors of the Egyptians and Israelites alike—practiced circumcision. Whether they learned it from the Egyptians is unknown. Some of Smith's colleagues argued that, instead of being born in Egypt, the rite began as a quasi-universal mark of slavery or the defilement of military prisoners. Maybe the only thing not in dispute is Herodotus's loathing of the practice, a view shared by all Greeks. "Other peoples leave their genitals as they were at birth," Herodotus wrote. The Egyptians say they "prefer to be clean [rather] than of seemly appearance."

Much of that Egyptian fastidiousness focused on body openings. One healer whose name has survived from Pharaonic times is Iri, Keeper of the Royal Rectum, who worked as Pharaoh's colonic irrigation specialist. Egyptians were extremely concerned with the free flow of natural excretions and may have started removing the foreskin because, in their hot climate, it often harbored smegma, sebaceous matter that could potentially impede the flow of urine and semen. But it is also possible that Egyptian circumcision was less about cleanliness than godliness. Although the rite existed in all social classes, it was required only of temple priests as a sign of affiliation with the sun god Re, who circumcised himself in an act described in *The Book of the Dead.* This created an unexpected dilemma for the Greek philosopher Pythagoras when he traveled to Egypt about 550 B.C. While visiting an Egyptian temple, Pythagoras asked to see the sacred books stored within. The chief priest agreed but with one condition: first the Greek had to have his foreskin cut off.

For the Hebrews, circumcision and the relationship it established among man, his penis, and God was a divinely mandated sign of affiliation with the Almighty—and with themselves. It was required not of priests alone, but of every Israelite male on the eighth day of life. The theological origins are spelled out in Genesis, where God offers a covenant to Abraham (née Abram), then ninety-nine years old, and his "seed." This covenant establishes the Almighty as sole deity of the Hebrews, who are promised a homeland in Canaan, where they will be "exceedingly fruitful," even Abraham, who is told that he, too, will once again become a father. The ancient desert dweller can only chortle at such a prospect. "Shall a child be born," he asks, "to a man who is a hundred years old?" This is no problem for God, of course, but in return he requires a sign: "Every male among you shall be circumcised. You shall be circumcised in the flesh of your foreskins, and it shall be a sign of the covenant between me and you." The Torah reports Abraham quickly cut off the foreskin from himself and every male that was born in his house, and all that were "bought with [his] money." (Left out is the reaction of those men and boys when this wizened goatherd emerged from his tent with a bloody stone in his hand and loudly declared what God had just commanded him to do.)

This strange commandment and the monotheistic covenant it sealed would have a lasting and controversial impact. Abraham, who was the father of Ishmael (founder of the Arab nation) as well as the Jewish patriarch Isaac, is revered by the Koran as "a guide for the people." Abraham circumcised Ishmael; consequently, Muslims also circumcise their males. (Many tribes in Africa, as well as Australian Aboriginals, practice circumcision with no link at all to the Old Testament.) Jewish circumcision, by spiritualizing the penis's procreative purpose, redefined the relationship between man and his defining organ. In return for becoming the father of God's Chosen People and a blessing of fertility that guaranteed the Israelites' eternal existence, Abraham agreed to worship no other deity and to cut off his foreskin. This act symbolically altered his penis, permanently exposing the glans—as happens when a noncircumcised penis is erect—a cosmetic change that has no effect on the organ's reproductive functioning. Some have argued that, by mimicking erection in this way, circumcision reveals the Hebrews to have been an early phallic cult. (This is not a widely held view.) Others note that Maimonides, the most influential Jewish thinker of the Middle Ages, declared the act's true purpose to be "decreas[ing] sexual intercourse" and "weakening the organ in question" so that Jews would serve God ahead of their own lusts. (Modern anti-circumcision activists make a similar argument on secular grounds: the operation, they say, removes much of the penile fine-touch neuroreceptors.) That the penis of Abraham would not "weaken," however, was clearly an essential part of the original agreement. We know that vigor was no problem for Abraham after his auto-circumcision, even after he celebrated his hundredth birthday. Not only did Sarah give birth to Isaac, as promised, but after Sarah's death Abraham took a much younger mate, Keturah, and produced yet another family.

Clearly, circumcision "worked" for Abraham. But its enduring fascination for religious scholars, historians, anthropologists, anti-Semites, public-health specialists, and even the zeal with which contemporary anti-circumcision crusaders now attack it, shows that circumcision "works" on many other levels as well. Few other rituals can match it for inherent contradictory psychological complexities—something physical yet not physiological, sexual without being erotic, not genetic but ge-nealogical, a mark but not a birthmark, made at the very place that distinguishes man from woman. This act of divine gender bias even makes sense to a leading feminist. "What is more log-ical and appropriate," Gerda Lerner asks in *The Creation of Pa-triarchy*, "than to use as the leading symbol of the covenant the organ which produces the seed and which plants it in the female womb? . . . The offering of no other part of the body could have sent so vivid a message to man of the connection between his re-productive capacity and the grace of God."

Some Old Testament passages, however, make circumcision a metaphor for holiness that can apply to any body part, as when Deuteronomy calls upon each child of Israel to "circumcise [your] heart." But there can be no doubt as to the authentic site of circumcision's meaning. The link between man and the most awesome mystery in the universe—God—was sealed by mark-ing the organ with whom man has his most awesome and mys-terious relationship: the penis.

———————

Not many of the Israelites' neighbors or conquerors saw it that way, however. The Greeks loathed Jewish circumcision every bit as much as they did that of the Egyptians. This presented a problem two millennia ago for socially ambitious Jews in Alexandria, Egypt, then the cultural center of the Hellenized world. If a Jew wanted to exercise in the gymnasium, the coun-try club of Greek society, where training was invariably done without wearing clothes, he knew his circumcised penis would offend Greek aesthetics. This was not because Greeks were un-comfortable with nudity—far from it. But the sight of the ex-posed glans was deemed unseemly by Greeks. For this reason, Greeks exercised naked, but with their penises "infibulated"—a process that pulled the foreskin forward over the glans, and then tied it closed with string or clasped it shut with a circular safety-pin-like instrument known as a fibula.

According to the Book of Maccabees in the Apocrypha, some Jews from the second and first centuries B.C. "remove[d] their marks of circumcision and repudiate[d] the Holy Covenant" in order to pass as Greeks. Most of them probably tried the *Pondus Judaeus,* a funnel-shaped weight made of bronze or copper that was attached to the penile shaft above the glans. The heavy metal then pulled and stretched the shaft skin forward to cover the glans. That was the hope, anyway: writing in 1999 in the *British Journal of Urology International,* Drs. S. B. Brandes and J. W. McAninch said, "It is difficult to see how this technique could have produced any durable success."

Some Hellenized Jews tried the surgical remedy known as *epipasmos,* Greek for "pull over." Two such procedures were described by the first-century medical writer Celsus in *De medicina* (*On Medicine*). Both required delicate incisions into the skin of the penis, which was pulled forward and over the glans. When the popularity of these operations began to spread, rabbis changed the circumcision laws. Where before it was necessary only to remove the distal part of the foreskin, an act that merely shortened the prepuce, rules promulgated around the year 140 required that the glans be left totally uncovered. This made *epipasmos* nearly impossible. (Even so, quite a few desperate Jews underwent the operation during the Nazi era.)

Some Greeks were more appalled by circumcision than others. Antiochus Ephiphanes, a descendant of one of Alexander the Great's greatest generals, turned his contempt into murderous rage when he ruled Judea. *Mohels,* the rabbis who performed circumcision, were stoned or fed to wild dogs. Mothers who permitted their sons to be circumcised were "garroted, their strangled infants strung about their necks, then hanged upon crosses as a terrible warning to others," the Book of Maccabees reports. According to the *Pesiqta de Rab Kahana,* a collection of traditional Jewish legends written centuries later, things were even worse during the reign of the Roman emperor Hadrian: Roman soldiers "would cut off the circumcised organ of generation from live Israelites and fling it heavenwards, taunting God: 'Is *this* what you have chosen?'"

Clearly, circumcision was a sign that brought Jews suffering as well as a special relationship with the Almighty. But there is no doubt that Abraham, by making that mark and that commitment, believed he was placing his penis in the service of God. Other ancient cultures placed the penises of the gods in service to them. Phallocentric myths such as the life-giving, universe-creating masturbations of Enki and Atum were staples of their religious literature. The penis of the Hindu god Siva is a key player in so much of that religion's sacred works that a book on Hindu aesthetics declares that Siva riding on a bull must be portrayed with an erection reaching his navel. Buddha was said to have a retractable member resembling that of a horse. But the Old Testament has no discussion of God's penis because the Hebrew god has no body. Instead, the focus is on the human penis, the mysterious organ spiritualized by God.

And that mysterious organ must be fully functioning. The Old Testament declares, "He whose testicles are crushed or whose male member is cut off shall not enter the assembly of the Lord." Rabbis had to show those parts were in working order before they could lead a temple. This same demonstration was later required of Catholic priests—even of the Pope. "On the 11th August, 1492, after Rodrigo [Borgia] assumed the name of Alexander VI, and made his entrance into the Church of St. Peter," British historian William Roscoe wrote, "he was taken aside to undergo the final test of his qualifications, which in this instance they might have dispensed with." That last comment no doubt refers to the fact that Cesare Borgia, the Pope's biological son, was then one of the most famous political figures in Europe.

The "final test" alluded to by Roscoe is said to have involved a piece of furniture called the *sedina stercoraria* (dung chair). This object, which resembled an ancient commode, was designed so that when the newly elected Pope sat on it, his testicles would descend through a specially placed hole, where their existence could be verified by a cardinal specially chosen for the task. According to legend, the origin of this practice was less the Old Testament proscription against eunuchs than a ruse played on the Church in the ninth century by a cross-dressing woman who, so the story goes, briefly ruled the Church as Pope John VII. True or not, the woman is now called Pope Joan—and the chair evidently exists. So says Peter Stanford, former editor of the London *Catholic Herald,* who says he sat in the chair in a backroom of the Vatican Museum. "I plonked myself down," Stanford writes in *The She-Pope.*

> It felt like a desecration. The Vatican Museum has the aura of a church and all my childhood training revolved around not touching anything in God's house. . . . Pulse racing, white-faced, I leant back and back. . . . The keyhole shape, I noticed as I brought my spine vertical, was in precisely the right place.

In biblical Canaan this link between the penis and divine power on Earth was understood literally by some of the Israelites' neighbors. Among these other tribes, Jungian analyst Sarah Dening writes in *The Mythology of Sex,* it was not unusual for a new king to eat the penis of his predecessor to absorb his sacred authority. That this practice existed, and that it was banned by the Hebrews, Dening says, is shown in the Genesis tale in which Jacob wrestles with God who, during that struggle, "touched the hollow of [Jacob's] thigh." Because of this touch, the Bible says, "the Israelites do not eat the sinew of the hip which is upon the hollow of the thigh to this day."

They did make oaths on that thigh, however. In Genesis, Abraham orders his servant Eliezer: "Put your hand under my thigh and . . . swear by the Lord, the God of heaven and of the earth, that you will not take a wife for my son from the daughters of the Canaanites." Later Jacob, now called Israel, asks of his son Joseph, "Put your hand under my thigh, and promise to deal loyally and truly with me. Do not bury me in Egypt, but let me lie with my fathers." This is puzzling language until you realize that "thigh" was often used by Bible translators as a euphemism for "penis." In Genesis and Exodus, Jacob's children are said to spring from his "thigh." It seems clear that sacred oaths between the Israelites were sealed by placing a hand on the male member. To swear on that mysterious organ was to swear to God. Could the penis as divine idea be expressed more clearly? Though few realize it, least of all in the courtroom, this idea of swearing a sacred oath by "placing a hand under one's thigh" (on or near the testicles) survives today—nearly four thousand years later—in the word "testify."

———————

There is no evidence that the Greeks testified this way. But the touching of a boy's testes by a man was so common in classical Athens that its failure to happen was made into a joke by the playwright Aristophanes:

"Well, this is a fine state of affairs, you damned desperado," says an Athenian father to a friend in the comedy *The Birds*. "You meet my son just as he comes out of the gymnasium, all fresh from the bath, and you don't kiss him, you don't say a word to him, you don't feel his balls! And you're supposed to be a friend of ours!"

This is a strange joke to modern ears. To us, pederasty—sexual relations between a man and a boy—is child abuse and a crime. Not in ancient Greece, however. There, pederasty was an institution sanctioned by Olympian gods and mythical heroes. Zeus, Apollo, Poseidon, and Heracles all had pederastic experiences. So did many of the most illustrious real-life Greeks, including Solon, Pythagoras, Socrates, and Plato. The act was part of the foundation of an elitist, military culture that elevated the idea of the penis beyond biology and religion to the rarified heights of philosophy and art.

The penis was not merely elevated in Athens—it was exposed. Men exercised naked at the factory of Athenian manhood, the gymnasium, a word derived from *gymnos*, meaning "naked." For a freeborn Athenian, nudity affirmed his position as a citizen-warrior. It was the "Athenian civic costume," historian Larissa Bonfante writes, the same one worn by the heroes vanquishing the city's enemies on the sculpted frieze adorning the Temple of Athene Nike. Some historians believe Greek males appeared naked outside the gymnasium as well. The evidence that they did "comes from Greek sculpture and the scenes on Greek pots," Oxford University's Robin Osborne writes. He warns, however, that "the relationship between [those representations] . . . and life itself is open to discussion." The nudity at gymnasia alone was sufficient to shock visitors to Athens twenty-five hundred years ago. But Athenians reveled in being different. Vase paintings from the classical period often depict a nude Greek exposing his penis to a fully clothed woman. What we call "flashing," they called "flirting." In Athens it was the man's attractiveness that provided the sexual spark, not hers.

This reverence for the male form was embodied in the thousands of *kouroi*, statues of nude young males, that stood throughout the Greek world. Though the penis on these sculptures was flaccid, the values projected by their hard, muscular torsos were clearly ithyphallic. Other Greek statues were not as subtle. *Hermae*—stone or wood columns topped by the head of the god Hermes and marked at the midpoint by an erection—dotted the Greek landscape. The tyrant Hipparchos had *hermae* erected at the midway point of every road linking Athens with the villages of Attica. By 500 B.C., historians tell us, most Athenians had a *herm* at their front door.

These statues, which had no body parts save a head and a penis, gave shape to the Greek understanding of the penis as an idea. Greek philosophy made a distinction between form and matter. Form, which Plato also called "idea," was active, fertile, and masculine—just like the penis. Matter was passive, non-generative, and female. Like a metal stamp into wax, an idea impressed itself on matter, giving it meaning. Nowhere was this more clearly expressed than in the Greek view of conception. In *The Generation of Animals*, Aristotle compared men to carpenters and women to wood; a child was created by the carpenter out of the wood. In *Eumenides,* Aeschylus had the god Apollo make the same argument:

> The mother is not the true source of life.
> We call her mother, but she is more the nurse,
> The furrow where the seed is thrust.
> The thruster, the father, is the true parent:
> The woman but tends the growing plant.

The erect penis also symbolized Athenian power. After the Greeks defeated the Persians at Eion, in 476 B.C., the generals who led that victorious army asked to be honored with a memorial. The resulting monument took the form of three marble *hermae* built in the Agora, the marketplace and center of Athenian civic life. Greek civilization and the victory that preserved it were symbolized by three stone erections. This is why one summer morning in 415 B.C. was so traumatic. Hours before an attacking Athenian army was to depart for Sicily, someone smashed off the erections on hundreds of the city's *hermae.* Whether this was a drunken prank or, as historian Eva Keuls writes in *The Reign of the Phallus,* an antiwar protest by Athenian women, there is no disputing the event's meaning to Athenian men. The city woke up to see itself emasculated—a terrifying omen. That the Sicilian invasion failed and ultimately hastened Athens's defeat by Sparta only confirmed those beliefs.

This Greek link between the penis and power was noted circa 275 B.C. by Kallixeinos of Rhodes, who left behind an eyewitness account of a Dionysian festival in Alexandria in which a "golden phallus, 180 feet long" and topped by a gold star was carried through the streets of that city as a half million people listened to poems sung in its honor. Preceding that golden erection, which if vertical would top a modern twenty-story building, were ten rows of ostriches ridden by boys dressed as satyrs, scores of adult Ethiopians hoisting elephant tusks, dozens of strutting peacocks, sixteen cheetahs, fourteen leopards, one white bear, one rhino, and a giraffe. Following the giant sacred penis was a golden statue of Zeus and more than fifty thousand foot soldiers.

Obviously, a Greek contemplated his penis with *aidos*—awe before that which is sacred and powerful. The Greek heavens were filled with gods born of (or with) magical testes. Aphrodite emerged fully formed from foamy semen after the titan Cronus castrated his own father and hurled his testicles into the sea. An affair between Aphrodite, goddess of love, and Dionysus, god of wine, produced Priapus, a minor fertility deity with a major (and perpetual) erection. Dionysus was honored each year in Athens with seven festivals, each marked by a procession of *phalloi* (penis replicas) held by *phallophoroi* (penis bearers) who walked through the city, holding aloft their wooden erections—none as large as the one seen by Kallixeinos in Alexandria, alas—as revelers drank wine and sang lewd songs.

Colonies and allies of Athens were required to send their own *phalloi* to the City Dionysia, the largest of the Athenian tributes to the god of wine. Records show that the Island of Delos on several occasions contributed a magnificent winged bird carved of wood; where its head normally would have been, the Delian bird had an erect penis. Many of the more conventional wooden *phalloi* in the procession had a large unblinking eye painted on the glans, with lines indicating a rolled-back foreskin, producing a penis with a head, neck, and "personality." The message of these anthropomorphic displays was clear to all Greeks and gave dramatic form to an eternal question: Does the possessor possess the penis, or does the penis possess its possessor?

Though Dionysus himself was never depicted with an erection, his link to the erect penis was well established in myth—actually, two of them. In the first, Pegasus, a missionary of Dionysus, took a statue of the god from Eleutharae to Athens, where both he and the image were rudely received. Giulia Sissa and Marcel Detienne write in *The Daily Life of the Greek Gods* that, as punishment, Dionysus "struck down" the impolite Athenians with a seemingly incurable "disease that afflicted the male organ.

> The Delphic oracle . . . made it known that a cure would only be forthcoming if the people of Athens paraded the god with all honors due his rank. The Athenians immediately set about constructing phalluses, . . . paying homage to the god with objects that commemorated their suffering.

In the second myth, Dionysus introduces wine to an Athenian farmer named Icarius who likes what he has tasted and soon invites nearby shepherds to join him. Before long, the shepherds have drunk themselves into slumber or incoherency, which is when they are discovered by other shepherds arriving late to the party. These men conclude that Icarius has poisoned their friends; in response, they murder him. This enrages Dionysus, who appears to those shepherds as a beautiful boy. Icarius's murderers are consumed with desire to make love to him, but—at the peak of their excitement—the boy vanishes, leaving the shepherds with huge erections that will not subside. Once again, the Delphic oracle is consulted, who divines that a cure can be effected only if the shepherds fashion phallic offerings to Dionysus and parade them in his honor.

As such stories show, a Greek saw his penis as a measure of his proximity to divine power, divine intelligence—and divinely inspired insanity. To a Greek, classicist Albert Henrichs writes, "erections are signs of a physiological and mental condition . . . that Plato identified as 'divine madness.'" In *Timaeus,* Plato located the divine in humans inside the spinal marrow, the same substance, he said, from which both the brain and semen were formed. This divinity within has "a vital impulse to gush forth," Plato wrote, which explains why the penis is "disobedient and self-willed."

Clearly, the Greeks used the penis to gauge their proximity to the gods, for better and worse. But size was not part of the equation—at least not in the way you might think. In real life, as opposed to parade floats, Greeks favored a small thin penis, as on an adolescent exercising at the gymnasium. This was the penis sculpted on *kouroi* and painted on vases throughout the Mediterranean rim. Greek artists showed their contempt for foreigners and slaves by painting them with large organs. Aristotle gave this aesthetic preference a "scientific" basis, writing that a small penis is better for conception because semen cools down in a large one, becoming "not generative." Whatever the rationale, Aristophanes had some fun with the subject in a pun-filled debate on pedagogy in *The Clouds*:

"If you do what I say," says one debater, "you will always have a rippling chest, glowing skin, broad shoulders, a small tongue, a solid rump, and a tiny pee-pee. But if you follow the modern practices . . . you will acquire a sickly complexion, narrow shoulders, a nothing chest, a large tongue, spindly thighs, and an enormous subpoena."

Large or small, there is no denying the importance of the penis in Greek educational philosophy. Whether one was from Athens or Sparta, a Greek was committed to a hierarchical belief system and aesthetics based on male supremacy, militarism, and the idealization of the naked male body, a system perpetuated by that now utterly indefensible institution—pederasty. Rather than a way of life, pederasty was a rite of passage in Greece. Nearly all Greek aristocrats, after their pederastic initiations in boyhood, married and raised families, and most retained a respectful relationship with their former mentors. (An adult male who allowed himself to be penetrated by someone else's penis, however, was scorned as a *kinaidos,* a man who played the role of a woman.) To understand Greek pederasty we must try to see it as the Greeks did: an institution more about pedagogy than pleasure, less about sex than class, and always about the nobility of the penis.

In Greece manhood was learned and earned, the first process instigated by a teacher, the second occurring in war. The pederastic act was the culmination of a one-on-one mentoring process aimed at passing on *arete,* a Greek word signifying a set of manly virtues that included courage, strength, fairness, and honesty. The link between pederasty and *arete* was given (literally) monumental form in the Athenian Agora. There the word *arete* was written on the three *hermae* erected to commemorate the Greeks' victory over the Persians at Eion. Nearby stood the even older, larger-than-life statues of Harmodios and Aristogeiton, a pederastic mentor and protégé depicted naked and extraordinarily well muscled, their penises clearly visible, as they were frozen in stone in the act that demonstrated their *arete*—their assassination, by stabbing, of the tyrant Hipparchos, in 514 B.C. Obviously, a man of *arete* personified the highest ideals of Greek democracy and manhood. And to the Greeks, a culture that marked its roads and military triumphs with *hermae,* all of those ideals were embodied in the penis.

Relationships between the *erastes* (older lover) and the *eromenos* (young love object) were forged at the gymnasium. According to legend, athletic nudity was born at the Olympic Games of 720 B.C., where a competitor named Orsippus dropped his loincloth in the middle of a race, which he won. It is unclear when gymnasia first appeared, but we know that Solon urged the death penalty in the sixth century B.C. for anyone stealing clothes there. The most famous gymnasia in Athens were the Academy and the Lyceum. Each had a track, wrestling room, general exercise room, baths, and areas for drinking and discussions of philosophy. Plato held forth at the Academy; Aristotle at the Lyceum.

The body of a young Greek aristocrat was a coat of arms and a work of art. Both were created at the gymnasium before an audience of appreciative older men. That appreciation, however, was not appreciated by everyone: Aristophanes snickered in *The Clouds* at the idea of an older Athenian melting from lovesickness in the wrestling room, gazing at the mark left in the sand by the dainty penis of his young beloved.

Whatever pleasure an *erastes* took from his sexual encounter with his *eromenos,* it was officially subordinated to the higher goal of passing on *arete*. "In Greece," Michel Foucault wrote in *The History of Sexuality,* "truth and sex were linked in the form of pedagogy by the transmission of a precious knowledge from one body to another; sex served as a medium for initiations into learning." Vase paintings show that intercrural sex (between the thighs) was common among Athenian men and boys. In *Pederasty and Pedagogy in Archaic Greece,* however, historian William Armstrong Percy III concludes that anal penetration was the preferred method. (This, too, brought out the homophobia in Aristophanes, who mocked those on the receiving end as *europroktos* ["wide-assed"] or *katapugon* ["butt-fucked"].)

Aristophanes' view was not the prevailing one among the Greek elite, however. When an *erastes* entered an *eromenos* with his penis, a symbolic and, to these Greeks, real act occurred—the full and final transfer of *arete*. That the vehicle for this transfer was semen accorded with the teachings of Aristotle, who believed sperm alone provided the soul of a child. With pederasty Greek men trumped nature: with a penis and without women they gave birth to other men. This was the penis's most awesome and mysterious power of all.

---

To a Roman, the idea that manly virtue was transmitted by anal penetration was unthinkable. His idea of manhood was measured by the power dynamic of sex. A Roman penetrated others with his penis; he was never penetrated by someone else's penis. A man who allowed that to happen endured *muliebria pati,* "a woman's experience." That man was no longer a real man. He was a *cinaedus,* a term taken from the Greek signifying males who enjoyed such humiliations. Romans felt so strongly about this that it colored their military operations. The Latin word for bullet, *glans,* also meant "head of the penis," as it now does in English. When launched by slings, these bullets often had lurid inscriptions written on them comparing their use to acts of rape. At the siege of Perusia in 41 B.C., forces supporting Mark Antony aimed their inscribed ammunition at Octavian's anus.

Like the Greeks, members of the Roman elite saw their peers' sons as objects of desire. But Romans saw these boys as *viri* (men)—or, more accurately, boys in the process of becoming *viri.* To a Roman it was anathema that this process be ruined by forcing a boy to have "a woman's experience." Because of this taboo a Roman boy was given a *bulla,* a locket containing a replica of an erect penis, to wear around his neck. Known as a *fascinum,* this penis replica signified the boy's status and power as a future *vir.* The *bulla* marked him off-limits to sexual approaches. The *fascinum* inside the *bulla* was probably the only penis replica not in public view in the city. Like Athens, depictions of erections were everywhere in Rome—on paving stones, at the public baths, on the walls of private homes—promoting good luck or warding off bad. A *fascinum* hung from a chariot shielded the triumphant general riding in it from the envy of his peers at a Roman victory parade. So enduring is the magic attributed to the erect penis in Rome that during World War I, the Italian prime minister, Vittorio Emanuele Orlando, wore a *fascinum* on a bracelet to ensure victory by the Allies. Today, fifteen hundred years after the fall of Imperial Rome, anything as powerful or intriguing as an erection is said to be "fascinating."

The ubiquitous presence of *fascina* in Rome was matched by that of Priapus, one of the smallest of the gods who nonetheless had the largest penis—an erection typically depicted as covering nearly half his body. Originally a Greek deity, Priapus was said to come from the city of Lampsacus in Asia Minor, where he presided over famous orgies. His mother, Aphrodite, was ashamed of her son's unattractive face and misshapen body. But not the women of Lampsacus; they thought he was configured just right, thank you very much. Priapus's problem was with the city's men, who, overcome with envy, had their eternally erect rival expelled. The result was a venereal plague that only attacked Lampsacan males. A cure was found only after those men begged Priapus to return, named him god of gardens and herds, and made macrophallic statues of him, which they placed in their yards. (There is an obvious similarity between this myth and those explaining the origin of the Dionysian penis parades in Athens.)

Priapus was a well-liked, if minor, deity in Greece. In Rome his popularity soared, largely because of his large penis. "Whereas the small, tidy penis of a boy [was] a cultural icon for . . . Athenian men," historian Craig A. Williams writes, "Priapus [was] the most salient Roman icon, amply capable of asserting his mature masculinity by penetrating others with his impressive member." Priapus performed his official function, as protector of property, as a small wooden statue standing at the rear of a citizen's home, or in his fields. His huge penis was often painted red and it was not unusual to see it supporting a bowl of fruit. This rustic nature enhanced Priapus's popularity during the Augustan period, when some social critics worried that the ostentatious splendor of Imperial Rome was contrary to more traditional Roman values. The crudely made statues of Priapus were a "foil to the adornment of Rome with gold and finely cut marble," historian Peter Stewart writes. With a sneer and a huge penis, Priapus "answered [these critics'] call for a return to Roman simplicity."

Roman brutality, too. Priapus is the star of more than eighty surviving Latin poems. Most purport to be written by Priapus himself as a warning to trespassers. Though the authorship of this verse is uncertain, there's no denying its aggressively macho tone:

> This scepter, which was cut from a tree,
> will now be able to grow green with no leaf,
> this scepter, which pathic girls seek out,
> which certain kings desire to hold,
> to which aristocratic fags give kisses,
> will go into the guts of a thief all the way
> up to my crotch and the hilt of my balls.

Such trespassers were assumed to be male. This does not mean Priapus had any warm and fuzzy feelings for women.

> For although I might seem well enough prepared,
> I would need ten handfuls of colewort,*
> for me to rub the ditches of your groin,
> and beat the swarming worms of your cunt.

These poems are fascinating for many reasons, not the least of which is the way they use a talking penis to paint a hardly flattering portrait of Roman society. As Otto Kiefer wrote in his landmark 1934 study, *Sexual Life in Ancient Rome,* cruelty pervaded Roman eroticism. This was nowhere more obvious than at the games at the Coliseum, where the love of violent spectacle focused on the gladiator, who penetrated with his weapon and lived, or was penetrated and died. A similar eroticized cruelty informed Priapic poetry. Though intended to amuse, Priapus's "contempt for lessers" and his "violence and cynicism," classicist H. D. Rankin writes, were "all too Roman."

So was the belief that a man with a Priapic penis possessed

---

*Colewort, a plant of the mustard family, was thought by Romans to have erection-enhancing properties.

exceptional strength. Roman generals sometimes promoted soldiers based on penis size; Emperor Commodus elevated at least one possessor of a prominent member to a special pagan priesthood. In *The Latin Sexual Vocabulary*, Professor J. N. Adams—clearly, a man with a lot of time on his hands—investigated more than one hundred Latin slang terms for penis. The word "penis" itself began as a slang term derived from the Latin word for "tail." It was not, however, the most commonly used term in classical Rome. That was *mentula*, a word whose origin is in dispute. Some scholars say it emerged from *menta*, meaning "spearmint stalk," but Adams is dubious. The more vulgar companion to *mentula* was *verpa*, which connoted "prick" to *mentula*'s "dick." Nearly every slang term studied by Adams showed a preoccupation with size. The poet Catullus mocked one Roman "whose tiny dagger, drooping like a flabby parsnip, never stuck halfway up his underwear." Those at the other end of the spectrum may also have been the butt of jokes, but the attitude was one of awe. The following ditty comes from the first-century wit Martial: "If from the baths you hear a round of applause, Maron's giant prick is bound to be the cause."

A large penis was Roman power become flesh: it was respected, sometimes feared, and always coveted. This made the Roman baths a dangerous place for someone like Martial's friend Maron. The naked truth was that his genital superiority incited *invidia*—envy of another person's wealth, power, or, as happened at the baths, his large penis. Romans believed *invidia* had pathological consequences, causing injury, illness, or even death to the person envied.

The penis was so much the symbol of Roman strength and power that some believe the architectural centerpiece of the Empire, the Forum of Augustus, may have been designed to resemble one. Though the building has never been fully excavated, a surviving blueprint shows a long hall flanked at the bottom by two hemispheres. When viewed from above, this plan suggests the grandest *fascinum* ever built. This seems only fitting, considering the rites of power and masculinity that took place there. It was at the Forum that Roman males came to exchange the robe of boyhood, the *toga praetexta,* with its purple stripe and *bulla* (the locket containing a replica of an erect penis) for the all-white *toga virilis.* The Forum was where emperors set up their tribunals, where the Senate declared war, and where triumphant generals dedicated their victories to the god Mars. The Forum of Augustus was a monument to masculinity, a proving ground and place of honor for powerful men of penetrating vision. Why wouldn't it be designed as a penis?

But Romans never forgot that the penis is an instrument of pleasure. We know this because of a calamity that occurred on August 24, 79 A.D., in Pompeii, a city in southern Italy that in a few hours was smothered alive by lava from Mount Vesuvius. A rain of ash preserved the place just as it was two thousand years ago, even the facial expressions of the dying. Many of the surviving homes in Pompeii are covered with exquisite murals and mosaics. A noticeably high percentage of them are about the penis.

Perhaps the most famous of those murals is in the entrance-way to the House of the Vettii. The artist's subject is Priapus, only this time the god is not a squat, ugly figure. Instead, he is of normal stature, with a face that seems handsome, even sensitive. On the floor to his right is the bowl of fruit that usually rests on his giant erection. Now Priapus has something better to do with that organ that reaches down to his knee: he is weighing it on a scale, balanced against a sack of coins. Apparently, Priapus's penis is worth its weight in gold.

The residents of Pompeii were pleasure lovers, but more so than other Romans? That's hard to say; other cities are not as well preserved. The chronicler Suetonius painted a penis-centric portrait of the ruling class in *The Twelve Caesars,* what with Emperor Tiberius having a painting behind his bed of Juno fellating Jupiter, and Empress Agrippina winning a sex contest by bedding fourteen men in one night, after which she placed fourteen laurels on a nearby *fascinum*. But how typical of anything is the court of the emperor? By contrast, Pompeii may have been staid. Still, the town credo seems to have been "Life is short. Have fun while you can." This philosophy, as it did all over the Roman world, found visual representation in the stiff penis. In one of the most famous wall reliefs in Pompeii, an erect member rises from two testicles. Written above and below are the words *Hic Habitat Felicitas*—"Here Lives Happiness."

---

Over time, some Romans began to question that idea, often by joining bizarre cults. The strangest of these honored Cybele, a goddess brought to Rome from Asia Minor during the Punic Wars Rome waged against Carthage in the third and second centuries B.C. According to legend, Cybele's love for her son Attis far exceeded normal maternal limits. This led her to strike her son mad rather than let him marry. In his madness—or, as others interpreted it, a state of religious ecstasy—Attis castrated himself. To honor this love between mother and son, initiates into the Cybele cult danced themselves into a frenzy on the Day of Blood. These priests ran through the streets of Rome, cut off their testicles with a consecrated stone knife, then threw the bloody parts into an unsuspecting Roman's house. The lucky residents of that dwelling were expected to give the priest women's clothing, which he wore from that day on. Known as *galli*, these cross-dressing eunuchs tended Cybele's temple, which stood until the fourth century on the Roman site now occupied by Saint Peter's Basilica.

Though Romans believed Cybele aided their final victory in the Punic Wars, they viewed the *galli* with loathing. Edmund Gibbon cited the following proverb in *The Decline and Fall of the Roman Empire*: "If you have a eunuch, kill him; if you don't have any, buy one and kill him." This homicidal humor arose from the Roman belief that potency was the sine qua non of manhood. Nothing was more unnatural to a Roman, or more worthy of suspicion, than a man without fully functioning genitals. The satyrical poet Juvenal mocked bored Roman women aristocrats for taking eunuchs as lovers.

> There are those who in soft eunuchs place their bliss;
> To shun the scrubbing of a bearded kiss;
> And escape abortion, but their solid joy
> Is when the Page, already past a boy,
> Is capon'd late; and to the gelder shown,
> With his two-pounders grown. . . .
> Seen from afar, and famous for his ware,
> He struts into the bath among the fair:
> The admiring crew to the devotions fall:
> And kneeling, on the new Priapus call.

Such hairless men, typically slaves, could achieve erections—even Priapic ones, Juvenal suspected. He was correct: a male whose testicles are removed or rendered inoperative after puberty loses the ability to produce sperm, and his natural appetite for intercourse, but not his ability to perform it. With no chance of conception, nor possible need of abortion, such men might be popular, indeed, with women living two millennia before the invention of the birth control pill.

Castrated slaves were also the erotic playthings of certain Roman men, as we read in Petronius's *Satyricon*.

> O fairies, O buggers
> O eunuchs exotic!
> Come running, come running,
> ye anal erotic!
> With soft little hands,
> with flexible bums,
> Come O castrati,
> unnatural ones!

The Emperor Nero, in whose court Petronius was *arbiter elegantiaei*, often invited eunuchs to his orgies and eventually married one. Nero "tried to turn the boy Sporus into a girl by castration," wrote Suetonius, "went through a marriage ceremony with him—dowry, bridal veil and all—which the whole Court attended; then brought him home, and treated him as a wife. . . . A rather amusing joke is still [being told]," Suetonius couldn't help adding: "The world would have been a happier place had Nero's father Domitius married that sort a wife."

According to most etymologists, the English verb "castrate" derives from the Latin *castrare*, meaning to geld, which itself is thought to derive from Hebrew and Sanskrit words meaning "eunuch" and "knife." A more creative, if not entirely credible, theory, however, holds that "castration" comes from the Latin word *castor*, meaning "beaver," an animal whose testicles were thought to have medicinal powers when consumed by humans, which made them a fiercely hunted creature two millennia ago. According to Greco-Roman folklore, a cornered male beaver would chew off his own testicles, then toss them to his hunter, hoping to save his life. If pursued later by another hunter, the beaver would roll over on his back, showing his pursuer that he was of no real value.

Castration in Rome generally referred, and still does, to the surgical removal or crushing of testes; a fully "shaved" eunuch, however, had his penis removed as well. (It is said that Sporos, the wife of Nero, was such a person.) "Eunuch" derives from the Greek term for keeper, or guardian, of the bed. Guardians of the harem beds in the great Moslem empires were typically "shaved." Only those without any manly equipment at all were allowed proximity to the Sultan's wives.

The Roman Senate forbade citizens from taking part in the bizarre and bloody initiation rites of the Cybele-Attis cult. They could be spectators, though. In *The Golden Bough*, James G. Frazer wrote that the sight of these public self-mutilations often had unexpected, and decidedly un-Roman, consequences:

as the flutes played, the drums beat, and the [new] eunuch priests slashed themselves with knives, the excitement spread like a wave among the onlookers, and many a one did that which he little thought to do when he came as a spectator at the festival. For man after man, his veins throbbing with the music, his eyes fascinated by the sight of the streaming blood, flung his garments from him, leaped forth with a shout, and seizing one of the swords which stood ready for the purpose, castrated himself on the spot.

It's hardly surprising that several psychoanalysts have weighed in on these rites. In her 1938 paper "The Cult and Mythology of the Magna Mater from the Standpoint of Psychoanalysis," Edith Weigert-Vowinkel was struck by Cybele's requirement of emasculation as the price of grace and the willingness of men to make themselves "females" to share women's superior powers. That this mutilation was self-inflicted, she wrote, suggested the impetus lay in the deepest layers of the psyche. Carl Jung was so moved by Attis's act that he wrote the words "To the Most Beautiful Attis" on a phallic-shaped road marker near his home in Switzerland.

The Cybele cult clearly shows that the Roman idea of the penis was evolving: the living symbol of Roman power was acceding to a "higher" power. At the same time Cybele and Attis were attracting initiates in Rome, followers of the Egyptian gods Osiris and Isis were also building temples in the city. These imported cults shared a concept new to Rome—the resurrection myth. Attis and Osiris suffered and died but were reborn. Both were castrated, a fate appropriate for a slave, perhaps, but never a freeborn Roman. Yet these new cults, with their strange initiations and periods of asceticism, slowly attracted followers. Without them it is unlikely another new religion from the East—Christianity—and its new concept of the penis would ever have been embraced by Rome. That turning point in history occurred after Emperor Constantine's battlefield "conversion" in 312, an event following centuries of brutal persecution that created countless Christian martyrs. Here begins the Christian idea of the penis, a concept of truly revolutionary consequences—politically as well as religiously.

As historians Aline Rousselle and Peter Brown have pointed out, the Roman penis was a tool of the state. At the height of imperial power, Roman life expectancy was less than twenty-five years. Only four in one hundred men lived to be fifty. It was a population grazed thin by death. Concerned with its own continuity, the Empire required its citizens to produce legitimate children. Properly channeled, a strong Roman penis built a strong Roman society. Augustus Caesar penalized bachelors and rewarded fatherhood. In anticipation of the latter, Romans celebrated a son's first ejaculation as part of a state holiday, the *Liberalia*. A Roman citizen's body was private property, off-limits to penetration, but his penis worked for the Empire.

Not the Christian penis. It broke the worldly chain of Rome and replaced it with a subversive and new spiritual connection. The true Kingdom was God's, not Caesar's; true freedom was freedom from lust—and from the mandate to repopulate the Empire. God's only son had been born of a virgin and walked the Earth. His sexless birth and life were a bridge between man's fallen state and his glorious future. Human spirit was divine but the flesh corrupt. And no organ, Augustine would establish, was more corrupt than the penis.

The foundation for this was laid by other Church Fathers. Clement of Alexandria compared semen to the froth of the epileptic. Tertullian taught that it is not merely semen that leaves the penis during orgasm, but part of a man's soul. Pope Siricius merged hatred of the penis and misogyny into one teaching. The subject was Mary's lifelong virginity, which, according to Siricius, Jesus demanded of her as a condition for becoming his mother. "Jesus would not have chosen birth from [her,"] Siricius wrote, "had he been forced to look upon her as so unrestrained as to let that womb from which the body of the Lord was fashioned, that hall of the eternal king, be stained by the presence of male seed."

Those looking for Jesus' thoughts on the penis and its seed will not find much. His most controversial words on the subject appear in Matthew, where he praises men who become "eunuchs for the Kingdom of Heaven." Around the year 206, a martyr's son from Alexandria named Origen, only a few years past puberty but already one of the Church's leading interpreters of Scripture, took that message to heart and had himself castrated. This act was not only rash, says Catholic theologian Uta Ranke-Heinemann, it was misguided. Jesus' subject in Matthew was not intercourse, she writes, but remarriage. "Whoever divorces his wife and marries another woman commits adultery," Jesus said in the same sermon. "Not all men can receive this saying." Those who can become "eunuchs for the Kingdom of Heaven." What stunned Jesus' listeners was not his teaching about sex, "about which he says nothing," Ranke-Heinemann argues, "but his teaching about marriage and divorce—and this was something new."

As Professor Gary Taylor notes in his book *Castration,* the word "eunuch" appears more than five hundred times in the surviving works of the Church Fathers—often, but not always, in a positive context. The Book of Acts states that Christianity's very first Gentile convert was a eunuch from Ethiopia who embraced the faith after the apostle Philip interpreted a passage from Isaiah for him. Even so, some early Christians had a contempt for the castrated almost rivaling that held by Romans. The fourth-century theologian Basil the Great, later canonized, referred to eunuchs as "lizards and toads . . . , effeminate, . . . money-mad, coarse, . . . disgusting, [and] jealous."

Such views, no doubt expressed more eloquently, eventually led the Church to denounce Origen's self-mutilation. The Council of Nicaea, convened in 325 to establish Christian orthodoxy, banned eunuchs from entering the clergy. The *Apostolic Consti-*

*tutions,* written roughly fifty-five years later, punished nonclerics who castrated themselves with three years' excommunication. Not everyone was listening, however. In 377 Epiphanius of Salamis wrote of one Christian sect, the Valensians, who believed castration was an indispensable condition of faith. Members of the group emasculated themselves and, according to Epiphanius, any traveler who accepted their hospitality, all in the name of assuring their eternal happiness. (The opinions of those unsuspecting houseguests on this matter has not made it into the historical record.)

Clearly the most bizarre pseudo-Christian castration cult was the Skoptsy. The story of this Russian sect, the largest of its type in Western history, requires a brief chronological detour. Founded in the second half of the eighteenth century, the Skoptsy believed original sin was brought to the world by sex. Many Christians thought that, too; where the Skoptsy differed was in their belief that Jesus came to bring salvation not by dying, but by castration. This, the Skoptsy said, was misunderstood by heterodox Christians, who failed to grasp that Jesus was not merely crucified, but castrated. To live in true imitation of Christ, said the Skoptsy's leader, Kondratii Selivanov, one must undertake a new covenant with God, which he called the "seal." This was a reference to the Book of Revelation where it is written that the "hundred and forty and four thousand" who accompanied the Lamb "had his name and his Father's name written on their foreheads." That the Skoptsy's seal was made on their genitalia, Laura Engelstein writes in her fascinating book on the sect, *Castration and the Heavenly Kingdom,* emerged from their belief that the penis was "the key to the abyss." (The "abyss," of course, was the vagina.) Males in the cult, Engelstein writes,

submitted to the removal of their testicles in a ritual called the "minor seal." The operator tied the scrotum at the base, sliced through the skin, cauterized the wound or applied a salve, and pronounced: "Christ is risen!" To achieve a higher level of purity, the penis itself was severed. This was the "major" or "royal" seal. For women, the rite entailed the removal of nipples, breasts, or protruding parts of the genitals.

By 1772 there were enough Skoptsy in rural Russia, east of Moscow, to cause the Orthodox Church to convene an investigation of their heretical activities. The sect survived, however, albeit with a dwindling membership, into the early twentieth century. Selivanov, who died around the year 1832, is said to have spent the last two decades of his life in Saint Petersburg where, according to Engelstein, "he was venerated by high-society figures fascinated with his charismatic charm."

———————————

The "true eunuch is not he who is unable, but he who is unwilling to gratify his passions," Clement of Alexandria wrote sixteen centuries before anyone had ever heard of the Skoptsy. Certainly no one wrestled with that teaching more memorably, or with greater impact, than Augustine. Of all the Church Fathers, we know the most about his sexual and spiritual journey. In *Confessions* Augustine wrote that he had several love affairs as a young man. After turning twenty, however, he chose one woman with whom he lived, apparently monogamously, for the next thirteen years. "Augustine chose [her] because he loved her; and he slept with her because he loved to," Princeton historian Peter Brown writes in *The Body and Society*. This sexual activity "was not shocking by any standards," Garry Wills adds in his biography of Augustine, "but those of a [future] saint."

While still living with his mistress, however, Augustine joined the Manicheans, a sect that saw the world divided into two realms, God's and Satan's, and taught that all sexual activity aided the powers of evil. Augustine was an auditor in the group, a rank below the Elect, who abstained from sex totally and ate as little as possible. At Manichean services auditors listened to prayers chanted by their emaciated superiors exalting the path of self-denial. Augustine, not yet the man he would become, responded with a now famous prayer of his own: "Lord, give me chastity," he said, "but not now."

In 384 Augustine moved from Carthage to Milan, where a prestigious career in imperial administration awaited if he made the right connections. His mother, Monica, already a convert to Christianity, found him a bride, a twelve-year-old whose family was close to Ambrose, bishop of Milan. Augustine consented. His concubine returned to Africa. Augustine resolved to wait two years for his wellborn fiancée to come of age. But "a slave to lust," as he later described himself, Augustine took a new mistress. He loved the sexual comfort but hated himself.

This led to a conversion experience rivaling Saint Paul's. While in a garden, Augustine heard a child's voice: *"Take up and read, take up and read."* Augustine picked up the nearest book. It was the New Testament, opened to Romans. "Let us conduct ourselves becomingly," he read, "not in reveling and drunkenness, not in debauchery and licentiousness. . . . But put on the Lord Jesus Christ, and make no provision for the flesh, to gratify its desires." Both the problem and the solution were revealed to him in that instant. Augustine was soon baptized by Bishop Ambrose, a famous eulogist of virginity. The new Augustine, who later became Bishop of Hippo, spent much of his life thinking about the old Augustine. Why had he been so powerless against lust? Augustine found his answer in Genesis. What he preached afterward redefined the Western idea of the penis for the next thousand years.

Augustine's epiphany was tautological: he was powerless to control the penis because he was powerless. Free choice is an illusion. Adam's birthright at Creation was freedom, defined by Augustine as the ability to obey God, yet Adam scorned that gift because he wanted the "freedom to do wickedness." Adam's sin deprived his descendants of the freedom to choose *not* to sin.

The ultimate embodiment of this, Augustine wrote, is "disobedience in the member." After Adam and Eve flouted God's will by eating the forbidden fruit, they experienced two new sensations: shame at their nakedness and sexual stirrings they could not control. "We are ashamed of that very thing which made those beings ashamed, when they covered their loins." That "very thing" is a spontaneous erection.

For Augustine the penis was for every man what, fifteen hundred years later, Dr. Strangelove's arm would be in Stanley Kubrick's black comic film—not just rising, but rising of its own will. "That is the penalty of sin," Augustine wrote, "that is the plague and mark of sin;

> that is the temptation and the very fuel of sin, that is the law in our members warring against the law in our mind.

Before sinning, Adam and Eve had mastery over sex, procreating as an act of volition, "the way one commands his feet when he walks." But since leaving Eden men have become powerless over, and tortured by, erections. "At times the urge intrudes uninvited," Augustine wrote in *City of God*. "At other times, it deserts the panting lover, and, although desire blazes in the mind, the body is frigid." For the Greeks and Romans, an erection was like a change in heartbeat: involuntary, and not susceptible to blame or praise. But for Augustine the cause *and* the effect of original sin is lust, the symptom *and* the disease is the erection. With this one stroke, this one man transformed the penis more than any man who had yet lived: the sacred staff became the demon rod.

"Everyone is necessarily evil and carnal through Adam," Augustine wrote. The agent transferring this stigma from one generation to the next is semen. This "astonishing argument," as historian Elaine Pagels describes it in *Adam, Eve, and the Serpent*, declared that "every human is born contaminated." In saying this, Augustine hammered cracks in two of the original pillars of Christian faith: the goodness of God's creation and the freedom of the human will. As an earlier Father of the Church had put it, the good news of Christianity was autonomy over the body. Sexuality was a beast but the Church was a lion tamer. Christian celibates were not "unmanly," as pagans mocked them. Sexually active men merely conquered weak females. Christian celibates subdued something far stronger—the penis.

Augustine's fellow bishop, the Italian Julian of Eclanum, criticized his peer's revision of this earlier Church teaching in a public letter, arguing that Augustine was wrong about original sin (no physically transmitted, hereditary condition infects human nature, Julian declared); wrong about free will (men *are* responsible for their actions); and wronger still about the penis: "God made bodies," Julian wrote, "distinguished the sexes, made genitalia, bestowed affection through which bodies would be joined, gave power to the semen, and operates in the secret nature of the semen—and God made nothing evil." Right, said Augustine, it was Adam who made it so. What Julian exalted as a "vital fire," Augustine scorned as "the diabolical excitement of the genitals."

This theological debate, as full of vitriol and ad hominem arguments as any political argument seen on CNN's *Crossfire* program today, went on for twelve years, until Augustine died. Augustine attacked Julian's "fragile mind," his "vanity," and his "madness." Julian, who was much better at this kind of thing, called Augustine the "guru of the outback," "what passes for a philosopher with Africans," a "wheezing old geezer," and "the braying spokesman of all donkeys." Even so, the Roman Church in the end sided with the wheezing and braying rube-guru, the sainted Bishop of Hippo.

Viewed in a modern light, Augustine's victory seems a triumph of medical marketing with a splash of proto-Freudianism. He taught that man is diseased by lust and semen, then established the Church as the Great Spiritual Physician. It is not your fault, Augustine told the sufferer. The blame belongs to your primeval father, Adam (tempted, of course, by Eve), and a penis you cannot control. Yes, you are suffering, but be assured that your pain is not without meaning and not without end—God's grace. The irony of Augustine's achievement is that his triumph belies his own belief in man's helplessness. The convictions of this one convert, rooted in his personal experience of the penis as an irresistible agent of sinful ecstasy and self-loathing, by the force of his *own* will he made universal.

From the fifth century on, Elaine Pagels writes, Augustine's negative views of erections, semen, and human nature would become "the dominant influence on Western Christianity, both Catholic and Protestant, and color all Western culture, Christian or not." His theory of Creation and Adam's fall, once espoused only by marginal sects, moved into the center of our intellectual and cultural mind-set.

The penis moved elsewhere. Once honored as the engine of life by the men who built the pyramids and the Parthenon, once revered as the god within by the desert tribe that gave the West monotheism and the idea of the Messiah, this sacred staff was toppled from its pedestal and erased from the Western cultural lexicon. In its place came the demon rod, the corrupter of all mankind.

———————

The English language, "with its elaborate generosity, distinguishes between the naked and the nude," art historian Kenneth Clark writes. "To be naked is to be deprived of clothes, and the word implies . . . embarrassment. The word 'nude,' on the other hand, carries, in educated usage, no uncomfortable overtone. The . . . image it projects into the mind is . . . of a balanced, confident body: the body re-formed."

The nude was invented by the Greeks. Christianity brought back the naked. The human body did not lose any of its power as an image, but its message was powerfully changed. Now the body was seen in Augustinian terms as a curse, "a vestment man had carried with him since the Fall," historian Michael Camille writes, "which in its uncontrollableness emblematized his sin and, in its decay, his death."

Medieval depictions of Adam and Eve reflected this seismic shift in consciousness. With the exception of Jesus, martyrs being tortured, and sinners burning in Hell, Adam and Eve were the only humans in that period rendered without clothes. Their bodies in these biblical illustrations are not Greco-Roman mirrors of divine perfection. They are objects of shame. And no part of that body is more shameful than the penis. A medieval drawing in the French National Library shows the first man born *without* a penis. This idea was expressed equally clearly in words by the mystic Mechthild of Magdeburg. The penis is not the cause of original sin, she wrote, it is the result:

> Their [Adam's and Eve's] bodies were to be pure, for God created for them no members of shame. . . . But when they ate the forbidden food, they were ignominiously altered in body, as we experience it even now. Had the Holy Trinity made us so ugly, we would have no cause to feel shame.

By the time that was written, around 1275, the penis had virtually disappeared from Western art for eight hundred years. This "rejection of the body in Christian art—an absolute reversal from the aesthetic standards of the ancient world"—Professor Camille writes in *The Gothic Idol,* "is one of the most crucial transformations in the history of the West." Even at the peak of the Italian Renaissance more than two centuries later, when artists reclaimed the nude, Michelangelo would learn how fickle opinion still could be on this subject. His nude statue of David was stoned by a Florentine mob in 1504. Thirty years later, after the great master finished *The Last Judgment* in the Sistine Chapel, Pope Paul IV ordered another artist to paint over the penises in it.

The penis was largely out of sight in medieval Europe, but

never out of mind. The demon rod became an obsession of the Church in the literature known as penitentials. Originating in sixth-century Ireland, these handbooks for confessors defined Christian behavior—especially the behavior of the penis. Penitentials proceeded from the Augustinian idea that sex was sinful precisely in relation to the pleasure it created. "Member not granted for this" was a key phrase in the books. "Member" meant "penis"; "not granted for this" referred to any sexual act not specifically aimed at procreation.

Violators had to do penance, which meant exclusion from Communion, undertaking long fasts and similarly extended periods of abstinence, and sometimes public floggings. The length of penance for each sin is revealing: English penitentials demanded ten years penance for coitus interruptus, fifteen years for anal intercourse, and a lifelong penance for oral sex. ("Those who put semen in the mouth commit the worst evil," said Theodore of Canterbury.) Yet these same guidelines required only seven years penance for premeditated murder. It seems the Church thought the penis a more heinous instrument of crime than a poleax.

Not every theologian agreed. One of the most insightful minds in the medieval Church, Peter Abelard, devoted his early career to fighting it. In the end, however, Abelard's saga only confirmed the teachings of Augustine and, even more hauntingly, Origen. A logician by training, Abelard criticized barriers to marital intercourse as illogical. "No natural pleasure of the flesh may be declared a sin," he wrote, "nor may one impute guilt when someone is delighted by pleasure where he must necessarily feel it." Since Creation, said Abelard, sexual intercourse and the eating of good-tasting foods—he was French, after all—were both naturally bound up with pleasure; God planned it that way. Abelard's ideas were attacked, which he expected. So was his body, which he did not.

Some might say he deserved both. In 1118 Abelard was tutoring Héloïse, niece of Fulbert, Canon of Notre Dame, in Paris.

During the lessons, Abelard later wrote, "my hand did more searching in her bosom than in her book.

To arouse less suspicion, I beat her now and then, not in hot temper but in love . . . and this beating surpassed all balms in sweetness. In short, we left no phase of love untried in our passion and if love-making could find the unusual, we tried this also. The less experience we had in these joys, the greater was our ardor.

Soon Héloïse gave birth to a child. The lovers were secretly married by the seething Fulbert, then separated. (Abelard was a monk, not yet an ordained priest, and therefore could marry, according to the rules of his time. He insisted the marriage remain secret, so as not to affect his teaching career within the Church.) Abelard returned to his quarters, Héloïse to her uncle. But when Abelard heard she was being mistreated there, he abducted Héloïse and moved her to the convent of Argenteuil, not far from Paris. Fulbert was "so embittered [he] decided on my destruction," Abelard later wrote. "My servant took a bribe and led [intruders hired by Fulbert] to my chamber, where I was sleeping. Then they took [his] revenge on me—so cruelly . . . that the world froze in horror. They cut off . . . the organs with which I had troubled him."

Naturally, Abelard was outraged. Not merely for the diminution of his sex life, but for the potential loss of his soul. As someone who had read the Old Testament, Abelard knew well the contempt eunuchs evoke in the eyes of God. But twelve years later a different Abelard emerged, one with a very different view of the penis. He wrote Héloïse, now a nun, and urged her to

remember God's mercy on us . . . the wisdom whereby he made use of evil itself and mercifully set aside our impiety, so that by a wholly justified wound in a single part of my body he might heal two souls. . . . So when divine grace cleansed rather than deprived me of those vile members . . . what else did it do but remove a foul imperfection in order to preserve perfect purity?

With these words the demonization of the penis marked a major milestone. The great liberal logician Abelard had come to see the logic of his own castration.

———————————

The Church, however, continued to be puzzled by the power of male potency. And nowhere was this confusion more obvious than in the Vatican's teachings on what we now call libido. Fornication—sex motivated by lust—was deemed a mortal sin; yet, to prevent that sin, the Church urged copulation. As absurd as this sounds to us, medieval theologians saw the distinction as rational. Copulation was without sin because it was supposedly accomplished without lust. The goal was not pleasure, but to honor God's commandment to be "fruitful." The ironic result of these teachings was to turn the Church into a diagnostic center for male sexual dysfunction. If lust was public enemy number one inside the Vatican, number two was impotence.

In Gratian's *Decretum*, the compendium of canon law published in 1140, impotence was declared grounds for annulment. Gratian urged the afflicted couple to live together as "brother and sister." If that could not be arranged, the wife was free to remarry, but not the impotent man. When Gratian's successors in the Church weren't wondering how many angels could dance on the head of a pin, they were debating whether Rome should honor the marriage of a eunuch. "Yes," said theologian Pierre de La Palude, if he can achieve an erection, penetrate the vagina, and ejaculate into it; "no," said William of Pagula, who insisted, however, that a marriage must remain valid for a man castrated *after* the ceremony.

There was one thing nearly all medieval clerics agreed on:

nonfunctioning husbands had to be properly examined, no matter how cruel or unusual the methodology. In the "cold water test," a man's penis was submerged in ice water, after which the veins in his scrotum were checked for constriction. Is it any wonder that one physician wrote of a tested man with "a penis the size of a two-year-old boy?" Even more humiliating, if that's possible, was a test in which an examiner known as an "honest woman" bared her breasts before the accused man, kissed and fondled him, stroked his penis, and did whatever else she thought might entice an erection. This was typically done in the presence of the man's wife and priest.

Some Church courts ordered an event known as a "congress" as part of any annulment proceedings arising from a charge of impotence. As we know from the *Chirurgia Magna,* written in the fourteenth century by physician Guy de Chauliac, the couple ordered to participate in such an event—the goal of which was successful penetration, so as to keep the marriage intact—had to "lie together on successive days" in the presence of "a matron used to such procedures." That matron, de Chauliac wrote, "must administer spices and aromatics to them, she must comfort them and anoint them with warm oils, she must massage them near the fire, she must order them to talk to each other and embrace. Then she must report what she has seen to the doctor." (Apparently not every New Age sex therapy was born in California.)

An illustrated manuscript from this period shows how embarrassing such a procedure could be. The drawing, which renders the matron reporting her findings, shows the accused man, his head hung in shame, his robe pulled open by two women (one the wife, the other, presumably, the matron), exposing his tiny limp penis to a doctor and priest. Some French congresses, historians Thomas Benedek and Janet Kubinec note, were witnessed by as many as fifteen people. Is it any wonder a German doctor later mocked the process for "converting a courtroom into a breeding stall?"

Any male forced into a congress in the late Middle Ages had obviously not read, nor consulted a doctor familiar with, the work of Constantinus Africanus, an eleventh-century monk-physician who made the prevention and cure of impotence a large part of his scholarly mission. By translating Arabic medical texts into Latin—the Arabic books were themselves translations of earlier Greek works—Africanus gave the West a new body of knowledge, collected as the *Pantegni* and the *Viaticum*, which became the core of European medical practice for the next four centuries. Book six of the *Viaticum* was titled *De Coitu* (*On Intercourse*). Inside Africanus listed dozens of "Foods and Herbs which Provoke Desire and are Good for Impotent Men," several of which, he wrote, "we ourselves have tried." One potion earned Africanus's personal imprimatur as amazingly stimulating.

> Take the brains of thirty male sparrows and steep them for a very long time in a glass pot; take an equal amount of the grease surrounding the kidneys of a freshly killed billy goat, dissolve it on the fire, add the brains and as much honey as needed, mix it in the dish and cook until it becomes hard. Make into pills like filberts and give one before intercourse.

Africanus was not merely interested in raising erections. He tried to decipher their hidden physiological processes as well, borrowing heavily from the Greek notion of *pneuma* (literally "breath" or "wind," but signifying the vital spirit within us all). "When the appetite arises in the liver," he wrote, "the heart generates a spirit which . . . fills the hollow of the penis and makes it hard and stiff." An erect penis is not filled with blood, the monk decided, but air, a view that would go unchallenged for nearly five centuries. Fascinating proof of Africanus's far-reaching and long-lasting impact can be found in Chaucer's *Canterbury Tales*. There, the merchant of "The Merchant's Tale" shows himself to be no fan of the priestly doctor's work, calling him a cursed monk, pimp, and sleazy purveyor of love potions.

Perhaps the most surprising example of the medieval Church's interest in sexuality was the work of Peter of Spain. Peter was actually a Portuguese priest who studied theology in Paris and became a professor of medicine in Siena. There Peter wrote *Quaestiones super Viaticum,* a commentary on Africanus in which he wondered, "Who experiences greater pleasure during sex, men or women?" (Men have a greater "quality" of enjoyment, Peter decided, but women have greater "quantity.") This inquiry predated the wired-up, fluorescent-lighted, pleasure-measuring experiments of William Masters and Virginia Johnson by seven hundred years. In his *Thesaurus Pauperum,* one of the most widely read medical books of the thirteenth century, Peter gave the ingredients for thirty-four aphrodisiacs and fifty-six prescriptions to enhance male potency. What makes Peter's research focus so fascinating is that, in 1276, Peter of Spain was elected Pope John XXI. Unfortunately for the future of Western sexuality, he died nine months later when the ceiling of his library caved in on him.

A message from God? John XXI's contemporary Albert the Great may have thought so. This future saint offered a litany of medical arguments against excessive potency. One piece of evidence was a story he heard about a monk who, after "visiting with and lusting for a beautiful woman sixty-six times" in one night, was found dead the next morning. (Who could blame him?) The monk's body was opened up, revealing a cerebrum withered to the size of a pomegranate. "This is the sign," Albert concluded, "that coitus drains the brain." Albert also claimed that people who have frequent sex are followed around by dogs. This is because "dogs love smells and run after cadavers," he wrote, "and the body of a person who has a great deal of intercourse approaches the condition of a cadaver because of all the rotten semen."

Every medieval theologian knew that semen was evil. But

when coupled with the belief that agents of the Devil had sex with humans, semen assumed an even worse aspect: it became diabolical. What churchmen were not sure about was how, or even if, demons produced semen themselves. The Vatican taught that demons were not flesh and blood; they were ghostly offspring of disgraced former angels who had fornicated with humans. These demons introduced evil into the minds of men— not just lust, but murder and war. That's a lot of power, but one question remained: How did they impregnate humans? Some believed demons recovered semen spilled by masturbators, or from spouses during coitus interruptus. The ejaculate from hanged criminals was thought to be a prime source. Demonologists urged the prompt burying of all dead males, lest demons milk the carcasses of their semen. Many believed a corpse left on the ground emitted vaporous semen, not unlike pollen, that demons collected.

The solution to this vexing issue was finally provided by Albert the Great's greatest pupil, Thomas Aquinas, in *Quaestiones Quodlibetales* and *Summa Theologica*. Demons took the form of a woman, known as a succubus, Aquinas said, and procured semen from a human male by tricking or seducing him into having sex. Later that same demon assumed the form of man, or incubus, and used the stolen semen to impregnate a willing woman. (Note the misogyny in Aquinas's construction.) Of all the sources cited by authors Heinrich Kramer and James Sprenger in their guidebook for witchhunters, the *Malleus Maleficarum*, no one is quoted more often, or with greater reverence, than Aquinas. It is Aquinas who answers their question about why God gave the Devil greater "power of bewitchment" over the penis than any other human organ. "He [Aquinas] teaches that the first corruption of sin, through which man has become the slave of the devil, entered into us through the act of generation," Kramer and Sprenger wrote. (Actually, Aquinas was just paraphrasing Augustine.)

Even so, it clearly was Aquinas who perpetuated the demonization of the penis that began with Augustine and culminated in one of the ugliest periods in history. Sigmund von Riezler, a German historian who studied the Bavarian witchhunts that burned the life out of Anna Pappenheimer and thousands like her, wrote that, "The persecutors based [their actions] on Thomas's authority. Wherever one checks the passages cited as evidence of their position, one finds that only the one from Thomas has the character of a clear doctrinal principle." With his teachings on demonized semen and the women who accepted it, Aquinas, "'the Angelic Doctor,' saint, and scholar of the Dominican order, must therefore," von Riezler wrote, "be identified as the one who contributed most to the establishing of the witchcraft hysteria."

———————

There was one penis, however, that remained a sacred staff, even at the peak of Aquinas's influence. This penis played no role in original sin, was not disobedient to the will of God or man, and definitely was not a tool of the Devil. Instead, this penis was an agent of redemption that, by its existence, proved that Paradise could be regained. The penis of this New Adam wiped away the sin of the first Adam. This was the most mysterious penis of them all, a mystery that signified salvation rather than Satan. This was the penis of Jesus Christ.

This exceptional organ was the only exception to the rule removing the penis from religious art. As historian Leo Steinberg has demonstrated in his eye-opening book *The Sexuality of Christ in Renaissance Art and in Modern Oblivion,* a large body of art was created between the fourteenth and sixteenth centuries devoted to the genitalia of Christ. These works, many of them displayed in church, often showed baby Jesus' penis proudly displayed by himself, his mother Mary, or his grandmother Anne. In some of them, Mary points to or protects the exposed organ with her hands. In others, Anne touches it with hers. Some pictures show Jesus' penis garlanded in flower petals. In paintings of the Magi, these seekers of Christ are often on their hands and knees, peering into Jesus' crotch as Mary extends it toward them. Their adoration is well focused, indeed.*

Reproductions of more than two hundred paintings document this *ostentation genitalium* that, until the original publication of Steinberg's book in 1983, was surely noticed but rarely discussed. These paintings of Jesus' penis, by masters such as Michelangelo, Titian, and Botticelli, cannot be explained by a commitment to "naturalism," Steinberg insisted. Nor were they merely "inspired by classical models." Instead, they reflect a contemporaneous theological trend that focused less on Jesus' divinity, which needed no demonstration, than on his humanity, which did, especially to counter the Catharian heresy, which taught Jesus had no body at all.

That the adult Jesus has a penis in the paintings cited by Steinberg, but chooses not to use it sexually, showed that lust can be conquered—and the sinister "mystery" of the penis can be solved. That the infant Jesus exposes his genitals in many of those paintings is not, as Freudians would say, proof of his polymorphous perversity. Instead, it proved that the penis of the New Adam was born without sin and, even more to the point, without the shame the Church says the rest of us rightly feel for our genitalia.

This thinking is vividly embodied by what may be the most shocking paintings in Steinberg's book, two pictures by the Dutch painter Maerten van Heemskerck, each called *Man of Sorrows*. In both paintings the risen Christ is a man of strength and obvious muscularity. A trickle of blood drips from the flesh wound on his side. He has turned his right palm outward to show the stigmata. Christ is sitting (alone in one, tended by angels in the other); he is naked in both, save for a crown of thorns

---

*Actually, the "sexuality" of Steinberg's title might be better put as "genitality." Jesus is not represented acting sexually in any of the paintings cited by Steinberg.

on his head and a loose cloth draped over his crotch. Clearly, van Heemskerck's intention was to draw the viewer's attention to that cloth. The penis underneath it is noticeably tumescent.

Steinberg's book is controversial, but there is no denying that the pictures exist, or their obvious focus. Interestingly, the penis of baby Jesus in these works is always uncircumcised, even though his circumcision is chronicled in the Gospels. Apparently, European artists could not conceive of the penis of the New Adam being anything but perfect—as original equipment, that is. No doubt anti-Semitism played a role in this. As a mark of Jewishness, circumcision epitomized the Jew's status as "the Other." It was deemed proof that the Jew's penis sinned against God's creation. Yet *The Golden Legend,* a popular religious book of the Renaissance era, declared that the day of Jesus' circumcision, when "he began to shed his blood for us . . . was the beginning of our redemption," a view shared by Aquinas.

That latter view had a bizarre, and probably unintended, result. In an age that prized religious relics, the most prized relic of them all was Jesus' foreskin. More than a dozen churches, including Saint John Lateran in Rome, the Pope's church, claimed to own a piece, or all, of the Holy Prepuce, the only part of Jesus that unequivocally remained on Earth. The foreskin relic at the Abbey Church of Coulombs, near Chartres, in France, was thought to cure sterility in females and render the subsequent delivery painless. It was said that Queen Catherine of England borrowed it for the second purpose in the early fifteenth century. So happy were she and her husband, Henry V, with the results—the future Henry VI—they built a special sanctuary to house the holy relic once they returned it.

Still, there was constant competition for the title of official Holy Prepuce, and these multiple sightings led to comparisons with the Miracle of Loaves and Fishes. John Calvin was dubious such a small piece of epidermis could be so often divided, and marveled similarly at the number of churches claiming to own vials of Mary's breast milk. "Had Mary been a cow all her life," Calvin wrote, "she could not have produced such a quantity." Martin Luther had similar scorn for relics, wondering how there could be twenty-six burial places in Rome for eleven apostles, or how there could be so many different Holy Foreskins, each of them claiming to be authentic.

This profusion of Holy Prepuces—all of them fetching high prices on the booming relics market—led to the rise of special connoisseurs and the development of certain tests to determine a specimen's authenticity. The most common of these tests was a *taste* test. A properly trained physician chosen by the local priest would chew the shriveled leather, historian Marc Shell writes, to determine whether it was wholly or partly human.

The Christian idea of the penis was now separate and unequal: demonic in humans, divine in Jesus. It was believed that Mary carried the foreskin of Jesus on her person for the rest of her life. In the fourteenth century, Bridget of Sweden had a vision in which Mary appeared to her with the relic in her hand and told the future saint she gave the treasure to the apostle John. Such visions were common in the Middle Ages, especially by women. Saint Catherine of Siena, one of only two females honored as a Doctor of the Church, claimed the ring she wore to signify her betrothal to Jesus was a mystical form of his foreskin. Saint Agnes of Blannbekin imagined she was swallowing the Holy Prepuce at Communion. In France it was said that the Holy Prepuce, protected by a shriveled leather pouch, had been brought to the court of King Charlemagne at Aix-la-Chapelle. This became known as the "Purse Reliquary of the Circumcision." Historian Marie-Madeleine Gauthier writes that the shape of this holy purse became the fashionable shape for all purses in medieval Europe.

Certainly no purse was more fashionable or valuable than the original, holding its tiny but prized contents. According to an article published in 1870 in the French *Journal L'Excommunier,* a thief stole the foreskin of Jesus that belonged to the Church of Saint John Lateran in 1527. The criminal hid his prize in a box, which was found thirty years later by a priest who carried it to the home of a female patron. The box contained a piece of Saint Valentine, the lower jaw of Saint Martha, and a small purse marked "JESUS." The lady opened the purse, the newspaper reported, and immediately "the most fragrant odor pervaded the apartment . . . while the hand that held it was seen perceptibly to swell and stiffen."

Not everyone had such a pleasant experience with the Holy Prepuce, however. In 1559, so the story goes, when the relic was back at Saint John Lateran, a priest "impelled by curiosity and untempered by piety" made an examination of it during which he had the temerity to break off a small piece. "Instantly the most dreadful tempest broke over the place, followed by crashing peals of thunder and blinding flashes of lightning, then a sudden darkness covered the entire country," said the account in the *Journal L'Excommunier.*

The blasphemer threw himself on the floor, sure that he had breathed his last. What he probably did not know was that, not far away, men of science had begun doing experiments and investigations that would change once again the way man saw his defining organ. No longer would the debate on man's link with his penis be dominated by competing religious conceptions—as divine or demonic. The mystery of the organ's power and potency would be examined under a new lens. Theology would slowly yield to biology.

# II

## The Gear Shift

Maybe he thought of Mona Lisa when he cut open the first corpse. Standing alone in a cold, dank hospital room filled with bloody entrails, inhaling the fumes of putrefaction, the silence broken only by the whine of his bone saw and scratch of his quill pen, Leonardo da Vinci no doubt had a lot on his mind. It was two years, maybe more, since he began his portrait of Signora Giocondo. She was an alluring subject, yet he went weeks without asking her to sit for him, sometimes longer without looking at her on the canvas. Clearly, the artist was distracted. The chance to look *inside* a human had that effect on him.

Da Vinci the painter marveled at the body as a work of art; da Vinci the scientist was thrilled by its bioengineering. He planned to merge those passions in a book on anatomy that would trace life from conception to death and depict every bone, muscle, organ, nerve, artery, and vein in the human body. Sometime around 1503 da Vinci was quietly given access to unclaimed corpses at a Florentine hospital. He had asked for it because he was convinced the only way to really know the human machine was to take it apart and examine the pieces. While still painting *Mona Lisa,* da Vinci started dissecting humans. This was difficult, disgusting work in an age without electric lights or refrigeration—somewhat dangerous, too, considering the Inquisition's dim view of the practice. "I destroyed all the [dissected] organs and took away . . . all the flesh," da Vinci wrote in his journal, perhaps mindful of the benefit of removing the evidence of his blasphemy. None of that flesh intrigued him more than the penis.

Though it is not widely known, the genius who painted *Mona Lisa* and *The Last Supper*, and who designed—five hundred years ago—fantastic machines that anticipated the helicopter and submarine, also investigated the male member as no one before him ever had. These inquiries, written right-to-left in "mirror writing," are recorded in da Vinci's notebooks, a mind-boggling collection of philosophical musings, military inventions, meditations on art and the scientific method, architectural designs, anatomical drawings, urban-planning systems, and elaborate sketches of penises that filled five thousand pages and authenticated its author as the quintessential Renaissance Man. Of the countless examples of brilliance inside those books, those concerning the penis—and there are many—show Leonardo to have been an early and eager promoter of the sea change that ultimately lifted the organ out of the realm of religion and into the world of science. After da Vinci, who died in 1519, there would always be an example for those who refused to see the penis as the gauge of man's proximity to the Devil. For these secular investigators the penis was something else entirely: a fascinating measure of man the machine. Man's relationship with his defining organ could not only be redeemed but scientifically understood. The demon rod became the gear shift.

It is not surprising that someone as creative as Leonardo would be fascinated by the penis. For him, the mystery of this organ existed on two levels: physiological and psychological. In one of his most famous journal drawings, known as the "coition figure," da Vinci imagined the mechanics of intercourse by drawing two people making love cut in half lengthwise, or hemisected. The penis in this unusual sketch—not only are the lovers sliced open, they are standing up—enters the vagina as a key into a lock. This reflected the artist's vision of genitalia as gears of the *machina mundi*, the "universal machine," in which all parts have their proper fit. (That's "proper" as defined by nature, not by humans.) "The woman likes the penis as large as possible, while man desires the opposite of the woman's womb. Neither gets his wish," da Vinci pointed out. Leonardo was similarly bemused by genital architecture. If the pubic bone did not act as the foundation for the erect penis, he wrote in his journal, "the force of coitus" would produce a queer result, indeed: "The penis would enter more into the body of the actor, than into the person acted upon."

If that penis failed to stiffen, there would be no action at all. Da Vinci's ideas on erection mechanics showed a precocious grasp of male sexual functioning. The Greeks taught, and medieval Europeans believed, that erection was "inflation by wind," a breathlike "spirit" from the liver that traveled to the heart then back through the arteries, filling the hollow of the penis. Da Vinci believed what he saw with his own eyes. In 1477 he attended a public hanging. At the subsequent dissection of this body by anatomists, a practice allowed twice a year by Florentine authorities on dead criminals, da Vinci saw what really filled the organ.

> I have seen . . . dead men who have the member erected, for many die thus, especially those hanged. Of these [penises] I have seen the anatomy, all of them having great density and hardness, and being quite filled by a large quantity of blood. . . . If an adversary says wind caused this enlargement and hardness, as in a ball with which one plays, I say such wind gives neither weight nor density. . . . Besides, one sees that an erect penis has a red glans, which is the sign of the inflow of blood; and when it is not erect, this glans has a whitish surface.

In 1585 Ambroise Paré, personal physician to four kings of France and often called the father of modern surgery, published the same conclusion in a medical treatise. According to the American Urological Association, this was the first accurate description of the role of blood in the erection process in official Western medical literature. What Dr. Paré did not know was that da Vinci, a medical amateur, had already written it a century earlier.

Modern urologists marvel at Leonardo's accurate drawings of the epididymis (the comma-shaped structure adjoining each testicle where final maturation of sperm cells occurs) and the vas deferens, the much straighter tube that conveys the spermatic fluid to the neck of the bladder for emission through the urethra during climax. But da Vinci did not get everything right. Several attention-grabbing errors occur near or in the coition figure. Not far from that undated drawing, on the same sheet, a different, freestanding penis is depicted in three-quarters perspective. Da Vinci drew many male organs in his journals; what makes this one memorable is that it is sliced nearly through at a point just behind the glans, which falls forward like the door of an open mailbox, a distressing image for any male eyes. The severed shaft behind the glans reveals two tubes inside, one for urine, the other for semen. This odd blunder—asserting there are two urethras inside every human penis—shows how Church dogma was still trumping science in the late fifteenth and early sixteenth centuries. Medieval anatomists felt the need to establish a boundary between urine, thought by the Church to be entirely polluting, and semen which, although the carrier of original sin, was still viewed by Rome as the source of a new human soul, however tainted that soul might be. Clearly, da Vinci's drawing of the twin-tubed penis shows the impact of such teachings.

Similar errors are drawn nearby. The semen tube in the coition figure originates at the base of the spine, a placement reflecting the teachings of Hippocrates, the Greek father of medicine who taught two thousand years earlier that semen enters the penis from the spinal marrow, something Plato believed as well. There is only one problem: this tube does not really exist. The coition figure also shows an artery linking the penis to the aorta, an explanation for male libido championed by Galen, the second-century Greek who wrote nearly five hundred Latin treatises on medicine and anatomy and counted Emperor Marcus Aurelius among his patients. Though it is unlikely that da Vinci (who read no Latin) ever read Galen, the Greek's ideas so dominated late medieval medicine that everyone then alive was a Galenist the way most today have a Darwinian outlook though few have read *The Origin of Species*. Galen's job at a gladiator school early in his career gave him ample access to body wounds in humans, but his medical books were based on classical metaphysics and the dissections of animals. It is not too surprising, then, that the artery drawn by da Vinci linking the human penis and the aorta, like Hippocrates' tube between the penis and the spine, does not really exist. Though Leonardo drew it as if it did, there is some evidence he doubted Galen on this point. "Are not the testicles the cause of ardor?" he wrote on the page. Five centuries later, when scientists isolated testosterone, the hormone from the testicles that *is* largely responsible for male libido, da Vinci was proved right.

---

But of da Vinci's many insights into the penis, perhaps the most impressive were psychological. His journals display a modern understanding of the penis as the key to the psychic vault of attitudes and anxieties that comprise the masculine mystique. As an artist, scientist, and engineer, Leonardo knew that mystique compels man to impose his will on the world. Yet as a male, da Vinci knew man cannot always impose his will on his penis. "Often a man is asleep and it is awake," he wrote, "and many times a man is awake and it is asleep. Many times a man wants to use it, and it does not want to; many times it wants to and man forbids it." There seems no doubt, da Vinci said, that the penis has a mind of its own.

The questions on the mind of da Vinci come through loud and clear in that passage: Do I control my penis or does it control me? And if I submit, to what am I yielding? Historian Sander L. Gilman has an intriguing theory on that last question. He believes da Vinci's lovers in the coition figure were deliberately drawn standing up to accentuate the bestial nature of male sexual desire. Leonardo's model, Gilman suggests, was the Greek myth of Leda and the Swan. In that legend, Zeus, after taking the form of a beast, rapes a mortal woman. Rape was always depicted vertically in classical art, Gilman says, unlike other classical depictions of sexual intercourse, which show lovers in the more conventional horizontal manner. There is no conclusive way to test Gilman's thesis. But there is little doubt that the questions raised by da Vinci concerning man's relationship with his penis are the very questions that make that relationship the most enduring mystery in every man's life. This da Vinci realized four centuries before Sigmund Freud.

Contained within those same journal musings are hints of da Vinci's discomfort with his own sexuality. Florentine court records show that Leonardo was arrested in 1476, accused of having carnal relations with the male prostitute and *sodomitari* Jacopo Saltarelli. Though details are sketchy, it appears two criminal hearings were held, after which da Vinci was released because of insufficient evidence. Some historians believe Leonardo benefitted from the intervention of the well-connected Tornabuoni family. Apparently, a young scion of that wealthy clan was a codefendant alongside young da Vinci.

Leonardo was described by Giorgio Vasari in *Lives of the Most Eminent Painters, Sculptors and Architects,* a book published in 1550 and based on interviews with people who knew da Vinci, as a man of "supernatural" beauty and strength who could bend a horseshoe with his bare hands. Da Vinci never married, fathered no children (that we know of), and surrounded himself with attractive, often effeminate, protégés. In *Leonardo da Vinci and a Memory of His Childhood,* Freud located the origin of da Vinci's erotic preference in a recollection the artist recorded in his journal. While still young enough to be lying in a baby carriage, da Vinci was attacked by a bird of prey. The animal "opened my mouth with its tail," da Vinci wrote, "then stuck me with the tail inside my lips again and again." The founder of psychoanalysis declared the tail to be a phallic symbol, a term he had recently popularized, and the dream to be a sexual fantasy, each showing his subject's latent homosexuality and subsequent fascination with flight.

Freud's use of the word "latent" was consistent with his belief that Leonardo had not been intimate with any of his male protégés, "choosing instead the cool repudiation of sexuality." But historian Kenneth Clark disagrees, concluding from the available evidence that the great master was, indeed, a homosexual. "We cannot look at Leonardo's work and maintain that he had the normal man's feelings for women," Clark wrote in *Leonardo da Vinci: An Account of His Development as an Artist*. But "those who wish, in the interests of morality, to reduce Leonardo, that inexhaustible source of creative power, to a neutral or sexless agency, have a strange idea of doing service to his reputation." Leonardo, himself, said little on the subject, other than a small note in his journal that seems to support the Freudian view: "Intellectual passion," he wrote, "drives out sensuality." We know that many Florentine artists were openly attracted to other men in this era without causing scandal. But "in contrast to this social acceptance," Gilman writes, such behavior was marked by the culture at large as a "loss of control over those forces that human beings must control."

It seems possible that, for da Vinci, the force resisting control—and threatening to turn a powerful man into a weakling—was his penis. Several journal drawings suggest this psychoerotic turmoil was still churning decades after his arrest on vice charges. One page of Leonardo's notebook shows an erect penis sketched near the bottom of the sheet. To its left is a muscular male torso, in profile, its back turned to the penis. Whether intentional or not, the penis is poised to enter the male's anus. Even more to the point, it appears a perfect fit, another "key and lock" mechanism, just like the penis inside the vagina depicted in the coition figure. Apparently for da Vinci the temptation to be weak was always strong. And his opponent rose up to meet him every morning.

This striking sketch shows da Vinci's grasp of the penis's defining paradox: it is the only organ simultaneously a part of, yet apart from, the rest of the body. The drawing also reveals a paradox about da Vinci himself. His work as a painter and sculptor convinced him of the ultimate power of sight. Leonardo believed it is through vision, not mental abstraction, that man gains the knowledge to master the environment and his individual fate. Yet da Vinci also understood, four hundred years before Freud, that fantasies and dreams, Herr Professor's unconscious, yield visions of the truth as real as anything seen by the naked eye. Da Vinci's recurring image of the penis unattached to a body—an independent agent, strong-willed and out of control—is a compelling example. The artist saw this in his mind's eye, yet he was certain this fantasy signified the truth.

The truth about the penis, Leonardo made clear in his journals, is that it is a mystery. And da Vinci loved mysteries, especially about himself. In *Lives of the Most Eminent Painters,* Vasari concluded that Leonardo's often eccentric personality and mannerisms were designed to cultivate an air of strangeness. According to Professor Henri Zerner, this quirk was the genesis of the mirror writing in da Vinci's journal, which was designed less as a code to protect indiscreet diary entries than to puzzle and amaze the artist's friends.

The mysterious powers of the penis puzzled and amazed Leonardo. But, no matter how ungovernable, the organ was never despised by him as a demon rod. "One has no right to love or hate anything if one has not acquired a knowledge of its nature," he wrote. The penis was the subject of a lifelong investigation by da Vinci, and no certainty was achieved beyond acceptance of its status as an enigma. The handsome, muscular man who surrounded himself with young, attractive protégés may have worried that the organ's power might weaken him. But the artist in him was moved by its spontaneity, and the scientist in him by its complex anatomical structure. Both were intrigued by its mystery.

The impressive insights and surprising errors in da Vinci's anatomical drawings, along with his grasp of the organ's role in the deepest workings of the male psyche, show that he viewed the penis while straddling two worlds, the medieval and the modern, and that he sometimes lost his balance. It is hard for us now to understand how the person who was so right about the anatomy of the testicle was so wrong about the anatomy of the penis shaft right next to it. One theory proposes that the testicle drawings were based on actual dissections, while the penis drawings were merely attempts to illustrate descriptions that da Vinci had read of the organ's interior made by scientists who had never cut one open. Why da Vinci never corrected those sketches remains a mystery.

We know, however, that on or around 1503 da Vinci began to dissect humans himself and to rely less on medieval anatomy texts, all of which were riddled with errors. This commitment to personal research unfettered by religious preconceptions, to physics over metaphysics, made Leonardo a pioneer in the secularization of the human body. No matter how many errors he made, Leonardo was the first person in Western history to even *try* to depict the internal organs with anatomical accuracy. According to the surgeon and medical historian Sherwin B. Nuland, "there is no medical textbook of [da Vinci's] time or previously in which the viscera are shown in anything but a diagrammatic or . . . symbolic form." In the late eighteenth century, Nuland writes, the Scottish surgeon William Hunter asked for permission to study some of Leonardo's anatomical drawings, which had just been discovered inside a locked chest in Windsor Castle. Hunter "expected to see little more than such as might be useful to a painter," he wrote at the time. Instead, "with astonishment," Hunter's own eyes "persuaded [him] that

Leonardo was the best anatomist at that time in the world." The twentieth-century historian H. Hopstock went even further in paying tribute to Leonardo's skills in that area.

> No one before him, so far as is known, made so many dissections on human bodies nor did any understand so well how to interpret the findings. . . . He was the first to give a correct description of the human skeleton. . . . He was the first to give a correct picture of practically all the muscles of the human body. . . . No one before him had drawn the nerves and the blood-vessels even approximately as correctly as he.

Though da Vinci's anatomy book was never finished, the process he started with those drawings was more than a great intellectual leap forward. It was an exorcism, one that liberated the penis more than any other organ because the penis had been demonized more than any other organ. We see some of the first signs of this sea change—unfortunately, one that would gain wide acceptance too late to save the "witch" Anna Pappenheimer—in da Vinci's notebooks. On those remarkable pages, unlike the writings of Augustine, another man of passion and intellect who struggled to understand the male organ's power and purpose, Leonardo finished his written thoughts on that subject not with religious rage, but worldly respect:

"A man who is ashamed to show or name the penis is wrong. [Instead] of being anxious to hide it, man ought to display it," da Vinci wrote, "with honor."

———————

Twenty-four years after da Vinci's death, a Belgian physician named Andreas Vesalius wrote the first illustrated anatomy book based on dissection to take a systematic secular look at the human body. *De humani corporis fabrica* (*On the Fabric of the Human Body*), published in 1543, was so well conceived and il-

lustrated that a historian later insisted, wrongly, that it was pla-
giarized from a lost work by Leonardo.

The son of an apothecary, Vesalius dissected cats and dogs as
a boy to prepare for his goal of exploring the human interior as
an anatomist. At the University of Paris, however, he was
greatly disappointed by the curriculum. Dissections of human
cadavers occurred but twice a year, and the professor did not do
the cutting himself. Instead, he remained at a podium, reading
long passages from Galen or another old source as a poorly educated assistant, often a barber, did the incisions and held up
the decomposing organs for inspection. Years later Vesalius
mocked such professors for "cackling like jackdaws from a
lofty chair about things they never tried." One of the books
from which they cackled described the male genitalia as follows:

> The testicles . . . are formed of glandular, white, soft, and
> spongy flesh. . . . The substance of the sperm, before it
> comes to the testicle, is received in a certain follicle, in
> which it is altered and whitened. . . . The penis [shaft] is
> fleshy, nervous, round and hollow . . . and is formed of two
> cords placed side by side transversely, which is necessary
> for double cause. First, that it may eject sperm into the
> vulva; for this reason it is made nervous. . . . It is hollow, in
> order that in the presence of ardent desire it may be ex-
> tended and erected with the greatest possible rigidity.

The penis in this passage, one of the Salernitan Demonstrations
taught at every medical school in sixteenth-century Europe, belonged to a pig. That the penis of man was considered anatomically equivalent to that of a barnyard animal—not just in
Church sermons, but in the greatest halls of learning in Europe—speaks volumes about the organ's debased status in medieval and early modern culture.

Vesalius rejected such "equivalence" and began an obsessive
pursuit of anatomical truth. While walking outside the city one

night, he came across a hanged criminal left to rot on a spike. Vesalius shinned up the pole and yanked off an arm, hiding it under his jacket until he walked home, where he cut it open and looked inside. Vesalius returned the next two nights and picked the corpse clean. What the Belgian saw in his secret dissections opened his eyes: much of what Galen wrote about the human body was wrong. Soon Vesalius demonstrated this publicly as professor of anatomy at the University of Padua. We are lucky to have an eyewitness account of Vesalius at work written by Baldasar Heseler, a German medical student in Bologna, where Vesalius was invited to lecture in 1540. The corpses of three dead criminals were made available to the professor on his arrival. Five days later a new one, freshly hanged, was added. One of the largest audiences in Bologna attended Demonstration XVII, Vesalius's dissection of the penis.

Hundreds of students hovered around the professor at his dissecting table, jostling one another to get a better view. Vesalius showed them how "the spermatic vessels . . . run in many bendings and convolutions . . . to the fleshy glands of the testicles," Heseler wrote, "and how from the testicles there are other vessels that convey the seed through the penis.

All this he showed in turn and especially how the vessels preparing the seed lie in many coils . . . around the testicles. . . . He demonstrated to us the great length of the spermatic vessels preparing the seed [by] stretch[ing] them out. . . . Eventually, he dissected the . . . penis [shaft] which he said was connected with the os pubis and the os sacrum. He showed us . . . the urinary duct by cutting it open, and then the duct of the seed. . . . And he showed us the spongy tube [inside the penis] which begins lower down around the anus.

After all this was done, and the hacked-up organ lay on the table, Heseler proved himself to be a worthy disciple of his new mentor: "I went up and took the dissected penis in my hands," he wrote. "I saw that the fistula spermatis was rather spongy, and I felt that the testicles were soft and light."

In August 1543 Vesalius published his *Fabrica*. Eleven inches wide, sixteen and a half inches tall, and bound in imperial purple silk velvet, the six hundred sixty-three pages within displayed the finest typography and hand-painted illustrations ever seen in a medical book—perhaps any book—to this point in history. Most of these drawings, it is believed, were the work of Jan Stefan van Kalkar, from the school of Titian. Where the frontispiece in older anatomy books paid tribute to the "cackling jackdaws" that Vesalius so despised, the *Fabrica*'s title page gave center stage to the cadaver. It—the body—is the authority. Vesalius is drawn on the frontispiece reaching inside the corpse to point out its contents to a throng of eager students. At the top of the page is Death, rendered as a skeleton. But this is not the Grim Reaper. His scythe is gone, replaced by a rod. This is Death domesticated by Science: not the punishment for original sin but the anatomist's path into the body and the truth.

The truth about the penis, Vesalius wrote, is that "to this organ was imparted so great a power of delight in the generative act that [men] are incited by this power, and whether or not they are young and foolish or devoid of reason, they fall to the task of propagating [as if] they were the wisest of beings." This is the only comment Vesalius makes about the penis's function. He focuses instead on its form: "The male possesses two testes covered by skin which is here called scrotum. . . . The semen, when it is created, is received by a strong vessel like a worm growing in the posterior region of the testes and complexly intertwined like a tendril. . . .

For the semen and urine there is a common channel which is led slightly downward and again bends back upward to the joining of the pubic bones outside, lying under the bodies which constitute the penis. There issues forth on either side of the pubic bone a nerve and a round sinewy body which is . . . very funguslike within. . . . United and fused together, they constitute the penis; by the aid of its substance it provides for erection and enlargement when it is about to inject semen. . . . Otherwise . . . it is flaccid and slender.

This description is not impressive by literary standards. But that is actually the point, and one of Vesalius's great achievements. To understand this, one must recall the world in which the *Fabrica* was written, the world of the *Malleus Maleficarum*, the guide for witch hunters that declared in a florid, grandiose style that God gave the Devil more power over the penis than over any other organ. The *Malleus* dedicated its most purple praise to men who cut off that damned organ, becoming "eunuchs for the Kingdom of Heaven." It is against this that the flat prose of the *Fabrica* must be measured. By deflating the religious rhetoric, by considering the penis as neither divine nor demonic, but human—by focusing on form not function—Vesalius's *Fabrica* took the giant step forward that Leonardo da Vinci planned to take but never completed.

The *Fabrica* corrected more than two hundred errors made by Galen, but Vesalius also repeated some. The most shocking was his depiction of the vagina as an inverted penis. This drawing in book five of the *Fabrica* shows a uterus presented vertically. The top of this organ is rounded to suggest the beginnings of a scrotum. The remainder is shaped like the shaft of the male member. The vaginal labia clearly mimic the head of a penis divided down the middle. This "monstrous" drawing, as one modern writer called it, reminds us that the chemistry of ideas is always catalyzed by the intellectual framework of a given era. In the sixteenth century the medical paradigm was still defined by Galen, who taught that all biology is governed by internal heat. The heat in males pushes the penis out from the body, Galen wrote. The lack of heat in women, he said, makes the organ grow internally as a vagina.

Biology was metaphor to Galen and conveyed a cosmic truth: man's superiority to woman. Women are imperfect men whose lack of heat resulted in the retention inside of an organ that is properly outside. For classical Greeks and medieval Europeans, man was the measure of all things, and the measure of man was the penis. It was the "standard operating system," defining not only masculinity, but, as Vesalius's drawing of the vagina shows rather well, all of human sexuality. A century later, one of the first sex manuals written in English, *Aristotle's Master-Piece,* a book clearly not written by Aristotle, used a poem to make this point:

> Thus the women's secrets I have surveyed
> And let them see how curiously they're made:
> And that, tho' they of different sexes be,
> Yet in the Whole they are the same as we:
> For those that have the strictest Searchers been,
> Find Women are but Men turned Out side in.

It was even thought a female could turn "right side out." In 1573 Ambroise Paré wrote of a peasant girl named Marie who was chasing a herd of pigs when, without warning, "the male rod came to be developed." After talking to a doctor and a bishop, Marie changed her name to Germain and became a soldier. (Marie/Germain's fame was such that Montaigne, the legendary French traveler and essayist, came to see him while on a trip from Paris to Rome. Marie/Germain was not at home, but Montaigne was told he had not yet married and had "a big, very thick beard.")

Even if Vesalius was wrong about the vagina by modern standards, he was right about the penis in the sixteenth century, and in a way that ultimately marked a major cultural advance. This we can see in another of his illustrations. In the companion volume to the *Fabrica* designed for students to bring to the dissection table, called the *Epitome,* there is a drawing of Adam and Eve. Unlike the depiction of them that had been the norm in

Christian Europe for a thousand years, they are nude, not naked. Their bodies are not sexless instruments of humiliation. They are imposing examples of beauty, grace, and precision bio-engineering. Eve's breasts are small but attractive and firm; Adam's torso is broad and muscular. This Adam and Eve represent not the pathology of human form, but its perfection. Yet this perfection is limited because man is mortal.

But the penis grants man "immortality." This is why the drawing of Adam is so noteworthy. He is not hiding his organ in shame behind a fig leaf. Instead, his right hand extends away from his body to make the organ clearly visible. This penis is flaccid but not weak. It emerges in a vital state of potentiality, like a sapling, from a bed of pubic hair. This penis is not a reminder of original sin, nor the agent of that sin's transmission. It is the perpetuator of human existence. Even if Vesalius never read Leonardo's journals, there is no denying the Vincian truth expressed here. Adam, the first man and father to all men, is displaying his penis "with honor."

———————

After Vesalius, anatomical research on the penis began to resemble the voyages of discovery made by Columbus and Magellan. But instead of a cross, these biological explorers planted their own names. Vesalius never claimed to have discovered a part of the human body; two of his most famous students, Gabriello Fallopio and Bartolomeo Eustachi, were not so modest. Nor were those who followed. Drawings of the penis in medical books today show such parts as Buck's fascia, Cowper's gland, Ebner's reticulum, and Lecat's gulf—each one named for the scientific explorer who "found" it. From the sixteenth century on, the penis was colonized by anatomists as science challenged religion as the primary lens to view the body. This new world was conceived of more as a machine than as a landmass, however. Fallopio took the penis-as-gear-shift metaphor more literally than most. He urged mothers to stimulate the penises of their young sons with vigorous strokes—to prime the pump, so to speak, to make those organs fit for their future role in propagating the human race.

To the Church, the body was not a machine at all. It was a sacred mystery, home to both the divine soul *and* vomit, feces, and the most contaminating substance of all, semen. To bolster its own explanation for this, Rome opposed most secular inquiries into the body. If any scientific schema was acceptable, it was Galen's, with its emphasis on the body's perfect design. Jacobus Sylvius, Vesalius's teacher in Paris, attacked his former student after the publication of the *Fabrica* and defended Galen in a manner that now seems totally absurd. If a penis dissected in the sixteenth century does not show the features described by Galen, Sylvius wrote, this only proved that the human body had deteriorated from the ideal form seen in the second century by the infallible Greek.

Vesalius's successors tried to erase ideal preconceptions from genitalia. For the Dutchman Govard Bidloo, whose *Anatomia humani corporis* (*Anatomy of the Human Body*) was the most ambitious atlas since the *Fabrica,* truth was beauty but not necessarily beautiful. He drew his specimens in 1685 nailed to the dissecting table, the spikes clearly visible. In one illustration the reader's attention was drawn to the penis by a housefly walking on the corpse. Bidloo exalted the rough and imperfect nature of the body. The penis was drawn not as the flawless work of the master sculptor—God—but as it is in real life: mutable and asymmetrical; not as spirit, as flesh.

In 1668 Bidloo's countryman Regnier de Graaf produced the most thorough investigation of the penis to date. *Tractatus de vivorum organis generationi inservientibus* (*A Treatise Concerning the Generative Organs of Men*) was the work of a physician and physiologist who obviously enjoyed his work. Despite its scientific rigor, *Tractatus* is a wonderfully unpretentious document, filled with humor, personal observations, a noticeable absence of religion (though de Graaf was a practicing Catholic), and unforgettable reports on bizarre experiments, including one in which he made a permanent erection, and teaching tool, from the member of a male cadaver. "Prepare the penis in the following way," de Graaf wrote.

First, gently express the blood which is always inside . . . and then insert a tube into the spongy substance, where it approaches the bones of the pubis. Half fill the cavity of the penis with water with the aid of a syringe and shake gently. When the water has run out stained with blood, fill again with fresh water and repeat the operation until the water is no longer stained. . . . [Then] gently express between two pieces of lint the quantity of water contained in the corpora nervosa. Finally, distend the penis, by inflating it, until it reaches its natural size . . . [and] tie it up. A penis blown up in this way . . . you can examine at will; everything is clearly and distinctly visible in the natural position it has during the sexual act.

Everything about the penis's role in intercourse piqued de Graaf's curiosity. Are large noses, as many believe, accurate predictors of penile mass? "In dissecting cadavers, anatomists frequently observe the opposite," he wrote. Some corpses did surprise him, though. "We have sometimes dissected cadavers in which the penis appeared at first glance to be quite small," de Graaf said, "but when inflated [with the method described above] extended like a . . . monstrous giant."

How important is penis size, really? Sometimes, de Graaf said, less is more. "There are families which excel mightily in the quality of their venereal armour," he wrote. "[A colleague] reports that a wellborn young man married a virgin . . . of excellent [family] who not only remained sterile into the second year but eventually developed cachochymia [an imbalance of humors].

This was because of the enormous length of her husband's penis, which caused her very great pain during and after intercourse. A kind of shield, however, with a hole embroidered at the corresponding place had the effect of shortening her husband's penis and freed her from these pains, making intercourse so pleasurable that she never afterwards complained about it.

While examining the testes of animals de Graaf observed what he considered to be his most important finding—that a testicle is not solid, but made of myriad tubules. This is how he described what he saw in 1668:

> If anyone asks us what is . . . the substance of the testicles we shall say that is simply a collection of minute vessels or tubules which confect semen; if these tubules were disentangled . . . and tied to one another, they would far exceed twenty Dutch eels in length.

De Graaf examined the entire penis as a well-designed tool. He noted the absence of fat under the member's skin, and how that skin is thinner, looser, and more elastic than just about any other patch of skin on the body, factors that enable the penis to change shape and consistency as no other organ can. The glans's efficient "sense of touch" earned his praise, too, as did the regulatory role played by the central nervous system, through which the "animal spirits" flow—or don't flow—into the penis. "It would be unseemly . . . and would totally impede one's conduct of worldly affairs to be like the Satyrs and have a penis always erect," de Graaf wrote. This understanding was prescient, indeed. It was not until two centuries later that physiologists began to document the role of the brain, the spinal cord, and other parts of the nervous system in establishing the penis's "default setting" at flaccidity.

As others had before him, de Graaf correctly described the role of blood in creating rigidity. Way ahead of those peers, however, he declared that the key event in erection is not getting blood into the penis, but keeping it there. His guess as to how that happens—the contraction of muscles surrounding the erectile bodies—turned out to be incorrect. De Graaf was also wrong about the function of the seminal vesicles, which he mistakenly believed to be storehouses for semen from the testis. But de Graaf can hardly be faulted for these false steps. Most urologists—using tools far more advanced than any available to de Graaf—believed the same things several centuries later. It is quite possible that many physiological mysteries regarding the penis would have been unraveled sooner had this pioneering scientist lived longer. But Regnier de Graaf died on August 17, 1673, reportedly of the plague, while treating patients. He was thirty-two.

Fortunately, his work did not die with him. The Dutchman Frederik Ruysch used a tool invented by de Graaf—the syringe—and a secret injecting fluid of Ruysch's own design to further explore the penis's interior. The syringe and the fluid enabled Ruysch to manufacture waxlike casts of body parts that revealed the internal workings of the penis with a thoroughness never before possible. After Ruysch it was patently ridiculous for anyone to speak of "wind" causing erection. Ruysch's wax replicas of actual dissected penises—with all the arteries, veins, and capillaries exposed—showed the expanding and shrinking organ to be a marvel of hydraulic engineering. He eventually made models of nearly every internal organ, displaying them for scientists in his laboratory and, later, for tourists in rented rooms. Before Ruysch, the primary use for such castings had been the manufacture of fake religious relics, crude reproductions of the bones and body parts of saints. Now the curious and the crowned heads of Europe, including Peter the Great of Russia, who purchased Ruysch's entire collection, gazed without shame at his amazing replicas of human genitalia. Formerly unmentionable, the penis was discussed by scientists and czars; once hidden, it was now displayed "with honor" as a wondrous machine.

Those exhibitions might never have happened were it not for another Dutchman. Even before intellectuals and thrillseekers began to stare at Ruysch's "cabinet of wonders," an autodidact named Antony van Leeuwenhoek was doing some gawking of his own. After watching spectacle-makers in his hometown of Delft, where his neighbors included de Graaf and a painter named Vermeer, Leeuwenhoek started making microscopes as a hobby. To the surprise of everyone but himself, this school dropout, drapery salesman, and part-time janitor at Delft City Hall created the most powerful microscopic instruments in Europe. Some could magnify an object more than two hundred fifty times, an amazing feat considering that when the century began the finest lenses in the world could barely make a pea look as large as a walnut. On April 26, 1673, de Graaf brought these microscopes to the attention of the Royal Society of London, then the world's leading scientific institution. The Fellows of that Society, who included Isaac Newton and William Harvey, were curious indeed to learn what Leeuwenhoek could see with his devices. (Unfortunately, de Graaf was never able to use those instruments himself in any systematic fashion; he died four months later.)

In 1675, after examining a drop of rainwater that had stood for days in a metal tub, Leeuwenhoek discovered the existence of bacteria. But it is another of his history-making discoveries that will occupy our attention, a breakthrough that put the penis at the center of three of the biggest and oldest questions ever raised by humankind: Who are we? What are we made of? How did we get here? This event occurred in 1677, when Leeuwenhoek reported his discovery of spermatozoa.

"What I describe here was not obtained by any sinful contrivance on my part," he wrote the Society. "The observations were made upon the excess with which Nature provided me in my conjugal relations." Having established that he was not a chronic masturbator, Leeuwenhoek recounted what he saw in his semen under his microscope. He called them "animalcules."

"I judge a million of them would not equal a large grain of sand," he wrote. "Their bodies were rounded, but blunt in front and running to a point behind, and furnished with a long thin tail. . . . [They] moved with a snake-like motion of the tail, as eels do when swimming in water."

———————

It is not easy for a person born in the twentieth century to grasp the immensity of this breakthrough. We are totally accustomed to the existence of microorganisms, cell biology, and the notion that even inanimate matter is composed of trillions of particles invisible to the naked eye. *None* of this was apparent before Leeuwenhoek. He saw something, a whole universe, that no one had ever seen.* This sighting changed everything: man's understanding of himself, his relationship to God, to nature, to reproduction, to sexuality, and, of course, to his penis. This is because Leeuwenhoek found this new world of animalcules, tiny "eels" whose hyperactive life cycle seemed anything but providential, inside the most mysterious human product of them all: semen.

Leeuwenhoek's most mysterious finding was yet to come, however. Inside the animalcules in the thickest part of the semen he saw

all manner of great and small vessels, so various and so numerous that I do not doubt that they be nerves, arteries and veins. . . . And when I saw them, I felt convinced that,

———

*Some believe that spermatozoa may have been first sighted by a Dutch medical student, Johan Ham, several months before Leeuwenhoek. It appears that Ham brought a sample of gonococcal discharge (not his own) to Delft for study under Leeuwenhoek's microscope. Ham had already observed "little animals with tails" in that sample, historian Edward G. Reustow writes; Leeuwenhoek confirmed their existence. (It is likely that the gonococcal sample included semen.) What we know for certain is that Leeuwenhoek was the first scientist to *report* the existence of spermatozoa.

in no full-grown body, are there any vessels which may not
be found likewise in semen.

With this last line Leeuwenhoek placed himself—and the
penis—at the vortex of a scientific, philosophical, and religious
debate on human existence that consumed much of the next
century. This debate was about "preformationism," defined by
historian Peter J. Bowler as "the belief that the generation of
new organisms is nothing more than the expansion of minia-
tures which have existed since the creation of the universe,
stored up one generation within another." Leading the anti-
preformationist camp was William Harvey, the first scientist to
correctly describe the circulation of blood. Harvey believed development to be the result of epigenesis, the process by which an
embryo develops from an originally undifferentiated structure,
the fertilized egg.

   Preformationism may seem ridiculous now, but it made sense
to many naturalists participating in the scientific revolution.
This is because they lived two centuries before Oscar Hertwig,
in 1875, declared fertilization to be the fusion of sperm and
ovum nuclei, a scientific fact observed for the first time in 1879
by Hermann Fol, using a microscope far more powerful than
any built by Leeuwenhoek in his home workshop in Delft. Until
technology made that possible, reproduction was as much a
philosophical mystery as it was a scientific one. Preformation
attracted followers because it explained reproduction without
challenging the primacy of mechanistic causes, and because it
agreed with Descartes's idea of the infinite divisibility of a natural world initiated, but not interfered with, by God. These
ideas were at the cutting edge of both science and philosophy in
the seventeenth and eighteenth centuries. When Leeuwenhoek
saw those vessels inside spermatozoa, he offered the most compelling proof yet for preformationism. He also allied himself
with one side in a dispute within the preformationist camp. This
debate was not about whether humans were preformed, but

where. "Ovists" believed it was in the egg; "spermists," the semen. Leeuwenhoek supported the penis position. Loudly.

The idea that sperm by itself could generate life—or, at least, manliness—was the philosophy behind pederasty in ancient Greece. In the Middle Ages and into the early modern era, the power of semen was thought to be awesome, indeed. The sixteenth-century Swiss-German alchemist and physician Theophrastus Bombastus von Hohenheim, better known as Paracelsus, claimed to have witnessed the ultimate organic transformation: "Let the sperm of a man be putrefied in a gourd glass," he wrote.

> Seal it up in horse-dung for forty days, or so long until it begins to be alive, move, and stir. . . . After this time it will be something like a man, yet transparent, and without a body. Now, after this, if it be every day nourished with . . . man's blood, and for forty weeks be kept in a constant, equal heat of horse-dung, it will become a true and living infant, having all the members of an infant born of woman.

According to legend, the dying Paracelsus had his penis cut into pieces and buried in bloody manure; the plan was to have himself resuscitated months later as a virile young man. Unfortunately, so the story goes, his bumbling servant opened the grave too soon, finding only dust.*

Leeuwenhoek never went that far. But his dissections of animal testes, where he saw more animalcules than ever, convinced him, rightly, that spermatozoa were produced there. This, too, marked a scientific advance. Ancient cultures had devised many theories to explain the origin of semen. The Sumerians said it

---

*Paracelsus was, indeed, eccentric. But he was also the first man in Western history to argue that disease is not a maladjustment of "humors" within the body, but a condition caused by agents from without. That revolutionary idea was one of the founding steps in the creation of modern medicine.

came from bones; the Egyptians, the spinal column; and the Hindus, food. Some Greeks pointed to blood, others to the brain or spinal marrow. Western Europeans were similarly divided on the subject. For Leeuwenhoek, his microscopic observation of testes and his ongoing observations of his own semen confirmed his belief that mammalian ovaries were useless ornaments, and that the sole function of the female sex was to receive and nourish the male seed where the future human was preformed in its entirety.

This belief that parenthood is really a male function—that man is the artist, the woman mere material—goes back at least as far as Aristotle. The artist's tool in this act is, of course, his penis. What convinced Leeuwenhoek of the primacy of the male in generation was the amazing motility of spermatozoa. Motion signified animal life, and animal life presumed a complex structure, and, in Leeuwenhoek's view, a soul, at least as far as human sperm was concerned. In 1685 Leeuwenhoek asserted the likely existence of a preformed man inside every sperm. He never claimed to see such "men," however, and, in truth, he had trouble replicating the sighting of the "vessels" that put him on the spermist side of the debate in the first place. Other men with inferior microscopes, but superior imaginations, were less hesitant.

At the end of the seventeenth century, two scientists released drawings of preformed men they had "observed." Nicolaas Hartsoeker drew a sperm that resembled a hot-air balloon with a tail. Inside was a tiny naked man sitting on his haunches, his head bent forward, and his knees pulled to his chest, held there by his hands clasped over his shins. A few years later François de Plantade drew several sperm cells, each revealing within a minuscule man standing on two legs, his two arms crossed in front of him, and his head encased in a hood. Midway through the next century, Gautier d'Agoty drew a tiny man-child inside a sperm with a gigantic bald head much like the intergalactic aliens featured in supermarket tabloids today.

These bogus sightings of "homunculi," as they were called, clearly damaged the cause of spermism, but in the end the movement died for more important reasons: It was unable to explain why so many preformed men died in the uterus without being "awakened" from inside the spermatozoa that encased them; and it was proved wrong by technological advances showing human development to be the result of epigenesis, the theory first postulated by William Harvey in 1651.

It is tempting to dismiss spermism as a quaint curiosity in the history of ideas, on a par, say, with believing that the Earth is flat. To do so would be to make an obvious point but to miss a deeper one. For all its flaws, spermism was a serious effort to understand the power and purpose of the penis, the mechanisms of its potency, and the meaning of man's relationship to God, nature, and the mysterious organ that raises these questions so persistently. The answers it provided, no matter how short-lived scientifically, had a lasting impact on Western culture. Even if spermism failed to explain generation, it succeeded in changing the terms of the discussion. Augustine taught that semen emitted during intercourse is the agent by which original sin passes from one generation to the next. This idea pervaded the medieval world and did more to demonize the penis than any other teaching. It denaturalized semen, transforming it from a biological agent of life into a theological instrument of damnation. To grasp the penis was to shake hands with the Devil; to spill one's seed into a woman was to ensure the perpetuation of man's fallen state. Man's link with his defining organ was a partnership with evil from which there were only two modes of escape: chastity and death.

But in the two centuries between Leeuwenhoek's discovery of spermatozoa and Fol's observation of fertilization, semen was transported out of the realm of theology and into that of biology. No longer was it an Augustinian agent of death, but a blameless instrument of reproduction. Like the body as a whole, semen had been secularized. A giant step forward in that process, ironically, was initiated by a Catholic priest. In 1769, nearly a century after Leeuwenhoek first saw his animalcules, Father Lazzaro Spallanzani, a naturalist at the University of Pavia, criticized the scientific establishment for doing so little to advance the understanding of their biological function. He dedicated himself to "following this race of little animals . . . and investigating . . . the laws they observe among themselves." In the course of his research, Spallanzani became the first scientist to prove that fertilization without semen is impossible. He did this by observing several groups of frogs engaged in reproduction, which, for nearly all members of that species, is external: the female emits thousands of eggs; the male sprays them with his semen. In every group of Spallanzani's frogs but one, the males were left to their own devices. Spallanzani dressed the remaining males in tight taffeta pants.

"The idea of the breeches, however whimsical and ridiculous it may appear, did not displease me, and I resolved to put it into practice," he wrote in *Dissertation Concerning the Generation of Certain Animals.*

> The males, notwithstanding this encumbrance, seek the females with equal eagerness, and perform, as well as they can, the act of generation; but . . . the eggs [from the female] are never prolific, for want of having been bedewed by semen, which sometimes can be seen in the breeches in the form of drops.

Only the eggs that came into contact with semen brought forth young, Spallanzani reported. Previously, the contribution of sperm to this process was said to be spiritual, rather than material. Now the reverse was a demonstrated fact. This was a terrifically liberating observation from which there was no turning back. The penis—and man's relationship to it—had moved from the supernatural to the natural.

But as Father Spallanzani was demonstrating the naturalness of the penis's most important product, there were *un*natural acts being committed on the penis not far from his laboratory. Historians estimate that five thousand European boys lost the use or very existence of their testicles each year of the eighteenth century, most of them in Italy. These procedures were not intended to make the boys harem slaves, as happened (most often to black Africans) in the Ottoman Empire, headquartered several hundred miles to the east. Nor were they done as punishment, as was the case with military enemies and adulterers since the beginnings of recorded history. To the contrary, the goal in eighteenth-century Europe was to create the possibility that these neutered boys would later become rich and famous beyond their wildest dreams. (Or, more accurately, the wildest dreams of their parents, who allowed the operations to happen.) All of these boys were castrated; the luckiest among them became castrati, professional singers in Italian opera seria, the greatest public art form of its time.

The original impetus for castrati, however, was religious. The development of complex polyphonic choir scores, many written for voices in the higher register, led Catholic choir masters to experiment with boys and adult falsettoists as soloists and choir singers. (A papal injunction banned females from singing in public in church.) But the sound of the falsetto was eventually deemed unsatisfactory, and boys could only sing like boys for so long. Unless . . .

Of course, no one then alive understood why castration had this "freezing" effect on boys' voices. There was no awareness of testosterone or other hormones, nor their role in expanding the larynx and pharynx during puberty, or the nonexpansion and soprano register that resulted if those hormones were not produced. But eunuchs had been around for thousands of years, and the results were clear enough to see or, in this case, hear. Canon law specifically forbid the amputation or destruction of any part of the body, except to save a life. But the Church toler-

ated castrati on the grounds that the music they created honored God.

At first the operations were done in secret. But as castrati became more famous and in demand, so did the castrators.
Records from Florence's Ospedale Santa Maria Nuova, the
same institution where da Vinci dissected his cadavers, show
that eight beds were allotted for this purpose in the early eighteenth century and that the Maestro dei Castrati, Antonio San-
terelli, was among the highest-paid surgeons on the staff. This
isn't to suggest that surgery was always involved; many testicles
were simply crushed. Either way, the operation was not considered major. A contract from 1687 cited by historian John
Rosselli shows that "13 days" was deemed a proper period of
convalescence. Such contracts were typically drawn between
the parents of the boy and the singing teacher paying for the
cost of the operation. Afterward, the boy would receive
instruction from the teacher, whom he would also serve as an
apprentice.

In 1589 Pope Sixtus V issued a bull providing for the inclu-
sion of four eunuchs in the choir of Saint Peter's. By 1640 castrati occupied places of honor in all the significant church choirs
in Italy. This marked a strange detour, indeed, from the course
charted a century and a half earlier by Leonardo da Vinci. In his
famous notebooks, the peerless genius and amateur urologist
urged man to display his penis "with honor." Now men with
key parts of the penis *removed* were working "with honor" in
some of the greatest churches in Europe, including the Pope's
private place of worship, the Sistine Chapel.

Other castrati worked in secular cathedrals. The heyday of
opera seria in the eighteenth century, "with its stylized plots involving legendary figures and gods lent itself especially to the un-
real sound of the castrato voice, even in the roles of heroic male
characters," historian J. S. Jenkins writes. The demand for and
appreciation of castrati reached unprecedented heights, and the
most accomplished among them became cultural icons and pop

stars of a magnitude not unlike today's Luciano Pavarotti and Placido Domingo—even Madonna and Michael Jackson. The Italian castrato Giovanni Manzuoli opened one opera season in London. According to Jenkins, he was paid fifteen hundred guineas to appear and another one thousand guineas for a single benefit performance. Not a bad payday now. And an even better one in 1764.

No doubt the most celebrated castrato of them all was Carlo Broschi, known professionally as Farinelli. Broschi had been castrated at age seven and made his singing debut in Naples eight years later. His incomparable voice spanned three octaves, and his thoracic development was such that it was said he could hold a note for a full sixty seconds without any need of air. In 1734 he made his debut in London, where orchestra members were so enthralled by his instrument they forgot to play their own. "One God, one Farinelli!" a British woman screamed during Broschi's performance. Perhaps the artist found her comment distracting. Still, it was no doubt sweeter to his ears than the oft-heard cry of opera lovers in Italy: *"Viva il coltello!"* (Long live the knife!)

Adoration from female admirers had tangible rewards, and financial patronage was only part of the story. Though their testicles were gone or inoperative, which made them sterile, castrati were still capable of raising functional erections, much like the handsome young eunuch-slaves prized by the bored wives of Roman aristocrats (and mocked by the poet Juvenal) during the Imperial Age. Many women in the seventeenth and eighteenth centuries threw themselves at castrati, the rock stars of their time, and many castrati were receptive. A contemporary of Farinelli's, Giusto Ferdinando Tenducci, caused an international scandal by eloping with an Anglo-Irish woman, Dora Maunsell, whose father sent the police to arrest his daughter's "seducer." The couple was quickly apprehended, but Mr. Maunsell relented and declined to press charges. Several years later, the most famous fully equipped seducer of his age, Giacomo Casanova, met Mr. and Mrs. Tenducci on the Continent. Much to his surprise, Casanova wrote in his *History of My Life*, the couple was traveling with two young children. When asked by the perplexed Casanova how this was possible, Tenducci answered that he was born with three testes, and that only two had been removed by the surgeon, leaving one for procreation. Apparently, Tenducci's talent for creativity—or, in this case, fiction—was not limited to the operatic stage.

Eventually the fad for castrati faded. Certainly one man cheering that development was the Swiss philosopher Jean-Jacques Rousseau, who heaped scorn on the "barbaric parents" who sold their sons' testes in such a cruel manner. "The voice of modesty and humanity," Rousseau wrote, "vociferates loudly against this horrid custom" so contrary to "the preservation of the human race." No doubt Rousseau would have been thrilled to get credit for the decline of the castrati. But many scholars cite Napoleon's invasion of Italy, in 1796, as the primary reason, for the disruptive effect it had on operatic training at Italian musical conservatories. Whatever the cause, by the mid-nineteenth century these strange but gifted creatures were generally regarded with disapproval, and opera composers were writing their best parts for tenors, men who could reach the desired notes without medical interventions. The last operatic castrato, Giovanni Velluti, died in 1861. Some castrati, however, continued to serve in the Sistine Chapel until 1902. The last castrato to sing there, Alessandro Moreschi, died in 1922 at the age of sixty-four, which means he was probably castrated around 1865. In 1902 Moreschi became the first—and last—castrato to make a recording. He made ten discs in the next two years. His credit line on each reads, *"Soprano della Capella Sistina."*

---

If you had a fully functioning penis when castrati were the rage, there was a natural way to use it—and an unnatural way. Homosexuality was years from becoming a social issue, or even a word, so the culture aimed its displeasure at a different practice involving man and his penis. This one, as old as the species, had long been vilified by the Church. But what makes its persistent condemnation in the eighteenth century so fascinating is that the rationale then was less about Hell than health. This act was masturbation.

A defining mark of the Enlightenment was the enthusiastic reception given didactic essays. One of the most passionately argued was *Onanism: Or a Treatise on the Maladies Produced by Masturbation,* published in 1758 by Dr. Samuel-Auguste Tissot. (Actually, the biblical "sin of Onan" was coitus interruptus. It is a sign of Tissot's enduring legacy that "onanism" is still a synonym for "masturbation.") Using case histories from his practice in Switzerland, Tissot spoke the unspeakable. He declared the sexuality of children and the need to control it on medical grounds. Consequences of self-pollution, he wrote, included a weakening of the digestive and respiratory apparatus, sterility, rheumatism, tumors, gonorrhea, priapism (prolonged erection), and an often irreversible decline of the nervous system, up to and including blindness and insanity. One of his patients dried out his brain so thoroughly via masturbation, Tissot said, it could be heard rattling around his skull like a rotten walnut.

These horrors occurred, Tissot wrote, because masturbation involves an abnormal loss of *liqueur séminale.* The loss of one ounce of semen, he claimed, equals that of forty ounces of blood. Masturbatory orgasms are worse than others because the polluter relies on fantasy for his love object, thus overheating the brain. The result, he warned, is not a pretty picture. One of Tissot's patients

less resembled a living creature than a corpse. A watery, palish blood issued from his nose; slaver constantly flowed from his mouth. Having diarrhea, he voided his excrement in bed without knowing it. He had a continual flux of semen. . . . It was difficult to believe he had once been a part of the human race.

*Onanism* was not the first tract to paint this portrait, but it was the most important. The author was no quack or religious nut. Tissot had written well-received papers on smallpox, epilepsy, and the plague (even becoming the Pope's personal adviser on such matters), and he counted among his close friends the writers Jean-Jacques Rousseau and Denis Diderot, two pillars of the Enlightenment who shared his views. Diderot's *Encyclopédie* had two entries for masturbation. The first appeared under "Pollution," a word that would not evoke images of shorelines soiled by oil, fecal matter, or used hypodermic needles until the twentieth century. In the Age of Reason, "pollution" meant "the effusion of seed outside the function of marriage," or "a disease of involuntary ejaculation of seed." A more detailed description of voluntary self-stimulated ejaculation, and the horrific medical consequences that ensued, was provided in the *Encyclopédie* under "manustupration" (violation by hand).

Rousseau wrote of his "nauseating" introduction to, and subsequent powerlessness before, onanism in *Confessions*, perhaps the most influential autobiography in the secular Western canon. After moving as a young man from Switzerland to Italy, where he served as a catechumen in a monastery, Rousseau was molested in church by a priest who masturbated in front of him. "I saw shooting towards the chimney, and then falling upon the ground, I don't know what sticky white stuff that turned my stomach," Rousseau wrote.

Soon the young Rousseau knew very well what that sticky white stuff was, and how to produce it. In *Confessions* Rousseau described how he tirelessly and shamefully "worked at destroying the good constitution that nature had established in me," a process of degradation made all the more irresistible because of his roommate, a beautiful woman whose image I caressed in the depths of my heart, seeing her constantly throughout the day; in the evening surrounded by objects that reminded me of her. . . . How many stimuli! The reader who imagines all this must already think me half-dead.

In *Émile* Rousseau denounced masturbation as an evil taught to children by modern civilization. "That Genevois is my hero," Tissot wrote in a letter to a friend. This admiration was mutual. Rousseau sought Tissot's medical advice and recommended his services and writings to many of his well-known friends.

Helped by the famous Rousseau, *Onanism* not only found an audience but kept it, staying in print in several languages for more than a century. But *Onanism* was more than an unexpected international best-seller. Tissot's screed earned a permanent place in the record of Western ideas because it used a new understanding of semen to reshape man's relationship with his defining organ. In the Middle Ages, semen was satanic; the Church taught that demons were literally made of the stuff. After Leeuwenhoek and Spallanzani, it became a mechanistic agent of generation. Now, after Tissot, semen was exalted as a substance essential to health and social productivity. This created a new body image for man. No longer was his body merely a machine, now it was also a bank. And any unnecessary withdrawal of capital—semen—was extremely ill-advised.

This marked a reversal in the cultural meaning of semen, from something evil to something precious. But, ironically, this shift reestablished an old relationship between man and his penis. The organ once again became dangerous, and man's connection to it a matter of great risk. To Augustine, semen damned the entire human race by passing on original sin. To Tissot, its emission jeopardized the health of men who would be better off conserving their "essence." In both views, the penis was the most perilous part of the body. Once this was asserted on religious grounds. Now it was said in the name of science.

To curb self-pollution, Tissot recommended drinking quinine, taking cold baths, and practicing "clean thoughts." Others used harsher therapies. German writer S. G. Vogel urged an updated version of infibulation, a practice invented by the ancient Greeks in which the foreskin is pulled forward and sewed, tied, or pinned shut. (Vogel closed it down with a wire ring.) Some physicians used straitjackets or gloves to stop the masturbation. Others applied ice packs or cold-water enemas. Some encased penises in metal cages, spiked rings, or plaster casts.

Other practitioners applied leeches to the patient's penis to suck out "congestion" or plugged the urethra with electrodes. Soon respectable physicians were blistering the penile shaft with acid, introducing small infections into its skin, and passing long needles into the prostate gland. According to one bibliographical survey of medical literature, these drastic measures comprised more than 50 percent of the recommended therapies in the eighteenth and nineteenth centuries.

These doctors were certain they were saving their patients from themselves. Unrestrained, boys were likely to re-create the terrifying example of a French shepherd named Gabriel Galien, whose case was described in 1792 by the surgeon François Chopart. According to Chopart, Galien became a compulsive masturbator at age fifteen. Over time, however, normal stimulation was insufficient for climax, and Galien began to tickle his urethral canal with a long wooden splinter. His occupation allowed him the solitude and free time to perfect that methodology. But eventually Galien became inured to this new technique as well. So he used a knife to make a long slit on the underside of his penis, attempting to enlarge his urethral passage. This (at first) shallow incision, Chopart wrote,

which in any other man would have produced the sharpest pain, instead procured for [Galien] an agreeable sensation and complete ejaculation. . . . Finally, given all the effort of his passion, he managed, perhaps, after a thousand instances, to slice his penis into two equal parts.*

But even at the peak of onanomania, it was clear to some physicians that cases like Galien's were exceptional. One call for common sense on the issue came from the Scottish surgeon John Hunter. If masturbation is so unhealthy, he wondered, and so many young men practice it, why aren't there more sick young men in the world? In 1836 French surgeon Claude-François Lallemand made sure there *were* more sick men, or at least more men diagnosed as sick. He did this by trumping Tissot. Sure, masturbation is unhealthy, Lallemand wrote. But so is the unintentional loss of semen, which he called spermatorrhea. A person with this disorder, most likely a chronic masturbator, lost all ability to control his seminal flow and was thus subject to debilitating seminal discharges and eventual impotence.

Spermatorrhea quickly became the diagnostic rage and a profit center for therapeutic entrepreneurs. One memorable device to treat it was invented by a Dr. T. H. Minière. Bearing a scary resemblance (in miniature) to an invention by yet another Frenchman—Dr. Guillotin—the Minière Alarm was a thin, electrified product roughly four inches square with a hole in the center containing a floating sleeve that looked like a tiny version of Guillotin's blade. This contraption was placed around the patient's penis. If the penis thickened, it pushed the sleeve upward, sending forth two metal spears to penetrate the skin and close the electric circuit. This connection then sent a shock into the "sick" man's organ.

---

*Galien's activities did not die with him. A 1988 article in *Urology* titled "Adolescent Males Who Insert Genitourinary Foreign Bodies" reported on patients who jammed sewing needles, straight pins, copper wire, pencils, and glass thermometers into their urethras—in some cases leaving the objects there for months.

---

Nowhere was this new "semen science" better received than in the United States. Masturbation phobia and the belief in spermatorrhea were in perfect pitch with a young culture based on mercantilism, machines, misogyny, and the belief that anything can be measured or made more efficient. America's secular religion, capitalism, rewarded constructive investments and penalized foolish ones, a metaphor that extended into sex. A then common usage referred to any ejaculation as something "spent." Masturbation offered no return and was therefore condemned as wasteful. This message was preached in numerous American best-sellers, some of which predated Lallemand. Sylvester Graham wrote *A Lecture to Young Men on Chastity* in 1834. A year later, the Reverend John Todd's *The Student's Manual* described masturbators as men who put a hole in their own ship, after which they leaked self-worth until they sank. Many of these books pointed to the semen-free lives led by great men as evidence. Isaac Newton supposedly "never lost a single drop of seminal fluid." Even the libidinous French, it was argued, recognized the value of semen retention. The proof was the following conversation between novelist Honoré de Balzac and his close friend, the poet Théophile Gautier, who passed it on to posterity.

"What's the matter?" asked Gautier.
"Matter enough," said Balzac. "Another masterpiece lost to French literature!"
"What do you mean?" cried Gautier.
"I had a wet dream last night," Balzac replied, "and thus shall not be able to conceive a good story for a fortnight."

Having accepted that the body is a machine, Americans now obsessed about its overheating. Graham and another chastity entrepreneur, John Kellogg, thought the problem could be solved by monitoring the engine fuel, keeping it bland so that one's body heat would stay out of the danger zone. Though it is not widely remembered, Kellogg's corn flakes and the Graham cracker were both designed to inhibit lust and masturbation. Kellogg and Graham were not the only experts to link foods with sexual behavior. Dr. W. F. Morgan warned readers of the *New York Medical Times* that the eating of watermelon caused unnatural excitement of the penis, "a fact that is fully appreciated," he wrote, "by our colored brethren."

The body-as-machine metaphor led some American physicians to believe they could eliminate masturbation by tinkering with the engine's original design. Circumcision was not unheard of in the United States; a Jewish minority had been there for years, removing the foreskin of their male infants on the eighth day of life in a rite demanded by the Old Testament. Beginning in the late nineteenth century, however, non-Jewish physicians in the United States began to recommend and perform "hygienic circumcision," as it was called, done in a hospital or doctor's office, as a prophylaxis against infantile self-abuse.

"Children under two years of age can and frequently do contract the habit of masturbation," J. P. Webster reported to the Ohio Pediatric Society in 1875—thirty years before Freud "shocked" the world by publishing "Infantile Sexuality," one of his *Three Essays on the Theory of Sexuality.* Dr. Webster described one of his self-abusing patients as "small, [with] a scowl on his face; wearied and bloated, nervous and fretful, a poor eater and a very poor sleeper," all "due to the condition of his prepuce." (The "condition" Webster was referring to was that of having a prepuce at all.) As infants could hardly be deemed immoral, this report implied that masturbation was less a character failing than a reflex response to a physiological problem— a design flaw, as it were, that could be corrected by surgery.

A best-selling book in 1896, *All About Baby,* told American mothers that circumcision was "advisable in most cases," and particularly recommended to prevent "the vile habit of masturbation." This same advice was given in 1902 by L. Emmett

Holt, a professor at New York's College of Physicians and Surgeons, who told his colleagues that while the prepuce can "hardly be called a malformation," it is nonetheless "a condition requiring attention in every male infant," lest he be subject to "priapism, masturbation, . . . and most of the functional nervous diseases of childhood."

At first, most circumcisions were done on boys, not infants, of the middle and upper classes. According to historian David L. Gollaher, a circumcised penis soon became a badge of status—proof of one's membership in the American elite. (Europeans, however, never bought this argument, though they were as phobic about masturbation as everyone else. As a result, circumcision failed to spread outside the Jewish community there.) In America the procedure typically involved an injection of cocaine to anesthetize the penis, after which the prepuce was removed by blade or specially designed scissors. Doctors called circumcision a "painless minor operation," which, as Gollaher points out, meant "any operation done on someone else." Dr. G. W. Overall claimed in 1891 that after injecting his six-year-old patient with cocaine, he removed the child's prepuce as the boy was "discussing with his mother the kind of toys he would get for Christmas." Not every boy was so lucky, however. Dr. J. Henry Simes, writing a year earlier in *Circumcision*, a book that praised the procedure's "unquestionably prophylactic importance," admitted he had seen several cases where clumsy surgeons had sliced off a piece of the child's glans.

Over time the operation became both safer and more democratic. By the outbreak of World War I, circumcision, done shortly after birth and without a cocaine injection, was the most common surgical procedure in the United States, as it still is today, though there is no conclusive evidence establishing its role in preventing masturbation—or, for that matter, any common disease. (This is one of many reasons for the growing anti-circumcision movement in the United States, which hopes to make routine neonatal circumcision a thing of the past.)

Many Americans were too old or too frightened to be circumcised when hygienic circumcision first swept through the medical establishment. But that establishment refused to turn its therapeutic gaze away from them completely. Many of those men, it was believed, were suffering from spermatorrhea, the unintentional loss of semen first diagnosed as a disease in 1836 by the Frenchman Lallemand. Dr. Homer Bostwick's *A Treatise on the Nature and Treatment of Seminal Diseases, Impotence, and other Kindred Affections* was intended as a guide to fellow spermatorrhea specialists in America. A century and a half later, it tells us a morbid tale of medical malpractice. In his book, Bostwick asked a patient to keep a journal of his emissions. This is a condensed version:

DEC. 21: Excitement—discharge of thin, sticky, colorless stuff. A few drops.

JAN. 9: Met Miss X. After an hour got erection; connexion; did not discharge.

JAN. 14: Feeling badly; Miss X sat on my lap, gave me erections—not firm, however—soon subsided; leaked, as usual, a few drops; drank brandy.

JAN. 30: Feeling so-so; met Miss X; semi-erection, subsided; by exciting myself got erection; attempt; discharge of semen; looked rich and thick; felt happy.

FEB. 5: No erections; penis a mere pinch—wilted up; after an hour tried to excite myself; could not succeed. I now dread I have no semen.

FEB. 8: On waking, found large and stiff stains of semen; thank God I am not dry entirely; parts look small, though; I think both testicles are shrinking.

Bostwick's patient was clearly depressed, a state exacerbated by the fact that he and his healer were at cross-purposes. The patient wanted emissions; his doctor wanted to end them. To achieve his cure, Bostwick inserted a long metal instrument, known as a bougie, into the hole of his patient's penis for the purposes of dilation, exploration, and medication. This medication was often sulphuric acid or silver nitrate, chemicals perhaps better suited for the development of photographs. Bostwick's goal was to cauterize the urethra's prostatic portion, which he no doubt did. After one treatment, Bostwick removed the spike from his patient's penis and saw it was dripping with blood and pus. As he wiped it clean, his patient fainted, falling to the floor, where he struck his head on the iron fender in front of the fireplace. After waiting for his patient to regain consciousness, Bostwick reinserted the spike for another fifteen minutes.

Pain was not the only by-product of spermatorrhea treatments. Misogyny permeated the new science. If semen must be preserved, and women entice its ejaculation, women are dangerous. This warning was issued in the aptly titled book *Conjugal Sins,* written in 1870 by Dr. Augustus K. Gardner, one of America's first popular sex experts. Proper intercourse, Gardner insisted, caused the smallest expenditure of semen possible. For this reason he urged wives to lie still during the act. In 1866 Dr. J. Marion Sims, then a future president of the American Medical Association and now the subject of a highly laudatory statue in front of the New York Academy of Medicine, quantified the health threat posed by the orgiastic penis. The average seminal emission was "a dram and ten minims," he wrote, a little more than one eighth of an ounce—equal, in Tissot's calculation, to the loss of five ounces of blood. Sims's sample was taken from the vaginas of married women, but his message was aimed at unmarried male masturbators, who were thought to have more emissions than their married peers. That these men were using their penises to kill themselves led one doctor to sound the alarm in a medical journal in verse:

> In vain we scan the springs of human woe,
> To find a deadlier or more cruel foe
> To erring man, than this sad self-pollution,
> This damning wrecker of his constitution.

[handwritten margin note: another way to discourage women from feeling pleasure in sex]

The fire of heaven on Onan quickly fell,
Cursed was the culprit ere he sank to hell,
Brief was the period 'twixt the noxious deed
And the dread chastisement, pollution's meed.

Just as certain now as then, is the indulger undone,
Not by ethereal stroke as there we see,
But equal in effect and certainty,
For death results although by slow degree.

---

This doggerel was not embraced by authentic American bards, however. Mark Twain mocked the medical condemnation of masturbation in "Some Thoughts on the Science of Onanism," a speech he gave in 1879 while on his second tour of Europe. Parodying the anti-masturbation crusaders' fondness for dubious quotes by great men of yore, Twain came up with a few of his own:

Caesar, in his *Commentaries,* said, "To the lonely it is company; to the forsaken it is a friend; to the aged and impotent it is a benefactor; they that be penniless are still rich, in that they have this majestic diversion. . . . There are even times when I prefer it to sodomy."

The purity crusaders' gruesome descriptions of the consequences of the "solitary vice" were also targets of Twain's wit. Yes, "the signs of excessive indulgence in this destructive pastime are easily detectable," Twain said.

They are these: A disposition to eat, to drink, to smoke, to meet together convivially, to laugh, to joke, and tell indelicate stories—and mainly a yearning to paint pictures.

Old Masters such as Michelangelo and Rembrandt were inspired thus, Twain declared. "Old Masters," he harrumphed, "is, in fact, an abbreviation, a contraction."

For Twain, the "science" of semen retention was just another example of bourgeois hypocrisy and an easy target for a man who loved nothing better than to prick such balloons. Twain poked his fun, then moved on. That would not be the case, however, for two other titans of nineteenth-century American letters—two men who made it their mission to fight the crusade against "self-abuse," using their formidable talents to glorify the image of the erect penis and its defining product. And unlike Twain, neither one was trying to be funny.

In Chapter XCIV of *Moby-Dick,* titled "A Squeeze of the Hand," Herman Melville presented a rapturous description of a part of the whale-harvesting process called "sperm-squeezing." At the same time physicians were demonizing semen loss in the name of science, Ishmael's encounter with spermaceti—the waxy white substance in whale oil used to make cosmetics and candles—triggers a religious experience.

"It was our business to squeeze these lumps back into fluid," Ishmael says.

A sweet and unctuous duty! No wonder that in old times this sperm was such a favorite cosmetic. . . . As I sat there at my ease, cross-legged on the deck; . . . under a blue tranquil sky; the ship under indolent sail, and gliding so serenely along; as I bathed my hands among those soft, gentle globules of infiltrated tissues; . . . as they richly broke to my fingers, and discharged all their opulence, like fully ripe grapes their wine; as I snuffed up that uncontaminated aroma—literally and truly, like the smell of spring violets; I declare to you that . . . I forgot all about our horrible oath. . . . Squeeze! squeeze! squeeze! all the morning long; I squeezed that sperm till I myself almost melted in it; I squeezed that sperm till a strange sort of insanity came over me; and I found myself unwittingly squeezing my co-laborers' hands in it, mistaking their hands for the gentle globules. Such an affectionate, friendly, loving feeling did this avocation beget; that at last I was continually squeezing their hands, and looking up into their eyes sentimentally; as much as to say,—Oh! my dear fellow beings, why should we . . . know the slightest ill-will or envy? Come; let us squeeze hands all round; nay, let us squeeze ourselves into each other; let us squeeze ourselves universally into the very milk and sperm of kindness.

Noticeably absent from this ecstasy is Ahab, whose terrifying powers of concentration, the very powers lauded by Sylvester Graham, John Kellogg, Homer Bostwick, and other champions of semen retention, will mutate into a deranged quest leaving only two survivors: Ishmael and the great white sperm whale.

Clearly, man's relationship with his penis and its most important product, semen, was not rendered by Melville in 1851 as something dangerous. To the contrary, it was glorified, even sanctified. Later, Ishmael looks back on that night as an experience of paradise gained and lost. "Would that I could keep squeezing that sperm forever!" he says less in joy than in sorrow at its impossibility. Then, in the surreal imagery of the religious convert, Ishmael declares his own understanding of the event, sounding every bit the man who has experienced God for the first time, no matter how peculiar the circumstances might seem to others. "In visions of . . . that night, I saw long rows of angels in paradise," Ishmael says, "each with his hands in a jar of spermaceti."

This curious image no doubt appealed to Walt Whitman, who published his first edition of *Leaves of Grass* four years later. In "Song of Myself," Whitman's signature poem, the masturbatory implications are no less insistent, and far more personal:

If I worship one thing more than another it shall be the
    spread of my own body, or any part of it, . . .

You my rich blood! your milky stream pale strippings of
    my life! . . .
Root of washed sweet-flag!' . . . it shall be you! . . .

"Root of washed sweet-flag" was but one expression for
penis favored by Whitman. Others included "thumb of love,"
"man-root," and "tooth-prong." Whitman was America's
greatest "spermatic poet," critic Harold Aspiz writes, combin-
ing the image of "the hero as sexually charged begetter . . . with
some [deeply felt] notions about the nature of sperm as the
quintessential distillation of the body and the mind." Kellogg
and Graham would have agreed with the second half of that
sentence. But for Whitman, it was not the retention of semen
that gave power to life and art. It was the release. This he made
clear in the following lines of "Spontaneous Me."

Beautiful dripping fragments, the negligent list of one
    after another, as I happen to call them to me or
    think of them,
The real poems, (what we call poems being merely
    pictures,)
The poems of the privacy of the night, and of men
    like me,
This poem drooping shy and unseen that I always carry,
    and that men always carry,
(Know once for all, avow'd on purpose, wherever are
    men like me, are our lusty, lurking, masculine
    poems,) . . .

The limpid liquid within the young man,
The vex'd corrosion so pensive and so painful, . . .
The young man that wakes deep at night, the hot hand
    seeking to repress what would master him,
The mystic amorous night, the strange half-welcome
    pangs, visions, sweats,
The pulse pounding through palms and trembling

> encircling fingers, the young man all color'd, red,
> ashamed, angry;
> The souse upon me of my lover the sea, as I lie willing
> and naked. . . .

Is it any wonder one critic said *Leaves* reeked from the smell of semen?

Some readers "got" Whitman, others did not. Ralph Waldo Emerson, whose essay calling for an American poet to celebrate the emerging nation led to the writing of *Leaves*, praised Whitman's "free and brave thoughts." This is not surprising considering the way Emerson issued his call:

> It is of the [ultimate] importance that these things get spoken. . . . that thought may be ejaculated as Logos, or Word. Doubt not, o Poet, but persist. Say "It is in me, and shall out."

But one critic's aesthetic ejaculation is another's uncivilized spray. "It is as if the beasts spoke," Henry David Thoreau wrote of *Leaves*. The *New York Herald* scorned Whitman's "disgusting Priapism," referring—and obviously not in a positive way—to the macrophallic Greek and Roman fertility god. Such criticisms were more on the mark than their writers probably realized. Whitman's praise of the penis *was* neopagan, particularly in the Priapic sense of being rough-hewn. In the splendor of Imperial Rome, Priapus stood for more than sex: he stood for simplicity and a return to nature. The animal urgency of the penis did not trouble Whitman. To the contrary, he dedicated his life to "singing the phallus" and "the body electric." To a life in which man is not debilitated by his penis, but invigorated by it.

This was the clear message of Whitman's poetry, now considered the most influential in the modern American canon. "My verse strains its every nerve to arouse, brace, dilate, and excite,"

Whitman wrote—the same goals of a modern urologist working in the field of erectile functioning. Whitman and Melville rejected the ostensible rationality of the new semen science in favor of a more spiritual vision. Yet neither favored a return of the Christian attitude. Their understanding of the organ was rooted in romanticism and a naturalistic, pagan past free of loathing for the penis.

We revere Whitman and Melville today, while Homer Bostwick, John Todd, and the other semen retentionists are long forgotten. It would seem that Whitman and Melville's romantic view of the penis "won" in the end. But when these artists were writing, their opinions were decidedly in the minority. Todd's *The Student Manual* sold thousands of copies more than Melville's *Moby-Dick*. Melville died forgotten and in poverty, a man who published ten books in eleven years yet ended up owing his publishers money. In the last nineteen years of his life Melville worked six days a week as a lowly clerk at the U.S. Customshouse in lower Manhattan. Melville's last great work, *Billy Budd*, in which the Jesuslike hero dies with an erection, from being hanged, was discovered in a tin bread box and published in 1924, three decades after Melville's own death.

Every edition of Whitman's *Leaves of Grass* was a commercial failure. The poet had ardent supporters, but like Melville, he lived in meager circumstances, especially after a stroke left him dependent on friends. The "rational" semen-retention movement, however, surged on. John Kellogg, Sylvester Graham, and their heirs got rich selling foods designed to quell masturbation (whether consumers knew it or not). The chief of an asylum in Worcester, Massachusetts, declared to his state legislature in 1848 that one third of his inmates were "insane from self-pollution." Several years later, the Charity Hospital of Louisiana reported that two patients *died* from the disease.

Looking for a cure, physicians filled journals with articles such as "Mechanical Restraint of Masturbation," "Infibulation and the Medical Profession," "Masturbation as the Cause of Insanity," and, most chilling of all, "Insanity Cured by Castration." According to the author of that last submission, J. H. Marshall, his patient was a once-respected physician who had spent seven years in an asylum for compulsive masturbation, where he failed to respond to any treatment. This is when Dr. Marshall decided to shear off his testicles. Soon the patient was "a changed man," Marshall wrote with remarkable understatement. The patient became "quiet and docile" and was able to "resume his own medical practice." Letters congratulated Marshall on his therapeutic breakthrough. Clearly, the science of semen retention, with its core belief that the "natural" penis is dangerous, its abiding faith in calibration, and its conviction that no treatment for such a grave problem is too extreme, prevailed in its own time.

These strange beliefs about the penis had huge implications when the most powerful nations in the West began colonizing Africa, bringing their assumptions of cultural superiority, their sexual insecurities, their shackles, their yardsticks, their knives, and their specimen kits along with them. Science and racism marched into the jungle, searching for wealth and truth. It wasn't long before most medical museums in Europe had an "Aethiopian Penis" in a jar.

# III

## The Measuring Stick

Travel is supposed to be an eye-opening experience. And so it was for Richard Jobson, a Bible-quoting, treasure-hunting Englishman who spent several sweaty months exploring what we now call the Gambia River in West Africa, an adventure he recounted in 1623 in his grandiloquently titled memoir, *The Golden Trade: or, A discovery of the River Gambra, and the golden trade of the Aethiopians. Also, The Commerce with a great blacke Merchant called Buckor Sano, and his report of the houses covered with Gold, and other strange observations for the good of oure own countrey; Set down as they were collected in travelling, part of the yeares, 1620 and 1621, by Richard Jobson, Gentleman.* That gentleman's eyes nearly left their Anglo-Saxon sockets when his boat was bitten by a hippopotamus, and Jobson was similarly stunned by the sight of an anthill taller than most London homes. But it was another display of local wildlife that opened his eyes wider still. The "blacke Lords of this countrey," Jobson wrote of the Mandingo tribesmen he met on both sides of the river, "are furnisht with members" so huge as to be "burdensome to them."

If Jobson was exaggerating—and he surely was—he was not alone. Reports of preternaturally macrophallic Africans peppered European travel writing once Portuguese ships landed on the continent's western shores in the early fifteenth century. The English did not sail for sub-Saharan Africa until many decades later, but their accounts were among the most expressive. Jobson's compatriot John Ogilby marveled at the natives' "large Propagators" in *Africa: Being an Accurate Description of the . . . land of the Negros,* written in 1670. So did the nineteenth-century explorer Richard Burton, who personally measured one such propagator, finding it to be six inches long—when *relaxed.* But French army surgeon Jacobus Sutor, whose travels in service to his country led him to categorize the penile endowments of several indigenous peoples, believed Burton's specimen was unusually modest. "In no branch of the human race are the male organs more developed than in the African Negro," Dr. Sutor wrote.

> It was among the Sudanese that I found the most developed phallus, . . . being nearly 12 inches in length by a diameter of 2¼ inches. This was a terrific machine, and except for a slight difference in length, was more like the penis of a donkey than that of a man.

Sutor's appreciation was not shared by everyone, however. One of his predecessors, the anonymous author of *The Golden Coast,* was so shocked by the "extraordinary greatness" of the Negro member that he (or she?) declared it a symptom of "the Pox," then a common synonym for syphilis.

Awed or appalled, it seems the first things noticed by any European when meeting an African male were his skin color and his penis. Would-be poet Robert Baker, who traveled to Guinea in 1562, was "inspired" to describe the natives this way:

> And entering in a river, we see
> a number of black soules,
> Whose likeliness seem'd men to be,
> but all as black as coles.
> Their Captaine comes to me
> as naked as my naile,
> Not having wit or honestie
> to cover once his taile.

"Taile" was a common sixteenth-century slang term for penis, an English word derived from the Latin word for "tail."

Explorers were not the only ones who stared. "That the PENIS of an African is larger than that of an European has . . . been shewn in every anatomical school in London. Preparations of them are preserved in most anatomical museums; and I have one in mine," the English surgeon Charles White wrote in 1799, expressing his awe for the African member in capital letters. White examined "several living negroes," too, and found their penile superiority to whites "invariably to be the case." Johann Friedrich Blumenbach, the father of comparative anatomy and the man who first classified "Caucasian" as a racial term, had a special specimen jar of his own at the University of Göttingen in Germany. "It is said that the penis in the Negro is very large. This assertion," Professor Blumenbach wrote in 1806, "is borne out by the remarkable genitory apparatus of an Aethiopian in my . . . collection."

It is hard not to recoil in horror when reading these reports now, nearly five centuries after some were written. Clearly, the line between fact and fiction was not observed with piety by several of the authors quoted above, least of all by the travel-adventure chroniclers, the pulp writers of their day. Even so, their work, which was widely read, reveals something significant about the way white Western man thought—and some would say still thinks—about the penis when comparing his "apparatus" to that of his African brother. The ongoing encounter between white Europeans and black Africans between the fifteenth and nineteenth centuries, a commingling more extensive and intimate than any that preceded it, led the European to examine his and "their" place in nature. This examination was made with great seriousness by men of God and by men of science. Despite the philosophical antipathies that divided those camps, the result was a largely unified position that, in the end, transformed the cultural role of the penis and significantly expanded its meaning as an idea. This cultural shift was cited by Europeans to justify not only colonialism and castration—those

black penises in the specimen jars had to come from some-
where—but slavery on a scale unprecedented in world history.
For better or worse, the penis was racialized.

Blumenbach's new field of comparative anatomy treated the
body as a legible text. Racial differences could be best understood not by studying language or behavior, scientists now believed, but by examining the interior and exterior of the human
form. "Every peculiarity of the body has . . . some corresponding significance in the mind, and the causes of the former are the
remoter causes of the latter," wrote the nineteenth-century
anatomist Edward Drinker Cope. Every quantifiable difference—whether skin color, skull shape, or hair texture—was
said to signify a defining racial characteristic. Differences in size
were given great weight by these theorists, generally in the "bigger is better" mode—with one glaring exception: the Caucasian's larger brain proved his intellectual superiority and
civilized status, but the Negro's larger penis proved his intellectual inferiority and innate savagery.

In this strange and, at times, sickening process the male organ
became a measuring stick. The black African's body was dissected by white anatomists, his intelligence gauged by white ed-
ucators, and the very existence of his soul debated by white
philosophers and theologians. Few of these Caucasians doubted
their racial superiority, or questioned its divine origin. Voltaire
and Thomas Jefferson believed Negroes were capable of only
limited mental achievement; so did Rousseau, despite his embrace of the Noble Savage ideal. David Hume, in his essay "Of
National Characters," wrote, "I am apt to suspect the negroes
. . . to be naturally inferior to the whites. There never was a civilized nation of any other complexion than white, nor any individual eminent in action or speculation." (Interestingly, one of
the only intellectuals of this era to reject the notion of African
inferiority was Professor Blumenbach, the man who created the
science of comparative anatomy in the first place.)

Despite their different starting points, most racial thinkers based many of their most important conclusions on the same criterion—the African's penis. It was stared at, feared (and in some cases desired), weighed, interpreted via Scripture, meditated on by zoologists and anthropologists, preserved in specimen jars, and, most of all, calibrated. And, in nearly every instance, its size was deemed proof that the Negro was less a man than a beast.

---

This notion that the observed are less human than those observing them was not new. To the ancient Greeks nearly all of life was based on comparisons of status. Man/woman and citizen/slave were two obvious examples. An even more decisive separation was Greek/barbarian. That final category included all non-Greeks, but black Africans—called Aethiops, from the Greek word for "burned by the sun"—earned more scorn than most. Rather than race, which is a modern concept, this was rooted in ancient ideas about climate. It was thought extreme temperatures caused grotesque, exaggerated bodies and savage, out-of-control behaviors. This is why Herodotus described Aethiops as beasts with dog heads who ate locusts, screeched like bats, and mated promiscuously, a view echoed in the Roman era by Pliny the Elder. Galen, who probably met quite a few Africans when he was a physician at a Roman gladiator school, declared there were ten traits common to all Aethiopian males: black skin, kinky hair, wide nostrils, thick lips, sharp white teeth, chapped hands, large black pupils, an offensive odor, inferior intelligence—and an oversized penis.

That last item, James Cleugh wrote in his history of ancient sex practices, gave Aethiops a virtual monopoly on a certain profession in Pharaonic Egypt. Egyptian males were so fearful of vaginal blood, Cleugh wrote, that they often hired an Aethiop to deflower the Egyptian's bride, thus saving themselves from the risk of "contamination." One such service provider, famous for his huge deflowering tool, was eventually

killed by a battle wound that mutilated his most valued possession. "Quite a number of women are alleged to have committed
suicide," Cleugh wrote, "when they heard of the destruction of
so tremendous an organ."

Cleugh's story sounds like a myth masquerading as fact. But
there is no denying the factual evidence of the fascination the
African's penis held for some Romans. Proof exists in three surviving houses of the Augustan period at Pompeii, where several
mosaics, nearly all of them in the bath, depict male black servants with organs of astonishing heft. In her paper "*Baiarum
Grata Voluptas:* Pleasures and Dangers of the Baths," classicist
Katherine M. Dunbabin said these images were intended to
ward off the Evil Eye, whose power to cause bad luck was a
constant source of concern for superstitious Romans. The best
deflectors of that Eye's gaze, Dunbabin wrote, were humor and
what we (but not the Romans) would call "obscenity." A citizen
of Pompeii "would have seen the Aethiop as more effective
against the Evil Eye than another Roman," says historian John
Clarke, "because his un-Roman body type caused laughter—all
the more so when he appears with an enormous phallus."

According to Pliny the Elder, who died from asphyxiation
after visiting Mount Vesuvius's eruption, the same one that
buried Pompeii, real-life blacks were often sent as erotic "gifts"
to lonely, wellborn Roman women. Stories like this no doubt
formed part of the source material for the depictions of
Aethiops in Pompeii. "The fact that the macrophallic black is a
traditional theme in Roman iconography," Lloyd A. Thompson
writes in *Romans and Blacks,* "underscores the image of black
sexuality which attributed to blacks . . . the possession of a sinister fascination for nonblacks."

That's "sinister," not "sinful." The ancients officially dis-
dained Aethiopian sexuality not because it was ungodly, but
because it was disorderly. It ignored Greco-Roman rules of deco-
rum, which, by the standards of many other cultures, were
hardly decorous at all. The idea that black sexuality—and the

black penis in particular—was sinful was an invention of the Judeo-Christian tradition. The source for that linkage was the Bible, where the battle between good and evil often took place between a man's legs. Some commentators read the story of the flood and its aftermath and saw a divinely ordained "stain" on the black body, which originally had been white. Calling this moral taint the Curse of Ham, after one of Noah's sons, these interpreters said God made a connection between blackness and hypersexuality—a sin situated in, and symbolized by, the African's huge penis.

As is often the case in biblical exegesis, the interpretation is clearer than the original text. The Curse of Ham occurs in the ninth chapter of Genesis:

> The sons of Noah who went forth from the ark were Shem, Ham and Japheth. . . . These three were the sons of Noah; and from these the whole earth was peopled. Noah was the first tiller of the soil. He planted a vineyard; and he drank of the wine and became drunk, and he lay uncovered in his tent. And Ham, the father of Canaan, saw the nakedness of his father, and told his two brothers outside. Then Shem and Japheth took a garment, laid it on both their shoulders, and walked backward and covered the nakedness of their father; their faces were turned away, and they did not see their father's nakedness. When Noah awoke from his wine and knew what his youngest son had done to him, he said, "Cursed be Canaan; a slave of slaves shall he be to his brothers."

"Nakedness" is clearly a euphemism for penis, as "thigh" is in other Old Testament passages. Between the lines, one hears Ham snickering at his father's embarrassing and inebriated state, inviting his brothers to join him. By staring at his father's penis, Ham mocked both patriarchal authority and the Mosaic laws of sexual modesty. His actions showed him to be a son without respect, a crosser of moral boundaries, someone unwilling or unable to contain the erotic beast within. Even so, it seems the curse of Ham is an unfair punishment of Ham's son, Canaan, who was not even there. That the Old Testament would condemn the Canaanites is not that surprising, however, because the Hebrews would eventually fight to remove them from the Promised Land. But where do blackness and large penises enter the picture? Some experts point to a passage written approximately seventeen hundred years ago in the Midrash, a commentary on the Old Testament that is one of the central works of Orthodox Judaism. There, in an interpretation that anticipated Freudian textual analysis by nearly two millennia, a rabbi declared that by seeing Noah's penis, Ham had, in fact, castrated him. This major crime, the rabbi wrote, required a major punishment.

"Now I cannot beget the fourth son whose children I would have ordered to serve you and your brothers!" Noah said when he awoke, according to the translation of the commentaries in *Hebrew Myths: The Book of Genesis*. "Therefore it must be Canaan, your firstborn, whom they enslave.

> And since you have disabled me from doing ugly things in the blackness of night, Canaan's children shall be born ugly and black! Because you twisted your head around to see my nakedness, your grandchildren's hair will be twisted into kinks . . . ; because your lips jested at my misfortune, theirs shall swell; and because you neglected my nakedness, they shall go naked, and their male members shall be shamefully elongated! Men of this race are called Negroes; their forefather Canaan commanded them to love . . . fornication.

This bizarre screed, a hundred words of opinion lacking any standing as Jewish law, out of several million in the rabbinic writings, had an impact on Western culture its author neither envisioned nor intended. When interest in the Bible as the Word of God led some medieval monks to learn Hebrew so they could read the Old Testament and commentaries in their original tongue, the racial interpretation of the Ham myth became part of the Christian oral tradition. The subsequent convergence of three events—the arrival of Europeans in sub-Saharan Africa in the fifteenth century, Gutenberg's invention of the modern printing press (circa 1436), and the resulting publication of the Old and New Testaments in English, French, and German in the sixteenth century—meant that more people were reading about the Curse of Ham just as more Europeans were meeting his "descendants."

Before the publication of those new translations, the Bible as we know it today did not really exist, at least not in a form easily accessible to the literate Christian laity. As historian Benjamin Braude has pointed out, "printing not only fixes words to the page, it helps fix meaning to those words." We know that the biblical meaning of the black penis was certainly fixed in the mind of the wide-eyed explorer Richard Jobson. In *The Golden Trade* he wrote that, as "Scripture testifieth," the Mandingo's huge and "burdensome" member was proof that God's curse on the "sonnes of Ham" had taken hold "where the originall cause began."

———————

Soon the English, richer and stronger than at any time in their history, began to see themselves as God's Chosen People. This elevated the Curse of Ham into a divine rationale for enslaving hundreds of thousands of black Africans, then shipping them off to work the tobacco, cotton, and sugarcane plantations in the English colonies in America, just as the Spanish, French, Portuguese, and Dutch did for their colonial holdings in the

New World. It was there, where the two races lived in proximity as never before, that the white obsession with the black penis reached an unprecedented malignancy.

One of the first self-proclaimed experts on that subject was Edward Long, an Englishman who published a three-volume *History of Jamaica* in 1774, based on his own life and research there as a slave-owning proprietor of a sugar plantation. In Long's view, Africans were "brutish," "thievish," and "superstitious people" with a "bestial, fetid smell" and inferior "faculties of mind." Their reproductive apparatus, however, struck him as more primitive yet, in some ways, clearly superior to that of whites. African women, Long said, gave birth without pain, a "fact" indicating they had escaped God's punishment on Eve's female descendants, which suggested they were not members of the human race. The relish with which African females mated with their macrophallic countrymen led Long to speculate that, back in Africa, those women occasionally sought out even better endowed sex partners. As "ludicrous as the opinion may seem," Long wrote, "I do not think that an oran-outang husband would be any dishonor to an Hottentot female."

In 1788 Long's book was excerpted and serialized in America in *Columbia Magazine,* giving his ideas even wider currency. Like their European peers, most whites in North America turned to religion for guidance on the subjects of race and sex. In *Slavery, as it relates to the Negro, or African race, Examined in the Light of Circumstances, History and the Holy Scriptures,* the Reverend Josiah Priest, a resident of central New York State, argued in 1843 that the "sexual member of the negro" was proof that the black African was at least as much an animal as a human. He proved this by referring to a Bible passage in which the Egyptians and Canaanites, two peoples descended from the accursed Ham, were said to have "the flesh of asses." "What do the Scriptures mean in [that] phraseology?" Priest asked. "Simply as follows. That between the sexual members of the negro and the brute called an ass, there is but little difference as to elongation and magnitude."

Priest, who also believed that a civilized white nation had populated the American West before "the present Indians," asserted that Ham's true crime in seeing "his father's nakedness" was the sexual violation of his own mother. This interpretation was based on a passage in Leviticus where it is written, "The nakedness of thy father's wife shalt thou not uncover; it is thy father's nakedness." Since that despicable act of incest, Priest said, all of Ham's black descendants, a group that included the residents of Sodom and Gomorrah, have had "the baleful fire of unchaste amour raging through their blood."

Tennessee clergyman Buckner H. Payne evicted blacks from the human race entirely. In his 1867 pamphlet *The Negro: What Is His Ethnological Status?*, written under the pseudonym "Ariel," Payne insisted that Negroes were not descended from Ham—that belief, he said, was based on a misreading of the Old Testament. Instead, Negroes were created *before* Adam. This made Negroes one of the pairs of animals Noah had carried onto the Ark. This "pre-Adamite" theme was picked up again three decades later by Charles Carroll, author of *The Negro a Beast* and *The Tempter of Eve*. Carroll set his exegesis in the Garden of Eden. Eve's seducer in Paradise was not a serpent, Carroll said. It was another, even more despicable, beast— a Negro-ape. This new scenario transformed the presumably red apple of Scripture into a large black penis, and redefined the cause of man's fall from grace as sex with an animal.

These narratives found an audience because they recalled some of the oldest psychosexual images in Western culture. Christianity declared a division between man and beast in the realm of sexual behavior. To be human was to contain one's animal passions; to accede to them was to sink to the level of a brute. But the Western imagination, shaped in Greece and Rome, was still haunted by pagan myths that spoke of satyrs, centaurs, and other beings half-man and half-beast. Implicit in those myths was the idea that to be closer to nature was to be closer to sex—and farther from civilization.

After whites reached black Africa, the Greco-Roman images

of natural sexuality were revived and infused with the Christian notion of sin, then projected onto Africans, people who, by European standards, seemed to live with no sexual inhibitions at all. Few Europeans objected to this because blackness was already loaded with negative meaning. It symbolized filth and death, while whiteness stood for purity and life. Even William Blake, in a poem calling for universal brotherhood, was not immune to such stereotyping. This is from *Songs of Innocence and of Experience*, published in 1789:

> My mother bore me in the southern wild,
> And I am black, but O! my soul is white;
> White as an angel is the English child,
> But I am black, as if bereav'd of light.

Christians linked blackness with sin and lust even before the Ham myth became part of their oral tradition. The fifth-century ascetic John Cassian, later canonized, described sexual temptation as a "Negro woman, ill-smelling and ugly." A thousand years later, nearly every European woman burned at the stake for consorting with the Devil described his penis as black. When Lady Alice Kyteler was tried for witchcraft in Ireland in 1324, a witness fond of visual allegory said she had seen the Lady with the Devil, who had magically materialized as "three large Negroes bearing iron rods in their hands." Each of those large, rod-bearing black men, the witness said, took their sexual pleasure with Lady Alice, who eagerly welcomed their blasphemous attentions.

All penises are ultimately tools of the Devil, taught Augustine, the Church's most influential theologian. But now some of them—those on Africans—were declared more satanic than the rest. The proof was in their size and color, each a punishment from God. It was not long before other experts, using the secular language of science, reached a similar conclusion.

In 1702 a paper presented at the French Academy of Sciences declared that the African male was born white except for some black spots that spread as the result of exposure to the sun. Those crucial bits of pigment, the author said, were on the African's penis. This theory is revealing, and not just about the foolishness of certain Frenchmen. It shows that the African's place in creation was becoming as much a biological question as a theological one. It also shows that this secular discussion, like its religious counterpart, focused much of its attention on the penis.

One of the most influential scientists to aim a spotlight there was Charles White of Manchester, England, a member of the Royal Society and author of *An Account of the Regular Gradation in Man, and in Different Animals and Vegetables; and from the Former to the Latter*, published in 1799. White did not believe all races were descended from the same source, as the Bible said. Rather, he saw multiple origins and a "great chain of being" in which different races occupied different, unequal "stations," with white Europeans at the top and black Africans at the bottom, just a link or two above the monkey. The evidence for this, White and others believed, was anatomical: the African's forehead, chin, jawbone, teeth, muscle mass, and even his way of walking were more like an ape's than that of a European. But the evidence that ultimately convinced Dr. White that he was correct about gradation was genital.

After examining many "parts of generation" himself—White had at least one African penis preserved in a jar—the doctor reported that the black member was "invariably" longer and stiffer than the white man's, even when relaxed. (In one memorable autopsy, the penis on an African corpse—an organ stiff *and* relaxed—was measured to be twelve inches.) But the typical African's testicles and scrotum, White found, were smaller in size and weighed less than the typical European's, as did the ape's. He also noticed that many African males lacked a frenulum—the wrinkly band of skin just below the glans—a lack shared by many species of apes but not by Europeans, except in rare instances of birth defects.

These observations constituted White's "Eureka moment." Whether larger or smaller, lighter or heavier, with frenulum or without, the African's genital parts—which, because of their role in reproduction, White deemed to be the most anatomically meaningful parts—were always closer to that of *simiae* than civilized Europeans. In reality, they are no such thing. The human penis, white *or* black, is larger than that of a gorilla or any other primate species, so any distinctive similarity between the huge Negro penis and the huge ape penis is based on a false premise. White's conclusions reflected the superstitions and bigotry of his age, an era when "lusty" tailless apes—animals that, to European eyes, greatly resembled Negroes—had just been "discovered" by those same white Europeans. It is obvious that White never examined such an ape himself. (Nor, for that matter, had many of his readers.)

Even so, White confirmed his gradation hypothesis by studying accounts of female genitalia. The clitoris of the African was larger than that of the European; larger still, he read, was that of the ape. A Negro woman menstruated less than a white woman; the ape, he learned, even less than the Negress. Wherever he looked, White found evidence of gradation. The African's "superiorities" to the European—in smelling, hearing, seeing, and sexual potency—were all in the brute senses. "In whatever respect the African differs from the European," White wrote, "the particularity brings him closer to the ape."

Which meant closer to the lascivious jungle. In 1607 the Englishman Edward Topsell wrote of a male baboon that had been brought to the court of the French king, where the ape "loved above all the companie of women and young maidens," proximity that often made his "great genitall member" even greater. One senses that Topsell found this amusing, but there is little chance that his king, James I of England, shared his mirth. In *Daemonologie*, which James wrote six years before he took the throne, he declared the lusty ape to be an emissary of Satan. The eighteenth-century French scientist Comte de Buffon—a hugely influential scholar in his day—commented often in his forty-four-volume *Histoire naturelle* on the black African's apelike lust, speculating that African women frequently copulated with gorillas. (Edward Long no doubt agreed.) For Buffon, such encounters showed male apes attempting to move up the great chain of being, a drive analogous to the rapacious sexual hunger he believed black men felt for white women. The asymmetrical depictions of these matings was consistent. "The sexual union of apes and Negroes was *always* conceived of as involving female Negroes and male apes," Winthrop D. Jordan writes in *White Over Black,* his National Book Award–winning history of American racism. "Apes had intercourse with Negro women. The aggressors were literally beasts; the sexual drive was conceived as thrusting upwards from below."

This was the scientific milieu in which Charles White wrote *An Account of the Regular Gradation in Man,* a work published with a large fold-out illustration of a naked, hairy chimpanzee presented as a quasi-human. This smiling man-beast was drawn walking upright down a city street with the aid of a cane, his penis prominently displayed, no doubt hoping to attract a white human female companion. When White compared the African to an ape, he was not expressing a brilliant proto-Darwinian insight. He was using science to link blackness with a large penis and sin.

Nowhere was this supposed link between the African's penis and his bestial sexuality cited more often, or more insistently, than in the United States. There, the image of the African slave as a walking penis had another origin separate from speculations emanating from specimen jars or the Bible. This was a strange fact of plantation life revealed to us by a semiliterate soldier named William Feltman. In an entry in his military journal dated June 22, 1781, Lieutenant Feltman, a Pennsylvanian, described a dinner party he attended on a large Virginia estate.

The splendor of the table certainly caught the young officer's notice. But what really got his attention was the scanty clothing worn by the slave boys serving the guests at that table.

"I am surprized this does not hurt the feelings of the fair Sex," Feltman wrote, "to see those young boys of Fourteen and Fifteen years old to Attend them, [their] whole nakedness Expos'd and I can Assure you It would Surprize a person to see those damned black boys how well they are hung."

Feltman was not the only tourist to notice. Letters from European visitors to the South cited by Jordan show that it was "common for mature Negro boys to wait upon tables wearing only a shirt not always long enough to conceal their private parts." These foreign visitors, Jordan wrote, were shocked by "the casualness with which this exposure was met by their [white] hosts, male and female."

"Casualness" would not be the word to describe the response of some abolitionists to those displays. As John Saillant points out in his essay "The Black Body Erotic and the Republican Body Politic, 1790–1820," quite a few abolitionist writings of this period were marked by an unmistakably erotic interest in the black man's body—especially his large black penis. The first of these works to claim an audience in America was written by a Frenchman, Joseph LaVallee, in 1789. *Le negre comme il y a peu de blancs* was translated into English in 1790, serialized by the magazine *American Museum* in 1791, and then published as the book *The Negro Equaled by Few Europeans*, in Philadelphia, in 1801. There was little doubt about the way in which LaVallee's hero, the African slave Itanoko, was rarely equaled by his white admirers: as LaVallee's first English translator put it, the finely muscled, naked Itanoko lacked "pudicity"—modesty concerning his penis.

*The Negro Equaled* presented its argument for the brotherhood of man in homoerotic terms. Itanoko is irresistible to every man he meets in LaVallee's book: the captain of the French slave ship that takes him to the New World, that captain's son, another Frenchman on the ship who tutors Itanoko in French and Christianity—even Itanoko's brutal slave master once the pudicity-challenged African disembarks in chains in the Caribbean.

Other abolitionist writings shared LaVallee's admiration for the black penis, but in a heterosexual context. The handsome and virile Selico, hero of "Selico, an African Tale," published in 1798 in *American Universal Magazine,* ends up "penetrating" a sultan's harem—the author's word, not mine—where he immediately becomes the illicit favorite of the women living there, who have never encountered such a well-endowed lover. Another heroically heterosexual African, Zami, was described in a story published in 1798 in the same journal as a black duplicate of the Apollo Belvedere. That a respected American magazine would link a well-hung black slave with the great god Apollo—the classical and divine exemplar of manly beauty—is clear evidence of what another historian, Eric Lott, has called "the white man's investment in the black penis."

That investment did not always produce goodwill, however. Once the boys described with awe by Lieutenant Feltman became free men after the Civil War, the black penis cast a large and alarming shadow over many whites, who feared that black emancipation meant the freedom of macrophallic black men to mate with white women—and, even worse, that white women might actually prefer them. In volume three of *Studies in the Psychology of Sex,* published in 1913, the British researcher Havelock Ellis wrote, "I am informed that the sexual power of Negroes and slower ejaculation are the cause of the favor in which they are viewed by some white women of strong sexual passions in America. . . . At one time there was a special house in New York City to which white women resorted for these 'buck lovers.' The women came heavily veiled and would inspect the penises of the men before making their selection."

Anxiety over the phallic appeal of those "buck lovers" prompted an ugly national outcry when Jack Johnson, a man who traveled openly with a beautiful white (unveiled) girlfriend and padded his already substantial crotch to make white men envy him all the more, became the first black heavyweight champion of the world, an event that in 1908 triggered the search for "The Great White Hope." The miscegenation practiced by Johnson and other buck lovers had to be discouraged, many whites believed, not merely by terror—the night rides of the Ku Klux Klan were largely created for that purpose—but by impartial science. The idea of proving a biological link between a large penis, a pathological sex drive, and blackness became an obsession during the Reconstruction era and beyond for a small but vocal number of American physicians.

An editorial titled "Genital Peculiarities of the Negro" ran in the *Atlanta Journal-Record of Medicine* in 1903 warning its audience of the "notorious hypertrophy" (the second word is a medical term for "excessive development") of the Negro's "virile organ" and the "exaggerated *libido sexualis* which is [his] conspicuous trait." These ideas were developed at even greater length that same year by Dr. William Lee Howard, of Baltimore, in the journal *Medicine*.

In "The Negro as a Distinct Ethnic Factor in Civilization," Howard used the size of the Negro's penis to prove that his subject was not civilized—or even capable of becoming so. There can never be mutually beneficial relations between the Caucasian and the African, Howard wrote. Such a bond is prevented by "their great sexual differences." The idea, spread by misguided Northern moralists, that the African can be elevated by education, Howard said, can only succeed if that education magically "reduce[s] the large size of the African's penis" and gives him the same "sensitiveness of the terminal fibers which exist in the Caucasian" but not in the Negro. That mysterious anatomical deficiency—Howard failed to further identify, or even locate, those crucial fibers—caused "all intellectual devel-

opment" in the black male to "cease with the advent of puberty." As a result, the "genetic instincts [become] the controlling factor of his life," leaving the Negro "with no morals. . . .
He will walk the alleys late at night with a penis swollen from
disease, and infect his bride-to-be with the same nonchalance
that he will an hour later exhibit when cohabiting with the
lowest of his race."

Because the genital organs in the African are "enormously
developed," and "as his whole life is devoted to matters per-
taining to the worship of Priapus," Howard wrote, "the sexual
centers in [his cerebral] cortex are correspondingly enlarged.

> Whether the persons who talk about elevating the negro
> . . . expect a diminution in the size of the sexual organs,
> thereby preventing excitation of sexual concepts; or
> whether having the negro boys brought up in schools with
> white girls is expected to inhibit cortical centers containing
> cells placed there on biologic principles, are questions not
> yet answered [by those persons].

Howard had his own answer. "What was decided among the
prehistoric Protozoa cannot be changed" by "act of Congress."
Only by shrinking the African's penis—a biological impossibility—could there be an end to "the African's birthright to sexual
madness."

Could the fear of the big black penis—or the belief in its accuracy as a measuring stick of bestiality—be expressed any
clearer?

In *The Negro: A Menace to American Civilization,* R. W.
Shufeldt, a physician practicing in Manhattan, argued that the
African-American's anatomy proved his status as a lower primate. "Many years ago," Shufeldt wrote, "I dissected an old
negro man in Washington, D.C. As a subject he was particularly
simian in his organization, and one thing I noticed about him, in
addition to his immense copulatory organ, was the structure of

his toenails, which were marvelously thickened and curved."
(No doubt to better enable its owner to swing from trees.)
Shufeldt also claimed to observe that blacks have a muscle of
the loin—the psoas parvus—"that is common in apes but virtually non-existent in [white] humans."

The African's "immense copulatory organ" was confirmed,
sort of, by an African-American scientist in 1942. This was
W. Montague Cobb, chief of the anthropology department at
Howard University in Washington, D.C. "So much has been
written of an incendiary nature on the sexual habits and capac-
ities of the Negro that almost all valid scientific information
would be welcomed," Cobb wrote in the *American Journal of
Physical Anthropology*. Yet Cobb's next sentence failed to meet
the standard he himself had just set: "It is said," he wrote, "that
the penis of the Negro is larger than that of the White." Cobb
cited the work of five scientists, published between 1863 and
1935, in a footnote as evidence. Yet a closer look at two of those
citations, the only two published in English, by W. L. H. Duckworth and Ales Hrdlicka, suggests their findings were far less
empirical than impressionistic. This is from Duckworth's *Mor-
phology and Anthropology*: "The relatively greater size of the
penis in Negroes has long been recognized." And this is from
Hrdlicka, for many years the editor of the *American Journal of
Physical Anthropology*: "The penis of the Negro boy is longer
than that of the corresponding white boy."

These hardly rigorous findings remind us that the subject of
race and penis size has a checkered history in science, one that
many (intimidated?) white scientists—even those ostensibly
committed to developing impartial statistical data—have chosen to avoid. In what seems to be the first attempt to create scientific phallometric data for American males, Lieutenant
William A. Schonfeld of the U.S. Army Medical Corps published "Primary and Secondary Sexual Characteristics: A Study
of Their Development in Males from Birth Through Maturity,
with Biometric Study of Penis and Testes," in the *American*

*Journal of Diseases of Children,* in 1943. Dr. Schonfeld measured "the genital status of 1,500 normal . . . boys and men from birth to 25 years of age." Amazingly, not one of those fifteen hundred males was black. The same glaring omission occurred in the penis-size survey published in 1949 by the pioneering sex researcher Dr. Robert Latou Dickinson, in the second edition of his *Atlas of Human Sex Anatomy.*

In *Black Skin, White Masks,* black psychiatrist Frantz Fanon cited two studies by French scientists that found no difference in size between the black penis and white penis. But *The Kinsey Data: Marginal Tabulations of the 1938–1963 Interviews Conducted by the Institute for Sex Research*—the 1979 follow-up to Alfred Kinsey's famous 1948 survey of male sexual practices in the United States—reported otherwise. From self-administered measurements given by roughly ten thousand whites and four hundred blacks, *Kinsey Data* authors Paul H. Gebhard and Alan B. Johnson found the average erect black penis to be longer in length (6.44 inches) and larger in circumference (4.96 inches) than corresponding white erections (6.15 and 4.83 respectively). Even larger differences occurred in the flaccid state. Blacks: 4.34 inches long, 3.78 around; whites: 3.86 and 3.16. (Some scientists are rightly skeptical of calling any self-measurements "scientific." Others suggest any and all self-measurements would more closely resemble reality if shortened by one inch.)

Psychologists J. Philippe Rushton and Anthony F. Bogaert accepted the Kinsey data in their 1987 paper "Race Differences in Sexual Behavior: Testing an Evolutionary Hypothesis," and supplemented it with reports from Dr. Jacobus Sutor, the same French army surgeon who marveled at the donkeylike twelve-inch penis he found on a Sudanese Negro just over a century ago. (Calling any data from Dr. Sutor scientific is another questionable practice, to say the least.) Rushton and Bogaert caused even more uproar by inferring certain social and sexual behaviors from those differences in penis size. The longer and thicker the organ, they said, the more likely its owner was to be promiscuous, to have children out of wedlock, and to take less responsibility for the raising of his children, whether legitimate or not. Of course, nearly all the longer, thicker, less responsible penises in their study were black.

Medical researcher Richard Edwards made no such behavioral inferences from his Internet survey of penis size, which collected more than three thousand self-reported penis measurings in the late 1990s. One of his most surprising findings, Edwards wrote on his website, was that although black penises were slightly longer than white ones in the flaccid state—3.7 inches for his black respondents, 3.4 for whites—the white erections were slightly longer than the black ones: 6.5 inches to 6.1. (Once again, keep in mind these reports were self-measured.)

This idea that whites are often bigger than any other race, even freakishly so, was embraced two centuries ago by one of the first modern Western writers to comment in public on penis size, albeit in fiction. In *The 120 Days of Sodom,* written in 1785, the Marquis de Sade described the attributes of several Caucasian "masculine deities" chosen to participate in an extravagant orgy. This is a sampling:

> *Hercule* . . . was endowed with a member eight and one-quarter inches around by thirteen long. . . . *Antinous* . . . wielded a device measuring eight inches in circumference and twelve in length. . . . *Bum-Cleaver* lugged a club so amusingly shaped it was nearly impossible for him to perform an embuggery without splitting the ass, whence came [his] name. The head of his prick . . . was eight and three-eighths inches around; behind it, the shaft measured only eight, but was crooked and had such a curve it neatly tore the anus when penetrating it, and this quality . . . made him singularly sought after.

None of the white respondents in Edwards's online survey were linked with any special acts or nicknames. What was spelled out, however, was the intriguing fact that—despite their superior self-measured erections—less than 20 percent of Edwards's white respondents believed themselves to be "well-endowed," while nearly 80 percent of his black respondents thought so of themselves, an opinion accepted as a fact of black masculinity by most whites.

That "Mandingo Myth" was called a patronizing insult by the African-American journalist McLean Greaves in his article "The Penis Thing: Measuring Up," published in *Essence* magazine's "15th Annual Men's Issue." "Like basketball, music and other areas where brothers dominate," Greaves wrote, "success is viewed as the result of raw, intuitive ability as opposed to hard work or intellect. Any carnal skills African-Americans are perceived to possess are considered—like Jordan on the court or Hendrix on stage—a 'natural gift.'" Subtle erotic talents and techniques "are viewed as the province of the cerebral [white man,] which brothers have yet to acquire."

In the end, it seems Dr. Fanon got it right in *Black Skin, White Masks* when he wrote that the "scientific" evidence regarding penis size is less important than people's attitudes about it. Whether the black penis really is larger than the white one is an unanswered, and maybe unanswerable, question. (It is highly unlikely any reputable scientific organization will fund a definitive study anytime soon.) What is a fact is that many people, white and black, believe it is larger. What is also true, and probably more important, is that many of those white people believe that "larger" black penis has a major—read: "dangerous"—cultural meaning.

There is no doubt that the unnamed author of the 1903 *Atlanta Journal-Record of Medicine* editorial thought so. In this person's view, the Negro's oversized "genital characteristic," along with his "stallionlike passion," had, after emancipation, transformed the harmless Uncle Tom of slavery into a lascivious free "menace" to all white women. This idea that most black men want to have sex with white women was (and still is?) so strong that it found its way seven decades later into the pages of *The Village Voice,* a journal not generally known for its racial bigotry or sexual prudery. "One of the great mysteries is why black women don't blow the whistle on some of their black brothers," Pete Hamill wrote in 1970.

> Everyone in the Village knows this scene: the black cat sitting in the Village bar, a copy of *Liberation* in his pocket, wearing Afro and shades, practicing his best surly look, nursing a warm beer, and waiting for the first guilt-ridden white chick to tumble in the door. It doesn't matter if [she] is the ugliest white broad since Ilse Koch, or that she is sodden with whiskey, or has a bad case of crabs. . . . What matters is that she's white.

It is unlikely that the following response from Cecil M. Brown in the newspaper brought much peace to Hamill or any other white males:

> The black brother with a white chick . . . is moving in terms of a political revolt. . . . He understands [that] politics deals with power, and power is what the black man wants; it is what all men want; not black power or white power—but cock power.

It is clear that many whites fear that black cock power is superior to their own. One "genital characteristic" that both impressed and alarmed white physicians in the late nineteenth century was the black's seeming immunity to impotence. In *American Nervousness* and *Sexual Neurasthenia,* New York neurologist George M. Beard—a man read by another soon-to-be-famous neurologist of that era, Sigmund Freud—invented a new disease state called neurasthenia. This was a debilitating depletion of energy, chiefly sexual, caused by "overcivilization" and the stifling quality of rationalized culture.

Beard believed, as did most Social Darwinists, that some ethnic groups and races had ceased to evolve. (Charles Darwin suggested no such thing in *The Origin of Species*. As a member of
the British aristocracy, however, Darwin did accept the social hi-
erarchy of the races then in place.) Because Beard believed
blacks were of a race that had ceased evolving, he declared they
were "undercivilized," a state that explained not only their
mental inferiority but their physical superiority—most of all in
the areas of sex and sex organs. Blacks had a "supernatural constitution" in the erotic sphere, Beard wrote, that made them
closer to nature, farther from civilization, and thus immune to
erectile dysfunction.

This supernatural constitution postulated by Beard, coupled
with the stallionlike passion noted in the *Atlanta Journal-Record
of Medicine*, led the *Virginia Medical Monthly* to solicit an article entitled "Sexual Crimes Among the Southern Negroes—Scientifically Considered." This consideration, published in 1893,
took the form of an exchange of letters between two physicians.
The first asked the second to give a "scientific explanation of the
sexual perversion of the negro." The seventeen-page answer that
followed gave a litany of causes, including "hereditary influences descending from the uncivilized ancestors of our negroes"
and the "defective development of their centers of psychological
inhibition." As a result, the respondent wrote, there is "no physical difference between the *furor sexualis* of the negro and that
[of] . . . a bull," a fact that explained the alarming increase in the
number of "negro rapists" throughout the South. "There is only
one logical method of dealing with [such] criminals," the doctor
wrote. Castration.

This method of punishment leaves behind it evidences
which will prove a wholesome warning to criminals of like
propensities.. . . . The violator loses not only the desire, but
the capacity for a repetition of his crime, if the operation
be supplemented by penile amputation according to the

Oriental method. . . . Executed, they would be forgotten; castrated and free, they would be a constant warning and ever-present admonition to others of their race.

Making this remarkable document all the more so is the identity of its coauthors: G. Frank Lydston, professor of Genito-Urinary Surgery at the Chicago College of Physicians and Surgeons; and Hunter McGuire of Richmond, Virginia, then the president of the American Medical Association.

———————————

There were Americans without medical degrees who shared this fear of free Negro "rapists" and their "stallionlike passion." Some of them turned their psychosexual paranoia into murder. According to Frank Shay, author of *Judge Lynch, His First Hundred Years,* more than four thousand Negroes were lynched in the United States between 1882 and 1937. (Shay was not suggesting that the practice of lynching ended in that second year; it most certainly did not.) At many of those illegal executions, death by hanging was the final act of something even more grotesque—a ritual castration. To really kill a black man, you first had to kill his penis.

Though many of those murdered blacks were accused of sexual activities with white women, the urge to mutilate black males was not prompted by rage against race-mixing in and of itself. White men were sexually involved with black women— with or without their consent—throughout slavery, and few neighbors threatened *their* manhood with a blade. But white paranoia about the black penis was so exaggerated it was believed the Negro organ inflicted a uniquely horrendous experience on white women. Many lynchers claimed the black penis was so monstrously huge, and the black rapist's lust so uncontrollable, he had to enlarge his victim's vagina with a knife before entering her. The woman in this scenario was nearly always a young, blond, beautiful virgin, her attacker a black macrophallic beast. These images, to use Professor Jacquelyn Dowd Hall's apt phrase, became "the folk pornography of the Bible Belt" a century ago.

Even if a sexual encounter between a black man and a white woman was consensual, some Americans were outraged to the point of genital mutilation. When white vigilantes in rural Georgia believed a black tenant farmer was having a more-than-agricultural relationship with the white woman whose land he was working, the black man was kidnapped and given a choice by his captors: castration or death. He lived to tell his decision to a Congressional committee investigating the Ku Klux Klan. Another black accused of consorting with a white woman had his penis—while still attached to him—nailed to a wooden board. His captors thrust a knife into the same piece of wood, then set the board on fire. The black man escaped, Martha Hodes writes in *White Women, Black Men,* by the only means provided.

No such choice was given a black man accused of raping a white, however. But death was merely the final act in a long and perverse drama. Only by stripping the "beast" of his primal power could that force be transferred to the white man, where it belonged. Eyewitnesses tell us that many lynchers took time to examine the penis of the black men they were about to kill. Professor Calvin C. Hernton found a weirdly religious aspect to that grim ceremony. "It is a disguised form of worship, a primitive pornographic divination rite," he wrote in *Sex and Racism in America.* "In taking the black man's genitals, the hooded men in white are amputating that portion of themselves which they secretly consider vile, filthy, and most of all, inadequate. . . . Through castration, white men hope to acquire the grotesque powers they have assigned to the black phallus, which they symbolically extol by the act of destroying it."

This vision of the hypersexed, macrophallic, free black man was seared into popular American culture by D. W. Griffith's groundbreaking film *The Birth of a Nation.* Released in 1915,

*Birth* was the first American film to use close-ups, crosscutting, rapid-fire editing, and realistic lighting. Audiences had never seen anything like it—and come to see it they did. According to historian Michael Rogin, *Birth* was one of the highest-grossing films in the first fifty years of the American film industry. A *Variety* poll later voted it the greatest picture in the first half century of American cinema. All this for a racist screed that portrayed blacks as drooling sex fiends obsessed with deflowering white virgins, a threat stopped by horse-riding knights in white hoods, their swords ready to castrate any black man who dared to insult white womanhood by even thinking about penetrating her with his huge bestial member.

Based on Thomas Dixon's novel *The Clansman*, *Birth* chronicled the travails of the Camerons, white South Carolinians besieged by free blacks and carpetbaggers after the Civil War. In one of the key sequences in the film, the family's virginal daughter is stalked by a black man named Gus, who is (literally) foaming at the mouth. Played by a white man in blackface, Gus catches "Little Sister" and rapes her. Later Gus is brought to justice by the Klan. As the storm music from Beethoven's *Pastoral Symphony* is heard in the background, one man in a white hood plunges his sword into Gus's loins. Griffith cuts to a close-up of the black rapist's face, blood pouring from his mouth and his eyes rolling in agony. In flash-cuts, the Klansman's sword plunges up and down on each beat of the tympani. On the final thunder crash, Griffith zooms in on Gus's twisted face. He is dead. And castrated.

This print of *The Birth of a Nation* was screened by Dixon on February 18, 1915, at the White House for President Woodrow Wilson, who was a friend of Dixon's, having attended graduate school with him at Johns Hopkins University. This was the first movie ever shown at the White House and it made quite an impression on the president. "It is like writing history with lightning," Wilson said of *Birth*. "And my only regret is that is all so terribly true." That second reference was not to Gus's brutal castration, but to his bestial lust for white women, a view of the Negro's intrinsic nature that Wilson, a Southerner by birth and temperament, shared with Dixon. According to historian John Hope Franklin, Dixon showed the film soon afterward in another private screening for Edward D. White, chief justice of the United States Supreme Court. "I was a member of the Klan, sir," White told Dixon, a sure sign of the favor in which he held Dixon's and Griffith's work.

After censors complained about the film's violence, an alternate version was released that had Little Sister hurl herself off a cliff rather than be caught by the black sex fiend. But the sexual nature of the film's racism was no less clear in this version, especially in the scene in which Lillian Gish is rescued by Klansmen from a forced marriage to a black politician. Griffith—not one to hold back in print, either—told the press that the aim of his film was "to create abhorrence in white women against colored men." The birth of this consciousness, he said, came from the night rides of the Klan. This suggests that the nation whose birth Griffith was celebrating was born in the original version of his film. There the castration of Gus showed the white man's power—Griffith would say his obligation—to stop the black penis.

With psychosexual issues such as this in the air, it is not surprising that they would be addressed by two of the most important figures in twentieth-century American literature. *Light in August,* by Nobel Laureate William Faulkner, told the brutal story of Joe Christmas, a man who looks white but believes himself black because of the presumed blackness of his dead father. After his mother dies in childbirth, Christmas is raised by a sadistic white farmer, whom Christmas slays during a fight over Joe's having sex with a white woman. Afterward Christmas lives as a black vagabond. He eventually meets a white spinster, with whom he begins an affair marked by her calling out "Negro! Negro!" when they make love. But remorse follows desire, and the woman withdraws from Joe sexually, then tries to "uplift" him morally. When Joe refuses to pray with her, she makes a clumsy effort to kill him. He kills her instead and again becomes a fugitive. When word of Joe's crime spreads, a mob corners him in a Mississippi farmhouse. One member of that group, Percy Grimm, shoots Christmas. But he's not finished.

> When the others reached the kitchen they saw the table flung aside now and Grimm stooping over the body. When they approached to see what he was about, they saw that the man was not dead yet, and when they saw what Grimm was doing one of the men gave out a choked cry and stumbled back into the wall and began to vomit. Then Grimm too sprang back, flinging behind him the bloody butcher knife. "Now you'll let white women alone, even in hell," he said.

According to John B. Cullen, a childhood neighbor of Faulkner's, this fictional account was inspired by a real-life castration and lynching that occurred in their Mississippi hometown when Faulkner was eleven years old and Cullen was a teenager. The victim of that extralegal activity—or, in Cullen's view, the righteously executed perpetrator—was a black sharecropper named Nelse Patton, accused of raping and murdering a white woman in a farmhouse just north of Oxford. After being arrested, Cullen wrote, Patton was placed in the local jail where, "from eight o'clock that night until two in the morning [a] mob [of local whites] worked to cut through the jail walls into the cells with sledge hammers and crowbars.

> When the mob finally got through and broke the lock off the murderer's cell, Nelse . . . was shot to death and thrown out of the jail. Someone (I don't know who) cut his ears off, scalped him, [and] cut his testicles out. . . . Then they hanged him [from] a walnut-tree limb outside.

A local paper, the *Lafayette County Press*, ran a story about the end of Nelse Patton's life. The headlines read as follows: "NEGRO BRUTE CUTS WOMAN'S THROAT / Mrs. Mattie McMullen, A White Woman The Victim — Lived but Ten Minutes After The Tragedy / Sheriff Hartsfield and Posse Give Chase and Land Negro in Jail / Mob Storms Jail and Kills Desperado / Officers and Guards Overpowered, and Failing to Find the Keys, the Orderly Mob Quietly and Deliberately Took Matters in Their Own Hands."

*right*

In 1963 the writer James Baldwin, born and raised in Harlem, went South for only the second time in his life. His objective was to help the civil rights activist James Forman in a voter-registration drive for rural blacks in Alabama. Two years later, Baldwin's short story "Going to Meet the Man" was published in a collection bearing the same name. In the title story, Jesse, a sheriff dealing with civil rights protesters in his small Southern town—a character inspired by the sheriff of Selma, Alabama, Big Jim Clark—remembers a lynching he witnessed as a child sitting atop his father's shoulders. In one powerful paragraph, Baldwin conveys the orgiastic ceremony and weird sexual transference taking place:

> [Jesse] turned his head a little and saw the field of faces. He watched his mother's face. Her eyes were very bright, her mouth was open: she was more beautiful than he had ever seen her. . . . He began to feel a joy he had never felt before. He watched the hanging, gleaming body, the most beautiful and terrible object he had ever seen until then. One of his father's friends reached up and in his hands he held a knife . . . ; as though this were a signal, silence fell. . . . Then the man with the knife walked up to the hanging body. He turned and smiled. Now there was a silence all over the field. . . . [He] took the nigger's privates in his hand, as though he were weighing them. In the cradle of the one hand, the nigger's privates seemed as remote as meat being

weighed on scales; but seemed heavier, too, much heavier, and . . . huge, huge, much bigger than [Jesse's] father's, . . . the largest thing he had ever seen till then, and the blackest. The white hand stretched them, cradled them, caressed them. Then the dying man's eyes looked straight into Jesse's eyes—it could not have been longer than a second but it seemed longer than a year. Jesse screamed, and the crowd screamed as the knife flashed, first up, then down, cutting the dreadful thing away. . . . Then the crowd rushed forward, tearing at the body with their hands.

Moments later, after Jesse stops screaming, his father spoke. "Well, I told you . . . you wasn't never going to forget *this* picnic.

His father's face was full of sweat, his eyes were very peaceful. At that moment Jesse loved his father more than he had ever loved him. He felt that this father had carried him through a mighty test, had revealed to him a great secret which would be the key to his life forever.

Fact was often worse than fiction. In 1932 a black laborer named Claude Neal was accused of raping and killing Lola Cannidy, the teenaged daughter of his employer, in rural Jackson County, Florida. After his arrest, Neal was taken to a jail in Brewton, Alabama, just over the state line, for his protection, only to be abducted from that location later that same night by white vigilantes. The plan was for Neal to be turned over by his captors to the Cannidy family. But on the day after the abduction, the *Eagle* of Dothan, Alabama, ran the following headline: "Florida to Burn Negro at Stake: Sex Criminal Seized from Brewton Jail, Will be Mutilated, Set Afire in Vengeance for Deed." As a result of this gruesome announcement, several thousand people, many of them drinking home-brewed alcohol, showed up at the Cannidy farm.

The "committee" that had taken Neal realized they could not produce Neal in front of that mob, for fear of a riot. So they killed him themselves, in the woods. Around one A.M., Neal's naked body, attached to a car and dragged along a dirt road, was brought to the Cannidy farm. Lola's father shot three bullets into Neal's head, after which children pushed sharpened sticks into the corpse, and several adults drove cars over it. Others hacked off ears and fingers for souvenirs. At sunrise, what was left of Claude Neal was hanging from a tree in front of the courthouse. An entrepreneur recorded the scene with his camera; he later sold picture postcards for fifty cents each.

Ten days after Neal's death, a white investigator for the NAACP interviewed several of the committee's leaders, who recounted their actions with pride. The last hours of Claude Neal's life, the report said, began like this:

> They cut off his penis. He was made to eat it. Then they cut off his testicles and made him eat them, too, and say that he liked it.

———————

Six decades later, another black American faced a committee of white men agitated about his penis. For hours those white men listened, many of them visibly appalled, to complaints from a woman about the black man's lewd behavior toward her, all of it, she said, unwelcome and unsolicited. They heard how he bragged about the size of his organ, comparing it to a supernaturally endowed porn star named Long Dong Silver. Now that same black man faced the same committee. Unlike Claude Neal, however, he was not dangling from a rope. Except, he said, metaphorically.

"From my standpoint as a black American," Judge Clarence Thomas told the senators considering his nomination to the United States Supreme Court, "[this] is a high-tech lynching for uppity blacks who . . . deign to think for themselves . . . and it is a message that unless you kow-tow to an old order, this is what will happen. You will be lynched, destroyed, caricatured by a committee of the U.S. Senate, rather than hung from a tree."

This image of Clarence Thomas, his teeth clenched in anger and his thick wrestler's body encased in a dark suit, made the front page of nearly every newspaper in America on October 12, 1991. In the days to come, the charge of sexual harassment raised by Professor Anita Hill, and Thomas's heated denial of it, were analyzed in editorials, living rooms, and workplaces all over America. So large was this media event that even TV sit-coms, not a place one ordinarily turns for political insight, got involved. A sketch on *In Living Color,* created by the African-American comedian Keenen Ivory Wayans, opened with an actor playing Thomas, after confirmation, fetching coffee for white justices. When one of them asks for his legal opinion, Thomas says, "I say whatever you guys say." Until, that is, an actress playing Justice Sandra Day O'Connor reminds him he has a lifetime appointment and urges him to relax. Now Thomas puts his feet up on the table and refuses to get anyone anything. When questioned about his abrupt personality change, Thomas says, "Five minutes ago, I was a black judge appointed by Bobo the white president. But now I'm your darkest nightmare: a black judge with a powerful hung jury."

*In Living Color* "got" Thomas's "high-tech lynching" speech in a way that few columnists at the *New York Times* or the *Washington Post* ever did. Virtually everyone agreed that Thomas's defiance on October 11 had won the day for him. A poll taken afterward showed that his support among African-Americans went from 54 percent to nearly 80 percent following the speech. This was duly noted in the mainstream press. But nearly all of those media outlets, from the beginning of the con-troversy right until Thomas's confirmation, framed the story as an either/or battle for prominence between two societal issues—racism versus sexual harassment. Thomas's victory, these pundits said, showed that the cause of fighting the former had trumped that of fighting the latter. But the Hill-Thomas story was not about race versus sex. As the writers of *In Living Color* understood, it was about the one place where race and sex have always intersected in American history. That place is the black penis.

That organ, and all that it stands for, stood at the center of Hill's accusations. The word "penis" was said more than ten times at the proceedings, surely a record for a confirmation hearing for a Supreme Court Justice, in all likelihood a record for *any* public activity by the United States Senate. Hill testified how, after going to work for Thomas at the Department of Education in 1981, he often turned work conversations into a discussion of "pornographic materials" starring "an individual with a very large penis . . . [named] Long Dong Silver" with whom Thomas "compared his [own] penis." This led to requests for dates, Hill said, none of which she accepted.

This remarkable testimony was, in itself, testimony to something larger: the enduring power of the black penis as a cultural signifier in America. If true, Hill's accusations did far more than alter our view of Thomas; they totally unmasked him. Beneath the persona of the highly educated, perfectly civilized jurist was the black man white America has always feared: the macrophallic, hypersexual beast, the same creature written about one hundred years ago in "Genital Peculiarities of the Negro." If true, this was no man of law. This was a crude creature who bragged about the one thing he possessed that whites envied and hated him for the most: his huge penis. And what was undeniably true was that he possessed a white wife sitting loyally behind him in the Senate hearing room. There she was, on national television: D. W. Griffith's worst nightmare come to life.

The power of that image was not lost on Anna Deveare Smith. The award-winning playwright was one of the millions of Americans transfixed by the Hill-Thomas hearings. Her fascination resulted in one of the most compelling portions of

*Identities, Mirrors, and Distortions,* a play written and performed by Smith soon after Thomas's confirmation. "There was
a moment where the camera went from Anita Hill and you saw
this wide shot of the panel," Smith said in her piece, "and you
looked at Orrin Hatch and Strom Thurmond, and in an instant
their faces dropped as they heard what she was saying and you
knew

> whether they were going to deny it
> to themselves
> that they realized she spoke the truth.
> And then there was another thing of perception
> in the minds of these white men:
> their friendly Uncle Tom
> is really
> when he leaves their presence
> and shuts the door
> he's a *buck!*
> You know Uncle Tom has this *penis*
> and he may have a *big* penis
> according to what Anita Hill is telling them
> so they've got a *buck* on their hands
> and *worse*
> he has one of their women!

But if the image of the black penis was powerful enough to
transform Thomas, it could also transform Hill. Any charge
that he bragged about the size of his penis, Thomas told Senator Hatch at the hearings, played "into racist, bigoted stereotypes." Language "about the sex organs of black men and their
sizes," Thomas said, "has been used about black men as long
as I've been on the face of this earth." Such accusations harmed
him, Thomas said, "worse than I have ever been harmed in my
life. I wasn't harmed by the Klan. . . . I was harmed by this
process."

By accusing Anita Hill of making false sexual accusations about him and his penis—and by linking those charges to the Ku Klux Klan—Thomas achieved the ultimate transformation of his opponent: he bleached and "de-raced" her, changing Hill from a soft-spoken, black professional woman into a hysterical white cracker falsely accusing him of rape, the very charge that, for several gruesome decades in American history, often culminated in a ritual castration.

The exchange between Senator Hatch and Judge Thomas about racial stereotyping ensured that no lynching would occur, high-tech or otherwise. If nothing else, the all-white members of the Senate Judiciary Committee were determined to show this was 1991, not 1891. At 10:34 P.M., on October 11, when Senator Biden recessed the hearings for the day, the verdict was clear. The nominee, so close to political extinction, had come roaring back to life. When Senator Hatch left the hearing room, he was stopped by Nina Totenberg of National Public Radio.

"Senator, you just saved his ass," she told Hatch.

"No, Nina," said the Utah Republican. "He just saved his own ass."

What both probably knew, but neither could say, was that it was another part of Thomas's body that had really been at stake all along.

---

If Clarence Thomas forced America to confront its anxieties about the black penis on a subliminal level, Robert Mapplethorpe shoved that same organ into America's face—as a work of art. Since 1980 Mapplethorpe's nude portraits of black men had been exhibited in museums and galleries in the United States, Canada, Japan, and Europe, earning lavish praise from such journals as the *New York Times, Artforum, Art in America, Time,* and *Newsweek.* In 1986 a collection of those photos was published by St. Martin's Press as *Black Book.* Exquisitely printed and composed, *Black Book* projected an undeniable elegance. Black nudes had rarely been presented this way, or in any way for that matter. Of the 134 images collected by Constance Sullivan in *Nude: Photographs 1850–1980,* a work considered canonical, not one of those portraits is of a black man.

Sullivan's selective vision was part of a well-established Western tradition. Hegel and Nietzsche denied the black any sense of the aesthetic. Blacks could neither create beauty nor could they be beautiful objects, they wrote. If the collective heir to that view, the twentieth-century art establishment, also thought the black male too ugly to be an aesthetic object, Robert Mapplethorpe did not. In several of his *Black Book* photos he literally put a black man on a pedestal; in others, nude black men re-created Olympian poses from ancient Greece. Mapplethorpe was already controversial for his photographs of the gay sadomasochistic subculture. Now his portraits of macrophallic black men made him *the* most controversial artist of his day.

In June 1989, three months after Mapplethorpe's death from AIDS, a retrospective of his work was canceled just before its scheduled opening at Washington's Corcoran Gallery. Because the exhibit was partially funded by the National Endowment for the Arts, the resulting controversy, like the Hill-Thomas hearings two years later, reached the floor of the U.S. Senate, where Senator Jesse Helms tore apart the show's catalog and denounced Mapplethorpe's work as "pornography." When the exhibit opened at the Contemporary Arts Center in Cincinnati, the museum's director was arrested on obscenity charges by local police. The subsequent trial, in September 1990, received enormous press coverage and gave an international forum to numerous experts on censorship, artistic freedom, photography as art, and pornography as the cause of criminal behavior.

Much of the testimony in that trial focused on a photograph titled *Man in Polyester Suit.* This was no conventional portrait, no matter what your beliefs regarding artistic freedom and/or license. According to Mapplethorpe's biographer,

Patricia Morrisroe, this image, considered by many to be Mapplethorpe's masterpiece, came about when an African-American boyfriend of Mapplethorpe's showed him a three-piece suit he had purchased while in the navy and stationed in Korea. "Mapplethorpe," Morrisroe wrote, "immediately spotted the flaws

> in the tailoring, and after persuading [its owner] to model the suit, he purposely emphasized the shoddy workmanship by lining up [the wearer's] thumb so that it pointed to the spot where the seam ended abruptly on the jacket. "Wouldn't a nigger wear a suit like that?" [Mapplethorpe] commented to [a friend,] when he showed him the picture.

Mapplethorpe cropped the photo so that its upper and lower borders cut the subject off at the neck and knees. The suit jacket parts like a curtain and the man's fly is open; emerging from within is an uncircumcised black penis. This organ is only semi-erect, but that merely underscores its exceptional length and girth. It hangs there, sullen and heavy, veined and pulpy. Unlike the men in Mapplethorpe's photos of the gay S&M world, the Man in the Polyester Suit isn't doing anything. He is just being. His massive black penis is simultaneously fascinating and frightening, suggestive of a primitive, even bestial, sexuality that no garment, polyester or cashmere, could possibly contain. The effect is startling, even viscerally so. As critic Arthur C. Danto writes in *Playing with the Edge,* this photograph "demonstrates what 'playing with the edge' means." It "keeps the viewer suspended between beauty and danger. It is *supposed* to be shocking." Three hundred years of American phobias and fantasies, a history marked by lynchings, castrations, and paranoid fears of black phallic superiority, had become a disturbing, unforgettable, and political work of art. "You want to cut off this penis?" the photo seemed to be asking. "You better bring a really big knife."

One nameless and faceless black man had been put forth to represent a truth about all black men, and about sexuality at its most basic, raw, and uninhibited. That place is a realm beyond morality and prohibitions, a place of erotic delirium both thrilling and terrifying to white America. At the gate to that mythic universe stands the black man, the natural incarnation of potency unlimited. The white man may be cerebral, Mapplethorpe's image said; the black man is definitely genital.

The fact that the Man in the Polyester Suit was shown without a head—and thus without a brain—only accentuated the work's self-evident "truth": He is black. He has a large black penis. He *is* a large black penis. Three decades earlier, Frantz Fanon had made the same point in print. Every intellectual gain requires a loss in sexual prowess—and vice versa. "An erection on Rodin's *Thinker* is a shocking thought," Fanon wrote in *Black Skin, White Masks*. But not on a black man, precisely because he is not viewed by whites as an intellectual equal. To the contrary, when a white man sees a Negro, Fanon wrote, he "is no longer aware of the Negro but only of a penis; the Negro is eclipsed. He is turned into a penis. He *is* a penis." And just as the American physician William Lee Howard wrote fifty years before Fanon, it is that large black penis that renders any chance of civilizing the black man absolutely absurd.

Only once before had this visual idea—that nothing defined blackness more than black genitalia—been delivered so forcefully. This was in the early nineteenth century, when the white man's fascination with (and fear of) the black penis was reaching its apogee. Specimens of male genitalia could be cut off, cut open, and preserved in jars, and, indeed, many of them were. But a live demonstration of the African's genital superiority to the European was more than the white man could handle. So, instead, the same "scientific" point was made, live and on stage, by an African woman.

Saartjie Baartmann, often called Sarah Bartmann, was exhibited virtually naked as the "Hottentot Venus" in theaters throughout Europe in the first two decades of the nineteenth century, a time when "Hottentot" was a synonym for the lowest rung in the "great chain of being" discussed by Charles White and others. What proved Saartjie's debased, apelike status on that ladder, along with that of all black Africans, was her genitalia, especially her "Hottentot apron," a hypertrophy of the labia and nymphae, and her advanced case of steatopygia (excessively protruding buttocks).

When Baartmann died in 1815 at the age of [twenty-five,] her body was subject to an extensive autopsy by Georges Cuvier, permanent secretary of the French Academy of Sciences and a leading racial theorist of his day. Nine of the sixteen pages in Cuvier's autopsy report focused on Baartmann's sexual anatomy—from her famous labia to the "elastic and shivering mass" of her buttocks to the "apelike" formation of her pelvis. Her brain, on the other hand, was described in one paragraph. Afterward, Cuvier prepared Baartmann's dissected genital organs for exhibition at Musée de l'Homme in Paris. The clear intention, Sander L. Gilman writes in *Sexuality: An Illustrated History,* was to document the similarities between the genitalia of "the 'lowest' human species" with that of "the highest ape, the orangutan." Saartjie Baartmann, like all Africans, was reduced to her sexual organ.

As was the Man in the Polyester Suit. This explains why the photograph caused as much controversy among black intellectuals as it did among prosecutors, U.S. senators, and First Amendment scholars. "The penis becomes *the* identity of the black male, which is the classic stereotype re-created and presented as art," the African-American essayist Essex Hemphill wrote of *Man in Polyester Suit.* "It is virtually impossible for [a black male] to view Mapplethorpe's photo" without feeling "exploit[ed] and objectifi[ed.]"

In the end, those were the emotions felt by the real man in the polyester suit. Mapplethorpe met Milton Moore in September 1980. According to Morrisroe, Mapplethorpe was then infected with what he called "jungle fever," spending most nights at a

Manhattan bar frequented by black homosexuals. There was something about the texture of black skin, Mapplethorpe later told art critics, the way it glistened against a black background and showed off the muscle definition, that he found aesthetically irresistible. With his close friends, however, Mapplethorpe talked about how there was an inverse relationship between penis size and brain size in black men. He was searching, Mapplethorpe said, for "Super Nigger," a man with the primitive masculinity and genital superiority of a gorilla. (On all these points Mapplethorpe was just as wrong as Charles White.)

What white America had historically turned into a phobia, Mapplethorpe turned into a fetish. Unlike Freud's explanation, however, this was not a substitute for genital satisfaction. This fetish was as genital as genitalia gets. The irresistible lure for Mapplethorpe, his friend Winthrop Edey told Morrisroe, was "the big black cock." Another friend once heard Mapplethorpe describe the perfect black penis in such precise detail that he had worked out the ideal measurement of the urethral opening on the tip of the glans. Few realized how hard Mapplethorpe worked to find the perfect specimen of that big black penis. According to Edey, "he examined thousands of them."

Mapplethorpe stopped looking after he met Moore, who had just finished playing pinball at a bar called Sneakers, hard by the West Side Highway, in Manhattan's Greenwich Village. When Moore noticed Mapplethorpe staring at him, he was so frightened by the strange man's gaze that he ran away. Mapplethorpe caught up to Moore near the Christopher Street subway station, introduced himself, and offered to buy him a late-night breakfast. Mapplethorpe's name meant nothing to Moore. Even so, he accepted the invitation, but only after saying, "I don't want no trouble."

An hour or so later, Mapplethorpe took Moore back to his apartment-studio, where, with the help of some cocaine, he convinced Moore, then a twenty-five-year-old AWOL sailor, to undress for some nude photos. Mapplethorpe's intuition had been correct: finally, he later told a friend, on a man with "the face of a beautiful animal," he had found the perfect penis. Moore, afraid of embarrassing his family back home in Tennessee, said he would not pose unless Mapplethorpe agreed not to show that penis and his face in the same photograph. Mapplethorpe went into his bedroom and returned with a [pillowcase] which he placed over Moore's head.

The resulting image, now on page 54 of *Black Book*, next to *Man in Polyester Suit*, shows a naked Moore as a near-perfect construction of human symmetry. His hands are clenched in front of his chest, his elbows extend equidistant from his solar plexus, his large penis hangs at the bottom center of the frame, his head is enclosed in a hood. The photo is an aesthetic triumph. It is also probably the second-most controversial image in *Black Book*, making a teasing reference to one of the ugliest periods in American history. Hoods, after all, conjure the unmistakable image of the Ku Klux Klan, the very group that institutionalized lynchings of black men and the ritual castrations that often went along with them.

Clearly, Mapplethorpe idealized the black penis as a thing of beauty, producing art that subverted the prevailing cultural view that deemed such an aesthetic a contradiction in terms. Yet, in some ways, his work confirmed that same racism—a view as old as the scientific exploration of the "gradation" in man by Charles White. This is because the intersection of sex and race has always been fraught with psychological tension in Western culture. As Sander L. Gilman points out, the African's debased status is what has always made him the exotic sexual object *par excellence* for some Caucasians. For these whites, the black is the their erotic alter ego, the Sexual Other. He is appealing because he is appalling.

This highly charged ambivalence comes through even in the celebratory art of Robert Mapplethorpe. In photos such as *Hooded Man* and *Man in Polyester Suit*, the black body is both attractive and frightening. It is closer to nature—which is to say, the jungle—and the fiery parts of Hell reserved for sexual sinners. And no part of that anatomy embodies more of those qualities than the huge black penis.

Mapplethorpe experienced all those contradictions in the "perfect penis" he found in Milton Moore. Once, when talking to his friend, the writer Edmund White, Mapplethorpe found himself too full of emotion to express his love for Moore in mere words. Mapplethorpe instead showed White a print of *Man in Polyester Suit*. "Now you know," Mapplethorpe sobbed, as he pointed to Moore's penis, "why I love him so."

But Moore rarely felt that weepy, emotional love from Mapplethorpe in person. Sure, he felt Mapplethorpe's sexual desire for him, and the artist's erotic-aesthetic obsession with his penis. But Moore also intuited the ironic link between Mapplethorpe's supposedly worshipful interest in him and, say, that of Charles White toward the black penis he kept in a jar of formaldehyde in his laboratory in Manchester, England, in 1799. For White, that huge penis said something scientific about the black man's subhuman status. It said the same thing to Robert Mapplethorpe, no matter how much he romanticized or aestheticized it.

In the end, Moore came to understand that Mapplethorpe's vision of him, for all its artiness, was not that dissimilar from that of the white men who studied the black man's place in nature centuries earlier, an examination that focused on the black penis and found its answers in comparisons with apes. Though he was no student of history, Moore sensed the larger meaning of what had happened to him, maybe better than his educated tutor, Robert Mapplethorpe, ever did. Posing for a series of photographs, rather than live on stage, Moore had become the male version of Saartjie Baartmann—the "Hottentot Adonis."

"We never had a real relationship," Moore told Morrisroe of the time he spent with Mapplethorpe. "He saw me like a monkey in a zoo."

The black penis was not the only penis imbued with a negative racial identity. There was another group so stigmatized. But these men were not found living in primitive sin on a strange and foreign continent; these men had been living among Europeans since the Greeks and Romans, as a part of Western culture yet apart from it. Their separate status, enforced from within as well as without, was symbolized by a strange mark on the penis. In the eyes of Christians, this mark of circumcision, like skin color, was the sign of someone cursed by God. Its bearer, the Jew, was the White Sexual Other who spread unspeakable perversions and terrifying diseases. If he was not black in body, he was certainly black in spirit. At the turn of the nineteenth century, one physician, himself a Jew, concluded there *is* a link between the idea of the penis and the etiology of certain illnesses. But this fact, he insisted, was not true merely for Jews, a race set apart by circumcision, nor only for hypersexed, macrophallic Africans. For Sigmund Freud, this fact was true for the entire human race.

This cigar smoker's views on phallic symbols, the stages of sexual development, the phallic nature of the libido, and the cultural consequences of penis envy are nearly as controversial today as they were when he formulated them in Vienna a century ago. They have been lauded and mocked, and everything in between. What they cannot be, however, is ignored. With the writings of Freud the idea of the penis was again transformed, moving a distance both vast and subtle: From the specific to the universal, from the concrete to the unconscious, from the specimen jar to the couch. Instead of differences, the focus would be on commonalities—starting with the penis, whether you were born with one or envied those who were. After being racialized, the penis was psychoanalyzed. It was a process that would recalibrate the measuring stick forever.

# IV

## The Cigar

Sigmund Freud was a good listener even before he invented psychoanalysis. In 1885, while still an unknown neurology instructor at the University of Vienna, Freud won a grant to work in Paris with Professor Jean-Martin Charcot, the most celebrated neurologist in all the world. Much of that fame arose from Charcot's pioneering work with hypnosis. In lectures attended by nearly as many French aristocrats as medical students, Charcot put hysterics into a trance, then caused their puzzling symptoms—tics and tremors with no apparent organic cause—to materialize and vanish at his command. This dramatic display of the power of the mind over the body made a vivid impression on all who witnessed it. Young Dr. Freud maybe most of all.

What the starstruck Viennese didn't know was that Charcot was putting on a bit of theater. His most animated "hysterics" were secretly paid a cash bonus. In the dark about that, Freud saw Charcot as a brilliant scientific beacon; he virtually hung on his mentor's every word. One night at a party in Charcot's home, Freud—his social anxiety masked by a few snorts of cocaine—stood next to his revered host as he spoke with another physician. "My attention was seized by their conversation," Freud later wrote. The subject was a patient being seen by the other doctor: a young woman, with severe symptoms of hysteria, married to a sexually inept man. Charcot's colleague wondered if her neurosis might be caused by that particular erotic circumstance. According to Freud, Charcot nearly leaped into the air when he replied, "But in this sort of case, it is always a genital matter—always, always, always!"

Freud was stunned. If the great Charcot really knows that, he wondered, why does he not say so in public? Soon Freud would pose the nearly identical question in Vienna. Having opened his own neurology practice there, Freud was asked to take over a patient by the gynecologist Rudolf Chrobak. Freud met his colleague at the patient's home, where he found a woman suffering from unusually intense anxiety attacks. Chrobak took Freud aside and told him what was, in his view, the certain cause of her pathetic state. "She ha[s] been married eighteen years" but "is still *virgo intacta*," he said. "Her husband [is] absolutely impotent." In such a case, Chrobak warned, all a doctor can do is "shield the misfortune with his own reputation, and put up with it if people say: 'He [must not be] very good if he cannot cure her after so many years.'" The truth, Chrobak said, is:

The sole prescription for such a malady is familiar to us, but we cannot order it. It goes: "*Penis normalis,* repeated dose!"

Today, more than a century later, it is clear that no one has written more, or more influentially, on the role of matters genital—especially the *penis normalis*—in the molding of individual psyches, family dynamics, societal norms, gender roles, art, religion, humor, aggression—the list goes on and on—than the cigar-smoking physician who listened to those stories told by his older colleagues. What Drs. Charcot and Chrobak lacked the courage to say in public, however, Dr. Freud said loudly and often, and there is little doubt that he was heard. "No twentieth-century writer rivals Freud's position as the central imagination of our age," says the literary critic Harold Bloom. And there is no denying the central place occupied in the Freudian imagination by the penis.

With his bedrock concepts of penis envy and castration anxi-

An Egyptian papyrus shows the mating of the Earth god, Geb, and the goddess of the sky, Nut. For Egyptians this wasn't pornography; it was a religious map of their universe. (© The British Museum)

*(left)* The Roman god Priapus weighs his most prized possession. From the House of the Vettii, in Pompeii. (Alinari/Art Resource, NY)

*(right)* The Egyptian god of procreation, Min, is on the left. Once a year, in an elaborate ceremony, Pharaoh thanked Min for granting him sons. (© The British Museum)

maleficiis impeditus uxori ſue debitu̅ redd̅

*Man of Sorrows,* painted in 1532 by Maerten van Heemskerck, shows the resurrected Jesus with a tumescent penis. (Museum of Fine Arts, Ghent, Belgium)

*(facing, top)* A medieval manuscript shows the humiliating results of a failed potency examination. The wife of an impotent man was free to remarry but not the man. (MS W133, folio 277. The Walters Art Museum, Baltimore)

*(facing, bottom)* This fifteenth-century drawing of Adam, Eve, and the Serpent shows Adam without his "organ of shame." (MS. FR. 17001, fol. 107v. Cliché Bibliothèque nationale de France, Paris)

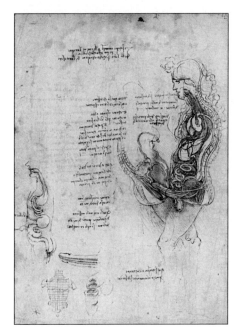

A page from the notebooks of Leonardo da Vinci shows several anatomical errors: the penis drawings have two urethras; the coition drawing on the right shows semen originating in the spinal column. (RL 19097v. The Royal Collection © HM Queen Elizabeth II)

*(below, left)* Adam, displaying his penis "with honor," in the *Epitome*, a companion volume to Vesalius's *De humani corporis fabrica*, the first anatomy text based on dissection, published in 1543. (Rare Book and Manuscript Collection. Cornell University Library)

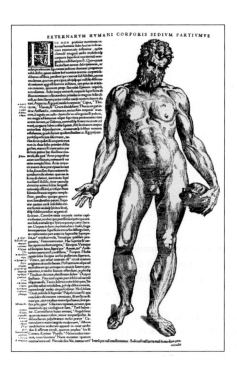

EXTERNARVM HVMANI CORPORIS SEDIVM PARTIVMVE

This drawing of a monkey as a quasi-human, originally published in 1699 in Edward Tyson's *Orang-Outang, sive Homo Sylvestris,* was included a hundred years later in Charles White's *An Account of the Regular Gradation in Man* to illustrate his thesis that Negroes were closer to apes than humans. (Olin Library, Cornell University Library)

*(below)* Antony van Leeuwenhoek, the Dutch microscopist who was the first to report the existence of spermatozoa, in 1677. (Museum of Comparative Zoology. The Agassiz Museum. Harvard University)

*(facing)* A drawing of the homunculus Nicolaas Hartsoeker claimed to observe inside a sperm cell in 1694. (Wellcome Library, London)

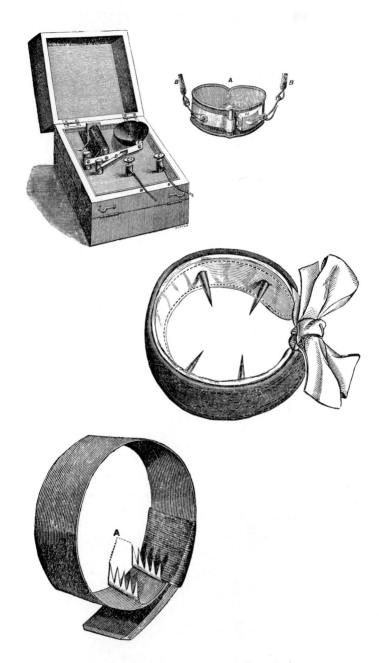

Three nineteenth-century devices used to treat masturbation and other "pollutions." (From J. L. Milton, *Pathology & Treatment of Spermatorrhoea* [London: Henry Renshaw, 1887]. Wellcome Library, London)

*Man in Polyester Suit.* (© 1980 The Estate of Robert Mapplethorpe)

Sigmund Freud in 1921 with his ever-present cigar. (Photograph by Max Halberstadt. Courtesy of W. E. Freud. Sigmund Freud Copyrights. Mary Evans Picture Library, London)

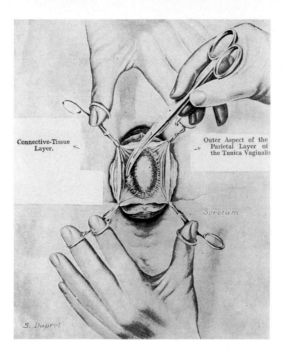

Two illustrations of Dr. Serge Voronoff's testicle-transplantation technique. The transplanted tissue came from chimpanzees. (From Dr. Serge Voronoff, *Rejuvenation by Grafting*. New York: Adelphia Company, 1925)

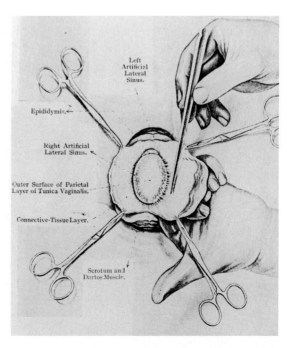

ety, his depiction of the unconscious as a realm made chaotic by penile lust, and his assertion that all libido, female as well as male, is phallic, Freud put the penis on the lips and minds of nearly every educated person in the Western world. In doing this, he became what another literary critic, Lionel Trilling, called a "figure": a man who "presides over certain ideas and attitudes." The ideas and attitudes Freud presided over tore away fig leaves left by fifteen hundred years of Christian civilization. To some this was an act of monumental courage; to others, an act of barbarism—to one Viennese contemporary, an act of Satanism. Psychoanalysis "proclaims the breakthrough of the Devil's Kingdom," Otto Friedell wrote in 1933. Just like a "connoisseur of the Black Mass," Freud "pay[s] homage to the phallus" as "the supreme Holy place." Freud did not heed his critics, but he heard them. Resistance to the penile thrust of analytic teachings was "unrelenting," he wrote in 1938, a year before his death. "People did not want to believe my facts and thought my theories unsavory." This is what happens, Freud said, when you "disturb the sleep of the world."

Of Freud's many upsetting insights, none is more basic than the idea that the body is more than a source of somatic stimuli. It is the author of one's character, he insisted, which is to say, everyone's character. Body-based drives are universal, Freud taught, and operate on the mind in meaningful ways, even if those meanings are not available to our conscious minds. We all go through an anal stage of development. We are all polymorphously perverse. We must all confront the Oedipus complex, named by Freud for the tragic hero who unwittingly killed his father and married his mother, then blinded himself—Freud would say castrated himself—in expiation. These are parts of our "common mental construction," common to us all because we all have bodies. What makes this link between body and mind "unsavory" to some is Freud's insistence that the pivotal organ in shaping character—for those who have the organ and those who do not—is the penis.

Born into a world of neat, ranked pairings (aristocrat over proletarian, West over East, Christian over Jew, and so on) Freud declared only one distinction really matters: having a penis or being castrated. This latter condition, which to Freud meant the lack of a penis and not just testicles, was conceived by him as much as a state of mind as a physical fact, and often just as castration anxiety. His views on the origins of that phobia were elastic and evolved over time. On the key point, however, Freud was consistent: There is no denying the psychic reality of castration or its consequences. For men, for women, for children, for everyone.

Freud's first reference to castration was somewhat choppy. In *The Interpretation of Dreams,* he wrote of a boy made anxious by nightmares filled with daggers and scythes. These frightening fantasies, Freud understood, were based in reality: the boy's father had threatened to cut off the child's penis if he did not stop masturbating. This remark resonated with Freud, Marianne Krull writes in *Freud and His Father,* because Freud's father made the identical threat to him. After Jacob Freud's death, Freud often referred to his father as a kind, jovial man. Krull speculates this was not his view when he was a boy. Young Sigmund seems to have been intimidated by his father, especially when, upon his return from frequent business trips, Jacob was called upon to discipline his children for behavioral infractions that, in Sigmund's case, may have included masturbation. Making Sigmund's early masturbatory life even more anxiety inducing is the possibility that the person who ratted him out for playing with his penis was the person who taught him how—the family maid, a Czech peasant named Resi Wittek. Years later, in a letter to his friend Wilhelm Fliess, Freud—then working out the founding ideas of psychoanalysis—referred to Wittek as his "instructress in sexual matters."

It seems the threat of castration delivered by Jacob Freud was a common response to masturbation in nineteenth-century Europe. One orphanage run by nuns dealt with this problem by making that very promise—then reinforcing it by blindfolding each trembling suspect and touching his penis with a lump of ice! How widespread such activities really were is hard to know, but we do know that Freud inferred a rule of psychic development from such situations. "The child, having been dominated by excitations in the penis, will have obtained pleasure by stimulating it with his hand," Freud wrote in *On the Sexual Theories of Children*. "He will have been detected in this by his parents or nurse and terrorized by the threat of having his penis cut off. The effect of this threat is . . . extraordinarily deep and persistent."

Freud was, for the moment, uncharacteristically silent about the specifics of that effect. But he made up for that lapse later, exploring in numerous papers—most notably *Some Psychical Consequences of the Anatomical Distinction between the Sexes*—the crucial link between castration anxiety and the psychic event he deemed to have the deepest effect of all, the Oedipus complex. There, Freud said, the son's fear of castration by his father, retaliation for the boy's sexual desire for his mother, acts as the "nucleus of all neuroses." Freud's description of this process was mostly psychological, partly biological, clearly mythological, and, more than a century later, still controversial. But one idea is as clear today as it was then: by insisting that the consequences of castration anxiety are inescapable, Freud assigned the defining role in human personality to the penis.

Every male infant, Freud said, assumes that everyone has the same organ he has. Seeing his sister's or mother's "castrated" state, something the boy assumes was done by his father, is terrifying proof of penile amputation. To save his own penis, the boy adopts a passive yet resentful attitude toward his father and one of bondage to his mother. He dare not desire his father's mate. But he cannot risk *not* being desired by her, lest she betray him and hand him over to his father for castration. In highly neurotic males, the reality of sexual difference can be a shock with significant fallout. Some become fetishists; others, Freud said, become homosexuals. But in non-neurotics these conflicts slowly evolve into a positive, humanizing experience. After the Oedipus complex is "smashed by the threat of castration," the boy internalizes his repressive father as his conscience or super-ego. Instead of killing his father and mating with his mother, he decides to be like his father and mate with someone like his mother. The boy's aggressive phallic energy is transformed into an "instinct for mastery" that later finds expression in meaningful work. It is in this socially acceptable way that a man penetrates his environment and leaves his mark.

Years later this same boy is now a man, presumably a productive member of society, a loving husband, and a father—and a tyrant who intimidates his own son and threatens *his* penis. This, Freud insisted, is the fate of all mankind and one of the primary reasons why civilized life causes so much psychic anxiety. The disclosure of this gloomy fact was Freud's proudest moment. "If psycho-analysis could boast of no other achievement than the discovery of the Oedipus complex," he wrote, "that alone would give it a claim to be included among the precious new acquisitions of mankind."

For a girl there could be no more precious acquisition than a penis. Castration is not a threat for her, it is a Freudian reality. Her trauma, then, is even greater. This is because the Oedipus complex coincides with the phallic stage of development experienced by both sexes, a stage marked by masturbation with the "active, penetrating, masculine genital organ"—the penis in boys and the clitoris in girls. Just like her brother, the sister desires her mother. This is her prevailing fantasy during masturbation. "The little girl," Freud wrote, "is actually a little man."

Until she realizes she is not and never can be. She "notice[s] the penis of a brother or playmate, . . . recognize[s] it as the superior counterpart to [her] own inconspicuous organ, and from that time forward fall[s] victim to envy for the penis." This envy hardens like a scar into self-loathing. Soon the girl shares "the contempt felt by men for her sex which is the lesser in so important a respect." Because she cannot internalize her father as her superego—something created by the fear of castration, Freud said, but not the reality of it—a female is morally defective. With no other options, a female must deal with her anatomical deficiency by substitution. Her wish to have a penis is satisfied by "extending her love for the organ to the bearer of the organ"—first her father, in Oedipal fantasies of being penetrated by him, then her husband. (Either way in the Freudian universe, a man is little more than a support system for the penis; he is attached to it rather than it to him.) The goal of vaginal sexuality for women is not love or pleasure, Freud said. It is to capture a penis.

These theories have taken as many shots as a rural road sign. Brain researchers and non-Freudian psychologists have declared them untestable and therefore unscientific. Historians note the blurring of nineteenth-century cultural biases, especially against women, with "objective" observation. Even many within the analytic community have protested. In 1932, four years before Gloria Steinem was born, the analyst Karen Horney argued that if anyone is ill-equipped it is men. Yes, the male's first sighting of a vagina causes a trauma, Horney wrote in "The Dread of Woman." But not the one Freud suggested. The real consequence, she said, is that the boy

> instinctively judges that his penis is much too small for his mother's genitals and reacts with the dread of his own inadequacy.

Perhaps the one thing not in dispute regarding Freud's ideas on the mind-body connection is this: their ultimate significance lies less in their accuracy than the fact that no modern thinker, certainly no one as influential as Freud, justified them in such a consistently and *in*sistently phallocentric way. By way of comparison, the oft-stated claim that Freud discovered the unconscious and infantile sexuality is greatly exaggerated. Other writers explored those ideas before Freud, though none as thoroughly as Herr Professor from Vienna. Among the core concepts of psychoanalysis, only two—penis envy and the castration complex—are without any precedent in the medical literature and thus stand as wholly original. In 1937 Freud called them the "bedrock" upon which all his theories were built and beyond which psychoanalysis was powerless to dig. If he were alive today Freud might call them "psychic DNA" or the "double-helix of human personality." One thing is certain: the focus on the penis in each of those concepts hardly requires demonstration.

These concepts were crucial to Freud because the penis—intact or amputated, erect or flaccid—always stands for something. The material reality of the organ encases its psychic reality; it links man with the external world and his internal drives and fantasies. The Freudian penis is a truth-teller, revealing man's brutish origins, showing his power and weakness, and reminding us all that we are not the master in our own house. Its rise and fall mirrors our own. The flaccidity that follows erection echoes human mortality, just as phallic lust shows our eagerness to use others, and masturbation our willingness to use ourselves.

This penis is far more than a body part. It is an idea and a symbol, a sign so powerful it is itself symbolized by other things. When this famous smoker who consumed twenty cigars a day said, "Sometimes a cigar is just a cigar," he still believed that most times it is not. By 1923 the roof of Freud's mouth was covered with cancerous growths, a clear result of his smoking. A surgeon removed nearly all of Freud's palate in thirty-plus operations that, afterward, required Freud to wear an oral prosthesis—a false roof, as it were—that made it difficult for him to speak. Even so, Freud refused to give up cigars, freely conceding that his habit suggested homosexual fellatio, a substitute for the primary human addiction—masturbation—and erotic sublima-

tion brought on by long periods of abstinence in his own marriage to the former Martha Bernays.

To Freud the penis itself represented the powerful, the creative, the intellectual, and the beautiful, as well as the ugly, the
irrational, and the beast within us all. Not since the Greeks had
anyone conceptualized the penis more forcefully, or with more
complexity, as an idea. It is no accident that Freud, with his repeated references to Oedipus, Medusa, and catharsis, took
some of his most important terminology from the Greeks.
Mount Olympus was home to gods with eternal erections, of divine castrations, of goddesses emerging whole from semen, of
satyrs and centaurs, of naked, masculine heroes comfortable
with their sexuality, even if bisexual.

Like that other great phallic "figure" Augustine, Freud saw
the penis as the key unlocking one's own history *and* the history
of the entire human race. Freud's concept of the primal horde,
where our prehistoric male ancestors murdered the father who
enforced his monopoly on the women of the group by threatening his sons with castration—a theory Freud advanced in *Totem
and Taboo* to explain the origins of civilization—took Augustine's central theme and stripped it of religion. Gone is Paradise
and a spiritual reason for man's fall. In its place is a "scientific
myth" (Freud's term) and a secular original sin. Where Augustine declared the punishment for Adam's crime to be erections
we cannot control, Freud's punishment for the primal parricide
is a civilization that controls our erections. The Freudian penis
has not been demonized; it has been psychoanalyzed.

Many have dismissed Freudianism as mythology, but no such
insult is intended here. Returning to the words of Harold Bloom,
Freud was "the most powerfully suggestive myth maker" of the
twentieth century, imagining a new map of the human mind.
Freud saw this work as completing a trinity with two of his idols,
the scientific revolutionaries Copernicus and Darwin. Bloom
proposes another lineage, putting Freud fourth in line after
Plato, Montaigne, and Shakespeare—not bad company, either.

"The neurologist who sought a dynamic psychology," Bloom wrote in his essay, "Freud, the Greatest Modern Writer," became "a mythologizing dramatist of the inner life."

The key player in that drama, Freud said, is the penis. That is a powerfully suggestive way of looking at human existence. The best way to understand it is to look at the mythology of the penis that produced Sigmund Freud.

---

That the penis is a marker, a body part with conscious and unconscious meanings of huge and enduring consequence, is an insight that was as much thrust upon Freud as it was created by him. Reaching manhood in late-nineteenth-century Europe, Freud knew well that his Jewishness defined him as diseased in the eyes of his Christian neighbors. He also knew those eyes focused on a part of him that "caused" his illness. This body part made him and all Jews a dangerous source of contagion to non-Jews. The organ that did this was the Jewish penis.

Fear and loathing of that organ had permeated European culture for two thousand years. In Imperial Rome the same insulting slang term—*verpa*—signified "Jew" and "prick," a reference to the common belief that circumcised Jews were pathologically lustful. In Augustine's *Tractatus adversus Judaeos* (*Treatise Against the Jews*), the future saint attacked circumcision as a sign that "carnal Israel" lived "according to the flesh" rather than the spirit. Another Father of the Church, Saint Jerome, wrote, "If you call [the Jewish synagogue] a brothel, a den of vice, [or] the Devil's refuge, you are saying less than it deserves." These libels explain why, centuries later, woodcuts often showed a Jew riding backward on a goat, the beast in whose form Satan appeared at Witches' Sabbaths, the sex orgies where the Evil One commanded every woman present to kiss his huge scaly member. By the twelfth century the penis was publicly identified as the source of the Jew's diabolical powers. The Abbot Guibert de Nogent learned this, he wrote in his memoirs, from a renegade monk who had begged a Jewish physician to teach him the secrets of his black magic and, better yet, to introduce him to the Devil. "First you must make a sacrifice to Satan," the Jew said, speaking for "the abominable ruler." "What kind of sacrifice?" asked the monk. "You will make a libation of your sperm," said the Jew. "And when you have spilled it before me, you will taste it."

The Jew was defined by his penis, and that penis was defined by circumcision. The ritual proved the Jew's perversity—removing the foreskin and thus hinting of castration, but exposing the glans, just as the penis looks when it is erect. Because of these mixed signals, the Christian idea of the Jew was sexually confused but uniformly negative. The Jew was seen as simultaneously effeminate and highly virile, a sly and cruel seducer, especially of Christian virgins, but a man whose manly tool was blunted by a barbaric rite that blurred sexual difference. It was even believed that Jews menstruated through their penises, a condition that, according to the sixteenth-century Jesuit Gottfried Henschen, led Jews to commit ritual murder: the only cure for the male Jew's menstrual cramps, Henschen wrote in *Acta Santorum* (*Acts of the Saints*) was drinking the blood of a dead Christian.

Even more widely believed was the idea that Jews murdered young Christian boys—always after circumcising them—then used the blood as part of the Passover celebration. Hartmann Schedel's *Nuremberg Chronicles*, published in 1493, wrote at some length on the martyrdom of Saint Simon of Trent. This was a two-year-old boy who was supposedly kidnapped just before Easter in 1475 in Trento, Italy, after which his dead body was found near the house of a local Jew, totally drained of blood, his penis freshly circumcised. A woodcut accompanying this grotesque tale in the *Chronicles* shows the alleged circumstances of Simon's death. The child is drawn standing on a table, his arms and legs restrained by smiling, bearded, caftan-wearing Jews. There is a gaping wound at the boy's throat; there are needles pricking into his neck. At the center of the woodcut is Simon's penis, which is being pulled forward by a kneeling Jew, holding a knife. Apparently, he's already done his dastardly deed. Blood is pouring out of Simon's penis into a bowl on the table, while another Jew looks on approvingly.

That circumcision was often equated with castration is seen in the plea of the sixteenth-century British poet Gabriel Harvey, who begged God to silence his enemies completely by "circumcising the[ir] tongues." Opponents of an English law granting citizenship to Jews added something new to this litany of libels—cannibalism. The *London Evening Post* sounded the alarm in verse in 1753:

> When mighty Roast Pork was the Englishman's Food,
> It ennobled our Veins and enriched our Blood.
> And a Jew's Dish of Foreskins was not understood.
>
> Then Britons Be wise at this Critical Pinch
> And in such a Cause be not Cowards and flinch,
> But the best of your Property guard ev'ry inch.

Clearly, when the Jew Shylock demanded a "pound of flesh" in *The Merchant of Venice*, Shakespeare understood the horror such words incited in those who heard them.

But nothing matched the horror incited by syphilis, a disease said to be spread by the Jew's penis. This slander, historian Sander L. Gilman writes, was rooted in Christian revulsion at *metitsah,* the ancient practice in which the circumciser, the *mohel,* after cutting off the foreskin, briefly placed the infant's penis in his mouth, which contained wine to aid clotting. This oral-genital contact, anti-Semites believed, made the Jewish penis a dangerous sources of contagion to non-Jews. The French essayist Michel de Montaigne, whose mother was of Spanish-Jewish descent, observed *metitsah* "very attentively" in Rome in 1581. As soon as the glans is uncovered, Montaigne wrote, "they hastily offer some wine to the minister, who puts a little in his mouth

> and then goes and sucks the glans of this child, all bloody, and spits out the blood he has drawn from it, and immediately takes much wine again. . . . He meanwhile still hath his own mouth all bloody.

(Despite his mother's ancestry, Montaigne was raised a Catholic and was not circumcised himself.)

Most Jews abandoned *metitsah* before the nineteenth century. Freud, however, was circumcised this way in Freiberg (now Pribor), the small Moravian town where he was born in 1856 in a one-room apartment above a blacksmith's shop. Nearly all the Jewish communities that still practiced *metitsah,* not including Freud's, insisted, for sanitary reasons, that the penis be covered with a glass tube when it was sucked—a change that rendered the act merely symbolic. Franz Kafka wrote an ironic lament for that shift in 1911. In his journal, Kafka contrasted the bland but safe circumcision he had just seen performed on his nephew in Prague with the weird but compelling ritual of the past, where the infant's penis was "sucked on by a half-drunken rabbi with a red nose and stinking breath." Kafka was not the only writer of genius to be riveted and repulsed by the rite's sexual ambiguity. In *Joseph and His Brothers,* Thomas Mann saw circumcision as a sign of a divine marriage between Jews and God that feminized Jewish men. But in *The Blood of the Walsungs,* Mann retold one of the oldest lies about Jewish hypervirility, writing of a Jew who cuckolded a German by seducing his fiancée—the Jew's own sister.

Seducing other Jews was one thing; seducing Christians, something else entirely. The Jew's penis was at the center of this anxiety, a fear showing the impact of one of the strangest genetic theories to emerge in the nineteenth century. Called telegony, this theory originated in a report sent by the Earl of Morton to the Royal Society of London in 1820. Morton had mated a chestnut mare with an African horse called a quagga, a now-extinct breed known for its zebralike stripes. After producing one striped colt, Morton's mare was sold and mated by her new owner with a black Arabian stallion. The offspring of those two horses, on two different occasions, also had quaggalike stripes, Morton reported, though neither of its parents was a quagga.

This evidence, later discredited, was used to assert that the offspring of any female—including humans—would forever resemble, externally and internally, the first male to enter her. This inflamed anti-Semitism all over Europe, but especially in Vienna, home of Freud and later Hitler, whose Nazi party newspaper, *Der Stürmer,* often presented cartoons depicting Jews with massive syphilis-spreading erections lusting after Christian virgins. Making this libel even more odious was the widespread belief that Jews themselves were immune to syphilis. It was the Jew's nature, his diabolical mission, such racial thinkers believed, to foster racial corruption by creating hidden Jews among the larger population with his large diseased penis. One cure for this threat to the Christian body politic was castration, which was occasionally administered to Jews via vigilante justice in a fashion not unlike lynchings in the American South. Just like the African penis, the Jewish penis was racialized, criminalized, and, on occasion, even excised.

These ideas and events colored the world in which Sigmund Freud grew up, studied medicine, treated patients, and thought about what he saw and heard. In a prodigious period of fertility that resulted in a corpus of several million words, Freud invented a new way of interpreting that world. This controversial method took many of the insults about the Jewish penis and, to use Professor Gilman's term, "universalized" them, rendering them into truths applicable to all. Psychoanalysis—Freud's way of reading the past, both of the individual and the entire human race—focused on the penis more than any intellectual system that preceded it. Whether we are conscious of it or not, Freud said, we all experience castration anxiety. We are all obsessed with sex. We all go through a phallic stage of development. We all have incestuous erotic desires. We all respond to phallic symbols. We are like this not because we are Jewish, but because we are human.

———————

In the summer of 1900, in the Alpine resort of Achensee, two friends met for the last time. That Sigmund Freud and Wilhelm Fliess were close is not surprising. Each was a German-Jewish physician pursuing research outside the usual channels, and both were viewed with suspicion by the mainstream medical community because of it. Though their friendship was undoubtedly personal, it was also functional, providing a greatly needed mutual-support system. Some of Freud's most controversial theories had just been published in *The Interpretation of Dreams*, where he asserted that dreams, considered meaningless by most of his peers, were in fact "the royal road to knowledge of the unconscious," a chaotic and unruly place, Freud said, preoccupied with phallic sexuality. Fliess, a nose-and-throat specialist from Berlin, had some provocative ideas of his own. One declared a biological link between the nose and the genitals, which Fliess discovered by curing menstrual cramps with applications of cocaine to the "genital spots" he located inside the nose. Another asserted the bisexuality of all humans. A third stated that all of human life plays out in periodic cycles, one of twenty-eight days' duration for women, and twenty-three for men.

For a while Freud was so open to Fliess's theories that he said he was impotent every twenty-eight days and was certain that he would die at age fifty-one—the sum of twenty-eight and twenty-three. No doubt some of Freud's open-mindedness was out of gratitude. In Vienna Freud had few listeners for his own strange ideas. But now, as Freud's faith in those ideas was growing, Fliess's ideas seemed more and more untenable. In Achensee Fliess insisted that all neuroses were tied to periodic cycles; they came and went on their own, with or without treatment. Such a belief, Freud said, denied the psychic dynamism he was witnessing in his practice. Freud was not seeing anything real in his consulting room, Fliess said. Freud was merely a "thought-reader reading his own thoughts in others."

The friendship between Freud and Fliess began to die right there. But their correspondence (Freud's half of it, anyway) survived. Like Leonardo da Vinci's notebooks, these letters—the fossil evidence of psychoanalysis—were not meant for publication. Proposing bold theories that were revised, discarded, and revived almost weekly, they display a fertile mind attempting to draw a map of the unconscious, especially as it relates to the human body. From 1892 on, Freud's letters show him narrowing his focus to a body-based power he eventually deemed more psychical than physical. This would result in one of the defining ideas of psychoanalysis and perhaps Freud's boldest conception of all: the mysterious *mental* potency of the human penis.

This insight—that the "idea" of the penis, through fantasies of penetration and castration, has a major impact on psychological functioning—emerged from Freud's neurology practice. Many of Freud's patients were hysterics and, at first, he treated them with the therapies then recommended in the medical literature: hydrotherapy (hot and cold showers), electrotherapy (jolts of current administered to the affected areas), and massage. Dissatisfied with the results, Freud began to experiment with hypnosis. He put suggestible patients into a trance, then questioned them about the origins of their symptoms. The result was exactly what Professor Charcot said it would be in Paris: a discussion of genital matters.

Freud's use of hypnosis showed the influence of Charcot and another early mentor, the Viennese physician Josef Breuer. As chronicled in *Studies in Hysteria,* which he cowrote with Freud, Breuer experimented in the 1880s with the pointed questioning of hypnotized patients, asking them to recall the precise moment their symptoms began, an approach he called the cathartic method. Breuer abandoned this technique when one of his patients, Anna O., developed a hysterical pregnancy and referred to her stomach as "Dr. B.'s child." Freud, too, was the object of a sexual advance from a hypnotized patient. Looking back years later, he saw it as an early hint that the etiology of neurosis is sexual.

Freud used and praised hypnosis for several years, on one occasion curing a patient who was sent into convulsions every time she heard the word "apple." A success like that was gratifying, Ernest Jones wrote in *The Life and Work of Sigmund Freud*, because it "replaced [Freud's] feeling of helplessness [with] the satisfaction of being admired as a magician." Not everyone was impressed, however. Dr. Theodore Meynert, chief of psychiatry at Vienna's General Hospital, denounced hypnotism as degrading to both patient and physician. Eventually Freud had doubts of his own. Some patients were easily suggestible, others were not, and even under the best of circumstances, the results were often temporary. So Freud dropped hypnosis in favor of "free association," a process in which the patient, lying down with his eyes closed, spoke unfettered by hypnotic suggestion but influenced by two phenomena whose importance would dawn on Freud later: resistance and transference. While using this technique, Freud had an epiphany. Charcot was right. The disturbances in his patients' sex lives were not the result of their neuroses. They were the *cause*. This "sex talk leaves patients stunned," he wrote Fliess in 1893. But they walk out "won over" after saying, "No one ever asked me that before!" Freud mailed Fliess his *Etiology of the Neuroses* (Draft B), warning him to keep it away from his young wife. By Victorian standards Freud's document was blunt, indeed: all neurosis, he wrote, "is sexual."

Though he said "sexual," Freud could just as well have said "penile." The two pathologies cited in Draft B each involved the penis and practices Freud said lessened its potency: masturbation and coitus interruptus, a term which, for Freud, not only signified the male pulling out before ejaculation but conventional intercourse with condoms. Each of those conjugal acts caused neurosis, Freud said, because both were fraught with dissatisfactory discharges caused by the fear of pregnancy.

Freud's objection to masturbation was based neither in morality nor a belief in conserving male essence. Rather, he thought it an unsatisfactory form of orgasm leading to a loss of vigor, premature ejaculation, or the inability to ejaculate during intercourse. These in turn created neurasthenia, a state of sexual weakness marked by depression and chronic fatigue. The psychiatrist and medical historian David J. Lynn recently uncovered an unpublished autobiography by one of Freud's early patients that shows the depths of Freud's commitment to this etiology. The writer, Albert Hirst, had been sent to Freud at age sixteen after a clumsy suicide attempt motivated by his sexual failings with girls. The first session with Freud began with the doctor offering his patient a seat in a chair opposite him. Then, Hirst wrote, Freud "ordered me to assume in that chair the position in which I masturbated."

If Freud saw a link between crippled psyches and crippled penises, not many others did. The Viennese "look upon me as . . . a monomaniac," he wrote Fliess, "while I [believe] I have touched upon one of the great secrets of nature." That Freud viewed sexual dysfunction from a physiological stance rather than a psychological one may seem strange to us now. But in 1893 Freud was not yet a psychoanalyst. He was a neurologist with an interest in psychiatry. Scientists in those fields did not study the mind. They studied the brain, which they saw as an organ of the body not unlike, say, the liver. Mental illness was caused, they believed, by lesions in the cerebral cortex or a weakness in the overall nervous system. "It is not our business, it is not in our power, to explain psychologically the origin or nature of the depraved instincts," the British psychiatrist Harry Maudsley wrote in 1874. "The explanation, when it comes, will not come from the mental, but from the physical side."

That Freud blamed the penis for mental illness shows the influence of this biological approach. *Psychopathia Sexualis*, the landmark study of perversion written in 1886 by Richard von Krafft-Ebing, chief of neurology and psychiatry at the University of Vienna, typified this school of thought. Krafft-Ebing's case histories described gruesome sex crimes with Teutonic thoroughness. Where possible, they also described the size and condition of the perpetrator's penis, implying a causal link. Rapist-murderer Vincenz Verzeni, who ripped out the intestines of his victims, then carried them home so he could smell them later, was noted by Krafft-Ebing to have a "greatly developed penis, missing the frenulum." That missing part is the small, wrinkly band of skin just below the glans and underneath the foreskin. It is fascinating to note that, a century later, a study in the journal *Brain Research* would show the frenulum to be one of the most sensitive parts of the penis. (It is equally interesting to recall that, in 1799, Dr. Charles White cited the frequent lack of a frenulum in black Africans as proof of their biological similarity to apes—and a reason for their shared lascivious nature.)

There is no evidence Freud examined the genitalia of his patients. But he did notice something odd: many of those patients had hysterical symptoms even though they were not sexually active. This puzzled Freud, who had concluded that "actual neuroses," his umbrella term for neurasthenia and anxiety, were linked to current sexual practices such as masturbation and coitus interruptus. Further work with his patients offered up a solution. Sex had taken place, Freud decided, but in the past— in childhood, sometimes even in infancy. These seductions, as he inaccurately called them, were not sugary persuasions. Most were assaults by fathers. No matter what the modus operandi, the key player was the penis. Girls endured "irritation of the genitals [in] proceedings resembling coitus" inflicted by an adult penis; boys had their penises fondled by nannies. These discoveries triggered elation and migraines in Freud, who wrote of both to Fliess. "Have I revealed the great secret to you?" he asked in October 1895. "Hysteria is the consequence of a presexual sexual shock. Obsessional neurosis is the result of a presexual sexual pleasure, which is later transformed into self-reproach." By presexual, Freud meant before puberty.

Freud went public with his discovery the following spring. On April 21, 1896, he spoke on "The Etiology of Hysteria" at the Viennese Society for Psychiatry and Neurology, chaired by Professor Krafft-Ebing. In his talk Freud used a metaphor he had already used in *Studies in Hysteria* and would return to often in his career. The scientist who looks at hysterical symptoms, he said, is like the archaeologist who discovers the ruins of an ancient city. He finds the psychic equivalent of columns without roofs, ceilings without walls, tablets with partially rubbed-out inscriptions, and objects whose very purpose is a mystery. Like the archaeologist, the mental investigator digs this material up, dusts it off, studies it, compares it with items found at other sites, and then, if his labors are met with luck, *"saxa loquuntur"*—the stones speak.

This image was old and literary, with antecedents in *Macbeth* ("The very stones prate of my whereabout") and the Gospel of Luke ("I tell you if they were silent the very stone would cry out"). But it was also modern and German. In 1871 archaeologist Heinrich Schliemann, one of Freud's heroes, found and decoded the marble ruins of Troy. Now in Vienna, using insights unearthed by free association, Sigmund Freud had listened to the stones in eighteen cases of hysteria. What he heard was unpleasant but important. The cause of hysteria, Freud announced, is the sexual abuse of children, often by penile penetration.

Having worked with most of the men sitting in his audience, Freud well knew the limits of their expressiveness. Still, he was shocked by their silence. "[My] lecture . . . was given an icy reception by the asses," Freud wrote Fliess. "Krafft-Ebing [said] 'It sounds like a scientific fairy tale.' This, after one has showed them the solution to a more-than-thousand-year-old prob-

lem . . . ! They can go to hell." A week later Freud's pique turned
to anxiety. "Word has gone out to abandon me. My consulting
room is empty." Self-pity and self-aggrandizement were recurring themes in Freud's life. How blank his appointment book really was is unclear. What is certain, however, is that not long
after his lecture debacle Freud began to work extremely hard
with a new patient, the most difficult, demanding, and reward-
ing patient of his career, a patient who would change forever the
way modern man viewed his defining organ:

Himself.

---

It is "hard for us to imagine how momentous this achievement
was," Ernest Jones later wrote. "What indomitable courage,
both intellectual and moral, must have been needed! But it was
forthcoming." This tone is not atypical. For Freudians, Freud's
self-analysis surpasses the sanctity for Jews of Moses' receiving
the Ten Commandments from God; after all, Freud played the
part of Moses *and* God. His self-analysis, one analyst has written, "accomplished for science the same liberating step that
Dante, Montaigne, Shakespeare, and Rembrandt took in literature and art: that of explicitly moving the self into the focus of
attention." This list overlooks Augustine, a key figure in the history of introspection *and* the penis, but the point is well-taken.
Today, when even twenty-five-year-olds write memoirs, Freud's
self-absorption does not seem remarkable. But in 1897 it was,
especially for an academic scientist trained to observe others.
We know that in the summer of that year Freud turned his back
on that training and began a period of intense self-scrutiny. We
do not know much about the particulars of the process—did he
put himself on the couch? did he fortify his mind with cocaine,
a drug he had used and praised in the past?—but we do know
this: His method was free association. The materials he worked
with were dreams, childhood memories, and the errors we now
call Freudian slips. This was no talking cure, however. Freud's

analytic rite of passage was a *write* of passage. His conviction that dreams are psychic transcriptions and wish fulfillments emerged from the act of transcribing his own dreams onto paper. (Many would be published two and a half years later in *The Interpretation of Dreams*.)

The turning point in this process occurred in 1897. "I no longer believe in my neurotica," Freud wrote Fliess on September 21, referring to his theory that neuroses originate with the sexual abuse of children. The idea that fathers were usually to blame was causing consternation Freud never anticipated. Several of his sisters had hysterical symptoms. If his neurotica was accurate this implicated his own father. Freud accepted this at first, calling Jacob Freud a "pervert" in an earlier letter to Fliess. But now he wasn't sure, and not just about Freud Senior. The sheer abundance of hysteria, Freud decided, worked against his theory. If true, paternal attacks must be virtually universal "and such widespread perversion is not very probable." His patients' incestuous "revelations," he told Fliess, were more likely the products of their imaginations.

A century later, Alice Miller and Jeffrey Moussaieff Masson attacked Freud's new theory as a cynical abandonment of the truth of sexual abuse. (And, in return, each was attacked for heresy by the Freudian establishment.) Masson was especially vilified for arguing that Freud was motivated not by ideas, but by the trauma of his rejection by his peers at the Viennese Society for Psychiatry and Neurology. Whatever the merits of that charge, it is clear that Freud was no more popular with his colleagues after he revised the seduction theory than he was when he proclaimed it.

Freud did not reject the seduction theory because he found new evidence to disprove it. In fact, he never completely rejected the theory at all. Twenty years after his famous letter to Fliess, Freud referred to three critical factors in the origin and development of neurosis: "observations of parental intercourse, *seduction by an adult* [italics added], and threat of being castrated."

What Freud did in September 1897 was come up with a new
theory to explain the old evidence. He did this by deciding that
Krafft-Ebing got it half right: many of Freud's patients had been
telling "fairy tales." But what Freud understood—in a way
Krafft-Ebing could not—was that there is truth in such fairy
tales. They are coded messages from the unconscious. As Freud
moved from psychiatry to psychoanalysis, he became less interested in the conflicts between individuals and more interested in
the conflicts within them. Even if most of the incestuous charges
made by Freud's patients were false, they were true expressions—evidence, in fact—of infantile sexuality, which to Freud
meant infantile sexual desire. These patients were not lying;
lying is a conscious act, fantasies are not. Freud was not denying
the reality of sexual abuse as much as he was declaring the existence of another reality: the realm of fantasy and conflict emanating from the depths of the id, a place where the prevailing
imagery is active and sexual, and the psychic potency clearly
phallic. Even for children.

Freud had been moving in this direction for some time. In
January 1897, he was struck by the similarity between the written reports of medieval witch hunters and what he was hearing
in his consulting room. "Why are [the witches'] confessions . . .
so like the communications made by my patients?" he wondered to Fliess. The Inquisitors "prick with needles" and the
"witches" respond with the "same old cruel story," an obvious
piece of fiction. But "why," Freud asked, "did the devil invariably abuse them sexually?" A letter sent the following week
proposed a solution: "Bringing in witches is [paying off],"
Freud wrote. Their flying and cruel stories can be explained as
fantasies. "The broomstick they ride," he told his friend, is "the
great Lord Penis."

Twelve years after the fact, Freud finally grasped the meaning
of what he had observed, or thought he had observed, at Charcot's lectures on hysteria in Paris. Whatever the unknown biological basis of mental illness might be, the symptoms had a

psychological origin and significance. They could be treated and, equally important, be understood, as ideas. But none of this could happen until Freud reworked his seduction theory. Where once the actual penis—through masturbation, coitus interruptus, or the sexual abuse of children—caused neurosis, now it was the *idea* of the penis, working through fantasies of penetration or castration. Sexuality became psycho-sexuality. "The tremendous advance accomplished by psychoanalysis," Simone de Beauvoir later wrote, was in understanding that "it is not the body object described by biologists that actually exists, but the body as lived by the subject." This was Freud's most revolutionary insight of them all.

Like all sea changes, this one, Freud's letters show, came with turbulence. Though he had not been much of a drinker beforehand, Freud now "sought strength in a bottle of Barolo" and companionship from "his friend Marsala." Neither tonic worked that well. His moods changed "like the landscapes seen from a train," as, night after night, his dreams revealed the coarseness of his own erotic desires. But as Freud shed more illusions about himself, he was certain he was nearing the truth, and not just about Sigmund Freud. On October 3, 1897, he wrote Fliess of his lust for his own mother, Amalia Freud, something that awakened, he now realized, between his second and third birthdays "on a [railway] journey from Leipzig to Vienna, during which we . . . spent the night together and [I must have] seen her *nudam*. . . . I have not yet grasped [what] lies at the bottom of [this] story," Freud wrote his friend. Twelve days later he had.

> I have found love of the mother and jealousy of the father in my own case, and now believe it to be a general phenomenon of early childhood. . . . If that is so, the gripping power of *Oedipus Rex* becomes intelligible. . . . Every member of the audience was once a budding Oedipus in fantasy.

Freud's idea of Oedipus' fate is not the same as Sophocles', however. It is not a force from outside; it is within. In our unconscious minds we all wish to penetrate our mothers. But we do not, for fear of castration by our fathers, the objects of our sexual (and homicidal) envy. Those who master this triangle, and solve the riddle, are healthy. Those who do not are neurotic. This, taught Sigmund Freud, is the enduring psychic potency—for better and worse—of the penis.

---

In October 1900, Freud wrote Fliess of a new patient, a "girl of eighteen" who "has opened smoothly to [my] collection of picklocks." This arrogant image, a Freudian boast if ever there was one, coming from Freud himself is almost laughable. But if Freud's language lacked subtlety, it did not lack foresight. The eleven weeks he spent with "Dora" produced one of the most phallic documents of his career. Freud merged three ideas—the significance of dreams, the instinctual nature of infantile sexuality, and the psychic potency of the penis—into the world's first psychoanalytic case history,* publishing his results even though the treatment was hardly a success and its history incomplete: Dora walked out on Freud before he was finished.

Freud wrote his report in January 1901, a time of great personal anxiety. His friendship with Fliess was in turmoil. (This may explain the boastful tone of his letter.) Freud's first major theoretical work, *The Interpretation of Dreams,* had not been as well-received as he hoped. And he had been passed over, again, for promotion at the University of Vienna, a snub he attributed to resistance to his analytic theories, exacerbated by anti-Semitism. In writing up his new case, Freud wanted to show his controversial ideas at work and justify their claim to serious scientific consideration. But the paper, published four years later, just as clearly showed *Freud* at work (and not al-

*Those in *Studies in Hysteria* were preanalytic.

ways in a flattering light), though it seems Freud was in the dark about that. The report also showed Freud's impressive skill as a player of literary tricks, so much so that eighty years later one literary critic compared his prose style to that of Vladimir Nabokov. Such is the strange and compelling performance that is *Fragment of an Analysis of a Case of Hysteria*.

Dora, "a girl of engaging looks," was brought to Freud against her will, twice, by her father, a wealthy manufacturer. Some years earlier Freud had treated the father for a "confusional attack, followed by symptoms of paralysis." Freud diagnosed the problem as a meningeal disturbance related to syphilis, which the businessman admitted he had contracted as a young man. Freud reveals this, but not the father's Jewishness, because he knows many of his readers already see a link between Jewish sexuality and mental illness. Freud has no interest in analyzing the psyches of Jews alone. The theories espoused in *Fragment,* he insists to a skeptical world, have a universal application.

The antisyphilitic treatment was successful, no doubt elevating Freud in the eyes of the father. Soon he brought his daughter in because of a mysterious cough that often robbed her of speech. Freud proposed psychotherapy, but Dora refused. Now, two years later, she was back—listless, depressed, perhaps suicidal, and definitely contemptuous of her father, someone she used to adore. Along with her cough and aphonia (loss of speech), Dora had a limp, painful irregular menstrual cramps, and abdominal attacks that mimicked appendicitis.

Freud's plan was to alleviate those hysterical symptoms by finding their psychological determinants, and it is this search that he chronicles in the central portion of *Fragment*. But first Freud has other things to tell us. His introduction is strangely titillating. What follows, he writes, will in the name of science reveal secrets typically kept safe by "a gynecologist." Thus he has changed the names of the participants and the places where they came into contact. To enhance this deception, Freud has delayed publication for four years and placed the case in a medical journal unknown to most of the general public. But even his medical readers are warned. If they have not read *The Interpretation of Dreams*—a book that had sold barely a hundred copies by this time—they "will find only bewilderment in these pages." Freud is sure even those who *have* read it will be baffled. "What is new," he roars in his best Alpha Male of Science voice, "has always aroused bewilderment and resistance."

In truth, even a dunderhead could see Dora was in trouble. The girl was involved in a drama worthy of Vienna's leading chronicler of bourgeois adultery, the playwright and novelist Arthur Schnitzler,* seasoned with the Hitchcockian terror of being the only truth-teller in a sea of liars. The cast was composed of two families: Dora and her unhappily married parents, and another mismatched couple Freud calls the "K.'s" The families were close, closest of all were Dora's father and Frau K. Dora's mother is described as a dull woman obsessed with cleaning. Six years earlier, when Dora's father was recovering from tuberculosis, he was nursed by Frau K. (Dora's mother was presumably too busy dusting.) Dora's father and Frau K. began an affair which, if Dora's mother didn't notice, Dora did.

Soon Dora, who had looked up to Frau K. almost as much as she did her father, started to suffer from chronic coughing and hoarseness. Years later, the love affair still on, Dora was out for a walk with Frau K.'s husband when he suddenly made a crude sexual pass. The girl slapped him, ran away, and told her parents. Dora's father confronted Herr K., who denied all. Even worse, he impugned Dora's innocence. Herr K. said his wife told him Dora was reading love manuals intended for newlyweds. Dora was "over-excited by such reading," he said, and had invented the scene she described. When Dora's father believed him, Dora's sense of betrayal was complete: Her lying,

---

*Eyes Wide Shut*, the last film directed by Stanley Kubrick, was based on Schnitzler's 1926 novella, *Traumnovelle*.

adulterous father was "giving" her to the lying, clumsy seducer, Herr K., in exchange for the lying, adulterous Frau K., who had betrayed Dora by exposing her secret reading material, books Dora had obtained from Frau K. herself! Not even the great Schnitzler could have imagined such a perverse plot.

After this, Dora's symptoms worsened, leading to her first abortive visit to Freud. When those ailments intensified later, she was forced to enter treatment. Dora's father thought the alleged lake incident was responsible for his daughter's depression. "[But] I believe [her] tale of the man's immoral suggestions is a fantasy," he told Freud. "Please try to bring Dora to reason." It is fairly obvious what Dora's father meant by that last line. Apparently, he did not know Freud as well as he thought.

But maybe we don't, either. For Freud, who reworked his seduction theory three years earlier, deciding his patients were usually fantasizing, tells us he believes Dora. But he does not think the lakeside proposition sufficient to have caused the particular character of Dora's symptoms. So he asks her to look deeper into her past. Perhaps there was a trauma, something she had put out of her mind, that does match the character of her illness, most of all the coughing and chest pains that were among the first of her symptoms to surface.

There was. One day, when Dora was fourteen, she was alone with Herr K. at his place of business. Dora was there to watch a holiday parade from Herr K.'s office window, and no doubt believed others would be there for the same purpose. But her host had arranged it otherwise. Eager to see the festival, Dora stayed. Suddenly, in the midst of meaningless small talk, Herr K. pulled Dora over to him and kissed her. Dora felt "a violent feeling of disgust," then tore herself free and ran away. Neither Dora nor Herr K. ever spoke of the event, not did Dora tell anyone else. It was then that Dora's chronic coughing began to turn into aphonia, a loss of speech that often lasted several weeks.

What follows in *Fragment* is an interpretation of these events formulated in such a jaw-dropping series of inferences that one can only marvel at Freud's ability to state them so authoritatively. Dora's reaction, he writes, was a case of "reversal of affect." Instead of the exciting genital sensation that would have been felt by a healthy girl, Dora felt disgust and thus showed herself to be mentally ill. At first this disgust localized in her mouth. Then it moved to another part of her body, which Freud identifies as another symptom: "displacement of sensation." Dora said she could still feel Herr K.'s embrace as an unpleasant tightness on her chest. That this tightness also accompanied Dora's cough caught Freud's notice. In accordance with "the rules of symptom-formation" that had revealed themselves to him—and, it goes without saying at this point in time, only him—Freud offers a psychoanalytic reconstruction of Dora's encounter with Herr K.

> I believe that during the man's passionate embrace she felt not merely his kiss upon her lips but also the pressure of his erect member against her body.

This "revolting" perception was "dismissed from her memory, repressed, and replaced by the innocent sensation of pressure upon her thorax."

When one looks at Freud's interpretation now, it is hard to believe that the man who stressed the role of symbols in everyday life was so oblivious to one meaning of Dora's aphonia. Clearly, here was a girl who felt she had no voice in the direction of her own life. The needs of her father and those of the K.'s took precedence. But in Freud's analysis it is the *penis* that takes precedence. Dora's illness, in fact, is presented as proof of the psychic potency of the penis. Her symptoms are physical manifestations of hysterical ideas created in response to Herr K.'s entirely nonpathological erection. What is pathological is her aversion to that erection.

For Freud the penis is not merely the message, it is the mes-

senger. The subject of erection explains some of the most fascinating hysterical symptoms, he writes in *Fragment*. "The attention that women pay to the outlines of men's genitals through
their clothing becomes, when it has been repressed, a source of
the very frequent cases of . . . dreading society." But what really
interests Freud is Dora's dread of the penis. When one feels disgust for that organ, he says, one is really experiencing disgust
for excrement. Crediting an unnamed Father of the Church as
his source, Freud repeats that Father's reminder that "*inter uri-
nas et faeces nascimur*" (between urine and feces we are born).
"It is scarcely possible," Freud writes, "to exaggerate the path-
ogenic significance of the comprehensive tie uniting the sexual
and the excremental."

But Freud is not certain Dora dreads every penis. Symptoms
result from conflict, and symptoms sometimes conflict with
each other. Dora seems less angry with her seducer, Herr K.,
than she is with her father for believing Herr K.'s version of
events. Freud also notices that Dora's coughing worsens whenever she repeats this wearisome complaint about her father.
(Freud often seems bored with Dora.) Even so, he is able to
overcome his tedium and notice the timing of his patient's
coughing fits. Freud "erects" (his word) a general principle from
this connection. A symptom such as Dora's cough, he writes, is
"the representation—the realization—of a sexual fantasy."

What kind of fantasy? In Dora's case, the answer comes from
a phrase she uses to describe her father. The only reason why
Frau K. is attracted to him, Dora tells Freud, is because her father is "*ein vermogender Mann*" (a man of means). For Freud,
the true meaning of this lies hidden within its opposite:
"namely, that her father [is] '*ein un*vermogender Mann*'" (a
man with*out* means). This meaning, Freud tells Dora, can only
be understood "in a sexual sense—that her father, as a man, [is]
impotent."

Amazingly, Dora confirms this, though we are not told how
or why she knows such a thing. Freud plunges ahead as if he

knew it all along. (And maybe he did, from his earlier treatment of the father for syphilis.) If her father is so impaired, Freud asks Dora, is it still possible for him to be carrying on a love affair? Of course, she says, raising the possibility of oral sex. This is Freud's eureka moment. When Dora has a coughing fit, she is acting out a sexual fantasy. Dora is imagining that it is she, not Frau K., who is giving "sexual gratification *per os*" (orally) to her father. This conclusion, Freud harrumphs, is "inevitable." Later, feminist analysts would raise the opposite possibility: that Dora's father was giving "sexual gratification *per os*" to Frau K., something that does not seem to have crossed Freud's phallocentric mind at all. Rather, Freud is convinced that Dora's hatred for Frau K. is the hatred of a "jealous wife." Dora's cough and persistent hoarseness is a "hysterical conversion," symptoms of her repressed Oedipal desire to be penetrated by her father's penis. If not vaginally, orally.

Even today, when "Lewinsky" is both a noun and a verb, this interpretation retains the power to shock. Years later, in *Civilization and Its Discontents,* Freud would argue that one of modern civilization's greatest "sins" is its failure to educate its children about the true aggressiveness of the human libido. Perhaps this is why he was so blunt with Dora. Even so, it is not difficult to imagine how shocking Freud's diagnosis was a hundred years ago to the "under-educated" Dora (Freud's term), a girl hearing such words from a man her father's age—a man who, in fact, knew her father—while lying down on this strange doctor's couch with her eyes closed as he placed his palm on her forehead supposedly to encourage a process he called "free association." All this—and sex talk, too—from a man she was seeing against her will, who claimed to be helping her by insisting that all of her problems, emotional and physical, arose from her thwarted desire to suck on her father's penis.

Not surprisingly, Dora loudly disavowed any such desire, thwarted or not—only to be met with one of the most famous passages in psychoanalytic literature:

The "No" uttered by a patient after a repressed thought has been presented to his conscious perception for the first time does no more than register the existence of the repression and its severity; it acts, as it were, as a measure of its strength. . . . In such a case "No" signifies the desired "Yes."

The psychic potency of the penis, Freud is saying, knows no "No." The doctor who doubted his own seduction theory is now doubting Dora's. Though he has been given ample evidence of the impact of external reality on his patient—the clumsy and repeated propositions from Herr K.—Freud's interpretation focuses on Dora's internal world. Other people are screens on which Dora projects her sexual fantasies. The unconscious is a cauldron of conflict and there is phallic energy concealed in all mental activity, even that of young girls—whether they admit it or not, Freud says; whether they like it or not.

———

It seems the person who best understood Dora's situation, and Freud's phallic formulation of it, was the person who objected most to that formulation: Dora herself. In Freud's postscript he called Dora's termination of therapy an act of self-injury triggered by his showing her the truth of her unconscious desires. But it seems Dora was more analytically aware than her doctor realized. For at the very moment Freud was at his peak of excitement—interpreting a dream Dora had just revealed to him—she severed their relationship and cut Freud off, leaving him totally impotent. You might even say Dora castrated him.

That's one way of looking at it. What is certain is that castration is the focus of Freud's next case report, *An Analysis of a Phobia in a Five-Year-Old Boy,* also known as the case of "Little Hans." If Dora was written at a time of anxiety for Freud, Little Hans was put to paper with relative cockiness. Freud's professional isolation seemed to be ending. In 1906 he attracted his first followers from outside Vienna—among them the highly regarded Swiss psychiatrist Eugen Bleuler, coiner of the term "schizophrenia" and director of the famous Burghölzli Asylum in Zürich, where his chief aide and fellow Freud enthusiast was an impressive young physician named Carl Jung.* Other new Freudians included Max Eitingon and Karl Abraham in Berlin, the Welshman Ernest Jones (after reading "Dora"), Eduardo Weiss of Italy, and the Hungarian Sandor Ferenczi. This inspired Freud to convene the first International Congress of Psychoanalysis in Salzburg in 1908. In 1909, the same year *An Analysis of a Phobia* was published, Freud was invited by G. Stanley Hall, president of Clark University in Worcester, Massachusetts, to give a series of lectures there. This honor gave Freud immense personal satisfaction, though he developed an immediate and lasting contempt for American food, drink, and bathrooms, the indulgence with which its citizens raised their children, and other (to Freud's mind) equally vulgar aspects of American culture.

Psychoanalysis was progressing as a movement, but its methodology still had many critics. The problem, even for those willing to accept a link between neurosis and childhood sexuality, was that Freudianism depended for its authority on the reconstruction of that sexuality from the debris of adult pathology. "Even a psycho-analyst may . . . wish for a more direct and less roundabout proof of these fundamental theorems," Freud wrote. This proof would take the flesh-and-blood form of Little Hans.

The boy's real name was Herbert Graf. His father, Max, was a respected Viennese musicologist and an early member of the Wednesday-night group that met at Freud's home and later evolved into the Vienna Psychoanalytic Society. Hans's mother, Olga Honig Graf, had been a patient of Freud's. The Grafs had agreed to raise their son as a kind of analytic test case, recording his dreams and childhood chatter, and keeping Freud abreast of noteworthy events in his development, his sexual development

*Both Jung and Bleuler would later break with Freud.

most of all. This was, depending on your point of view, a very progressive thing the Grafs were doing, or an utterly perverse thing. In 1903, when Hans was born, most physicians denied the very existence of childhood sexuality.

What those physicians, the Grafs, and Freud himself probably did not realize was how new that official view of childhood innocence really was. As historian Philippe Ariès later pointed out in *Centuries of Childhood*, a far different opinion on this question prevailed in Europe as late as the seventeenth century. Ariès set his proof at the court of King Henri IV of France, where the king's physician, Dr. Heroard, kept a diary recording the details of the childhood of Henri's heir, Louis XIII. "No other document," Ariès wrote, "can give us a better idea of the non-existence of the [chaste] idea of childhood at the beginning of the seventeenth century." One can challenge the larger validity of any thesis on behavior, erotic or otherwise, set at Versailles. One cannot, however, dismiss the reality of the proto-Freudian acceptance of infantile sexuality shown on nearly every page of Heroard's journal.

When Louis XIII was one year old, Heroard wrote, the future ruler "made everybody kiss his cock." At the age of three, he called his governess's attention to his erections. "My cock is like a drawbridge," he told her. "See how it goes up and down!" Once he tried to show this trick to his father, the king, only to be embarrassed by a momentary attack of "impotence." "There's no bone in it, Papa," young Louis moaned. "But there is sometimes!"

It is unknown whether Max Graf, for all his open-mindedness, expected to report on this kind of behavior to Freud from his own son who, while comfortable, was hardly growing up in a royal palace. Though Graf later broke with Freud, he wrote a kind reminiscence of him, and the Wednesday-night discussion groups at Freud's home, after Freud's death. Without question, the penis and phallic potency were frequent topics at those gatherings. Freud's belief in the sexual etiology of neurosis was certainly one reason. Perhaps another was the fact that the man who urged Freud to host the group in the first place, Dr. Wilhelm Stekel, had embraced psychoanalysis after Freud cured him of impotence.

Freud's salon was home to sexual candor rarely heard in Vienna or anywhere else. One memorable session was dominated by Rudolf von Urbantschitsch, director of a local sanatorium, who recounted his own sexual development before marriage, focusing with extravagant precision on his adolescent career as a masturbator. At another meeting dermatologist Maximilian Steiner spoke of how a period of abstinence caused him to suffer a series of crippling psychosomatic symptoms that vanished once he began a love affair with the wife of an impotent friend. Thus it was probably not too shocking, to Graf or Freud, that Graf came to Freud in 1908 with the following problem: His young son had become obsessed with his own penis, then the penises of animals, and had then developed a strange phobia. Once an extremely outgoing boy, Little Hans was now afraid to leave his house. His fear was that, once outside, a large well-hung horse would bite him.

It was decided Graf would act as his son's analytic facilitator, asking questions posed by Freud, to whom Graf reported the answers. Hans went only once to Freud's office as a patient. Freud believed a child at this age could be treated only by his or her parent, a view he later dropped. In effect, Little Hans was analyzed by proxy. "I never got a finer insight into a child's soul," Freud told Ernest Jones. Maybe so. But that insight was indirect.

Actually, Little Hans had been aiding the Freudian cause for years. He was the "delightful little boy" in *The Sexual Enlightenment of Children,* who showed a keen desire for sexual knowledge once his little sister was born. Likewise, he was the child in *On the Sexual Theories of Children* who, in one of Freud's most famous and controversial assertions, "attributed to everyone, including females, the possessions of a penis." This mistaken notion, Freud said, once a boy is presented with visual proof to the contrary, triggers the onset of the castration complex, a trauma experienced, Freud insisted, by all boys. But it is not until *Analysis of a Phobia* that this complex gets a detailed discussion, or maybe "exposition" is a better term. For this time Little Hans is a named player in his own psychic drama, speaking and writing his own lines of dialogue.

*"Mummy, have you got a widdler?"* Little Hans asked just before his third birthday, a period marked by a masturbatory fascination with his own widdler—that is, his penis. (Caught off-guard, Mrs. Graf made the mistake of answering Hans's question somewhat glibly: "Of course," she said.)

Hans (aged three): *"Daddy, have you got a widdler?"*

Hans (still three, seeing a bloody bowl outside the room where his mother is giving birth to his sister): *"But blood doesn't come out of my widdler!"*

Hans (shortly after his sister's birth): *"Her widdler's still quite small. When she grows up it'll get bigger."*

In Little Hans's world everyone has a widdler—men, women, boys, girls, even a locomotive he sees draining water from its engine. But no one has a widdler like those he sees on the mighty horses pulling carts through the streets of Vienna. At first Little Hans is fascinated by those large impressive organs. Then he becomes frightened of them. This fear reaches its zenith when Little Hans, out for a walk with his mother, sees a horse fall down in the street while attempting to pull a trolley. After this, Hans does not want to leave his house at all.

These details fascinated Freud because they confirmed his ideas regarding childhood sexual development, many of which had been published in 1905 in *Three Essays on the Theory of Sexuality*. Little Hans's mind was overflowing with sexual curiosity, sexual fantasies, and, now it seemed, sexual phobias—all resulting from his infantile efforts to understand his own penis, its role in reproduction, its significance in determining his own identity, and that of others around him. Such issues, Freud later wrote in Hans's case history, are "the common property of all men, a part of the human constitution." Freud was thrilled to observe, even secondhand, these "sexual impulses and wishes"—the existence of which his opponents so vociferously denied—in Little Hans, where they were churning with "the freshness of life" one only finds in a child. Here was the direct proof even Freud's supporters were looking for.

The key moment in Hans's treatment, Freud tells us, occurred during a talk between Little Hans and his father. Following Freud's suggestion, Graf gave his son a brief lesson on reproductive biology, informing him that, despite what he thinks (and what his own mother had unthinkingly told him), neither his mother nor his sister has a widdler. Graf also tried to calm his son's fear of animal widdlers. "Big animals have big widdlers" he said, "and little animals have little widdlers," to which Little Hans responded: "Everyone has a widdler. And my widdler will get bigger as I get bigger. It's attached."

To Freud, who believed in the truth-telling power of words as few have before or since, Hans's answer was the occasion for a major diagnostic breakthrough. Hans was not afraid of the huge widdlers on horses, Freud decided. He was afraid of losing his *own* widdler, a fear motivated by the troubling news he had just learned and, at first, refused to believe, from his father. This alarming news, Freud wrote,

> was bound to have a shattering effect upon [Hans's] self-confidence and to have . . . aroused his castration complex. Could it be that living beings really existed which did not possess widdlers? If so, it would no longer be so incredible that they could take his own widdler away.

Hans's horse phobia showed he was going through his Oedipal phase, an analysis of which Freud is eager to provide. But first he interjects a strange footnote, the first paragraph in all medical literature to assert a psychological link between circumcision and anti-Semitism, two subjects that have no bearing on Little Hans's case, other than the fact that Little Hans is himself a Jew, a fact Freud does not mention at all. "The castration complex is the deepest unconscious root of anti-Semitism," Freud writes at the bottom of the page.

> For even in the nursery little boys hear that a Jew has something cut off his penis—a piece of the penis, they think—and this gives them the right to despise Jews.

It is hard to find more direct proof of the impact of anti-Semitism—and the specific role played in it by the Jewish penis—on Freud's thinking.

But, then, just as suddenly, Freud returns to Little Hans and his Oedipal issues. The horses who are scaring the child, he says, represent Hans's father, who, like the intimidating beasts with black muzzles, is an imposing man with a black mustache. Hans was afraid that his father was upset with him because Hans could not restrain his erotic feelings for his mother, who, against her husband's wishes, allowed Hans to cuddle with her in bed. Soon Hans was wishing his father dead, a wish that caused him even more anxiety. The biting horse was a stand-in for his furious, castrating father; the falling horse symbolized the father Little Hans hoped would die. Hans experienced these conflicts with anxiety because he loved his father at the same time he hated him as a rival—ambivalence he acted out by punching his father in his stomach, then kissing the spot he had just assaulted. On the one occasion Little Hans was brought to Freud's consulting room, Freud explained to him why he was feeling that way.

"I . . . disclosed to him that he was afraid of his father precisely because he was so fond of his mother. It must be, I told him, that he thought

> his father was angry with him on that account; but this was not so, his father was fond of him in spite of it, and he

might admit everything without any fear. Long before he was in the world, I went on, I [knew] that a little Hans would come who would be so fond of his mother that he would be bound to be afraid of his father because of it; and I had told his father this.

"Papa, does the Professor talk to God?" Hans asked on the way home.

(That would have been a local call, of course.) Soon Hans's symptoms began to disappear. These outward changes were accompanied by psychic adjustments. In a dream Hans was visited by a plumber who took away his penis, then replaced it with a larger one. "Just like yours," Hans told his dad. Exit castration anxiety, enter psychological growth. Like all non-neurotics, Freud wrote, this little Oedipus decided not to fear or kill his father, but to be just like him.

---

A postscript to the Little Hans case, added thirteen years later, told of a visit Freud received from the real Little Hans, Herbert Graf, then a young man hoping for a career in music. (Graf eventually became stage director of New York's Metropolitan Opera.) Enemies of psychoanalysis had predicted the worst for Hans, a child exposed, in their view, to the prurient excesses of Freudianism when he was powerless to resist. Freud delighted in reporting that no such calamity had occurred, though he conceded that Graf said he did not recognize himself as the boy described in such detail in Freud's analytic report.

This second fact exacerbated the fears Freud already felt about his case histories. Though he saw them as a necessary demonstration of his therapeutic method, Freud worried as far back as *Studies in Hysteria* that they read like "short stories." Maybe it is only fitting, then, that conflict—physical and psychical—over reality, repression, and the penis would inform one of Freud's most controversial works, a case history of the entire human race that one contemporary critic mocked as a "just-so story," an insult inspired by the title of a children's book by Rudyard Kipling offering fanciful explanations for the leopard's spots and other zoological curiosities. This boldest of all of Freud's case histories—a blend of biology, anthropology, psychoanalysis, and, some would say, nonsense—was published in 1913 as *Totem and Taboo*.

Apparently, Little Hans had served the analytic cause once again. Minutes taken at the Vienna Psychoanalytic Society show that insights from that case had been pushing Freud on to something larger for some time. Hans's castration anxiety, Freud told his Wednesday-night colleagues, was more evidence that neurosis arose from the "ruin of sexual impulses" in the past. The way Hans merged his love-hate relationship with his father into a fear of horses, Freud said, resembled the way primitives worshiped their totem animal, a beast they revered as their common father yet, on somber religious occasions, they killed and ate. That totem clans had a taboo against incest, the psychic fuel of the Oedipus complex, also caught Freud's notice. Was there an analogy between the psyches of primitives, children, and neurotics? Freud wasn't sure. But in his practice and meetings with fellow analysts, several of whom he had treated for impotence, two conclusions seemed likely: The child is afraid of losing his penis. The neurotic adult is afraid of using it.

Perhaps psychoanalysis, which found its truths in the psychic rubble of the individual's past, could explain this by studying the past of mankind. The challenge was irresistible. Years later, Freud confessed that medicine had been a "detour" from his true passions—cultural problems and philosophy. So Freud started his research, reading dozens of fat books on anthropology and religion—among them, Edward Tylor's *Primitive Culture*, James G. Frazer's *Totemism and Exogamy*, and Robertson Smith's *Lectures on the Religion of the Semites*—before choosing a Darwinian setting for his speculation, the primal horde postulated by the groundbreaking British evolutionist in *The Descent of Man*.

"We may conclude from . . . the jealousy of all male quadrupeds," Darwin wrote, "that promiscuous intercourse in a state of nature is highly improbable."* It is more likely that "primaeval man lived in small communities, each with as many wives as he could obtain and support, whom he would have jealously guarded." Or "he may have lived with several wives by himself, like the Gorilla; for all the natives agree that . . .

> but one adult male is seen in a band; when the young male grows up, a contest takes place for mastery, and the strongest, by killing and driving out the others, establishes himself as the head of the community.

It is not surprising that Freud started with Darwin. Freud's academic training was steeped in evolutionary theory, and three Darwinian ideas had a lasting impact on his thinking: first, that every physiological detail has meaning that can be deduced from its function; second, that if this meaning cannot be found in the present, it must be sought in the past; and third, that the driving force of natural history is conflict. Freud adapted this approach to psychology. Darwin's physiological details became Freud's neurotic symptoms. All, he insisted, even the most seemingly trivial—dreams and slips of the tongue—have meaning, a meaning *always* found in the past. But where for Darwin the essential conflict was between species and environment, for Freud it was between sex and death. This eternal and unavoidable contest, he would show in *Totem and Taboo,* was as old as human life itself, and nowhere were the stakes higher: the winner kept his penis; the vanquished lost it.

In Freud's reconstruction, the primal father was even more brutal than Darwin imagined. The sons who were driven away

---

*Obviously, Darwin died before he could see a film documentary on bonobo chimpanzees, whose seemingly inexhaustible appetite for sex is now a staple of PBS pledge-week programming.

or killed were lucky. The less fortunate became walking, wounded symbols of the price exacted for challenging the old man's sexual monopoly. They were castrated. Over time, Freud speculated, this system sparked history's first political revolt. The banished brothers, along with the eunuchs living in humiliating submission, banded together and overpowered the father, castrated him, then put him to death. "It goes without saying," Freud added, "that they devoured their victim." The father "had doubtless been the feared and envied model of . . . the brothers: and in the act of devouring him . . . each one acquired a portion of his strength."

But why settle for a portion? The noncastrated brothers soon realized their common biology—having a penis and wanting to use it—did not unite them. Each wanted to be father-king and have the sexual perks that went with it. Sexual rivalry and fratricidal violence ensued, until the brothers, who had achieved a sense of community while in exile, decided to restore that bond. This pact, Freud wrote, prompted the birth of organized religion. Remorse over the murder they had committed led the sons to resurrect, and then collectively worship, their father as a totem animal. Each son gave up any plan to become the new father, an oath that made all of the horde's women—the young men's mothers, sisters, and cousins—taboo. Mates would have to be found outside the clan. With this act of sexual renunciation, Freud said, law, morality, religion—and all the neuroses attached to them—were born.

This "just-so story" explained the origin of man as a social animal. But, in so doing, *Totem* went through an evolution of its own. A speculation on Darwinian biology and cultural anthropology became a secular retelling of Genesis and a psychoanalytic update of Augustine. This trip began by veering off the Darwinian path. For Darwin, sex is a natural act; for Freud, it is clearly not. If the dreams and verbal slips of his patients had taught him anything, it was that civilized man is excruciatingly self-conscious about his sexuality. This *un*naturalness—the psychological content expressed as guilt or shame—is what defines man as man and divides him from the rest of the animal world. It is also, Freud said, the turning point of human history.

For Freud, the sexually motivated murder of the primal father, an act echoed in the Oedipus complex, is the dawning of civilization. That crime, after all (just like the "nucleus of neurosis" he was so proud of having discovered), is composed of two fantasies—elimination of the father and intercourse with the mother—that repeat the acts committed by the primal brothers. This led Freud to make his boldest assertion yet. The Oedipus complex is not merely a universal fact, he wrote in *Totem*. It is a memory of a real event. In his practice, Freud saw that personal history never died; it lived on in his patients' unconscious minds. Neurotics "suffer . . . from reminiscences," he wrote in *Studies in Hysteria*. Now he said this was true for mankind as a whole. There "exists in the mental life of the individual not only what he has experienced himself," Freud wrote, "but also what was brought with him at birth, . . . an archaic heritage," a concept not dissimilar to Jung's "collective unconscious." To use a term not yet invented when *Totem* was written, this heritage, Freud was suggesting, has seeped into our genetic code. The primal parricide, an act motivated by castration anxiety and phallic libido, has been passed from one generation to the next in our unconscious as the Oedipus complex, making that crime and its consequences as real to us as it was to the actual participants.

Freud's belief in the inheritability of acquired characteristics shows he was a poor geneticist. But the sex scandal that resulted in the only presidential impeachment trial of the twentieth century suggests he was a very prescient psychologist, indeed. In many ways, the life-and-death political struggle between Bill Clinton and his accusers was nothing less than a modern replay of the primal drama described in *Totem and Taboo*. One of Freud's main points in that work, repeated in *Civilization and Its Discontents*, is that civilization requires sexual renunciation. Thus, for one man to act as though he has sexual access to all women without fear of challenge is to threaten the very foundation of public order. Seen in this light, Clinton's mistake was less political than psychological. Consciously or not, he allowed himself to become the target of an unconscious fantasy in which he was the primal father and, as such, had to be taken down if civilization was to endure.

Clinton's real crime was not perjury, the American psychoanalyst Jonathan Lear wrote in a provocative 1998 essay, but believing himself to be "omni-potent—able to fuck anyone. Only a God," or the primal father, "can get away with that." And only for a while, before the brothers band together to emasculate and kill him. The fact that some of the most vocal Congressional brothers—Newt Gingrich, Henry Hyde, and Bob Livingston—were themselves accused of sexual misconduct only supports Freud's setting the drama as a sexual contest. The televised criticisms of Clinton made by several of his former employees—Dee Dee Myers, George Stephanopoulos, Robert Reich, and David Gergen, to name the most vocal—show that the castrated brothers joined in the revolt, too.

Were he alive, Freud surely would have taken satisfaction in seeing his primal drama played out, again, on national television. What is equally certain is that he would have been appalled by Clinton's behavior. Oral sex, in the Oval Office or anywhere else, was repellent to Freud. "Perverse forms of intercourse between the two sexes, in which other parts of the body take over the role of the genitals, have undoubtedly increased in social importance," he wrote in *"Civilized" Sexual Morality and Modern Nervous Illness*. "These activities cannot, however, be considered harmless. . . .

> They are ethically objectionable, for they degrade the relationship of love between two human beings from a serious matter to a convenient game.

When Freud wrote *Totem and Taboo*, however, he was not trying to explain American presidential politics or the perversions of one particular president. He put forth *Totem*'s thesis—that acquired psychic characteristics are inherited—because it explained evolution psychoanalytically, showing it to be "nothing more than the power unconscious ideas have over the body," the same proposition demonstrated by Charcot in his lectures on hysteria. Freud's belief in this inheritability gave the Oedipus complex, his most cherished discovery, a new mystique of origins. The unconscious mind, the ancient psychic "stones" Freud urged his skeptical colleagues to listen to, were now older by countless millennia and packed with historical-evolutionary power.

For a secularist, however, Darwin gave that power an oddly religious cast. His primal parricide resembles Augustine's original sin, and *Totem* often seems a psychoanalytic reworking of Genesis. But for Freud, what has been created isn't human life and the subsequent fall from grace; it is civilization and neurosis. The story of mankind parallels the story of each man. It is the same psychic drama—a sex crime/murder mystery motivated by castration anxiety—performed on a larger stage. Two men who could not seem more different, Freud and Augustine, meet on a crucial point: Each recognizes the psychic and historic potency of the penis. For the Bishop of Hippo, original sin is passed from one generation to the next by semen, and the punishment for Adam's insult against God is erections we cannot control. For Freud, the killing of the primal father and the sexual appropriation of the mother is passed on as the Oedipus complex, and the punishment is a civilization that controls our erections.

The legal structure of that control is unequivocal. Laws and cultural norms demand sexual renunciation, as witnessed by the modern world's restrictions against rape, adultery, pedophilia, and incest, acts that man in his natural state committed regularly and without compunction. However, for Freud, these laws tell only half the story. The most intrusive method of penile control is indirect. It is the "psychical impotence" fostered in men by civilization, the problem that, as Freud wrote in 1912, led more men into his consulting room than any other.

Civilization has made man "capable of his highest and noblest achievements," Freud wrote, for which he, as a buttoned-up, tie-wearing member of the urban bourgeoisie, was duly appreciative. Yet this gratitude was tinged with despair. "We [are] forced to become reconciled," he wrote, to the following "gloomy prognosis." It is "impossible to adjust the claims of the sexual instinct to the demands of civilization"—or vice versa. The erection of culture, and the erection of man's defining organ, Freud said, are inevitably—and permanently—at cross-purposes.

---

Throughout the Clinton sex scandal, the president's defenders criticized his attackers for confusing the personal with the professional. Whatever Clinton's sins, this argument went, they were committed in the private sphere, even when committed in the White House. No matter how objectionable, they did not affect his job performance and, for that reason, were irrelevant. In the end, polls showed that most Americans agreed. Freud has his attackers and defenders, too, of course. But these camps that clash on nearly everything, often more vehemently than even politicians, on one point find common ground: to understand psychoanalysis one must acknowledge the relevance of the messenger to the message, and the personal to the professional.

Psychoanalysis was born of Freud's self-analysis—for Freudians, an act of unprecedented intellectual courage and strength. It was in the most personal parts of himself that Freud unearthed the truths, many of them unflattering, that he later discovered in others to be universal. Anti-Freudians also stress the importance of this self-scrutiny, but the similarity ends there. They do not see a brave clinician exploring inner space, then finding corroboratory evidence in his patients. They see a sex-obsessed charlatan planting bogus evidence *on* his patients. Pro or con, each side agrees that to know Freudianism one must know Freud, a man who viewed psychic life through the foggy prism of the mind-body connection.

But to know Freud is to know that, for him, all parts of the body are not created equal. The relationship between man and his penis, a link as self-conscious as it is unconscious, is the driving force of psychic history, Freud insisted, a fact as true for mankind as it is for each man. This powerfully suggestive view of human existence suggests that one further question be addressed: What was Freud's relationship with his own penis?

Which is another way of asking, What was Freud's sex life like? We know he was routinely denounced in the press as a libertine and a sexual adventurer. But Freud's own estimation of his erotic life was quite different. In a 1915 letter to James Jackson Putnam, the Harvard professor who wrote the introduction to the American edition of Freud's *Three Essays on the Theory of Sexuality,* Freud allowed that, "[although] I stand for an infinitely freer sexual life, I myself have made very little use of such freedom." Apparently, this was true both before and during his marriage. Freud's official biographer, Ernest Jones, believed his subject was a virgin when he wed Martha Bernays in September 1885, at age thirty.

According to Peter J. Swales, a revisionist historian reviled by most Freudians, much of Freud's early libido theory, based on the premise that obstructed sexuality is physically and psychologically toxic, was conceived by Freud under the influence of cocaine—while masturbating before his marriage, and, later, while lamenting the frustrations of his own unfulfilling marriage. Before that wedding, however, cocaine and sex seemed a happy mix, indeed, to young Freud. In a letter written in June 1884, he warned his future bride, "Woe to you, my Princess, when I come [to see you]. I will kiss you quite red. . . . And if you resist you shall see who is stronger, a gentle little girl . . . or a big wild man who has cocaine in his body."

With or without that drug in his body, "wild man" Freud fathered six children in the first nine years of his marriage. This would seem to indicate a lively interest in using his penis. In reality, however, Freud's fertility was less about libido than an aversion to condoms. In 1893 Freud, then thirty-seven, informed Wilhelm Fliess that he and his wife were "living in abstinence" to avoid pregnancy and the methods of preventing it. Four years later, Freud told Fliess that "sexual excitation is of no more use to a person like me." Later, Freud hinted that his nuptial abstinence was less about birth control than controlling his fear that his penis might kill him. He made the bizarre claim in 1909 in *Some General Remarks on Hysterical Attacks* that every sexual climax causes an "unmistakable lapse of consciousness." Fifteen years earlier, Freud had written about his "death deliriums"—fears of expiring from a coronary, especially during intercourse. It all seems so ironic. Freud's critics attacked him for seeing all of life as sex, while Freud looked at sex and frequently saw death.

———————

It appears Freud's relationship with his own penis was similar to the one he found in his patients. In his practice, Freud worked to make his patients conscious of their unconscious fears, and thus less likely to be victimized by them in their daily lives. (In his own life, however, Freud was content to sublimate his sexuality and castration issues into work and cigars.) With *Totem and Taboo*, Freud began a long investigation of the larger cultural consequences of this most intimate predicament. The structure of organized society, what we call civilization, was born of castration anxiety, phallic lust, and murder, he declared, followed by remorse and instinctual renunciation, often leading to impotence. We tote this heavy psychological baggage—as real in our minds today as it was in our prehistoric past, Freud wrote in *Totem*—as the Oedipus complex. Not since Augustine, the most influential Christian theologian of them all, had anyone placed the penis so completely at the center of man's individual and collective fate. Nor had anyone, since the sainted Bishop of Hippo, held such pervasive intellectual sway over Western life and culture.

We are civilized. And we are neurotic. We are afraid to use our penis. And equally scared to lose it. The personal is political. And the political is personal. No one knew these facts better than Freud. In *Civilization and Its Discontents*, he restated the insight in his title. But Freud's political analysis was never translated into political action. He thought it enough to tear off our cultural fig leaf and expose the truth for all to see. Instead of calling for a revolutionary remake of civilization, Freud treated its discontents. The groundbreaking psychologist was a civic conservative. The Freudian penis was psychoanalyzed but never politicized.

That latter process would only happen in earnest after Freud's death, led by radicals who considered Freud's phallocentrism a pillar of the structure they were trying to pull down. These feminists redefined the penis as an instrument of political and sexual oppression. They felt neither castrated nor envious, but they did feel condescended to and lied to. Once again the idea of the male organ went through a tumultuous shift. The battle of the sexes moved from the unconscious to the conscious, from the couch to the bed, from the psyche to the streets. It was not an easy time to own a penis.

# V

---

## The Battering Ram

In 1962, a year before Betty Friedan's *The Feminine Mystique*, Helen Gurley Brown told women in her own book, *Sex and the Single Girl*, that they could find fulfillment whether they were married or not. This claim, quaint by today's standards, made Brown both revered and reviled. She was pelted with fruit at one public appearance, given a regular's chair on *The Tonight Show*, and hired by the politically conservative but fiscally savvy Hearst family to remake one of their failing general-interest magazines, *Cosmopolitan*, into that Single Girl's checkout-rack bible. Soon Mrs. Brown—this Single Girl was actually married—was one of the highest-paid executives in America when the boardroom seemed an impregnable fortress of phallic power. None other than Gloria Steinem honored her a decade later as a "feminist pioneer," and in 1999 *Ladies' Home Journal*, another Hearst publication, named Brown one of "The 100 Most Important Women of the 20th Century." Thus it was hardly surprising that the first year of the next century found Brown, then seventy-eight, publishing a memoir offering even more advice on the subject that had already made her rich and famous.

"Sex is one of the three best things we have, and I don't know the other two," she wrote. Brown mentioned a plaque in her office that read, "Good Girls Go to Heaven, Bad Girls Go Everywhere." But it was another piece of advice that got the most attention in the press:

"Spread semen on your face," Brown urged. It's "probably

full of protein, as sperm can become babies. Makes a fine mask—and he'll be pleased."

It is hard to imagine Ms. Steinem or Ms. Friedan giving such counsel, no matter how that lotion was obtained. And, in truth, Brown's defense of sexual harassment in the workplace during the Senate's investigation of serial groper Bob Packwood had, with other heresies, already toppled her from whatever precarious perch she once occupied in the feminist pantheon. Even so, Brown's career in the advice business is more than a testament to one woman's search for fame, fortune, and a grateful, grinning man. It serves as a bracket around one of the most tumultuous periods in the cultural history of the penis.

This was a period in which the old truths about that semen-making machine were reexamined by people who did not have one. A new generation of women, better educated and more politically potent than any before it, rejected the notion that they were castrated men. They embraced their erotic potential but denied the thrusting penis was their only route to a "mature feminine" orgasm—or any orgasm for that matter. Women who chanted "Make Love, Not War" at Vietnam-era peace rallies started to wonder how different those activities really were. Instead of feeling made whole by the penis, they often felt degraded by it, entered and occupied as if by a foreign army. To them an erection seemed less an object of pleasure than a battering ram.

This new critique did not limit its focus to the bedroom. For the first time in history an organized movement questioned if the relationship between the vagina and the penis was really a private matter at all. To the contrary, these new feminists argued it was political: that the domination of women by men in most facets of modern American life, from the monotony of middle-class marriage to the limited possibilities available to women in the workplace, a portrait painted so memorably in *The Feminine Mystique*, was shaped by the sexual act itself. What men saw as biology—intercourse as a dominant-submissive polarity in which the penis penetrates and the vagina receives—was seen by feminists as ideology. Heterosexuality was attacked for artificially defining female eroticism in terms of male needs. As the counterculture evolved into feminism's second wave—the first having achieved suffrage half a century earlier—many women came to think the only real beneficiaries of sexual liberation were men. That males in the New Left were as misogynistic as those in the Old Right seemed clear enough, especially to women who joined the former to bring about social change only to find themselves expected to be perpetually available to their male leaders for sex. When asked to define the position of women in the civil rights struggle, Stokely Carmichael famously answered "Prone."*

In time, anger over such treatment focused more and more on the penis. For centuries man's relationship with his defining organ was framed by one question: Am I in charge of "him," or is "he" in charge of me? Now women saw their relationship with the penis in that same context—in their case, refusing to let the organ limit *their* sexual and political independence in any way. Starting in the 1960s, the prevailing cultural images of the penis, all conceived by men, were scrutinized through a new lens, this one held by women, who used it to deconstruct the phallic excesses that exploited them most—rape, pornography, even consensual intercourse. Viewed this way, the penis was neither divine nor demonic, neither biological nor psychological. What men jokingly called their "tool" was seriously (and at times humorlessly) critiqued as a tool of oppression. The meaning and purpose of the penis—not just in the bedroom but in the culture—were debated as never before. The age of Freud was forced to yield to the age of Friedan, and then became NOW. If the first half of the twentieth century saw the penis psychoanalyzed, the second saw it politicized.

---

*Carmichael, then head of the Student Non-Violent Coordinating Committee, actually meant to say "supine."

That Freudians and feminists ended up in rival camps on these issues would have surprised many who helped start those movements. The anarchist and free-love advocate Emma Goldman, the most notorious feminist in America in 1909, eagerly attended Freud's lectures that year at Clark University in Massachusetts, sitting in the front row, according to one newspaper account, "chastely garbed in white with a red rose pinned to her waist." Goldman was especially impressed by Freud's critique of "civilized" morality, a code that insisted "good" women had no libido yet scorned those supposedly sexless creatures for unleashing the erotic beast within men. For pointing out the hypocrisy of that view, and for appearing to link the social liberation of women with their sexual emancipation, Freud was, in Goldman's eyes, "a giant among pygmies," a view she held until her death in 1940.

Perhaps she should have read his work more carefully. Freud's insistence on the "primacy of the penis" made him a dubious sexologist indeed, and hardly a friend of feminism. Beginning in 1905, Freud asserted, and later often repeated, one of his most controversial claims. This was the idea that femininity—and in particular the "mature feminine" orgasm—was produced by a physiological transfer with no parallel in the sexual development of men. A "girl's becoming a woman," Freud wrote, depends "on the clitoris passing on its sensitivity to the vagina completely." Freud's notion of penis envy already defined femininity as a series of private humiliations that, in the public sphere, rendered women incapable of advancing civilization in any meaningful way. Now he was saying something equally condescending: that a woman, left to her own devices, doesn't even know how to *be* a woman. Instead, she is taught how by an act of male penetration. It is the thrusting penis, Freud said, that awakens the true site of feminine eroticism— not the clitoris, the vagina.

If not, they are ill. New York analyst Sandor Lorand's "Contribution to the Problem of Vaginal Orgasm," published in 1939 in the *International Journal of Psychoanalysis,* reported on several patients who complained of "absence of sensation in the vagina" during sex. Somewhat magically, that sensation returned in Lorand's consulting room, though it is not clear how pleasurable that development really was. In analysis, Lorand wrote, "pulsations may occur during the analytical hour accompanied by an insatiable desire to feel the penis constantly within the vagina. . . .

> The vagina was called a monster, constantly hungry, by one woman. . . . Coitus was always very painful to her, but the desire to have the penis inside her made her endure it. . . . When later [after extended analysis] she was able to achieve orgasm [during coitus], it was accompanied by angry shrieking.

There was surprisingly little shrieking from female Freudians about these ideas. Though Karen Horney challenged the concept of penis envy in 1922 at the Seventh International Congress of Psychoanalysis, chaired by Freud, not many followed her lead. In fact, two of the movement's most influential women, Helene Deutsch and Marie Bonaparte, insisted Freud got it just right. Before moving to America in 1934, Deutsch had been president of the Vienna Psychoanalytic Society, where she formalized the training of analysts. She herself was one of the first female graduates of the University of Vienna medical school. Despite these professional achievements, Deutsch believed a woman served her true function under a man—often literally. In *The Psychology of Women,* Deutsch argued that women have a "deeply feminine need to be overpowered" by the thrusting erect penis. "Woman's entire psychologic preparation for the sexual and reproductive functions is connected with masochistic ideas," she wrote. Childbirth, Deutsch said—even when painful—is the "acme of sexual pleasure."

Masochism was a concept familiar to Marie Bonaparte as

well. In *Female Sexuality,* this great-grandniece of Napoleon—
and Freud's savior (she financed his escape from Nazi-occupied
Vienna)—described intercourse as an act in which a woman is
given "a beating by the man's penis" and "loves the violence."
Decades earlier Bonaparte's quest for psychoanalytically sanctioned orgasms led her to praise a certain Dr. Halban, who had
devised a new treatment for frigidity, defined by Freudians as
the inability to climax from vaginal penetration. From research
and her own experience, Bonaparte knew that many women
found the clitoris stubbornly unwilling to give up its sensitivity.
Freud declared this a symptom of neurosis; Bonaparte, analyzed
by Herr Professor himself, agreed. Still, she thought the problem might have a physical basis as well: that, in some unfortu-
nates, the clitoris was simply too far from the vagina to effect
the required shift.

The cure for such a *fixation clitoridienne,* Bonaparte wrote in
*Bulletin de la société de sexologie,* was the surgical procedure
invented by Dr. Halban in which the misplaced clitoris was cut
out and then reattached at a spot closer to the vaginal opening.
(The article was illustrated by several gruesome photographs of
the procedure.) No dilettante on this issue, Bonaparte personally measured the distance between the clitoris and the vagina in
two hundred corpses. Then, in 1927, she underwent Halban's
"corrective" surgery herself.

---

Four decades later, feminists sought sexual satisfaction through
a different route. They made a political cause out of it, sometimes deciding to leave men—and the penis—out of the
equation completely. As part of the American Left, feminists
were supposedly focusing on other issues, and in 1968 there
was no lack of them. North Vietnam's Tet Offensive, launched
in January, belied the boasts of imminent victory made by
American General William Westmoreland. Inner cities erupted
in April after Martin Luther King was murdered. Robert

Kennedy was shot dead in June moments after winning the California primary. July produced a nationally televised police riot at the Democratic Convention in Chicago. Then in November, after a bitter and raucous presidential campaign, prowar candidate Richard Nixon threw his hands in the air in a V-for-victory sign, apparently unaware the same sign now signified "peace" to anyone under thirty. For many leftists, Armageddon no longer seemed a religious concept.

For some women, however, there was a growing awareness that the final conflict would not be about government or religion. It would be about the penis. These women wondered who their oppressor really was—"The System" or the men they were allied with to fight it. At consciousness-raising sessions, those who had supposedly benefitted from sexual liberation admitted that they often felt abused by the sexual demands of radical men. The transcript of one session, full of stories of phallic intimidation and faked female orgasms, was published as "When Women Rap About Sex," by Shulamith Firestone, in June 1968. The message seemed clear: women weren't merely getting fucked by men, but fucked over. Four months later this idea gained a prominence in the feminist movement it never had before when 150 women met at the first National Women's Liberation Conference, near Chicago. There were arguments between political leftists and cultural feminists, but there was one thing nearly every participant agreed on: the best-attended workshop was led by Anne Koedt. Her topic: "The Myth of the Vaginal Orgasm."

We live in a male world, Koedt said, that fights any change in the role of the penis in that world. The real issue in sex is power. "Women are defined sexually in terms of what pleases men," she said. "Men have orgasms by friction with the vagina. . . . Frigidity [is] defined as the failure of women to have vaginal orgasms. Actually, the vagina is not constructed to achieve orgasm. It is the clitoris which is the center of sexual sensitivity" in women. These last two facts were hardly new. They had been confirmed by Kinsey in 1953 and Masters and Johnson in 1966. It also seems to have been quite obvious to the ancient Greeks and Romans. But until Koedt's lecture, it had never been said in a feminist context.

Because a clitoral orgasm does not rely on penetration, she said, it "threatens the heterosexual institution." It makes men "fear they will become sexually expendable," which is why men prefer to ignore it. Koedt was not arguing for sexual secession from men. She was calling for an erotic coalition between equals based on sound sexual knowledge and respect, even if that respect had to be wrested from men against their will. When men are forced to share power in the bedroom, she said, men will have to share power everywhere else. If Koedt's listeners had not already grasped that the personal is political, they did now. From this point on, the galvanizing issue for many feminists was overthrowing the primacy of the penis.

In August 1970, the press anointed a leader of that revolution. The coronation took place in the *New York Times* where, for the first time in anyone's memory, a book critic devoted two columns on successive days to the same book. "*Sexual Politics* is a radical feminist's view of the infinite variety of man's exploitation of women," Christopher Lehmann-Haupt began, "and it should be said at once that the book is supremely entertaining, brilliantly conceived, overwhelming in its arguments, breathtaking in its command of history and literature, filled with shards of wit and the dry ice of logic, and written with [the] fierce intensity of a . . . blowtorch."

Kate Millett's blowtorch was aimed at patriarchy, the institution in which all power goes to men, enforced by a rigid code of status framed by intercourse. Millett's focus was on sex, but not the biological disparity in genitalia between the sexes (Freud's starting point). Rather, Millett looked at how those differences were interpreted in Western culture: how, for instance, the penis was typically seen by writers and philosophers as a symbol of power, competence, and integrity, while the vagina nearly always indicated weakness, greed, and deceit.

Ironically, Millett's guiding spirit in *Sexual Politics* was a man: Jean Genet, the French novelist and playwright. Millett saw that Genet's greatest works—*Our Lady of the Flowers, The Thief's Journal,* and *The Balcony*—drew a picture of the "barbarian power structure of masculine and feminine" revealed by a homosexual, criminal underworld mimicking the straight world around it. The pimp Armand in *The Thief's Journal* is gay. But his attitude toward his penis, Millett understood, is universally male.

> "My cock," Armand once said, "is worth its weight in gold." He boasts he can lift a heavy man on the end of it. [He] associates sexuality with power [and] his pleasure. . . . Intercourse is an assertion of mastery, one that announces his own higher caste and proves it upon a [person] who is expected to surrender, serve, and be satisfied.

Virtually identical attitudes could have come from the cock-crazy heterosexuals Henry Miller and Norman Mailer. As Millett showed in *Sexual Politics,* they often do.

For Miller, women are objects of lust and/or contempt. For Mailer, they're bloody combatants. One of Mailer's most graphic sex bouts takes place in "The Time of Her Time," a short story in *Advertisements for Myself,* which Millett saw as typical of his sexual politics. Mailer's stand-in in "Time" is Sergius O'Shaughnessy, who spends his days running a bull-fighting school in his Manhattan loft, a conceit perhaps less laughable then than now, and his nights as the "messiah of the one-night stand," preaching and teaching sexual ecstasy to leggy NYU students. Sergius's prey in "Time" commits her first incitement to erotic battle when she holds forth on T. S. Eliot at a party. A duel with her can only be fought with one weapon.

"Her college-girl snobbery so inflamed the avenger of my crotch that I wanted to prong her then and there, right on the floor," Mailer wrote. "I was a gorged . . . phallus, eager to ram her." But Sergius has to wait. Now, back at his loft, in bed, that time has come. He begins to work on her, Mailer wrote, "like a riveter. . . .

> I went, and I went, and I went. I bore her high and thumped her hard . . . and then . . . I turned her over on her belly, my avenger wild with the mania of a madman . . . I drove into the seat of all stubbornness, tight as a vise, and I wounded her, I knew it, she thrashed beneath me like a trapped animal, . . . forced to give up . . . her symbolic and therefore real vagina. . . . [It] took ten minutes . . . but as the avenger rode down to his hilt . . . she gave at last a little cry . . . and I could feel a new shudder which began as a ripple and rolled into a wave. . . . So I turned her once again on her back, and moved . . . to love's first hole. . . . I said into her ear, "You dirty little Jew." That whipped her over. A first wave kissed, a second spilled, and a third and a fourth and a fifth came breaking over, and finally she was away, she was loose in the water for the first time in her life. . . . I was nothing but a set of aching balls and a congested cock, . . . looking at the contortion of her face and listening to her sobbing sound of "Oh, Jesus, I made it, oh Jesus, I did."

Mailer's chest-pounding, Millett understood, is the jungle display of an exceptionally insecure primate. His erotica is clueless and clumsy, reading "like the sporting news grafted onto a series of war dispatches." These were not words Mailer was used to reading about himself. A year earlier he won the Pulitzer Prize and the National Book Award for *The Armies of the Night*. There was even talk of a Nobel. Even so, Millett was thoroughly unimpressed. Mailer's sex writing isn't merely awful, she said. It's not even about sex. It is about "fucking for conquest," where the victory "is not only over the female, but over the male's fears for his . . . erection." Women, Mailer said, are on their backs during "the only significant moments of their lives," but "the male is forced to exert himself," risking a condition Mailer described as "fucking your head off," "wrecking your brains and body—eternally."

This would be comical, Millett said, if the consequences were not so serious. Still, she guessed there were times the author might be laughing at himself. "But the comprehension of folly is so little guarantee of its renunciation in Mailer," she wrote. Instead, his relentless machismo reminded Millett of a gag gift sold on the Coney Island boardwalk not far from Mailer's home in Brooklyn. This was the "Peter Meter," a piece of "folk art," she called it, stamped in the "shape of a ruler with printed comments equating excellence with penis size." Man is the measure of all things, men have been telling women since the Golden Age of Greece. Millett couldn't help wondering why they measure themselves with such a silly stick. Nor could she help noticing that men habitually blame their shortcomings—penile and otherwise—on women.

The *New York Times* was not alone in noticing this critique of the male mystique. Two weeks later, Millett's face was on the cover of *Time*. "It was not so long ago that the battle of the sexes was fought in gentle, rolling Thurber country," the unsigned, six-page cover story began. "Now the din is in earnest, echoing from the streets where pickets gather, the bars where women were once barred, and even connubial beds." Radical feminists want "to topple the patriarchal system." Until *Sexual Politics,* this movement "had no coherent theory to buttress its intuitive passions [and] no ideologue to provide chapter and verse for its assault." Now those holes were filled by Kate Millett, "the Mao Tse-tung of Women's Liberation." That *Time* understood her politics to be an attack on men in general—and the penis in particular—was made clear in the following sentence:

"Reading [her] book is like sitting with your testicles in a nutcracker."

There is no doubt Norman Mailer saw it that way. In 1971 he responded with *The Prisoner of Sex,* where he referred to himself as "the Prizewinner," alluding as much to his view of his own sexual prowess as to his status as the 1969 Pulitzer and National Book Award recipient. Part confessional, part screed, and wholly self-aggrandizing, *Prisoner* argued that feminism had changed man's relationship with women, and his defining organ, in catastrophic ways. Authentic male sexuality, Mailer insisted, is no longer possible now that women have control over contraception, because that means female control over the penis. Before, man's sexual power was absolute. A man could fuck a woman to death, if not immediately, nine months later, during childbirth. The penis was designed to exercise that god-like power, Mailer said. But now—after the Pill, Anne Koedt, and Kate Millett—man has suffered the ultimate humiliation. He has become expendable and his penis irrelevant, replaced by his "superior," the vibrator.

On this last point, Mailer wasn't being entirely paranoid. A 1974 piece in the *Journal of Popular Culture* noted that the beginning of that decade saw a proliferation of advertisements for battery-operated "female facial massagers" that were clearly not aimed at relieving tics. One advertisement from the *New York Times* was illustrated by a sketch of a woman holding an unmistakably phallic-shaped device to her cheek. The text declared the "Body Beautiful" machine ready to "massage [its owner] delightfully all over." The $8.95 item was 7½ inches long and 1⅝ inches in diameter, about two inches longer and a half inch thicker than a typical human erection. (Like many mail-order products, the "Body Beautiful" was selling fantasy.) Its "unique shape"—as unique as any stiff penis—"and smooth contours," the text said, "were designed to concentrate helpful, penetrating massage right where you need it, when you need it." That would probably be some quiet time at home, the copy said. "You'll be amazed at how private toning sessions can become a delightful part of your life."

Mailer preferred to tone up a woman the old-fashioned way. Or at least try to. A few years before *Prisoner* was published, the Prizewinner and his mighty avenger found themselves in bed with Gloria Steinem, then a magazine journalist as famous for her long legs and short skirts as she was for her budding role as a feminist spokesperson. What an opportunity for the avenger, indeed. According to one biography of Steinem, however, the Prizewinner was more booby than prize in the sack, failing to raise an erection.

Though it will come as small consolation to Mailer, he was not alone. In October 1971, a panel of male physicians addressed the question "Is Impotence Increasing?" in the journal *Medical Aspects of Human Sexuality.* All but two answered yes. Speaking for the majority—but citing no data to support his conclusion—Dr. B. Lyman Stewart blamed "the Women's Liberation Movement."

---

*Sexual Politics* stayed in print throughout the 1970s, but Millett's personal time in the spotlight was brief. Three months after the *Time* cover, Millett, then married to sculptor Fumio Yoshimura, reluctantly outed herself as a lesbian at a forum on sexual liberation at Columbia University. (Millett was more comfortable with the term "bisexual," but the woman who challenged her mocked that choice as a "cop-out.") That feminism's rising star was pushed into this by a lesbian separatist shows the bind that feminism's new focus on the male organ had created for itself. How can you overthrow the primacy of the penis if you're "sleeping with the enemy"? some feminists asked. But others, Betty Friedan chief among them, were insistent that feminists not be dismissed in the media as penis-hating lesbians. Friedan would lose this particular battle in that war. A *Time* reporter showed up at Millett's Manhattan loft the next morning. Her confession, the resulting article said, "discredit[ed] her as a spokesperson for her cause." Apparently only full-time heterosexual women could comment on the penis and expect to be listened to.

That requirement was met by Shere Hite. As part of her

doctoral-thesis research at Columbia, Hite stood up at NOW meetings in New York and asked those present to fill out a questionnaire on orgasms. In 1974 Hite published preliminary findings based on forty-five responses. *Sexual Honesty* was ignored by the press. This would not happen when Hite's finished project came out two years later.

*The Hite Report on Female Sexuality*, based on three thousand responses, found that seven women in ten did not achieve orgasm from a thrusting male penis. Most men were unaware of this, Hite said, because intercourse was deemed successful once a man had his orgasm. This erotic inequality was fast becoming a political issue for women, she wrote. "We're expected to serve men their orgasms, just like we're expected to serve them their coffee," one respondent complained. Another said the thrusting penis made her feel "like a punching bag"—apparently without the thrill experienced by Marie Bonaparte or Helene Deutsch.* Hite's book, filled with compelling testimony from the bedroom, along with a matter-of-fact acceptance of masturbation and lesbianism as alternatives to penis-dominated sexuality, eventually sold 20 million copies worldwide. After *The Hite Report,* the "din" noticed by *Time* in 1970 got a lot louder.

*The Hite Report* made its author rich, famous, and an inviting target for some male critics, several in the employ of the well-known phallic supremacist Bob Guccione, founder of *Penthouse*. Nude pictures of Hite were printed in girlie magazines, and she was barraged with leering questions about her own orgasms. Others belittled her methodology. *The Hite Report* was unscientific, these critics said, because the sample was not random. Instead, it was dominated by penis-fearing, NOW-meeting-attending, nonorgasmic feminists (and probable les-

---

*That "punching bag" complaint was probably not entirely political. In 1992 British scientists placed an ultrasound monitoring device inside the vaginas of two female volunteers, who then had intercourse with their regular partners. "Penile thrusting," the study found, "was associated with considerable displacement of the female pelvic anatomy."

bians)—women who exaggerated the sexual selfishness and incompetence of men. Hite countered that her report was not meant to be a conventional sociological survey. It "was intended as a new kind of social science" providing "a forum for women to speak out freely. . . . No one can be sure if the seventy per cent figure for women who do not orgasm from intercourse is exactly correct." But *The Hite Report* "has been published in seventeen countries," she wrote, "and in not one have women disagreed with its basic findings."

If Hite thought this would quiet her critics, she was wrong. The attacks continued until Hite moved to Europe. The goal of that onslaught was as old as the battle of the sexes: If you can't kill the message, kill the messenger. Another historical analogy is equally apt. Stone monuments in Egypt tell us that Pharaoh's soldiers often cut off the penises of their dead foes, no doubt to discourage future enemies. Hite's enemies attempted a similar kind of intimidation—metaphorically—when she was still alive. They tried to castrate her credibility.

———

Susan Brownmiller filled out Hite's questionnaire. "But I was so absorbed with my own piece of the puzzle," she later wrote, "that I rarely saw the significance in what others were doing." A former *Newsweek* writer turned *Village Voice* reporter, Brownmiller had been active in leftist politics in New York for years. In 1971, the same year the gruesome exploits of a Beethoven-loving rapist were dramatized in *A Clockwork Orange,* Brownmiller helped organize a speak-out on real-life rape at a Manhattan high school. Up on stage a female karate instructor demonstrated flips and kicks to enable those present to defend themselves from any such attack. Most of the day, however, was devoted to testimony from those who had not been so lucky.

Germaine Greer, in America to promote *The Female Eunuch,* told of her rape in Australia when she was eighteen, pregnant, and desperate to find an abortion. Other women told of assaults occurring at an even younger age. One speaker attacked the insensitivity of psychoanalysis to that subject. Orthodox Freudians believed the child was often responsible for the attack; she was the seducer, not the victim. Rubbish, said Florence Rush, who later wrote *The Best Kept Secret: Sexual Abuse of Children*. Nearly all of those assaults were by grown men on young girls, nearly all of them unprovoked. Those and every other form of rape, Rush said, were "weapons of a male-dominated society that subjugates women," a statement met by a standing ovation.

Suddenly Brownmiller's piece of the puzzle became clearer than ever to her. Two days later she had a book proposal in hand for a feminist investigation of rape. Simon and Schuster gave her a contract. Four years later Brownmiller handed in *Against Our Will*. With its publication in October 1975, the politicization of the penis took a major, and controversial, step forward.

This is because Brownmiller argued that rape is not a sexual crime, but a political one—and that even if the rapist uses a knife, his real weapon is the blunt object rising between his legs. History's first rape, Brownmiller guessed, was unplanned. But the second, she was sure, was not. The ability of man to penetrate a woman's body, against her will, became "the ultimate test of his superior strength, the triumph of his manhood." And still is. "Man's discovery that his genitalia could serve as a weapon," she wrote, "ranks as one of the most important discoveries of prehistoric times, along with the use of fire and the first crude stone axe."

This idea of the "penis as weapon" was central to Brownmiller's thesis. The rapist is not a drooling sex fiend, she said. He is indistinguishable from any other man, just as his victim is from any woman. She can be young or old, attractive or not. To a rapist it makes no difference, because the act is not about sex. It is about control. "From prehistoric times to the present, rape has played a critical function," she wrote. "It is . . . a conscious process of intimidation by which *all* men keep *all* women in a state of fear."

One problem with this theory is that the incidence of rape is not a constant—the same year after year—nor is it universally prevalent. Reported rapes in the United States are nearly twenty times greater than in the United Kingdom, when measured per one hundred thousand women. In some Asian cultures rape hardly exists at all. Still, Brownmiller cited two well-known cases to back up her case. Albert DeSalvo, the "Boston Strangler," raped and murdered eleven women that police know of. Nearly half his victims were older than sixty. Some were nearly eighty. When a police interrogator expressed surprise at that, DeSalvo set him straight: "Attractiveness had nothing to do with it," he said. Rape "made me feel powerful." That DeSalvo preferred his victims power*less* was proved by his modus operandi. Nearly all his victims were tied up when he penetrated them. Some were already dead.

Eldridge Cleaver began his career as a rapist attacking black women. But that was just practice for his ultimate prey. Raping white women, Cleaver wrote in *Soul on Ice,* was "an insurrectionary act" in which he used his black penis to "defile" the white man's most prized possession. This too was cited by Brownmiller to prove her "rape is political, the penis is a weapon" thesis. And perhaps it does, for one rapist. But the most original example of Cleaver's playing penis politics with rape would happen years later—and on national TV.

In 1968 Cleaver was wounded in a shootout between Black Panthers and the Oakland, California, police. He jumped bail and spent several years abroad. When he returned in 1975 to face trial, the rapist and Marxist revolutionary was a changed man, indeed—a soon-to-be born-again Christian and cheerleader for entrepreneurial capitalism. In that second mode Cleaver reinvented himself as a fashion designer, selling a line of "anatomically correct" pants for men. What made those slacks

"A.C." was the codpiece in front, a huge pouch designed to contain, and call attention to, the organ that makes a man a man. In October 1976, producers at *The Phil Donahue Show,* then television's leading talk program, took in all of the above, as well as the controversy created by *Against Our Will,* then coming out in paperback after a successful run in hardcover. Someone got the idea to do a show in which the feminist author of that book on rape, Susan Brownmiller, would debate the rapist who created those pants, Eldridge Cleaver. Amazingly enough, they agreed.

The result was the most bizarre instance of sexual politics ever seen by a national viewing audience until the Clarence Thomas hearings introduced the American public to Long Dong Silver. The studio audience for the Cleaver-Brownmiller debate was composed of members of the Green Bay, Wisconsin, chapter of the La Leche League, a pro-breast-feeding group. "Uh-oh, white women in polyester," Cleaver said as Brownmiller and he walked onto the *Donahue* set. "They're your people, Susan." Brownmiller thought so, too. When the show started, she asked Cleaver to apologize to black women. He did. She asked him to apologize to white women. He did that, too. But penitence was "an unaccustomed role" for Cleaver, Brownmiller later wrote. Her opponent tacked to the hard phallic right. Sure, the beast within him had emerged when he was a rapist, Cleaver said. But someone had lured him out.

"Aww, you know what those young girls are like," Cleaver said of the women he had raped. "There's a word for it—I can't say it here but you all know it. [The initials] are C.T." The audience laughed. Shocked, Brownmiller reminded them that no one asks to be raped. Cleaver kept to the "Aww, shucks, I couldn't help myself" act, which only made her angrier. After Brownmiller interrupted him a few times, Cleaver jumped up from his chair. "Damn, woman," he barked, "you won't let a man speak!"

The Leche Leaguers burst into applause. Phil Donahue—the

very model of the sensitive seventies guy—came to Brownmiller's aid, but it was too late. The women in the audience turned on her. For the rest of the show Brownmiller faced a barrage of hostile questions. Cleaver strutted like a cock in a henhouse, urging his new friends in the audience to buy his anatomically correct pants for their penis-packing husbands and sons. Later, when the show was over, and the two debaters were backstage, Cleaver gave the visibly upset Brownmiller some advice. "Don't make the mistake I made" in the sixties, he said. "Don't get too far ahead of the people."

———————

There are scientists who think Brownmiller got too far ahead of the facts. Her assertion that rape is always about power—and never about sex—is wrong, they say, and not even proved by her own evidence. Though some rapists, like the Boston Strangler, do attack older victims, police reports show that most rapists choose a young fertile woman, even though she is more likely to resist, and ejaculate into her vagina. This last fact, coupled with the victim's fertility, is significant, these scientists say, but not as evidence of the rapist's desire for orgasm with an attractive woman. Rather, it suggests that rape is about reproduction, whether that event occurs or not. A rapist is not, to use a vulgarism, merely trying to "get his rocks off." Nor is he making a political statement, even if he brutalizes his victim. Instead, he is using his penis to try to spread his genes. In whatever way he can.

This explanation is based on the Darwinian model, which argues that back in our primeval past, men and women evolved different mating strategies shaped by the different roles played in reproduction by the sperm and the egg. Because carrying a child requires a huge commitment from a woman, starting with the long gestation period and continuing with the birth of a helpless infant, evolutionary woman learned over time to be particular, choosing a mate that she believed would help and protect her. No "rambling guys"—thank you very much. To ensure her genes were carried into the next generation, a woman needed her man to stick around.

A man, however, has different priorities. He does not have to stick around to see his genetic investment turn profitable. He can leave the care of the infant to the woman, someone he can usually count on to do her best to keep the baby alive, even without his help. From a Darwinian standpoint, the man's genetic goals are better served by doing the opposite of sticking around—that is, using his penis to inseminate dozens of women, thus, by sheer numbers, increasing his chances of reproductive success, the sine qua non of Darwinian fitness.

Some scientists call this asymmetry in attitudes "the Coolidge Effect," after a story told about President Calvin Coolidge and his wife. One day, the story goes, the Coolidges visited a farm, going their separate ways once on the property. When Mrs. Coolidge passed the chicken pens, she couldn't help noticing a rooster enthusiastically copulating with a hen. "Does he do that more than once a day?" she asked. "Sure, dozens of times," the farmer said. "Please tell that to the president," said Mrs. Coolidge. Later, when the president stopped by the chickens, the farmer did just that. "Same hen every time?" the president asked. "Nope, different one each time," said the farmer. The president nodded. "Please tell that to Mrs. Coolidge."

Fact is, seeing evolution as a sexual battleground can explain some pertinent and peculiar facts about the human penis, including why the women of *The Hite Report* were so unhappy with the staying power of their men. We will start, however, on a more positive note: the unusually large size of the human penis—unusual in that the erection of a 160-pound man is larger than that of a 400-pound gorilla—is something men can probably credit to natural selection.*

*Give five and a half inches to the man, just over one inch to the supposedly mighty ape. Source: "Sexual Selection and Its Component Parts, Somatic and Genital Selection, as Illustrated by Man and the Great Apes," by R. V. Short, *Advances in the Study of Behavior* 9 (1979).

Some scientists assert a large penis acted as an evolutionary turn-on long ago to women who interpreted a huge organ to indicate strength, something they hoped to pass on to their children, and, for that reason, chose the best endowed of their suitors. But other scientists, after watching monkeys, guess the original function of a large penis was to impress other males—and intimidate them from becoming sexual rivals. In the 1963 study "Display of Penile Erection in the Squirrel Monkey," zoologists Detlev W. Ploog and Paul D. MacLean observed numerous instances in which "the [dominant] male [monkey] approached . . . the other male head-on, placed one or both hands on its back

> and thrust [his] erect penis toward the [other male's] face. . . . The animal receiving the display sat in a cowering position while ducking its head as if dodging a blow. . . . If it does not remain quiet during the display, it may be viciously attacked.

It may be hard to imagine humans acting this way, but as anyone who has been in a boy's high-school locker room can attest, the difference is one of degree.

Zoologists link penis size, testes weight, and volume of ejaculate to frequency of copulation. The reason why gorillas carry such a small stick, R.V. Short wrote in 1979, is that they rarely have sex. Humans have sex often and, equally important, are descended from humans who had sex even more often. In the earliest stages of our evolutionary past, the theory goes, a woman probably mated with many men, often in rapid sequence. (Some of our closest relatives still do: primatologist Jane Goodall saw the same female chimpanzee copulate eighty-four times with seven different males over eight days.) Thus the man with the largest penis, which theoretically would transmit his sperm closer to the female's cervix, and the most semen (which would probably contain the most sperm) was more likely to win the competition to fertilize evolutionary woman because he was best equipped to deliver his reproductive payload.

Unfortunately, and this is where those unhappy *Hite Report* respondents reenter the conversation, the man who ejaculated fastest also had an edge in that prehistoric insemination contest. This was because of the very real chance that another man might pull him off that female and take his place inside her before he released his sperm. Men who took too long, therefore, could be eliminated from the competition completely. This suggests that every man now alive is descended from countless generations of well-hung, fast-spurting men. This second trait, and the Darwinian explanation of it, reminds us that in nearly all cases of penile shortcomings, men eventually find a way to blame their failures on sex-crazed women.*

The Greeks certainly did. According to one myth, Erichthonius, a king of Athens, was conceived from the seed of a premature ejaculator, a god driven to that lamentable state by his divine wife's infidelity. The male deity was Hephaestus, the divine metalsmith and god of fire who was crippled (apparently not just in bed) when his father Zeus threw him down from Mount Olympus after Hephaestus sided with his mother Hera in a domestic dispute. Though considered repulsive by his own mother, Hephaestus married Aphrodite, goddess of love and beauty, who neglected her own marriage bed in favor of affairs with other gods. Forsaken and frustrated by his wife, Hephaestus, the myth says, tried to rape Athena. The virgin goddess broke free, but not before her attacker left behind a trail of semen on her leg. Athena wiped off the seed in disgust, threw it on the ground, and, where it landed, arose the fully formed Erichthonius.

---

*Humans, with an average time of four minutes, according to physiologist Jared Diamond, are actually among the slowest to climax among male primates. Gorillas normally ejaculate in one minute. Chimpanzees have been timed at seven seconds.

But what about mere mortals living today, even those who are not premature ejaculators, who nonetheless find it difficult to find a sexual partner? They too are operating under the Darwinian imperative to spread their genes. One scientist has come up with a theory to explain the behavior of some of these men. He says evolutionary pressures may lead them to become violent sexual predators—and politics has nothing to do with it, no matter what Susan Brownmiller thinks.

In several controversial papers published between 1979 and 1991, entomologist Randy Thornhill examined the sexual activities of the *Panorpa vulgaris* scorpionfly. When the male *Panorpa* wants to mate he has two strategies. He offers a female a "nuptial gift" of food (a dead insect or a mass of hardened saliva), which usually makes her quite receptive; but if he has no food, the male rapes any female he is lucky enough to catch.* Evolution has made this second option easier for the empty-handed *Panorpa*. Males are equipped with a special "notal organ," a clamplike structure near the penis that enables them to immobilize the female's forewing, thus making it impossible for her to flee once forced copulation has begun. *Panorpa*s who mate with receptive females, Thornhill's experiments showed, do not use their special rape tool.

In *A Natural History of Rape*, cowritten with anthropologist Craig T. Palmer, Thornhill made his most controversial claim yet. This is the assertion that human males, even without a notal organ, have adapted to female choosiness by overpowering them in a way not unlike the *Panorpa*. We call it rape. Thornhill calls it a genetically programmed, adaptive reproductive strategy—as much a product of evolution as the giraffe's elongated neck—created by the sexual asymmetry between men and women. Women are selected by evolution to resist men they do

---

*Several biologists—most notably Anne Fausto-Sterling, author of *Myths of Gender*—are disdainful of Thornhill's use of the term "rape" to describe sexual acts committed by animals. To these critics rape is an act of conscious will, thus the term properly applies to humans alone.

not want. Men are selected by that same irresistible force to mate regardless of what a woman wants. This is a formula for conflict because "those [men] unable to compete for resources and status necessary to attract and reproduce successfully" will be left out of the reproductive cycle unless they force the issue. This makes *all* men potential rapists. Sexual violence is biological, Thornhill says, which is not to say it is socially acceptable. But, unfortunately for women, biology ignores morality. The result, Thornhill says, is a sexual arms race—a heated-up Cold War with no end in sight.

---

Andrea Dworkin would not disagree with that assessment. But she would argue men have never needed a new organ to be violent sexual predators. They already have a penis.

Making that case in books such as *Intercourse, Our Blood,* and *Pornography* made Dworkin one of the most controversial feminists in the world. This notoriety emerged from her work in the anti-pornography protests of the 1970s, a movement that tried to prove, in Robin Morgan's famous formulation, that "Pornography is the theory, rape is the practice." There was no convincing data to back up that claim, which is one reason why the anti-porn movement fizzled. Studies have not found a consistent correlation between exposure to pornography and sexual assault. In Japan, where violent porn is easily accessible, rape is nearly nonexistent.

The movement also failed because it was out of step with the '70s Zeitgeist. The defining aspect of hard-core porn was, and still is, showing an erect penis in real sex acts, culminating in real orgasms—often in the woman's face—known as "money shots." A 1971 piece in the *New York Times*, of all places, praised the availability of hard-core porn as "a sign of health." Thousands of Americans, most of whom had never seen another man's erect penis penetrating a woman, saw *Deep Throat* in 1972, generating a million dollars at the box office—a wildly unprecedented sum for a porn movie. (The film eventually made more than $25 million.) Film scholar Arthur Knight praised it in *Time* for "acknowledging the importance of female sexual gratification." This was an oddly optimistic view, considering that the film's star, Linda Lovelace, "found" her clitoris in her throat, then spent the rest of the movie sucking the penises of men.

*and was forcibly violently & made to do the movie*

One thing is certain: *Deep Throat* made pornography chic. By the late-1970s, porn actors were celebrities, escorted beyond the velvet rope into Studio 54 and similarly exclusive bastions of trendiness. Before, a porn star—if that term was not oxymoronic—was by definition a woman. Men in such films were often nameless and at times literally faceless. Now men were porn stars, revered and envied for their superhuman phallic endowment (Marc "Ten and a Half" Stevens was one of the first to be so honored) and their gravity-defying, on-demand staying power—the latter no easy feat considering this was decades before Viagra. Of course, all the stars in gay porn were men, and there too size ruled, as evidenced by the imposing Jeff Stryker, who later marketed a massive dildo supposedly cast from his own penis.

Dworkin's involvement in the anti-porn movement began in 1976, when the film *Snuff* opened in Manhattan. *Snuff* was a crass attempt to cash in on rumors that the New York Police had confiscated underground films from South America in which women were "snuffed"—murdered—on camera by men with whom they had just had sex, a concept that, if true, gave grisly life to some of Norman Mailer's most excessive rants about phallic power.

It was *Snuff*'s epilogue that caught Dworkin's attention. The camera dollied back from the previous shot to show a movie set, replete with crew members and the director. A script girl tells the director she was turned on by the last sex scene. Soon they begin to have sex, themselves. She tries to push the director away, however, when she realizes they are being filmed. To stop her, the director grabs a knife, looks directly into the camera, and says to the cameraman, "You want to get a good scene?" Seconds later the camera "shows" the director forcing himself on the woman, then, when he is done, using that knife to cut open her abdomen, after which he reaches in and pulls out her throbbing entrails. Suddenly the screen goes black. "Shit, we ran out of film," the audience hears the cameraman say. "Did you get it all?" the director asks. "Yeah, let's get out of here," says the cameraman. Then silence—and no credits.

Dworkin's well-publicized demonstrations against the film led the *New York Times* and the Manhattan District Attorney's office to look into *Snuff*'s reality. As the *Times* concluded, "No one [was] vérité killed." The D.A.'s office found the actress playing the woman whose intestines were supposedly displayed in the epilogue. Dworkin had made her point, however, drawing attention to violent pornography in a manner that raised feminism's involvement in that issue and her own profile within that movement. Two years later she gave a rousing speech before the first-ever "Take Back the Night March" through the red-light district of San Francisco. In October 1979, when a Women Against Pornography rally brought five thousand sign-waving protesters to New York's pre-Giuliani Times Square, her stature in the feminist movement was a visible fact. Dworkin held up the organization's banner while marching in the first row next to Gloria Steinem and Bella Abzug.

Soon after the Times Square march, Dworkin met Linda Marchiano, the real name of Linda Lovelace, at a press conference where Marchiano revealed she had been drugged, beaten, and sexually brutalized by her former husband-manager before she appeared in *Deep Throat*, experiences she later chronicled in her book *Ordeal*. Dworkin, whose own books later revealed that she too had experience with wife beating, asked attorney Catharine MacKinnon if Marchiano had grounds to sue her ex-husband. MacKinnon thought several civil rights statutes might apply.

In 1983 Dworkin and MacKinnon tested that theory when they were hired by a city councilman in Minneapolis to draft anti-porn legislation based on their civil rights model. Their bill made pornography an actionable offense on the grounds of sex discrimination. It defined injured parties as anyone coerced into performing in porn, those assaulted by porn consumers after viewing or reading such works, and those offended by having porn forced on them in their homes, jobs, or public places. The bill passed by one vote but was vetoed by the mayor. In 1984 the women introduced a similar bill in Indianapolis that was signed into law, only to be struck down by a local court as unconstitutional. (The U.S. Supreme Court refused to hear the case.) Dworkin also testified before the Meese Commission on Pornography, lending her support to a process many feminists considered a tool of the anti-feminist Religious Right.

Today there are hundreds of references to Dworkin on the Internet and nearly as many opinions about her. Some praise her as a social critic of towering courage. ("In every century there are a handful of writers who help the human race to evolve. Andrea is one of them," says Gloria Steinem.) Others attack her as a puritan confusing her own experiences with everyone else's. ("Dworkin," Camille Paglia writes, "boasts of her bizarre multiple rapes, assaults, beatings, breakdowns, and tacky traumas as if her inability to cope with life were the patriarchy's fault rather than her own.") Men who despise Dworkin *really* despise her. Some threaten to violate her body in precisely the way Dworkin has condemned in her writing.

Obviously, there is little that these camps agree on. But they are responding to the same message. Dworkin's work reconceptualizes intercourse from penetration to occupation and, ultimately, infestation. In doing this she has moved the feminist idea of the penis to its most pessimistic place yet—not just politicized, but pathologized. Heterosexuality, she implies, is toxic: the penis invades a woman's body, contaminates it, and, unchecked, eventually kills it. In Dworkin's universe any man with a penis is a real or potential rapist. An actual rapist is merely following a diseased phallic imperative he was born with. And so oppressive is the simple act of intercourse that the difference between a husband and a sex criminal is nearly impossible to discern.

Though she insists she does not believe that anatomy is destiny, Dworkin's writing seems to indicate otherwise. This passage is from *Our Blood*:

> I suggest to you that the transformation of the male sexual model under which we now all labor and "love" begins in the place [men] most dread—that is, a limp penis. I think that men will have to give up their precious erections, . . . that they will have to excise everything in them that they now value as distinctively "male."

This is from a speech given in 1980 at Yale Law School:

> The penis conquers and possesses; [it] distinguishes the male conqueror from the female conquered. . . . The use of the penis to conquer is its normal use. In the male system, rape is a matter of degree.

This is from *Pornography*:

> Violence is male; the male is the penis; violence is the penis or the sperm ejaculated from it. What the penis can do it must do forcibly for a man to be a man.

And this—apparently unread by Helen Gurley Brown—is from *Intercourse*:

> In some pornography and in some sex murders, semen is spread all over the woman's face . . . [because] to ejaculate is to *pollute* the woman. Women's magazines sometimes recommend spreading semen on the face to enhance the complexion, pushing women to submit to a practice from

pornography. . . . [In] real life . . . men use the penis to deliver death to women. . . . The women are raped as adults
or as children; prostituted; fucked, then murdered; murdered, then fucked.

As is this:

[The erect penis causes] a literal erosion of the [female]
body's integrity. . . . Her insides are worn away over time,
and she, possessed, becomes weak, depleted, usurped in all
her physical and mental energies . . . until it ends in death.

It would seem the penis isn't merely a battering ram, as
Dworkin sees it. It is a corrosive battering ram that kills.

It is impossible to believe that such ideas, expressed so ur-
gently and covered so widely in the press, failed to influence the
culture. One piece of evidence that they did is the following
poem by National Book Critics Circle Award winner Sharon
Olds, published in her collection *The Gold Cell*, in 1987. These
are the opening lines:

Outside the operating room of the sex-change doctor, a
    tray of penises.
There is no blood. This is not Vietnam, Chile, Buchen-
    wald. They were surgically removed under anaes-
    thetic. They lie there neatly, each with a small space
    around it.
The anaesthetic is wearing off now. The chopped-off
    sexes lie on the silver tray.
One says *I am a weapon thrown down. Let there be no
    more killing. . . .*\*

*From *The Gold Cell* by Sharon Olds, copyright © 1987 by Sharon
Olds. Used by permission of Alfred A. Knopf, a division of Random
House, Inc.

But perhaps the ultimate evidence of Dworkin's influence was the vigilante justice achieved by a sexually brutalized wife who probably never heard of Dworkin, an immigrant from Ecuador named Lorena Bobbitt. Bobbitt's explanation of why she attacked her husband reads like a passage from one of Dworkin's autobiographical novels. Seconds before Bobbitt left her bed for the kitchen on the night of June 23, 1993—after her intoxicated husband forced himself upon her but before she noticed the shining knife near the kitchen sink—she lay there thinking. "I remember many things," Bobbitt told the jury in her imperfect English.

> I remember the first time he raped me. I remember the first time he forced me to have anal sex. I remember the abortion. I remember everything.

It was after remembering all this, Bobbitt testified, that she went back to the bedroom where her husband John was sleeping, pulled down the sheets, and sliced off his penis.

---

Meeting Andrea Dworkin in person, one gets the impression that the last person she expected to become is, well, . . . Andrea Dworkin. "When I first heard of feminism it seemed ridiculous. It wasn't political enough," she said in a lattè shop not far from her home in Brooklyn, New York. Dworkin was wearing overalls on top of a blue sweater. She spoke slowly, almost inaudibly. "I was raised [in Camden, New Jersey] in a political family. My father was a schoolteacher, postal worker, and union organizer. My mother marched for contraception rights when abortion was still illegal. Feminism seemed pointless to me. I thought, 'These are women who don't know how to have sex.' You have to realize, before 1972 I was not the person I am today. I loved Norman Mailer. I wanted to *be* Henry Miller. People would say, 'They're such shits to women.' I'd day, 'But they're such great writers.' Their idea of sex was my idea of sex. It took me a long time for me to realize that what was good for them was not good for me."

Dworkin started to learn that, she said, on the streets. In 1964 she enrolled at Bennington College, a school in Vermont known for academic excellence and a bohemian environment. Bennington's school calendar called for a nine-week off-campus work period during the winter. Dworkin went to Manhattan's East Village, occasionally having sex for money, she said, when she ran out of cash. In the winter of 1965, Dworkin was arrested near the United Nations during a protest against the Vietnam War. While in custody at the Women's House of Detention, Dworkin says, she was given an internal examination by two doctors who ripped her vaginal walls with a steel speculum, then left her bleeding. Traumatized, Dworkin left school and took off for a brief stay in Greece, then returned to New York—once again homeless, hungry, and doing whatever she had to in order to stay alive.

"I slept with hundreds of men. I thought I was Henry Miller—'fuck bourgeois culture, I'll do what I want.'" In 1968 Dworkin moved to Amsterdam, getting involved with a sex commune called Suck. Most of its members had been political activists in the United States; others were Dutch, British, or Australian. One of that last group was the yet-to-be-famous Germaine Greer. *Suck* was also the name of the group's newsletter, a journal filled with images of women sucking penises and men with their heads buried in vaginas. At first Dworkin was exhilarated by this atmosphere. But soon what was inspiring became intimidating. "There was pressure to pose for those pictures. The men in the group would say, 'This is the next liberation struggle, after Civil Rights and Vietnam.' I remember being in someone's house. There were naked pictures of Germaine on the kitchen table. I wasn't offended. I just didn't want to be pressured."

In 1971 Dworkin married a Dutchman several years younger

than she. It was a relationship of opposites. "He was a virgin. I'd slept with hundreds. I figured, 'Fine, I'll teach him what I know.'" Everything *was* fine, at first. But intercourse, Dworkin soon learned, brought out the brutality in her husband. "I think male contempt for women comes from being inside her body. The dynamics of intercourse are such that it's an act of owner-ship for men. My husband thought my vagina belonged to him.

"I believe it is more true than untrue that men have a propen-sity for sexual violence. I believe it is more true than untrue that women experience the penis as something invasive. I'm not say-ing every erection is bad. It's what you do with it that counts. Lorena Bobbitt isn't my hero, but I understand her. Most men think only of finding a hole to stick it in whether the person with the hole wants to be stuck or not. That was the problem with my husband, who became a batterer when I refused him.

"I was on the run for months. Sometimes he'd find me and beat me nearly to death. The people who finally helped me in Amsterdam—the only people who helped me—called them-selves feminists. They were the only ones who didn't say, 'Your husband wouldn't be hitting you if you didn't like it.' One of them gave me a book called *Sexual Politics*. Until then I thought oppression meant apartheid in South Africa, or America in Viet-nam. Now I knew better. I made a vow then, which I have kept, that I would use everything I know in behalf of women's libera-tion. And what I know is this: I know what men are like. I know what intercourse is like. And I know what it means to be bat-tered by a man drunk on testosterone and obsessed with his penis."

*He's being so condescending*

——————————

It is impossible to meet Andrea Dworkin and not be impressed with her intelligence, sincerity, and surprisingly gentle nature. But does she really know what she thinks she knows? *Is* there something pathological about the human penis? Can a tendency toward aggressive, antisocial behavior be measured in that organ? Is there a physical difference between the penis of a sex offender and the penis of a normal man? Do they respond differently to the same stimuli? Can a rapist's penis be reprogrammed? And if there is no difference, does that mean, as some feminists say, that *all* men are potential rapists? At the same time Dworkin was writing her books, scientists were doing equally controversial experiments trying to address those very questions.

This search began with the invention of a machine that some call "the penile lie detector." Its scientific name is the penile plethysmograph, the second word derived from two Greek words: *plethysmos,* meaning "enlargement," and *graphos,* from the root word meaning "to write." The inventor was Kurt Freund, a Czech psychiatrist who announced his new device to the English-speaking scientific community in 1965.

"The availability of an objective method to determine the objects of arousal in the male is of considerable importance [as a diagnostic tool] for research," Freund wrote in the *Journal of the Experimental Analysis of Behavior.* "[My] method is based on the measurement of volume changes in the male genital while the patient is viewing . . . possible erotic objects on the screen, . . . photos of nude men, women, and children of either sex." Freund was trying to understand deviant male sexuality by measuring it.

His invention was a glass tube shaped like an oversized condom, which was placed over a man's flaccid penis, filled with air, then sealed with a rubber cuff and an ominous-sounding "locknut." This apparatus was linked by electric wires to a machine configured to measure changes in the air volume inside the glass. The examination went like this: attach the subject to the penile plethysmograph, show the subject the suggestive pictures or reading material, give him a few moments to respond, measure the displaced air. "A stiff prick has no conscience," Norman Mailer once wrote. Dr. Freund was saying Mailer was even smarter than he realized.

That's because a pedophile *is* likely to have a conscience—enough of one to deny his pedophilia. As a psychiatrist told the *New York Times* in Freund's 1996 obituary, "The problem [addressed by the penile plethysmograph] is that people are not going to tell the truth. If someone is charged with approaching a child, they don't have much motivation to say, 'Yes, I did it. And, moreover, I'm more attracted to children than to adults.'" Like George Washington, a stiff prick cannot tell a lie. (Or can it?)

This may sound like a modern update of the Inquisition, when a strange growth on a fifteenth-century woman's body was used to prove she had been sexually intimate with Satan. But Freund was no Inquisitor. Frustrated with the subjectivity of standard research into deviant sexuality, which often relied on case histories, he was looking for a more objective way of measuring and, he hoped, preventing such behavior, especially the sexual abuse of children. Unfortunately for Freund, he was living in a communist country where military service was compulsory, and many Czech men, the government suspected, were falsely claiming to be homosexual to avoid conscription. Soon after Freund invented his machine* he was forced by the Czech government to use it to weed out malingerers. Freund was also compelled to use his invention to "cure" genuine homosexuals via aversion therapy—giving the patient an electric shock whenever the plethysmograph showed he was responding to men. This experience led Freund to become one of the first psychiatrists to conclude that homosexuality is neither a pathological condition requiring treatment nor a crime worthy of punishment.

In 1968 Freund fled Czechoslovakia, eventually settling in

---

*A simpler device, using a mercury strain gauge inside a stretchable band wrapped around the subject's penis, was invented in 1966 by Dr. John Bancroft, now head of the Kinsey Institute, in Indiana. Freund's device measured changes in penile volume; Bancroft's calibrated changes in penile circumference.

Toronto. Much of his research there was on pedophiles. But a significant portion of Freund's work from that point on was focused—along with his plethysmograph—on a subject of great interest to Andrea Dworkin and Susan Brownmiller: men who use their penis as a weapon against women. Throughout the next two decades, professional journals in psychiatry and criminal justice were filled with articles such as "Penile Responses of Rapists and Non-rapists to Rape Stimuli Involving Physical Violence or Humiliation," "The Measurement and Generation of Sexual Arousal in Male Deviates," and "Differentiating Sexual Aggressiveness with Penile Measures." All of these studies used a penile plethysmograph, either Freund's or Bancroft's, but that was about the only thing they agreed on. Some found a high correlation between violent sexual stimuli and penile erection in rapists that was not produced in nonrapists; others could not find a statistically significant phallometric difference between those two groups at all.

In one controversial study, UCLA psychologist Neil Malamuth had male college students, none of whom had ever been arrested for a sex crime, read accounts of two sexual encounters, one consensual, the other coerced. The students were asked to give a written response to what they read, then they were hooked up to a plethysmograph and asked to read the same accounts again. In their written reports, the students claimed to be far more turned on by the consensual encounter. But the readings on the plethysmograph showed they were equally turned on by the rape. This finding was trumpeted by some feminists to prove that all men, no matter what they say in polite company, have a propensity for sexual violence.

But scientists without a political agenda to advance—including, eventually, Malamuth himself—noted that such tests do not establish a link between arousal and behavior and therefore have no predictive significance. It is, after all, the behavior that is the crime, not the arousal, some of which can be attributed to unconscious fantasies that a wired-up man, no matter how large his erection might get during the experiment, would never act out in real life. It is also relevant to note that nearly all the phallometric experiments in the scientific literature took place in prison, an environment raising two serious validity issues: first, it is by definition a place inhabited by men who have already demonstrated a lack of self-control; second, it is occupied by men with little (or no) exposure to heterosexual stimulation at all—therefore any depiction of women and sex, coerced or not, would be likely to raise an erection.

For reasons such as this, evidence from the so-called penile lie detector, just like the "real" one, the polygraph, is not admissible in court. In a 1993 case covered by the *Wall Street Journal*, a police officer in Maine lost his job, and then successfully sued to get it back, when he refused to submit to a penile plethysmograph after he was accused—falsely, it turned out—of taking part in a sex orgy with local teenagers. The officer refused the test not on Fifth Amendment grounds, but because he found the methodology "disgusting."

Perhaps the suspect would have been less repulsed had he been aware of the Association for the Treatment of Sexual Abusers' "Guidelines for the Use of the Penile Plethysmograph," then (and still) in effect. Among the organization's recommendations:

The client should attach his own gauge in private, at midshaft of the penis.

Client space must be separated form the clinician's work area by at least an opaque wall, which is a minimum of seven feet high. A stationary wall is preferred.

A disposable cover on the chair seat is required for each client.

Gauges will be disinfected prior to use.

Disgusting or not, disinfected or not, reliable or not, the penile plethysmograph continues to be used in some psychiatric hospitals to screen out "potential" pedophiles from easy access to minors. It is also used in behavior-modification centers that employ aversion therapy to rehabilitate sex offenders. Just as Kurt Freund was ordered to do with homosexuals by the Czech government, these centers use electric shocks or other unpleasant sensations to treat patients who, according to the plethysmograph, respond to inappropriate sexual stimuli with an erection. The long-term success rate of such treatment is, like the penile plethysmograph itself, a matter of some controversy.

---

Even if a plethysmograph cannot predict who will become a rapist—or cure one—the fact that rape is nearly always male-against-female suggests that the sexes have different libidos, a dissimilarity that may have influenced the size of the penis that the plethysmograph was created to measure. Should sexual conflict, then, be recognized as something that contributes to evolution just as surely as the usual suspects—climate, landscape, vegetation, and so on? Several years ago a geneticist decided to test the idea that one's environment includes the sexual behavior of the opposite sex. If the erotic activities of males affect the evolution of females, and vice versa, William Rice thought, there should be a way to prove it with the geneticist's favorite guinea pig—the fruit fly.

Exploiting that species's short life span, which enables a scientist to breed many generations (and see many mutations) in just months, Professor Rice used genetic engineering—*un*natural selection—to breed "superfly" males exhibiting a hyperaggressive sexuality. These little tough guys totally dominated normal males, denying them access to female flies, who were similarly intimidated. These supermales were so ultramacho, in fact, they often fathered only males. They thus became the fittest of the fit—re-creating themselves abundantly in subsequent generations—while killing most of the females in the process.

This happened because of a peculiar aspect of fruit fly semen which, even under normal circumstances, is slightly toxic. Evolution has enabled female flies to cope with standard toxicity levels. But the levels reached by Rice's superstuds were way beyond—and, equally important, arrived at much faster—than anything those females could adapt to in so short a time. So they died, Rice reported, like flies. This experiment, as Deborah Blum notes in her book *Sex on the Brain,* reminds us that males and females do not necessarily work as partners, even when coming together to reproduce. Feminists may be happy to know there are "superfemales" in the insect world who flaunt a similarly imposing superiority. During copulation, the female biting midge (*Johannseniella nitida*) traps the male inside her. Then, after he releases his sperm, she eats him—except for his penis—which remains packed in her genital opening to facilitate fertilization.

We are not biting midges, thank God. Nor, of course, are we fruit flies. But Professor Rice's research with that second species raises some intriguing questions: Is there anything in or about human semen that tells us something about *our* sexual behavior? Or male aggression? Is it possible that it is in sperm, a substance produced exclusively by male genitalia, that the penis's true "pathological" nature is revealed?

Fascinating answers to those questions were proposed by British scientists R. Robin Baker and Mark A. Bellis in their book *Human Sperm Competition: Copulation, Masturbation and Infidelity,* published in 1995. The authors' interest in the subject emerged from one of biology's great mysteries: Why is it that during copulation the human penis expels enough sperm—about 350 million—to theoretically fertilize every woman in the United States twice? Their answer is "sperm competition," a theory that says the sperm of one man must be prepared to do battle with the sperm of another inside a woman's vagina because of the real possibility that she has "double-mated." By that term Baker and Bellis mean that the female had unprotected sex with another man within ten days, the outer limit of a sperm's fertility, in the same reproductive cycle. Evolution, the

[handwritten margin note: Notice he doesn't say thank God about the species in which the female is killed]

authors suggest, has selected all sperm cells, and the entire penis, to fight that battle—a conflict that requires a huge army of sperm with specially trained "soldiers" for different aspects of combat.

Based on a sex survey done by a British women's magazine, Baker and Bellis guessed that between 4 and 12 percent of British children are conceived to a sperm that prevailed over rivals from another male. The idea of sperm competition was conceived in 1970 by British scientist Geoffrey Parker, who was studying the sex lives of insects. Baker and Bellis's highly controversial contribution was to declare that Parker's theory unequivocally applies to humans.*

Along with the quantity of sperm in human ejaculate, the authors' investigation was prompted by the equally impressive variety of shapes exhibited by those cells. The man on the street may think all human spermatozoa resemble tiny tadpoles, each with an oval head at one end, a midpiece, and a long tail at the other end. But Baker and Bellis identified at least eight different types of sperm head, four types of tail, and two types of midpiece, with many variations among those types, not to mention in size. Why such variety? is a question that has many scientists scratching their heads. Baker and Bellis were also intrigued by a related question: Why do so many of those sperm cells appear to be "mistakes"?—that is, sperm with misshapen heads and/or tails.

The conventional wisdom starts its answer to that second question by noting that sperm are difficult to produce. The manufacturing process, which takes almost eleven weeks, starts in

---

*Some would argue that the existence of sperm competition in humans—and the "winners" and "losers" produced by it—was confirmed by a study done by the American Association of Blood Banks. The organization reported that 280,000 paternity tests were done in the United States in 1999. In 28 percent of them, the man tested was found not to be the father. One must keep in mind, however, that such tests are not likely to be done unless there is doubt about paternity in the first place.

the seminiferous tubules inside the testes—the same ones described by Regnier de Graaf in 1668—where the sperm head is made, and then moves to the epididymis, a commalike structure adjoining each testicle where the sperm cells slowly mature, gaining motility and the biochemical properties necessary to fertilize an egg. The optimal temperature for sperm-cell manufacture is three or four degrees lower than the rest of the human body. This is why testicles are enclosed outside the body in the scrotum, stored in a cool, dark place, just as you might read on a warning label.

Unfortunately, natural selection is not so powerful as to make that assembly line totally efficient, no matter what the temperature. Like birth defects in humans, developmental errors in sperm—sperm with misshapen bodies—are inevitable, says the conventional wisdom, which is one reason we emit so many: the greater the number, the greater the chance of having more perfect sperm in that ejaculate, swimming next to all those mistakes.

But Baker and Bellis say it is wrong to think of those "mistakes" as mistakes. They argue in their controversial "Kamikaze Sperm Hypothesis" that the great variation in size and shape of human sperm cells reflects a brilliant division of labor. Some sperm cells, usually the younger well-formed ones with large heads, are "egg getters"; others are "kamikaze sperm," whose job is to block sperm from other men, or "seek-and-destroyers," whose function is to disable a rival's sperm by spearing them in the head, then injecting a tiny dose of acrosomal enzyme, the same substance used by the successful egg getter to melt the membranes surrounding the female egg.

Sperm competition not only affects the amount of sperm in an ejaculation—more if the male intuitively suspects the presence of another man's sperm, less if he does not—but the types of sperm inside that ejaculation. If competition is likely, the more likely it is there will be more kamikazes. The authors speculate the purpose of masturbation by males is to maximize the number of young, fit, egg-getting sperm available for the next competition. A typical man has 2 to 3 billion sperm cells in production at any given moment. Roughly 300 million finished cells emerge from that assembly line every day. Some of them could grow old and weak waiting to be used. Those who saw Woody Allen's *Everything You Always Wanted to Know About Sex (But Were Afraid to Ask)* will no doubt recall his depiction of sperm cells, sitting like anxious paratroopers in an airplane.

Baker and Bellis argue that women double-mate to promote sperm competition, so that their sons will inherit the ability to make victorious sperm from their victorious-sperm-making fathers. In this view, women are not being promiscuous; they are being genetic entrepreneurs. The authors speculate that the purpose of the female orgasm, as well as "flowback," the process in which a woman expels some of the semen a man has just ejaculated in her, is to influence that competition. This influence occurs because the orgasm helps to retain, and flowback discards, some or all of the sperm that a woman is rooting for or against.

The male, of course, is never a bystander in sperm competition. Baker and Bellis propose that, along with the makeup of his sperm, something else has evolved to help him get an edge over his rivals—the very shape of his penis and the way he likes to use it. Other biologists have pointed to the length of the shaft and the weight of human testicles as evidence of natural selection at work. Baker and Bellis add three more items to that list: the hefty girth of the human penis (thicker than any primate, including the much larger gorilla and orangutan); its large smooth, acorn-shaped head; and the repetitive, plunging fashion in which men use it during intercourse.

To see the evolutionary advantages of these adaptations, we must look at other mammals. The penis of a male rat, after copulating with a female, ejects a substance into her reproductive tract that coagulates into a hard plug. The point of this is to emerge as the undisputed champion in sperm competition. The plug is designed to ensure the plugger's sperm are the only ones in play. Other male rats are aware of this, of course, so before any self-respecting male rat starts copulating with a female, he checks to see if she is carrying a plug. If not, no problem. If she is, he tries to remove it with a series of rapid, spearing thrusts with his penis, which is equipped with tiny spines for this very purpose, after which he withdraws without ejaculating. If this exercise is successful, he removes the plug from his penis, grooms his organ, then gets busy on his own behalf—after which he leaves behind his own plug. According to one study, rats are successful at unplugging another rat's plug nearly 70 percent of the time.

Baker and Bellis hypothesize that current human males evolved from an ancestral anthropoid primate that left behind a soft plug in the vagina of his female partners, a situation with far-reaching consequences for the human penis and human sexuality as a whole, for better and worse. It explains, they said, why the penis shaft is shaped like a piston, straight and thick, topped by a smooth, acorn-shaped glans—and why men are so eager to start thrusting with that device once inside a woman's vagina, whether that thrusting stimulates a woman's clitoris or not. That repetitive motion, the authors write, was not designed to bring about female pleasure. It was intended to remove a competitor's soft plug and now functions as a pistonlike "push-pull-suck-push-pull-scape" mechanism—their words, not mine —to remove competing sperm.

"Backward and forward thrusting of the penis during copulation," Baker and Bellis write, "combined with the [long, thick] shape of the penis in a distended vagina

> should successfully remove a major part of any soft copulatory plug or liquid seminal pool [left by another man]. The shape of the glans seems perfectly adapted to such a push-pull-suck-push-pull-scape function. Depending on the suction pressure that the thrusting penis can generate,

the penis may even successfully remove the older part of the cervical mucus column along with any contained sperm.

In this way of looking at human sexuality men *do* use their penis as a "battering ram." But not out of misogyny or to exercise domination. Rather, to advance their own evolutionary agenda, just as women act to further theirs. The battle of the sexes is real, Baker and Bellis say, and the penis is a major participant in that war. Politics, however, has nothing to do with it.

———————

It would be stretching things to say *Human Sperm Competition* has met with universal acclaim. "An important part of scientific progress is the generation of new ideas, especially in relatively new areas of research. In this respect, Baker and Bellis have been eminently successful," biologist T. R. Birkhead wrote in *Trends in Ecology and Evolution*. But "scientific progress is made only when ideas are fully tested. . . . All that was required [of Baker and Bellis] was a clear statement that [their] claims are not facts, but ideas. . . ." By not saying this, "they have misled the public on a grand scale."

A similar charge was made against Andrew Sullivan, former editor of the *New Republic,* after he wrote about his experiences with male-hormone therapy—part of his treatment for HIV infection—in a *New York Times Magazine* cover story headlined, "Why Men Are Different: The Defining Power of Testosterone." For Sullivan, testosterone shots were nothing less than rocket fuel, supercharging his sex drive, muscle mass, energy level, confidence, competitiveness, impulsiveness, and propensity for violent confrontation, the last of which, he wrote, led to a vein-bulging encounter with a fellow dog walker who had the temerity to criticize Sullivan for smacking his own pooch after she ate a discarded chicken bone found on a Washington street. Seconds after his judgment was challenged, and only minutes after his last testosterone shot, Sullivan was in his accuser's face, threatening to pummel him in what would have been, he wrote, "the first public brawl of my life."

Such aggression may explain why Adolf Hitler was a huge believer in testosterone shots. It is quite possible, in fact, that *Der Führer* was one of the first men in the world to get such injections. Though it was roughly nine thousand years ago that man learned he could calm a surly bull (and, several millennia later, cause similarly eye-opening changes in a human) by cutting off his testicles, it was not until 1935 that teams of scientists, each financed by rival drug companies (one of them in Hitler's Berlin), fully understood why. The first step in this process occurred in 1931 when German chemist Adolph Butenandt, backed by the Schering-Kahlbaum (now Schering-Plough) Corporation, isolated a tiny amount of androtesterone, a nontesticular male hormone, from fifteen thousand liters of boiled-down urine from German policemen. In May 1935, a Dutch team sponsored by Organon, using ground-up mice testicles, was the first to describe the molecular structure and give a name to the substance we now call testosterone. In August of that same year, two years into Hitler's "Thousand Year Reich," Butenandt informed a German scientific journal—and maybe *Der Führer*, too—that he had discovered a method of preparing testosterone from cholesterol. A week later, another journal received a nearly identical paper from Leopold Ruzicka, a Croatian working in Zürich for the Ciba Corporation. In 1939 Butenandt and Ruzicka shared the Nobel Prize for Chemistry.

In his *Times* piece, Sullivan conceded that culture and socialization have a significant impact on male behavior. But he gave the lion's share of the credit, and a roaring lion at that, to testosterone, a hormone that aids muscle growth, helps to manufacture red blood cells, and carries messages to the brain, where special receptors read them. These messages are responsible for many of the attitudes and behaviors we consider "male," such as aggressiveness, self-confidence, impulsiveness, dominance, risk-taking, physical intimidation, and violence, up to and including rape and murder. It should come as no surprise, Sullivan suggested, that inner-city males, a group occupying most of the cells in our nation's prisons and responsible for much of our country's "illegitimate" births, generally have higher testosterone levels than young male suburbanites who are not incarcerated.

That women show confidence, take risks, can be impulsive, and commit violent crimes only reminds us that they too produce testosterone. Women make the substance in their adrenal glands and ovaries; nearly all the testosterone in men is made by the testes. Either way, there isn't much there. A typical man has about 60 millionths of an ounce in his body at any given time. That level fluctuates throughout the day—higher in the morning than in the evening—and begins a steady decline after age forty. By the time a man turns eighty, his serum testosterone level might be half what it once was. A woman has around 6 millionths of an ounce of the substance inside her, a level that also drops over time.

The fact that women make testosterone at all came as a great shock to those who assumed its discovery meant that scientists had finally found the pure, unadulterated, biological essence of masculinity. That assumption, after all, was at the cutting edge of modern biology in the early twentieth century. But, beginning in the late 1920s, European biochemists found incontrovertible evidence of "female" secretions in healthy, normal males, and vice versa. A 1929 article in the *Journal of the American Medical Association* found these discoveries "disquieting." It is unlikely, however, that anyone was more disquieted than Eugen Steinach, the director of the Biological Institute of the Viennese Academy of Sciences.

In a series of odd, gender-bending experiments that began in 1895 and continued for several decades, Steinach, a friend and colleague of Sigmund Freud's, tried to prove his theory of "sex hormone antagonism," which held that male and female gonads secrete utterly opposite, totally antagonistic substances. To demonstrate this idea, Steinach transplanted male organs into female lab animals, and vice versa. In one experiment, Steinach removed the testicles of a rat and replaced them with ovaries. Then he compared the growth rate of this rat's penis with another rat who only had his testicles removed. The first rat's penis, Steinach reported in 1912, shrunk under the influence of the female organs until it was smaller than the penis of the rat eunuch. Two decades later, however, subsequent discoveries rendered the "sex hormone antagonism" theory untenable.

Before that happened, however, Steinach's "successful" experiment with mice led him to experiment with a cure for homosexuality. Convinced that the testicles of homosexuals were made defective by the presence of "F-cells"—F for "feminine"—Steinach had a surgeon remove one testicle each from seven homosexual men, implanting in its place an undescended testicle from seven heterosexuals. Afterward, the "improved" homosexuals, Steinach reported, were attracted to women for the first time in their lives. As time went on, however, this "Steinach Procedure" showed itself to be just as falsely effective as the other one—except as an equally potent testament to the power of the placebo effect. In 1923 Steinach abandoned his gender-identity experiments.*

The paean to testosterone-defined masculinity in the *Times Magazine* and the criticism it engendered are relevant to our discussion of the "politicized" penis because many of the article's conclusions about male behavior echo those reached by feminists. The personal is political, these women insist, using the dominant-submissive, penetrator-penetrated model of intercourse to illustrate their point. Some feminists go further. Man's oppression of woman isn't merely political, they say. It is pathological. Andrea Dworkin's inquiry into man's diseased nature

---

*Steinach also believed, wrongly, that a vasectomy could rejuvenate a man's libido and sexual potency. Among the many patients who underwent this "Steinach Procedure" were Sigmund Freud and William Butler Yeats.

focused on the erect penis. Andrew Sullivan's article suggests she might have been better off looking slightly lower, at the testes.

Is it possible that feminists could learn all they need to know about sexual politics, as practiced by men, by studying testosterone—a substance that by itself does not create an erect penis but boosts the sex drive that, in men, ends up as one? Biologist Ben Greenstein, author of *The Fragile Male*, certainly thinks so.

> Men exercise seemingly absolute power over the lives of women . . . to the point [where some women] suffer crippling violence [from men], in silence. . . . What gave man this edge? How was he able to establish and maintain for so long an absolute supremacy over women? The answer is not to be found in arguments about power structures, politics, or sociologically based theories but in the human body. The plight of women can be ascribed to a single chemical, . . . testosterone.

If true, this is hardly cause for hope in men or women. But is the link between testosterone and aggressive male behavior, especially criminal behavior against women, as clear as Greenstein, Sullivan—and even Adolf Hitler—think it is?

Studies by biologists, psychologists, and criminologists in peer-reviewed journals bring a cloud of conflicting results to that question. One of the most prolific researchers in this field is James M. Dabbs, professor of social psychology at Georgia State University, coauthor (with his wife Mary) of *Heroes, Rogues, and Lovers: Testosterone and Behavior*, and the principal investigator in dozens of scholarly articles on that hormone, a life's work that has prompted the *New York Times* to say of him, "Professor Dabbs is to testosterone what Oliver Sacks is to madness. Champion. Iconoclast. Philosopher. Friend."

Yes, Dabbs says, testosterone levels are generally higher in physically imposing, aggressive, highly competitive men, the kind said to be "macho." But, after two decades of trying, Dabbs reports, no one has been able to distinguish criminals from noncriminals by their testosterone levels. In his study "Testosterone, Crime and Misbehavior Among 692 Male Prison Inmates," Dabbs and his coauthors found that murderers in a Georgia penitentiary tended to have higher T levels than embezzlers, and that prisoners with higher levels got into more scrapes with guards and other inmates. So far so good for those who believe in the "testosterone poisoning" theory. But Dabbs also found that the readings for *all* of the felons, violent or not, were in the same normal range as levels found outside the prison in successful, law-abiding citizens. If testosterone is poison, there are a lot of men who are immune.

In the early 1980s, psychologist Robert Prentky received a grant from the National Institute of Justice to write "The Neurochemistry and Neuroendocrinology of Sexual Aggression." Prentky's aim was to find a causal link, if one existed, between testosterone and rape. His report anticipated the blurry results found later by Dabbs. Yes, most violent rapists tested by Prentky had high T levels—the highest in his study came from the only rapist who killed his victim. But the overall levels found by Prentky among rapists were, just like Dabbs's prisoners, the same found in the overall male population in the United States. Two years later the link thought by many to exist between high T levels and violent crime took an eye-opening blow in the *British Journal of Psychiatry,* where researchers reported on two unusual criminals. One had been castrated years before he committed his crime. The other had Klinefelter's syndrome, a genetic disorder whose symptoms include smallness of testes and a correspondingly low level of androgen production. Yet these two testosterone-deprived men were each incarcerated for a sexually motivated murder.

Days after Sullivan's piece on testosterone appeared, it was challenged in *Slate,* an Internet magazine, for overstating its case in two ways. However true Sullivan's experiences were for him, Judith Shulevitz wrote, they established no truths about the hormone's impact on anyone else. She also criticized Sullivan's reading of evidence that, to him, suggested a link between testosterone and violent behavior. Even if such links can be demonstrated statistically, Shulevitz added, they establish a correlation—but not causality. In saying this, Shulevitz was echoing Robert M. Sapolsky, professor of biology and neuroscience at Stanford University (and 1987 winner of the MacArthur Foundation "genius grant"), who made the same point in *The Trouble with Testosterone,* his book on the biology of the human predicament.

"Suppose you note a correlation between levels of aggression and levels of testosterone among normal males," Sapolsky wrote. "This could be because . . .

(*a*) testosterone elevates aggression; (*b*) aggression elevates testosterone secretion; (*c*) neither causes the other. There's a huge bias to assume option *a,* but *b* is the answer. Study after study has shown that when you examine testosterone levels when males are first placed together in a social group, testosterone levels predict nothing about who is going to be aggressive. The subsequent behavioral differences drive the hormonal changes, rather than the other way round.

The elevated T levels found in inner-city males are not the cause of the violence in their lives. It is the violence that causes the rise in their testosterone levels. Getting a hiccup in testosterone is not what makes a guy go postal—or, for that matter, pick a fight with a stranger at the neighborhood dog run. If Sullivan really wants to understand why that happened, Sapolsky urges him to look in the mirror. "Testosterone doesn't cause aggression," he wrote. "It exaggerates the aggression that's already there."

So we cannot say testosterone creates violence in men. What we can say, though, and without any fear of contradiction, is that testosterone creates the organ that many men refer to as their manhood, the same organ many feminists liken to a battering ram. That, of course, would be the penis.

For the first eight weeks after conception the human embryo is neither male nor female. It has gonads and tissue called the genital ridge, but they are of no particular sex—just a "blob of cells," science writer Deborah Blum calls them, "with unlimited potential." There are also two ducts in that embryo—Wolffian (male) and Muellerian (female)—existing in a state of pregendered readiness, waiting to go to work. If the embryo has a Y chromosome (XX = female, XY = male), a gene issues a call for testosterone, which is when the construction site comes alive. The gonadal blobs turn into testes, where cells called Leydig cells start producing testosterone, which serves as site foreman. Testosterone causes an expansion of the Wolffian duct, which produces the epididymis, vas deferens, and seminal vesicles. The penis shaft and the acorn-shaped glans sitting at its top emerge from the genital ridge once some of the testosterone in the embryo is converted into a closely related, even more job-specific hormone called dihydrotestosterone.*

While all this is happening, other cells inside the testes—the Sertoli cells—emit a misogynistic hormone called Muellerian inhibiting factor (MIF), which causes the female ductwork, still on standby, to disappear. There's no union job security on this work site. But feminists will be happy to know that a very similar thing happens to the Wolffian duct if the embryo is XX. In fact, if no

---

*It is the lasting impact of this prenatal testosterone, it seems, that made it impossible for David Reimer, a boy raised as a girl after his penis was surgically removed after a botched circumcision, to successfully live as a girl—no matter how many dresses or dolls he was given. Reimer's story is told in *As Nature Made Him,* by John Colapinto.

call for testosterone goes out, *nothing* happens in the eighth week. With no testes pumping out male hormones, the gonads automatically evolve five weeks later into the ovaries, the genital ridge becomes the clitoris and labia, the Muellerian ducts become the uterus, Fallopian tubes, and upper part of the vagina. The Wolffian ducts vanish. To borrow a phrase from the digital world, the human embryo's default setting is female.

What this teaches us is that, even more than chromosomes, it is the hormone environment in the womb that determines the sex of the fetus. In the animal kingdom, it also determines what we humans might call sexual "attitude," occasionally in rather bizarre ways. Certainly the most famous example of this is the female spotted hyena (*Crocuta crocuta*). To mix an animal metaphor, this is one hyena you want in your foxhole—as long as she's on your side. In Africa it is not unusual to see a hyena, no bigger than a large dog, attack a wildebeest five times its size. A pack of them will eat an antelope in less than an hour, leaving behind only hooves and antlers. What is unusual about all this is that the largest and most aggressive of the spotted hyenas— the ones leading the hunt and the feeding frenzy—are the females.

The odd gender situation among hyenas is a testament to the power of evolution—and testosterone—working in tandem. The blood circulating in a female hyena contains a large amount of androstenedione, the same substance baseball player Mark McGwire took in 1998, the year he broke the sport's single-season record for home runs. During a hyena's pregnancy, "andro," as McGwire called it, is converted by the placenta into testosterone (as it was in his body too except not by a placenta). Thus every hyena fetus, male and female, is exposed to that hormone during gestation. The result is "the most aggressive infant animals known to science," Robert Pool writes in *Eve's Rib*, infants that often maim or kill their siblings, apparently just because they can. Because males leave the natal clan when they reach two years of age, that clan is dominated by females who fight among themselves to establish a pecking order, a struggle that, thanks to evolution, has made female hyenas larger and stronger than hyena males, who do not participate in that status war. As a result, females, no matter what their status inside the clan, dominate each male hyena who returns to mate.

It is in the context of mating that things in the hyena world really turn strange. Because of that long testosterone bath in her mother's womb, the sex organ of the female hyena is not exactly what you would call feminine. It is a hollow cylinder that grows out from her body, assuming the identical length, width, and shape of the penis on the male hyena. This makes intercourse for hyenas no laughing matter. First the female, using muscles that exist specifically for this job, must retract her "penis" and draw it into her abdomen in a manner not unlike what we do when we turn our socks inside out. This forms a somewhat smallish vaginal opening into which the lucky male must try to maneuver *his* penis—no easy feat, according to zoologists who have watched inexperienced males trying to do it. Females give birth through their "penis" as well, which must stretch a considerable amount to accommodate the emerging pups. Amazingly, hyena cubs are patiently mothered and nurtured by the same female who dominates and/or terrorizes all the males in the pack and, in the past, probably killed several of the siblings she herself was born with.

---

It is unlikely the lifestyle of the female hyena will shock Andrew Sullivan. After all, his own experience with testosterone shots has convinced him of that substance's irresistible power to foster aggression in humans. It is fascinating to note that, a century earlier, one of the greatest names in the history of medical science—the first man to analyze the physiology of the spinal cord and, later, one of the founders of modern endocrinology—made a similar well-meaning mistake.

His name was Charles Brown-Séquard. On June 1, 1899, this

seventy-two-year-old scholar, whose teaching career had taken him from Harvard Medical School to the Collège de France, gave a lecture before the Société de Biologie in Paris on some recent experiments he had performed. According to one account of the evening, Brown-Séquard pushed aside his notes and spoke with great animation to his audience, most of whom were his own age. He had injected himself ten times with a remarkable potion, the tall, bearded scientist told his listeners. This substance, which had been filtered through paper, he said, contained "a small quantity of water mixed with . . .

first, blood of the testicular veins; secondly, semen; and thirdly, juice extracted from the testicle, crushed immediately after it was taken from a . . . healthy young dog [the source of the testicular veins and semen, as well].

No doubt this, in and of itself, was enough to shock Brown-Séquard's audience. But, like any good showman, Brown-Séquard had prepared a finale. The injections had improved his energy levels for work, he said. His ability to run up stairs had returned. He no longer suffered from constipation. Even the arc and force of his urinary stream had shown a marked improvement. But, best of all, Brown-Séquard said, after ten shots of ground-up dog testicles, coming after ten years of involuntary abstinence with his much younger wife, the professor had been able—just that very morning—to retake his proper place as his wife's fully functioning husband. In bed.

Normally, the French press paid little attention to the goings-on at the Société. But this story was too big to ignore. After a report appeared in *Le Matin*, a "geriatric horde" descended on Brown-Séquard's laboratory at the Collège de France, demanding that he share his miracle potency-restoring elixir with them. If the public was convinced, along with Brown-Séquard, that the professor had found the sexual fountain of youth, the professor's peers were far more skeptical. A scientific journal in Vienna described Brown-Séquard's claim as "proof of the necessity of retiring professors who have attained their three score and ten years."

Other scientists tried to reproduce Brown-Séquard's results but could not. A century later we know why. Even if the substance in those dog testicles—testosterone—had the miraculous rejuvenating qualities Brown-Séquard said they did, which they do not, there is no way he could have experienced them. This can be said without fear of contradiction because one thing scientists learned when they did isolate testosterone in 1935 is that it is not water soluble.

Brown-Séquard's mistake reminds us of the power of the mind to convince the body of what the mind believes. Still, the practice of self-experimentation, especially via self-injection, has a long and splendid history in medical science. Only two decades ago a very famous self-injection helped usher in what may be the final chapter in the history of man's relationship with his penis. After five thousand years of asking, "Who's in charge here—him or me?"—man has finally found the power, through chemistry, to answer, "I am."

# VI

## The Punctureproof Balloon

Farther down the Strip, Siegfried and Roy were making a tiger vanish into thin air, Sammy Davis Jr. was belting "I Gotta Be Me," and two circus aerialists—one sitting on the other's shoulders—walked fifty yards of tightrope without a net. But even in Vegas they'd never seen a show like this.

The year was 1983, the showman a complete novice. But this was no Open Mike Night. The person on stage, a Briton named Giles Brindley, was a professional—a physician, in fact. The Nevada desert was blooming with conventioneers and Dr. Brindley was in town to address several thousand members of the American Urological Association. That's a hall full of men who examine prostates for a living. In Vegas they call this a tough room. Even so, Brindley wasn't nervous. He had presented numerous papers at scientific meetings like this in Europe, where his reputation for original research, especially in bioengineering, was legendary. In 1964 Brindley invented the world's first visual prosthesis. Three pairs of electronic eyes were implanted in human volunteers before the project was terminated because of high costs and low effectiveness. Still, Brindley's design concept impressed his peers as a major theoretical breakthrough, perhaps a work of genius. Unusual physiological questions had always piqued Brindley's curiosity. Once, while traveling in a car, he dropped a rabbit from the roof to the floor whenever the auto made a sharp turn. Brindley wanted to see how centrifugal force affected the creature's ability to land on its feet. The car, it should be noted, was moving nearly eighty miles per hour at the time.

On this particular night in Nevada, Brindley was standing still behind a podium. Lately he had been concentrating on physiological problems of the male human. The buzz from London was intriguing. Brindley, who begged off speaking at a similar conference months earlier because of pressing research, was rumored to be experimenting with drugs that produced an eye-opening result: when injected in the penis they created an erection that lasted for hours. This supposedly had occurred in men who were impotent for decades, even in men who were paralyzed. If Brindley had really done this, he had solved a physiological mystery that had been unsolved for thousands of years. But the full significance was even greater. If true, Brindley's feat did more than stretch the limits of being a medical man. It stretched the limits of being a man.

Impotence had only recently become a serious subject of inquiry for urologists. For much of the previous century, they had waged a halfhearted, and ultimately unsuccessful, struggle with psychiatrists for primacy in the field of male sexual functioning. After Freud, impotence was seen by most patients and healers as a mental problem. This was fine with most urologists, who were happy to specialize in removing stones, treating incontinence, and shrinking swollen prostates. In the 1970s, however, technical advances gave these surgeons new impotence therapies that, while extreme, actually worked. One was the inflatable penile implant. The other was revascularization, a procedure that rewired the arteries through which blood enters the penis in an operation not unlike a heart bypass.

In 1983 rumors of Brindley's drug experiments provoked skepticism among doctors committed to those new treatments. One urologist approached Brindley at the Las Vegas convention and challenged him to prove his drug therapy's effectiveness beyond charts, tables, and graphs. Brindley, a former competitive athlete, decided to do just that. The result was perhaps the most memorable public moment in all of modern medicine. After calmly presenting his data from behind the podium, Brindley stepped in front of it and pulled down his pants. Moments earlier, you see, he had gone to the men's room and secretly injected *himself*. And now, before a room full of strangers, there it was: the, uh, "evidence."

The audience gasped. Brindley did not want the urologists to think he was fooling them with a silicone prosthesis, so he headed into the crowd, proof in hand, and asked them to inspect it. "I had been wondering why Brindley was wearing sweatpants," says Dr. Arnold Melman, chief of urology at New York's Albert Einstein College of Medicine, who was there. "Suddenly I knew." Some urologists accepted Brindley's offer, slipping on their eyeglasses to get a better look. Never before had so many penis doctors seen another man's erect penis. And in this singular moment, human sexuality, the healing profession, and man's relationship with his penis underwent a huge transformation, the consequences of which are still being felt today.

This is because Brindley did more than give new meaning to the term scientific presentation. He gave birth to the newest idea of the penis: a totally medicalized organ stripped of its psychic significance and mystery and transformed into a tiny network of blood vessels, neurotransmitters, and smooth-muscle tissue knowable only to a credentialed scientist. This white-coated expert sets standards for the organ's size and rigidity against which all erections must be measured, and decrees any variation from that norm is a disease. The organ's intrinsically finicky nature—that constant of human history—has been redefined as a pathology addressable only by drugs and/or surgery.

This penis is impervious to religious teachings, Freudian insights, racial stereotypes, and feminist criticism. It is no longer part of a human dialogue. It is a thing—a virtually punctureproof balloon that can be reinflated at will, no matter how often it has gone flat in the past, or why. Man's testy relationship with his defining organ has been medically pacified. The longest power struggle in every man's life is over, the uncontrollable has been brought to heel, and the ultimate male fantasy has come true: A penis that is hard on demand, potentially hard for hours, and definitely hard enough to satisfy the most demanding women. Maybe even a bunch of them.

Now urologists see erect penises all the time. They create them in their offices, then show patients how to re-create them at home using the drug therapy pioneered by Brindley and others. Transurethral pellets can now achieve the same result without a needle, and, on March 27, 1998, the Food and Drug Administration gave its sanction to Viagra, the first oral agent approved to treat erectile dysfunction (ED). The astonishing medical, social, and commercial success of Pfizer's little pill—Viagra has been taken by nearly 10 million men, producing annual revenue estimated at $1 billion—has led to the rapid expansion of an erection industry.* This commercial alliance of ED specialists and drug manufacturers (the latter hire the former as consultants and supply the funding for nearly all the research done in the field) is now seeking faster, longer-acting, and even more profitable medications, a quest the psychologist and social critic Leonore Tiefer has called "the pursuit of the perfect penis."

The lucrative new therapies developed and marketed by Pfizer and others are covered by the media as a personal-hygiene update for the estimated 30 million Americans who struggle with erectile dysfunction, a number supplied (critics say "fabricated") by the very erection industry that profits from identifying those men as patients. There is no doubt that these erection drugs have helped millions—Viagra works—not to mention the millions more who own drug-company stock. But this coverage misses the larger point. The erection industry is more than just a

*These numbers, from August 2002, do not include those who have purchased Viagra without a prescription, or users from outside the United States.

health or business story. It is the latest, and perhaps final, chapter in the story of man's relationship with his penis.

———————————

The recorded history of impotence treatments is nearly as old as recorded history. Ancient medical texts reveal that not long after man discovered his penis could get hard he began to fret about it staying soft. Respect for the former condition, and fear of the latter, led to numerous cures, many applied to the organ directly. An Egyptian papyrus from around 1700 B.C. recommended the following poultice: "One part leaves of Christ's-thorn; one part leaves of acacia; one part honey. Grind the leaves in this honey and apply [to penis] as bandage." Clay tablets from the Tigris-Euphrates Valley (ninth century B.C.) tell us that Assyrian physicians had their limp patients eat dried lizard and cantharides. That second substance, made from crushed beetles, has an inflammatory effect on a man's genitourinary system that the ancients and not-so-ancients mistook for revived vigor. (Many centuries later Europeans called it Spanish fly.) Those Assyrian healers also urged an impotent man to have a woman rub his penis with a special oil flecked with bits of pulverized iron. For best results it was recommended she do this while chanting "Let this penis be a stick of martu-wood" and "Let this horse make love to me." Apparently the power of positive thinking—and flattery from females—has a long history indeed.

The Hindu *Samhita of Sushruta* (circa 1000 B.C.) mentioned several impotence remedies, most of them to be eaten. "By eating the testes of a he-goat . . . fried in clarified butter prepared from churning milk," the *Samhita* said, "a man is enabled to visit a hundred women one after the other." Early Western cultures also consumed animal testes to restore or improve potency. The Greek physician Nicander (second century B.C.) recommended those obtained from a hippopotamus, a prescription that no doubt required a wealthy client list. It seems there

were many industrious erection entrepreneurs among our ancient ancestors, but the true forefathers of the modern erection
industry are found in the nineteenth century, when some Western urologists devised treatments that today seem (at best) hilar-
ious and (at worst) barbaric. It was not a good time to be an
impotence patient. But it was an excellent time to be a quack.

This was because even well-educated, legitimate doctors did
not understand the physiology of erections very well. Thanks to
pioneers such as Leonardo da Vinci, Ambroise Paré, and Regnier de Graaf they knew an erection was produced by a surge of
blood. But they did not know how that blood got there or what
kept it there once it arrived. The sixteenth-century anatomist
Costanzo Varolio attributed the ability of the penis to rise to
"erector muscles." Most doctors still believed this three centuries later, though the mechanism of those muscles had never
been conclusively demonstrated. It was not until 1863 that German scientist Conrad Eckhard showed the role of the nervous
system in erectile functioning. He did this by applying electric
current to the pelvic nerves of a dog, who responded by becoming erect. "That there is a neurological aspect to the erection
process seems like common sense now," says Dr. Arthur L. Burnett, director of the Male Consultation Clinic at Johns Hopkins
University. "But you have to realize our understanding of erections has gone through a long evolutionary process. It was once
thought that spirits controlled erections and that the penis was
filled with air. Much of our scientific information about erections is less than two hundred years old. A lot of it is less than
twenty years old."

In the nineteenth century this combination of some good information, with lots of bad, led to some bizarre and painful impotence treatments. One of the most honored physicians in
America then was Samuel W. Gross, author of *A Practical Treatise on Impotence, Sterility and Allied Disorders of the Male
Sexual Organs*, published in 1881. Gross was professor of
surgery at Jefferson Medical College in Philadelphia, just as his

father, Samuel D. Gross, had been before him. (The artist Thomas Eakins immortalized both doctors—focusing on the father, from whom he had taken an anatomy class—in his 1875 painting *The Gross Clinic*.)

The younger Gross, like many of his peers, was convinced of the link between erectile failure in intercourse and masturbation. Gross specifically attributed impotence to "strictures" inside the base of the penis, where the urethra is ringed by the prostate gland. These strictures, Gross said, were the result of inflammation and swelling of the prostatic urethra, a condition he called "prostatic hyperaesthesia," caused by self-abuse or involuntary night "pollutions." Gross made this diagnosis by inserting a long, thin, nickel-plated instrument called a bougie down his patient's urethra. As he conceded on page 34 of *A Practical Treatise,* this procedure was not always a pleasant experience for the person bougied.

> Case XIII. A mechanic, twenty-three years of age. . . . Examination with a No. 25 explorer [the bougie] disclosed intense hyperaesthesia of the entire urethra, and particularly of its prostatic portion. . . . As soon as the instrument entered the passage it occasioned tremor and retraction of the testes, and when it reached the prostatic portion [the patient] shrank from the excessive suffering from which it awakened, and the muscles of the lids, nose, and mouth twitched convulsively. On its withdrawal, the bulb [at the tip of the bougie] brought forth a considerable prostatic discharge. [The patient] afterward rode to his home on street cars, and about two hours later, after urinating, was seized with a curious crawling sensation in his arms and legs, lost consciousness, and, when found by his friends, was lying on the floor, his face livid.

Amazingly, this patient returned to Dr. Gross to have his condition treated, which meant several more intimate invasions.

Blasts of hot and cold water were sent down his urethra, a hot rubber plug was jammed into his rectum, and the bougie was reinserted after being dipped in corrosive chemicals.

In cases that still failed to respond, many urologists used a method inspired by Varolio's sixteenth-century anatomical speculations and Eckhard's more recent experiments on dogs: they applied electricity to the (mythical) erector muscles inside the penis. The first step in this procedure required the doctor to insert a twin-pronged metal instrument, shaped like a tiny pitchfork, handle-first into the meatus (pronounced me-ATE-us) of the penis, the place we nonurologists call "the hole." The prongs were connected to a small generator, which was then turned on and off. An illustration in a contemporaneous urology textbook shows the treatment to resemble our current practice of restarting a car battery with jumper cables. Many doctors touting electrotherapy sold the machines providing current to the disabled penis or wrote books extolling the virtues of the treatment. Very few of them lost money at it.

---

You might think impotence therapy couldn't sink lower than penile electroshock or chemically spiked bougies. But you would be wrong. In the early twentieth century, doctors began doing testicle transplants.

What seems Frankensteinish to our ears had its roots in a mixed soil of old superstitions and new science. In Emperor Nero's day, orgies were often fueled by the Viagra of ancient Rome—liquids made from the crushed testes of goats or wolves. Such preparations could not have had any real effect, except as early testimony to the power of placebos. But the enduring nature of that effect no doubt explains why medieval physician Johannes Mesue the Elder was still prescribing testicular extracts eight centuries later—or why, eight centuries after that, the English medical reference *Salmon's Dispensatory* endorsed the use of testes extracts from dozens of species.

Aper, the boar: the stones and pizzle dried, and given in powder, help weakness and barrenness. Canis, the dog: the testicles and secretion provoke lust. . . . Buteo, the buzzard: the testicles help weakness of generation.

An understanding of the true androgenic role of testicles (that is, on secondary sex characteristics such as facial hair) was not achieved until 1848, when the German physiologist Arnold Berthold did the following experiment on six freshly castrated roosters. Two of these birds had one of their own testicles returned to their abdominal cavity; two others had testes from another bird in the experiment implanted in them; the remaining two were left castrated, as controls. Berthold saw that the comb and wattle of his castrated birds quickly deteriorated after surgery, but returned to normal in the birds that had been "re-testified." He attributed this, correctly, to "the productive function of the testes, i.e., by their action on the blood stream, and then by the corresponding reaction of the blood upon the entire organism."

This experiment is now considered one of the founding acts of modern endocrinology. Unfortunately, it was ignored for the next fifty years. As a result, ignorance of the testes' true function, and misconceptions about their potency-restoring properties if eaten, continued. Thus, when Charles Brown-Séquard, one of the world's most respected physicians, said he had rejuvenated his own sexual powers in 1889 by ingesting a potion made of crushed dog testes, one circle dating back to the ancients was completed, and a new one, thankfully of much shorter duration, was about to begin. Weeks after his "rejuvenation," Brown-Séquard was mailing vials of his *liquide testiculaire* (obtained from dogs or guinea pigs) to any physician who wanted to experiment with it. When these doctors were unable to replicate his results, they concluded the problem was not with the concept, but with the materials: the extract was too weak. What was needed, they thought, were actual testes.

As it happened, the first testicle transplant in the medical literature was not about sex. At least not directly. The patient seen by
Drs. Levi Hammond and Howard Sutton in Philadelphia in November 1911 was a nineteen-year-old boy who had been kicked
in the scrotum, after which one of his testes had swollen by more
than ten inches. The doctors' original plan, motivated primarily
by aesthetic concerns, was to replace that testicle with one from
a sheep. But a day before that was to happen, a human testicle
became available from a young man who bled to death. Somewhat impulsively, the surgeons decided to use it. They removed
the testicle from the donor, flushed it with sterile saline, stored it
overnight in a glass jar at forty degrees Fahrenheit, then transplanted it into their patient the following morning. (This appears
to be the first transplant of any human organ in the medical literature.) A month later, however, the doctors were disappointed to
see that their transplant had atrophied considerably. Hammond
and Sutton never published a follow-up. Knowing what we
know now, it is safe to say the transplant was rejected.

But the fact of tissue rejection—indeed, the very idea of the
body's immune system—was not yet well-understood, so testicle transplants continued. Chicago urologist Victor Lespinasse
claimed to have performed a transplant several months before
Hammond and Sutton, reporting his results in *Journal of the
American Medical Association* and *Chicago Medical Report* a
few years later. Unlike Hammond and Sutton, Lespinasse's goal
most definitely was improving sexual function. But rather than
transplanting an entire testicle, as the Philadelphians had done,
he carved the donor's testicle into slices, then grafted them into
muscle tissue in and around the recipient's scrotum. This is how
Lespinasse described the procedure in 1914:

"A man, aged 38, consulted me in January, 1911, to find out
if anything could be done for the loss of both testicles. One testicle was removed during a hernia operation; the other had been
lost in [an] accident. . . . He was unable to have intercourse,
which was his chief reason for seeking medical advice. . . .

A testicle from a normal man was easily obtained. . . . The two patients were anesthetized at the same time, and the recipient prepared as follows: The scrotum was opened high up and a bed prepared in the same way as we prepare the bed for the reception of an undescended testicle. . . . The fibers of the rectus muscle were exposed and separated . . . and then the testicle to be transplanted was removed. It was stripped of the epididymis . . . and then sliced transversely to its long axis [in slices] approximately 1 mm. thick. The central slice and the one next to it were taken out and placed among the fibers of the rectus muscle. Another slice was placed in the scrotum.

Lespinasse wrote that he was "surprised at the number of testicles that are available for transplantation purposes." He made no mention, however, if (or how much) those living donors were paid for their services.

Four days later Lespinasse's patient "had a strong erection accompanied by marked sexual desire. He insisted on leaving his hospital bed to satisfy this desire." This the patient did—and continued to do so, Lespinasse reported, for the next two years, after which the surgeon lost contact with him. Even so, Lespinasse was reluctant to take all the credit. "The sexual function is about nine-tenths psychic," he wrote, "and how much is due to the strong mental stimulus engendered by the operation, and how much to the actual functioning of the [grafted testicular] cells, is impossible to determine."

That uncertainty did not stop Lespinasse from doing more transplants. In 1922 one of his gland-grafting cases made the front page of the *New York Times*, no doubt because of the identity of his patient, the chairman of the International Harvester Corporation—the IBM of that era—Harry F. McCormick. The fact that McCormick, then fifty-one, was married to Edith Rockefeller, daughter of John D., made him one of the richest men in the world twice over. That he was carrying on a well-publicized love affair with a beautiful European opera star made him even more newsworthy. The headline and subheads in the *Times* piece read, "SECRET OPERATION FOR H. F. M'COR-MICK / Family Refuses to Say Whether His Stay in Hospital is for Gland Transplanting / KEEPING YOUNG IS HIS HOBBY / Lespinasse, His Surgeon, A Leader in Rejuvenation, Also is Silent on Case." The donor was rumored to be an Illinois black-smith. True or not, the following ditty, inspired by verse by Henry Wadsworth Longfellow, was soon heard in taverns all across America:

> Under the spreading chestnut tree,
> The village smithy stands;
> The smith a gloomy man is he,
> McCormick has his glands.

Lespinasse was certainly getting famous for his work, but a colleague in Chicago had gone him one better. In 1920 Dr. G. Frank Lydston informed the press that he had transplanted a testicle into *himself*. Lydston wrote in the *Journal of the American Medical Association* of nine other grafts, eight done by him on volunteers, the other done by Leo L. Stanley, chief surgeon at California's San Quentin prison. Dr. Stanley had no shortage of freshly deceased donors—inmates were executed often at his place of work. Lydston's *JAMA* report on one of Stanley's cases, based on facts given him by the prison doctor, is a peerless blend of optimism and condescension:

Case 9—A man, aged 25, evidently a moron, committed for burglary, had been kicked in the testicle five years previously. . . . At the time of operation the testes were the size of olive pits. The patient was tall, thin, anemic, very dull and apathetic. . . . The donor was a negro hanged for murder. The glands were removed . . . fifteen minutes after death . . . refrigerated . . . [and implanted several hours later. . . . ] Seven weeks after the operation the doctor reported that the testes were firm and . . . "resting nicely in the scrotal sac." The patient gained fifteen pounds and had become active and alert—in fact, he was improved in every way—and sexually had become very active. . . . Dr. Stanley said: "He now has erections nightly and in the daytime, something he never had before."\*

In the "comment" section of his *JAMA* piece, Lydston noted the cross-racial aspect of Stanley's case. Lydston's fascination with the donor's race and the recipient's improved sex life (in an all-male prison population!) reflected an enduring interest of his. In 1893 he cowrote "Sexual Crimes Among the Southern Negroes—Scientifically Considered," an article calling for the full "Oriental" castration—testes and penis—of any Negro convicted of raping a white woman as the only effective punishment. Clearly, Dr. Lydston spent a *lot* of time thinking about black genitalia.

Lydston went public about his surgery on himself because, as the 1920s moved along, the most celebrated testicle transplanter in the world became a publicity-seeking, Russian-born surgeon working in Paris named Serge Voronoff. Ever the jingoist, Lydston wanted to remind the world that gland grafting had started in the good old U.S.A., where dozens of surgeons were doing the procedure and promising great results to all comers. That fact was certainly true, but it failed to halt Dr. Voronoff's publicity juggernaut. This wasn't because Voronoff was doing more testicle transplants than anyone else. It was because he didn't bother to use humans as donors.

---

\*Stanley's concern with his patients' well-being did not end with testicle transplants. Convinced that crime was often the result of psychological pain caused by physical unattractiveness, he gave nose jobs and face-lifts to several San Quentin inmates.

In 1925 a book newly translated from French into English opened with perhaps the most jaw-dropping first paragraph in all of medical literature. "Between the 12th of June, 1920, and October 15th, 1923, I performed fifty-two testicular grafting operations" on human males, Serge Voronoff wrote in *Rejuvenation by Grafting*. "In all [but one case], the grafts were obtained from apes."

It is impossible to exaggerate the shock and fascination with which these words were received. Though other surgeons had preceded him, Voronoff instantly became the most famous testicle transplanter of them all. He had not been totally unknown; in France Voronoff had grafted testes tissue from young rams into older ones, after which, he told the press, the recipients showed clear signs of rejuvenation. When asked by a *New York Times* reporter in 1922 when he would start working with humans, Voronoff said, "Soon." "Grafting can only be done with beings of the same species," the Russian said, "but with men it is a rather difficult situation, as you cannot remove the source of vigor from a young man for the sake of making an old man young." (Clearly, Dr. Lespinasse in Chicago felt differently.) "But it is possible," Voronoff said, "to use monkeys, as they are akin to men." This was not the answer the *Times*man was expecting.

"But if you graft a monkey's glands in the body of a man, [won't he] become a monkey?" he asked.

"It would not be the case at all," Voronoff promised.

About that, and not much else, Voronoff was correct. On June 20, 1922, he was again quoted in the *Times*, saying he had made good on his vows. Voronoff had placed testicle grafts in several men who, afterward, remained totally human but dramatically improved over their previous state, especially sexually. The donors for all these transplants, Voronoff said, were African chimpanzees.

Voronoff had become interested in a possible link between testes and rejuvenation in 1898, while working as a physician in

Egypt, where he examined several eunuchs. He was struck by their obesity, hairless faces, and developed breasts. But, most of all, Voronoff was impressed by how old they looked. "The hair grows white at an early age, and it is rare for them to attain old age. . . . Are these disastrous effects directly due to the absence of the testicles?" he later wondered in print. And might not aging in a normal man be attributable to old, weak testes?

Voronoff was certain his subsequent animal experiments proved his Egyptian musings had been prescient. Actually, they proved no such thing, though the blame for that error must be shared with Edouard Retterer, a Parisian pathologist. In France Voronoff had operated a second time on one of his first patients—Old Ram No. 12—a year after the initial surgery and removed the graft for examination. Because Voronoff was not an experienced microscopist, he turned this tissue over to Retterer, who was. Unfortunately, Retterer mistook the invading cells of the sheep's immune system at the graft site as evidence of the survival of the graft itself.

Once he started operating on humans, Voronoff, as Lespinasse had before him, grafted thin slices of a testicle into the recipient. Unlike Lespinasse, however, Voronoff sutured his monkey tissue directly onto the tunica vaginalis, the thin serum-filled pouch that encases each testis, rather than embedding it in muscle tissue inside the scrotum. Voronoff prepared the tunica for the graft by gently scratching its surface with a sharp surgical instrument. The resulting grooves formed a bed for the monkey graft; equally important, the flow of blood serum out of the scratches, Voronoff believed, nourished the graft and kept it alive. He had raked the tunicae of his rams in his first experiments. The fact that Retterer pronounced those grafts still functioning years later convinced Voronoff his theory was correct.

*Rejuvenation by Grafting* is a thoroughly compelling document, made all the more so by its unpretentious style. "It is not possible to get the ape onto the table while conscious, as even the gentlest subjects fight desperately [any] attempt to tie their limbs," Voronoff wrote. "They are extremely suspicious and, in order to anaesthetize them, it is necessary to resort to strategy." One of Voronoff's associates designed a strategic cage that closed by means of a double trapdoor.

One shutter of the trapdoor is an open trellis permitting free access of air to the ape, while the second shutter is solid. The latter is lowered just before the cage is saturated with the anaesthetic.

A small window in this "Anaesthetizing Box" enabled Voronoff to see when the ape was dazed. "No time must be lost" at this moment, he warned. The ape "must be got out of the cage and onto the operating table . . . before he is sufficiently recovered to get his teeth into the hands of those who control him."

Once there, the ape was administered chloroform, after which his four limbs were spread out and tied down. Then an extensive pre-op session began. "Owing to [the ape's] uncleanly habits, meticulous care" was taken to shave the "scrotum, the lower part of the hypogastrium and the upper portions of both thighs; they must be well scrubbed with soap and hot water, washed with plenty of ether or spirit, and carefully painted with tincture of iodine," Voronoff wrote. On a table several feet away, the human recipient was similarly prepared. One assumes he escaped the indignity of the "Anaesthetizing Box" and—it is hoped—required less scrubbing and shaving.

After this, a testicle was removed from the ape by Voronoff's cosurgeon, who cut that testis into two halves, then cut three slices from each half. As this was happening, Voronoff prepared the human recipient, opening his scrotum, and exposing the tunicae vaginalis inside. Voronoff scratched the first tunica, prompting the flow of blood serum. Then he took the three monkey grafts prepared by his cosurgeon and sewed them onto its grooved surface, ensuring that none of the grafts was in contact with another. He then repeated this procedure on the other tunica. All of these steps were demonstrated in *Rejuvenation* with lifelike illustrations.

Most people, however, learned about Voronoff's operation in the popular press. Several monkey-gland recipients were practiced boulevardiers before the surgery; afterward, newspapers noted approvingly, their success rate as seducers soared even higher. The German humor magazine *Simplicissimus* ran a cartoon showing Voronoff's operating room crowded with a pregnant woman and dozens of her scrawny children, many with their hands in a supplicant's position, begging the surgeon not to operate on the ape sitting on his operating table, or their father, lying nearby. "Professor, please," the caption began, "wouldn't you rather use a method that prematurely makes our father *older*?"

Voronoff's operations were soon mimicked in America. Max Thorek, the esteemed physician who later wrote *The Human Testis*, spent much of the 1920s supplying his patients with slices of monkey testes. He had a small zoo built on the roof of a Chicago hospital to house his donors. One Sunday morning the monkeys escaped, gathering minutes later, for no known reason, at a nearby Catholic church. In his memoirs Thorek declined to describe in print "the sacrilegious actions" of those beasts, witnessed by a packed house of shocked congregants. Strange things with animals were also occurring in rural Kansas. There "Dr." John R. Brinkley got rich grafting *goat* testes into human patients. Unlike Voronoff and Thorek, however, Brinkley's credentials were highly suspect. In fact, it appears he bought them.

In England Voronoff's procedures inspired a novel called *The Gland Stealers*, issued by the same house that published P. G. Wodehouse. "Gran'pa is ninety-five, possessed of £100,000, a fertile imagination, and a good physique," the promotional copy on the book jacket began. "He sees in the papers accounts of Professor Voronoff's theory of rejuvenation by means of gland-grafting. Nothing will satisfy him but that the experiment should be made on himself. . . .

> He acquires a gorilla, a hefty murderous brute, and the operation is performed with success. That is only the beginning. . . . Inspired to philanthropy by the thrill of regained youth, Gran'pa decides to take a hundred or so old men to Africa, capture a like number of gorillas, and borrow their glands. . . .

In this case fiction reflected fact: Voronoff's operation became so popular that the French government felt compelled to ban monkey hunting in its African colonies.

The press marveled at Voronoff's extravagant lifestyle—the huge hotel suite on the Champs-Elysées, where he lived with his wife and a staff of servants, his holiday home on the Riviera, the fancy cars and parties, etcetera. Voronoff could certainly afford it. He charged $5,000 per surgery, a prodigious sum eighty years ago. By the end of 1926, Voronoff said he had done one thousand of them.

The enduring power of the placebo effect is certainly one reason why Voronoff was so successful. The surgeon's career was also given a boost by the then-burgeoning eugenics movement. Because World War I "destroyed a fit elite and left behind a degenerating, elderly rump," David Hamilton writes in *The Monkey Gland Affair,* "Voronoff's efforts at rejuvenating the aging wealthy classes was [seen as] a step in the right direction." At the same time, recent advances in plastic surgery and orthopedics led many to believe, as British scientist Julian Huxley did, that "biological knowledge enable[s] us to modify the processes of our bodies more in accord with our wishes." Just about everything was deemed malleable in the hands of the scientist. Why not add man's testes to that list?

Because, in the end, it was proved that Voronoff's operation did not work. One would hope to learn this sorry episode was ended by one of Voronoff's medical peers, after putting Voronoff's claims to rigorous scientific scrutiny. But that was only partly the case. In truth, few medical doctors ever challenged Voronoff's claims. The scientist who finally did prove the futility of Voronoff's testicle grafts was a French veterinarian, working in Morocco, named Henri Velu. In the late 1920s, Velu re-created Voronoff's early experiments on rams. After performing his own testes grafts, Velu removed them months later and examined them himself under a microscope. He concluded, correctly, that the "graft" was really a scar plus some inflammatory cells, the latter a remnant of the "invading force" that had successfully rejected the graft. Testicle grafts, Velu wrote in 1929, are *"une grande illusion."*

Skepticism regarding Voronoff's work finally began to grow, and Velu's findings were confirmed by subsequent medical advances. After testosterone was isolated in 1935, scientists demonstrated its inability to reverse the aging process or, by itself, to restore potency to a dysfunctional man who was otherwise healthy. In the next decade biologist Peter Medawar's work on the immune system proved that any and all of Voronoff's grafts would have been quickly destroyed by the host. (Professor Medawar was later awarded the Nobel Prize.)

There are conflicting reports of Voronoff's state when he died in 1951, at eighty-five. In *Medical Blunders,* Robert Youngson and Ian Schott wrote that "Voronoff lived to be ridiculed, but bore it with dignity." But Patrick McGrady, in *The Youth Doctors,* quoted a Swiss physician who knew the monkey-gland doctor as saying Voronoff was severely depressed near the end. Not because of what happened to him, the Swiss said—because of what may have happened to his patients *because* of him. Apparently, Voronoff feared that several of his grafts may have transferred syphilis from his apes to his human recipients. Voronoff was horrified by this thought, the Swiss said, and spent much of his final days in depressed isolation because of it. Only one thing is certain: depressed or not, the pioneer in the erection industry named Serge Voronoff died an extremely wealthy man.

———————

In 1934 a psychiatrist stood up at a meeting of primary-care physicians in New York and urged them to refuse to send any of their impotence patients to a urologist—or any surgeon for that matter—for fear of doing them irreparable harm. This skirmish in the turf war between psychiatrists and urologists had begun in earnest seven years earlier. In *Impotence in the Male*, psychiatrist Wilhelm Stekel declared there is no such thing as "organic impotence," save for the 5 percent of cases in which patients have damaged or diseased genitals. Stekel was extrapolating from personal experience: his own impotence had been cured on the couch in Vienna by Sigmund Freud. (Interestingly, Freud later came to despise Stekel, and banished him from his inner circle.)

Stekel's personal problems with Freud did not lessen his enthusiasm for Freudianism. Stekel insisted that, in the remaining 95 percent of impotence cases, the disease is entirely psychological, caused by self-hatred produced by unresolved Oedipal issues, unconscious fears and anxieties arising from childhood sexual disturbances, and inhibitions reinforced by religion and/or secular morality. The physical power of erection in men is given to them at birth, Stekel wrote, and is "preserved until death."

Stekel's 95 percent figure was soon accepted as fact, though there was no epidemiological evidence to support it. Nor was there any hard data that the talking cure used by psychoanalysis was of any lasting benefit in impotence cases, either. Many of the case reports in the medical literature now seem comical, misogynistic, or both. The following was written by Dr. B. S. Talmey, in the *New York Medical Journal*.

Mr. X., thirty years of age, was as a young boy regularly taken to the Tyrolean mountains [for his] vacation. When he was fifteen . . . he lived with his parents near an Alpine dairy where he roamed around among the cows and became quite attached to a pretty, twenty-year-old dairy maid who, on her side, took an erotic fancy to the handsome boy.

One day, while young Mr. X. was sunning himself near the grazing cows,

she joined him and taught him the *ars amandi*. This she repeated every day as long as the vacation lasted. [Later,] when Mr. X. married, he found that conjunction was possible only if his wife was attired in Tyrolean peasant costume and assumed the same posture as his pretty dairy maid years ago. . . . In the beginning of their married life . . . the wife granted his requests. The erections were perfectly normal, and two children were born. Lately the wife has rebelled against the masquerade, and Mr. X. found himself completely impotent. In the lupenar* where, for a remuneration, anything can be obtained, he has violent erections with a [prostitute] dressed as an Alpine dairy maid.

Dr. Talmey's response was to accuse Mrs. X. of a "sanctimonious frigidity" he said he often found in upper-class wives. Such women think that "assuming the supine position and [a state of] femoral divergence are the only contributions" to intercourse required of them. To help her husband's impotence, Talmey said, Mrs. X. must improve her attitude and don that damn peasant blouse. If not, she was dooming him to more visits to the lupenar, where the outcome would be even *more* impotence. "Extreme excitement after long abstinence," Talmey wrote, causes serious erectile dysfunction.

*An archaic word for brothel, from *lupa,* Latin for "she-wolf."

The expectancy and joy over the final reaching of the goal causes a great nervous disturbance within the inhibitory center which becomes overexcited, and at the critical moment the erections fail, the penis becomes flaccid, and shrivels to half its normal size.

In 1936 New York urologist Max Huhner had read enough. He challenged Karl Menninger, head of the famous psychoanalytic clinic in Kansas that bore his name, to a debate on impotence therapy in the *Journal of Urology*. Menninger, who went first, argued that even when interventions such as the cauterization of the prostatic urethra produced the resumption of erectile functioning, they only did so because of their psychological effects. "The patient thinks there is something wrong with his genitalia," Menninger wrote. Urologists "know this is not true, or at least, that the organ pathology is secondary to the psychopathology, but experience has taught them the curative value of treating the genitalia locally, and by its suggestive value reassuring the patient and relieving his anxiety and thereby his impotence." The reality of the situation, Menninger said, is that impotence is caused by anxiety, a condition best treated by psychoanalysis. The talking cure made conscious "the unconscious emotions that often (always?) determine the inhibition of sexual functioning." The specific nature of those negative emotions, Menninger wrote, include "fears, especially of punishment or injury; hostility toward the love object; and conflicting loves, particularly parental and homosexual fixations."

Dr. Huhner responded by dismissing psychoanalysis's claim that impotence is psychological in 95 percent of the cases as less a scientific fact than a philosophical assertion. Huhner did not rule out the possibility of psychogenic impotence. He argued that urologists can discern such a patient from one with organic disease because they do a medical examination, something a psychoanalyst never does. What would one think, he asked,

if a patient with an undersized penis complained of his inability to perform the sexual act and consulted a physician
who, without even looking at that organ, informed him
that his condition was purely psychic and due to some unresolved complex from his childhood days? This certainly
seems ridiculous . . . but it is exactly the procedure that is
followed daily by psychoanalysts.

Huhner also wrote that, while he was not "doubting the psychoanalyst's findings" regarding the prevalence of unresolved
Oedipal issues in impotent men, he doubted their methodology
in asserting it.

Just as in other branches of medical science, a control
should be established to determine the possible presence of
such an unresolved Oedipal complex in men who are not
impotent. . . . In any other branch of medical experimentation, such a system of control would be the obvious rule.

On these two points, Huhner was on solid ground. Unfortunately, he weakened his case, from our viewpoint today, by insisting on the reality of the link between masturbation and
impotence, and the efficacy of treating that condition with jolts
of electric current to the penis. (It goes without saying, of
course, that he was wrong on both counts.) Equally distressing
to contemporary eyes is Huhner's qualified endorsement of the
"clinical observations of Stanley," the San Quentin prison doctor, "and Voronoff," Mr. Monkey Gland—each of whom, Huhner wrote, had scientifically established the "endocrine action"
in erectile physiology.

Both of these operators have had [temporary] success in
producing sexual desire and erection in impotent persons
. . . . And yet, in the face of all these modern observations
on the influence of sex hormone, psychoanalysts still be-

lieve that everything sexual comes from the brain, and simply ignore the fact that we have been endowed with sexual organs as well as brains.

The fact that a scientist as serious as Dr. Huhner wrote these words in 1936, several years after the Frenchman Henri Velu proved that testicle grafts were *"une grande illusion,"* is troubling. It is also one more reason why urologists lost the early battle for therapeutic control of erectile functioning to psychotherapists and, for several years after the 1970 publication of *Human Sexual Inadequacy,* by Dr. William H. Masters and Virginia E. Johnson, to sex therapists. Urologists would not, however, lose the war.

———————————

A real war—World War II—put them on the path to victory. In 1944 the *American Review of Soviet Medicine* translated an article that appeared in Russian the previous year. "The use of new weapons in the present war has resulted in . . . wounds which were unknown during World War I," A. P. Frumkin wrote. "The rapid fire of automatic weapons and mine and bomb explosions, with their spray of fragments, have [caused] . . . the destruction of whole organs. It is not surprising, therefore, that a complete loss of the external genitalia is a frequent occurrence."

In "Reconstruction of the Male Genitalia," Dr. Frumkin offered an extreme solution to an extreme problem. He removed a section of the patient's rib, then made two parallel incisions into the patient's abdominal wall. The flap of skin between those incisions was pulled up, then curved inward into a tube, in which the rib cartilage was inserted. This "tube flap," with the rib inside, was then sewed shut. The resulting product, Frumkin wrote, resembled "a suitcase handle." After a healing period of several weeks, this handle was carefully removed from the patient's midsection and even more carefully attached to whatever remained of his penis. A new urinary canal, made of scrotum skin, was sewed to the outside of the reconstructed penis, running along the bottom. (Frumkin's article included a photograph of a reconstructed patient urinating into a glass beaker.)

Though it may sound freakish to a nonscientist, it is not surprising that Dr. Frumkin experimented with a rib bone. Most mammals, including many of our primate cousins, are born with a bone in the penis called the baculum or os penis. The "little stick" of the fox was described by Aristotle twenty-four hundred years ago. Much more recently the British zoologist W. R. Bett noted that "in the whale [the baculum] measures 2 metres in length and 40 cm. in circumference at the base, and in the walrus it is 55 cm. long." When male otters fight, they have been known to bite an opponent's penis, snapping the bone inside in two. Anyone desiring more information on this subject would do well to visit the Icelandic Phallological Museum in Reykjavík, where more than eighty penis baculae—from sixteen varieties of land mammals, twelve different whale species, seven types of seal and walrus, and one rogue polar bear—are preserved and displayed on wall plaques.

Because of examples like this from the animal kingdom, the idea of a penile bone implant in humans made some biological sense. Even so, the results were disappointing. Most bent noticeably within eighteen months; later, nearly all were absorbed into the recipient's body. These problems led urologists to experiment with artificial materials. This research would mark the first major step forward in the medicalization of the erection.

In 1948 Dr. Willard E. Goodwin of the University of California at Los Angeles became the first surgeon to use a synthetic substance to make a baculum in a human. He replaced a patient's bent rib cartilage implant with a single rigid acrylic rod. Not long afterward, however, he had to remove it because of complications. In 1973 Drs. Michael P. Small and Hernan M. Carrion of the University of Miami invented the first device made of paired sponge-filled silicone rods. These flexible, semirigid rods were inserted alongside the corpora cavernosa—the two spongy bodies that fill with blood inside a normally functioning penis—and underneath the tunica albuginea, the membrane encasing those bodies. This created a more "natural" appearance than any single-rod implant. Well, maybe "supernatural" is a better term. The Small-Carrion implant did not leave the patient's penis in a constant state of elevation, but it did leave him in a state of perpetual expansion. Some patients, but not all, found this embarrassing.

A solution for that predicament was devised later that same year by F. Brantley Scott of the University of Minnesota, who led a team that created the first inflatable prosthesis. This device, which also used silicone rods, was manipulated up and down by a small pump placed inside the scrotum. Nearly all prostheses in use today are updated versions of Dr. Scott's design, manufactured by American Medical Systems or Mentor, Inc.

Six years before Scott's breakthrough, however, Dr. Robert O. Pearman, a private practitioner in Encino, California, had invented a single-rod silicone implant, which he placed atop and in between the corpora cavernosa and underneath the tunica, a position that caused his patients to complain of pain. Even so, Pearman was a major force in the medicalization of erections—not for his faulty technique, which he soon abandoned, but for the definition of erectile dysfunction he published in the *Journal of Urology.*

Pearman defined ED as the "loss of ability to produce and maintain a functional erection due to pathology of the nervous or vascular system, or to deformation or loss of the penis." He did not mention psychological causes at all. This declaration encouraged other urologists to believe what they were already seeing with their own eyes. "Anyone doing implants could see the penile tissue of an impotent man was scarred," says Dr. Arnold Melman, coeditor of the *International Journal of Impotence Research.* "How could you explain that psychologically?"

Another prolific researcher, Dr. Irwin Goldstein of Boston

University, pays homage to Pearman as well. But for Goldstein the big breakthrough was made by Scott's inflatable prosthesis. "Finally we had a therapy that produced reliable, lifelike erections. Before we had nothing to offer, so we left the field to psychiatrists." Most doctors are "acceptors," Goldstein says. "If they read impotence is ninety-five per cent psychological, they accept it." Not Goldstein. "My undergraduate training was in engineering. Engineers do not accept things. They take working machines apart and try to make them work better." The subcutaneous pump in Scott's prosthesis was an inspiration to Goldstein and like-minded urologists "It reminded us that the penis is like a tire. An erection must be pumped up—with blood instead of air, of course. And when it goes flat, just like with a tire, you have to look for a leak or check out the pump."

In the 1970s the Czech surgeon Vaclav Michal did autopsies on male diabetics, many of whom were impotent when alive. Nearly all, he discovered, had a pump problem—blocked cavernosal arteries. In "Arterial Disease as a Cause of Impotence," Michal asserted that ED is often the result of this insufficiency. Michal experimented with revascularization procedures on live diabetics to surgically enhance their arterial blood supply, getting good results. In 1978 Dr. Adrian Zorgniotti summoned urologists from Europe and the United States to a conference in New York to discuss Michal's work. "That meeting was a turning point," says Dr. Gorm Wagner of the University of Copenhagen, who was there. "It changed forever the old, erroneous way of thinking of impotence as exclusively a psychogenic problem." Another meeting was held in 1980 in Monaco and, in 1982, in Copenhagen, where participants agreed to exchange scientific information every two years at a World Meeting on Impotence and formalized their organization as the International Society for Impotence Research, the first group of its kind in the world.

In 1981 Michal taught his revascularization procedure to Irwin Goldstein, who became an enthusiastic supporter. Two years later Giles Brindley gave the most startling scientific presentation in medical history—and in so doing not only launched the erection industry but, even more important, helped scientists to finally understand the mysterious hemodynamic process that makes an erection possible.

---

Brindley would have to share credit for the second feat with another European. In October 1982, the French surgeon Ronald Virag published a short paper that, in truth, not many urologists noticed at the time. This was several months before Brindley's display in Las Vegas—something everyone in attendance noticed. While doing a routine surgical procedure at his Parisian clinic, Dr. Virag mistakenly injected papaverine, a chemical that causes body tissues to relax, into an artery leading into his patient's penis, rather than his intended target, another artery nearby. Much to Virag's surprise, his patient, still under anesthesia, responded with an erection that lasted more than two hours.

Virag later tried to duplicate this result in thirty impotent men—awake, this time—and was successful. His paper, published in *Lancet,* was titled "Intracavernous Injection of Papaverine for Erectile Failure." Brindley bared his results in Las Vegas the following spring. Later Brindley would publish "Pilot Experiments on the Actions of Drugs Injected into the Human Corpora Cavernosum Penis." This paper reported on thirty-three injections resulting in erections lasting between several seconds and forty-four *hours*. A close reading reveals that Brindley did all the experiments on himself.

Before Virag's and Brindley's experiments, the picture urologists had of erectile functioning was still a little fuzzy. "There was a taboo against studying male sexual biology in detail," Goldstein says. "If you studied the heart everyone applauded. But the penis? People thought you were a pervert." Still, urologists had poked around enough to know most of the basics. They knew, for instance, that neurological signals caused the organ to fill with blood. They knew about the cavernosal arteries bringing that blood in and the smaller arterioles branching out into the surrounding corpora cavernosa, the two spongy bodies that expanded once the blood got there. They knew the corpora were composed of smooth-muscle tissue, thin sheets that line blood vessels and most of the hollow organs of the body. Inside the corpora they saw this smooth muscle formed a meshwork of linked spaces called sinusoids. They also knew the corpora were encased by a thin but tough membrane called the tunica albuginea.

What they did not really understand was the most important event in the process—the mechanism that enabled the penis to trap the blood once it came surging in. Virag's and Brindley's experiments confirmed what some scientists already suspected: the importance of smooth-muscle relaxation. Papaverine, which Virag used, and phenoxybenzamine, the drug injected by Brindley in Las Vegas, were both powerful smooth-muscle relaxants. When injected in the penis, each mimicked the body's own erectile methodology and thus gave urologists a view—a pharmacological magnifying glass—into the penis's inner workings.

"We learned that what we learned in medical school [about blood trapping] was wrong," says Dr. Arthur L. Burnett of Johns Hopkins. And had been for a long time. In 1900 a German anatomist named Von Ebner found what he called "pads" lining the arteries bringing blood into the penis. He concluded that those pads enabled the arteries by themselves to regulate blood flow into the penis—opening up to allow blood in and closing down later to trap that blood and cause an erection. Von Ebner's theory was the prevailing wisdom until 1952, when it was updated by a French urologist named Conti, who said he found shunts, soon called "Conti's polsters," in veins outside the tunica albuginea that carried blood out of the corpora. Conti concluded that these were the mysterious shutdown valves urologists had been searching for for so long. Blood entered the penis, the corpora expanded, and those polsters outside the tunica closed down, Conti said, giving that blood nowhere to go. Result: erection.

Papaverine proved this was not the case at all. "We saw that the key to the trapping of blood is the rapid relaxation of the smooth-muscle tissue in the corpora," Burnett says. "Once that tissue is relaxed, the resistance to blood flowing in is greatly reduced. So the blood comes in, the corpora suck it up like two thirsty sponges, and the tissue expands so quickly that it flattens the exit veins against the tunica."*

Those exit veins inside the penis are there for a reason: an erection is not supposed to be a permanent event. It is through those veins that blood leaves the corpora—after an orgasm, or when a man loses his erection because the telephone on the nightstand starts ringing. That second example of shrinkage occurs because the ringing startles the man, which triggers the release of epinephrine, a smooth-muscle constrictor that causes tissue to tighten. That reaction sends the blood through the suddenly no-longer-flattened exit veins and down the drain, as it were. This is part of the "fight or flight" response sometimes known as an adrenaline rush. It is sexually counterproductive by evolutionary design. All men today are descended from cavemen who successfully got away from a saber-toothed tiger precisely because they were not impeded by an erection. Those who could not lose their erection fast enough were caught and eaten.

When there is smooth-muscle relaxation—and no saber-toothed tiger—"the blood that has just entered the penis is trapped, so pressure inside builds by a factor of about ten," Burnett says. Urologists call this process "venous occlusion." We call it getting hard. It doesn't take much blood: less than two ounces, says Dr. James H. Barada, treasurer of the Society for

---

*Urologists later determined that Von Ebner's pads and Conti's polsters were atherosclerotic debris, much like that found in the chest of heart-disease patients.

the Study of Impotence. But that is enough to make the typical human penis—roughly three and a half inches long and one and a quarter inch thick when flaccid—get two inches longer and more than a half inch thicker, boosting its total volume by around 300 percent. That expansion and rigidity is the difference between a penis with some extra blood, called "tumescent" by urologists, and a bona fide erection. The problem with many impotent men is not that blood is failing to enter the penis; it is that, because the smooth-muscle tissue has not relaxed properly, that blood is draining out immediately after getting there.

Within days of Brindley's demonstration in Las Vegas (and months of Virag's article in *Lancet*), urologists all over the world were prescribing injection therapy. Papaverine, Virag's drug of choice, was preferred over Brindley's phenoxybenzamine because the latter was shown to be carcinogenic and often caused priapism—an utterly unfunny condition marked by an erection lasting four hours or more, which can do permanent damage to penile tissue. Reached on the telephone in London, Brindley said that he had suffered "no negative consequences" from his injection experiments in the 1980s, which numbered, he said, "in the hundreds." But then he added: "Well, that's not quite true. I do have a small case of Peyronie's disease," a curvature of the penis, caused by internal scarring, that can cause impotence. "I don't think my experiments are the reason," said Brindley, now professor emeritus of physiology at the University of London. "But who knows?"

Papaverine occasionally causes priapism, too, so urologists experimented with other smooth-muscle relaxants such as prostaglandin E-1, or a mix of papaverine, prostaglandin E-1, and phentolamine as their injection drugs of choice. None of these substances was FDA-approved for use as a medication for ED. They were, however, approved for other uses in the human body, so few doctors were hesitant to prescribe them. This off-label use, as it is known, is common medical practice. In 1995

Pharmacia & Upjohn received FDA approval for the first drug specifically approved for impotence—Caverject, a synthetic form of prostaglandin E-1, injected into the corpora cavernosa. Two years later Vivus received approval for the same medication delivered by a transurethral pellet. In 1998 both would lose market share to Viagra.

Approved or not, those first-generation erection drugs certainly worked—in some ways far better than original equipment. A penis injected with a smooth-muscle relaxant could stay hard for hours and remain hard after orgasm, a lure some men found irresistible. Glossy magazines reported on a black market for the drug in Hollywood, where it became a favorite of aging producers "forced" to entertain young starlets. "Girls love the shot," Dr. Uri Peles, a Beverly Hills ED specialist, told me at the 1996 World Meeting on Impotence. "They might not want a hard man, but they want a man hard." What seems funny can, and occasionally has, turned tragic. According to Dr. Goldstein, several Hollywood types have come to his Boston office with serious pathology. "One patient was having an affair with a younger woman. He was perfectly healthy but wanted a little 'performance enhancer.' He injected himself with forty micrograms of prostaglandin—a proper dose for a man with impotence, but about four times higher than anything he might have easily tolerated." The result, Goldstein said, was "a forty-eight-hour erection. That's like having a tourniquet on down there."

After Brindley and Virag, urologists not only began prescribing smooth-muscle relaxants for at-home use, but injecting them in a hospital or consulting-room setting for research purposes. If medical remedies such as drugs and surgery were the primary products of the new erection industry, the secondary products were expensive tests designed to find the vascular problems requiring those remedies. For much of the 1990s, urologists routinely gauged their patients' erectile functioning by injecting their penises with smooth-muscle relaxants, then measuring the arterial blood flow via ultrasonography, a method that sends sound waves into the chemically erected penis and then converts the returning sound waves into an electronic image on a monitor. If the flow after an injection is low, the doctors said, it indicated an arterial-supply problem that possibly required surgery.

Another, even more extensive and expensive, test is called dynamic infusion cavernosometry and cavernosography—or DICC (pronounced "dick"), for short. Irwin Goldstein, a champion of this procedure, told me, "Just like with a tire, you can't always find the leak when it's flat. You have to inflate it and put it under water. We inflate the penis with drugs, then we do our version of the water test."

In the first part of a DICC study, Goldstein records the blood-pressure response inside the corpora after the injection of smooth-muscle relaxers. The goal is to see how closely that penile pressure approaches the mean pressure of an artery in the patient's arm. Next he tests the patient's blood-trapping mechanism by injecting saline solution into the corpora until the patient's penis reaches a defined pressure. Goldstein then charts how fast the erection pressure drops after the infusion is stopped. In a normal man, the saline flow needed to maintain pressure, and the resulting pressure drop after the flow is terminated, are both small. In a man with ED they are quite large. In the third phase of the DICC study, ultrasound charts the blood pressure of the penile arteries. Finally, an X-ray is taken of the erect penis, providing the physician with additional anatomical data.

By the late 1990s, however, there was a feeling such tests were neither essential nor very accurate. "I haven't done a DICC in years," says Dr. Barada. "They make some sense in an academic setting, where you're collecting data and trying to stratify patients"—factors that do apply to Goldstein's work, by the way. "But I've been to Boston," Barada says, "and it seems to me that if you're secretly hoping to find pathology that setting will probably deliver it. The patient is lying on a cold hard table. People he doesn't know are walking in and out. There's no soundproofing. Screens are flashing nearby. Doctors are ostensibly checking for normal smooth-muscle relaxation in a totally abnormal situation."

Viagra would render this debate moot. Nowadays urologists do little or no tests on ED patients. They take a medical history, then, in most cases, write a prescription. "Once I determine [from an interview that] the patient is a good Viagra candidate," says San Francisco urologist Ira Sharlip, president of the Society for the Study of Impotence, "I say, 'You probably have an organic disease. Do you need to know that it's sixty-five percent arterial and thirty-five percent venous or vice versa? Or are you interested in taking a pill that will probably give you an erection adequate for penetration?' You can guess the answer."

This is why millions of Viagra users, whether they know it or not, are taking part in one of the largest unsupervised (or barely supervised) medical trials in history. Only a few thousand men took Viagra in the trials run by Pfizer in the mid-1990s. In the months after the drug's approval, in March 1998, that number jumped more than a thousandfold—with little or no tests to determine whether those patients had a genuine erectile disease or possibly dangerous preexisting conditions.

This seems to have had fatal consequences. In November 1998, Pfizer agreed to augment and expand the warning label included with every Viagra bottle alerting users and physicians to the danger of mixing Viagra with heart medications containing nitrates. Between late March and mid-November 1998, more than one hundred Americans died within hours or days of taking Viagra. Half those deaths, the FDA reported, were associated with heart attacks. (The reason for many of the other fatalities could not be conclusively determined.) According to a World Health Organization report, none of the patients in Pfizer's clinical trials for Viagra had suffered a heart attack, stroke, or life-threatening arrhythmia within six months of taking the drug. It appears that some Americans who *had* may have been prescribed and taken Viagra—incurring the most permanent side effect of them all.

Pfizer and the urological establishment insist that Viagra is safe for men not taking nitrates. And it appears they are right. For now. But the financial ties between urologists and drug companies make some critics worry that a doctor's ability to speak the unvarnished truth has been compromised. Manufacturers pay urologists in the area of $5,000 per patient enrolled in a clinical trial for an impotence medication. Some, like Irwin Goldstein, have hundreds of patients taking part in different trials at once. Many urologists own stock in the companies whose products they test. Others serve as paid consultants to those firms, in some cases signing nondisclosure agreements that prevent them from divulging data that might conflict with that company's marketing statements about new drugs. "It isn't possible to go to anybody in this field right now for a neutral opinion," Dr. Jeremy Heaton told *Fortune* magazine recently. (Heaton, a respected impotence researcher at Queen's University in Kingston, Ontario, is himself a paid adviser to a drug company trying to bring a new erectile medication to market.)

This is not to imply that Drs. Goldstein or Heaton, or any other ED researcher, entered the field just to get rich. They could earn far more if they left academic medicine altogether, closed down their expensive laboratories, and ran a purely private practice. Nor is anyone suggesting they are shills for Fortune 500 companies hoping to get into the Fortune 5, or that they would ignore a dangerous side effect of a drug they were being paid to test. Helping patients—whether by drugs, surgery, or a sympathetic ear—is, without question, the top priority of just about every physician in the ED field. (Goldstein's attentive manner with patients, which I have witnessed, could be a model for the entire medical profession.) Indeed, it is because of the missionary zeal of Goldstein, Arnold Melman, and others like them that drug companies were awakened, often against their will, to the fact that erectile dysfunction is a serious condition with consequences meriting serious attention.

But there can be financial consequences to breaking ranks with the erection industry. Dr. Ronald Lewis of the Medical College of Georgia was cut loose by a drug company testing an impotence medication after he expressed doubts about its efficacy. "They read my skepticism and figured I wouldn't be out there pushing," Lewis says. "So I was out." Nothing like this happened during the Viagra trials, that we know of, and Viagra's problems for the approximately 9 million American men taking nitrates is now a well-disseminated fact. But *Maxim, Details,* and other slick magazines aimed at young, sexually active men—a group decades away from serious cardiac worries—report that Viagra has become a drug of choice for their club-crawling audience, often taken in conjunction with Ecstasy, a party drug that enhances sexual desire but can inhibit sexual performance. Viagra, because it solves the latter problem—without the priapism risk of injectable drugs—has become de rigeur among the party-hearty set. But the long-term effects of Viagra on this nonprescribed, nonclinically tested population are unknown.

Several weeks after Viagra's approval, Dr. Robert Kolodny of the Behavioral Medicine Institute in New Canaan, Connecticut, a former partner of the famous sex researchers William Masters and Virginia Johnson, told the *New York Times,* "Whenever a new drug is introduced, pharmaceutical companies tout it as extraordinarily effective and without side effects." But "years later . . . side effects emerge that were not previously seen. There may be interactions between Viagra and other drugs. . . . Men may use it at higher doses. . . . And it will undoubtedly be used by a wide range of people, not all of whom are suitable or adequately screened beforehand." Kolodny's words proved to be prescient. A different set of questions was raised by San Francisco attorney Michael Risher, legal adviser for the Lindesmith Center, a think tank on drug policy. "There are striking similarities between the recreational use of Viagra and, say, anabolic steroids and tranquilizers," he wrote. "It is legally considered drug abuse if a man ingests steroids simply to look virile. So why isn't it illegal to take a pill to become virile?"

Not everyone was alarmed by Viagra's appeal to John Doe, or its risks. "Feminism has emasculated the American male," *Penthouse* founder Bob Guccione told a *Time* reporter. "And that emasculation has led to physical problems. This pill will take the pressure off men . . . and undercut the feminist agenda." Hugh Hefner gave similar interviews praising the drug. In most of them he was accompanied by three statuesque women, each young enough to be his granddaughter, whom he was said to be dating simultaneously.

---

In September 2000, Dr. Milton Lakin of the Cleveland Clinic welcomed several hundred scientists, and a smaller number of science reporters, to his home city for the Fall 2000 Research Meeting of the Society for the Study of Impotence (SSI). He reminded them that several decades ago he had predicted that people would be having sex on the moon before there would be an impotence pill that actually worked. He then invited the audience to listen to a few "can't miss" stock tips. When the laughter ended, Lakin got serious. "The ability of researchers, many of them in this room, to devise new treatment options for erectile dysfunction is one of the great achievements of modern medicine," he said. Clearly, the treatment that has astounded Lakin and the media the most—Viagra—never would have been found had it not been for the research that followed the groundbreaking work of Brindley and Virag nearly two decades earlier.

Once urologists grasped the importance of smooth-muscle relaxation, they focused on identifying the primary neurotransmitter that initiated that process. They had a good lead. Three scientists working independently, Robert F. Furchgott, Louis J. Ignarro, and Ferid Murad, had already established the role of nitric oxide in relaxing smooth-muscle cells in the vascular system. This led urologists to examine the role of that molecule in the penis, where they confirmed the findings of those three scientists. (In 1998 Furchgott, Ignarro, and Murad were awarded the Nobel Prize for medicine.)

The link between nitric-oxide-signaled erections and Viagra (sildenafil citrate) was discovered by accident. In the mid-1980s, Pfizer developed a new compound that it hoped would be an effective drug for angina pectoris—severe chest pain caused by deficient oxygenation of the heart muscles. This drug was sildenafil citrate, which inhibited the production of phosphodiesterase-5, an enzyme also known as PDE-5. Studies on sildenafil's effectiveness, overseen by Dr. Ian H. Osterloh, began in England in 1990 and two years later produced results both disappointing and intriguing: males taking sildenafil reported their angina was as bad as ever, but there was this not unwelcome side effect. . . .

At first Osterloh and his team though it was a fluke. But recent papers on the function of nitric oxide made them realize they might have stumbled onto something important. (This gets a little technical, but bear with me.) Scientists now understood that the presence of nitric oxide inside the corpora cavernosa caused an increase in the levels of another substance called cyclic guanosine monophosphate (cGMP). It was cGMP that directly relaxed the smooth-muscle tissue inside the corpora, thereby making an erection possible.

But scientists also noticed there was another substance in the corpora—PDE-5—that reversed this process by breaking down the cGMP. Because it is a PDE-5 inhibitor, Viagra prevented that from happening. It did not so much create the erection as it stopped that erection from wilting. Just like those pesky exit veins, PDE-5 is in the penis for a good reason. The organ's default setting, as it must be in a civilized world, is flaccidity. Considering the sexual stimulation that exists in places one does not always expect to find it—the elevator, for instance—it is a good thing that the erection-inhibitor is there. Except when a man is having sex, when the signals to relax and expand in the corpora cavernosa overwhelm those to tense up and constrict. (At least they do in a normally functioning man.) "The beauty of Viagra," says Dr. Andrew R. McCullough, a urologist at New York University, "is that it enhances a man's natural response to sexual stimulation by diminishing its equally natural inhibiting process." This cross talk between signals urging a penis to become erect, and others demanding it go soft, creates a constant state of static inside every man. Not only does a penis have a mind of its own, it has *two* minds.

The approval of Viagra, the first oral medication for ED, on March 27, 1998, marked the biggest moment yet in the erection industry. Along with enhancing the sexual performance of millions of men, that industry and the research that produced it accomplished something almost equally dramatic—making urologists even more in awe of the penis than they already were. "The penis is an anatomical marvel," says Dr. Arthur L. Burnett. "It can change size and shape, become rigid and flaccid, and expel semen and urine through the same collapsible tube. What other organ goes through so many changes or has so many functions? It is clearly one of the most cleverly designed organs in the body."

That cleverness begins on the outside and moves in. The skin of the penis shaft is thinner, looser, and more elastic than just about any patch on the human body. The glans is hairless, putting it in direct contact with everything it touches. A 1986 study in the journal *Brain Research* found sensory receptors distinctive to the penis in the glans, the corona (the fleshy lip on the outer edge of the glans), and the frenulum, the small, wrinkly band of skin just below the glans. All three of these areas enlarge when aroused, creating more surface area—and more erotic sensation.

The result is a unique neurological hot spot, one more about quality than quantity. Sensitivity is measured by density of nerves, says Dr. Claire C. Yang, coauthor of "Innervation of the Human Glans Penis" (*Journal of Urology*), and one of medicine's rarest breeds, a female neurourologist. Nerve density is pretty good in the penis, Yang says, but it is far greater in the face and hands and there are larger areas in the brain working to process signals from those places. This makes sense, considering we are descended from apes that lived on all fours and spent much of the day sniffing for food in the rain forest. But no one is suggesting that signals from, say, the palm are more vivid than those from the penis. Messages from the male member are so powerful, in fact, that Dr. Yang thinks they can do something no other body part can: temporarily alter the brain itself. "Stimulation from the penis seems to expand and enhance the brain's ability to process that stimulation," she says. Yang, a researcher at the University of Washington, has not proved this yet, but she's working on it.

The urethra, the penis's internal transport tube, runs from the meatus (the hole) to the bladder, a distance of about six inches—nearly half of that inside the body—and stretches when the organ is erect. It is surrounded by the corpus spongiosum. Together, they lie beneath two larger, even spongier bodies, the corpora cavernosa, which sit above them to the left and right; all of these bodies are encased by a lining called the tunica albuginea. The corpora cavernosa, which fill with blood when one has an erection, extend down the shaft into the body, where ligaments tie them to the pubic bone. These ligaments are severed in patients undergoing penile-extension surgery. Afterward gravity pulls the penis down, making it "longer"—and a lot wobblier, which is why most urologists neither recommend nor perform the procedure.

The tunica albuginea, the lining that surrounds the penis's internal workings, is another structural marvel—up to a point. "It is about as thick as a magazine cover," says Dr. Ajay Nehra of the Mayo Clinic, in Rochester, Minnesota. "It's very strong, but not very flexible," factors that enhance erectile firmness but create a potential for a serious injury called penile fracture. Actually, this is more like a muscle tear than a cracked bone. The cause is usually overly athletic intercourse, typically with the woman on top. Such fractures are rare, and if treated within twenty-four hours the tunica can usually be repaired. If not, injection drugs help in most cases. Major tears may require the insertion of a penile prosthesis.

Of ejaculation and orgasm, only the first takes place in the penis. The second occurs in the brain. But ejaculation is, of course, triggered by the brain, which receives pleasurable stimulation from the penis—sometimes only for a minute or two, as women well know—until it passes a certain threshold. As the brain erupts into orgasm, it still has the presence of mind to send signals to the genitalia. Sperm cells have already been produced by the testes and are in the epididymis. Another tube, the vas deferens, connects the epididymis to the urethra and transports the sperm there. (This is why ligating those tubes, in a vasectomy, makes a man sterile.) Glands called seminal vesicles meet the vas just before they enter the urethra. These provide fructose and other secretions required for the sperm to exist outside the body. The prostate, which surrounds the base of the urethra like a donut, also provides chemicals enabling the sperm to complete their trip.

At "show time," sperm are moved from the epididymis, through the vas, and deposited at the bottom of the urethra, near the prostate. At the same moment, the seminal vesicles and prostate contract, emitting their fluids. These secretions mix together, then are forced out by a series of convulsions by the bulbourethral muscle, which surrounds the urethra, near the bottom. (Imagine holding a sausage with the casing cut open at one end in your fist, then squeezing.) "Sperm make a journey the equivalent of a marathon in two to five seconds," says Dr. Abraham Morgentaler, a urologist at Harvard Medical School. Is it any wonder men fall asleep so soon after sex?

Ask Leonore Tiefer about that and you will get a different explanation. Tiefer is a psychologist, feminist, sexologist, sex therapist, former newspaper sex columnist, and author of *Sex Is Not a Natural Act & Other Essays*, a collection published in 1995. (Yes, she thinks about sex a *lot*.) Tiefer is a serious person, but not so much that she cannot enjoy a good laugh. She just doesn't think the urological takeover of male sexuality—the "pursuit of the perfect penis," she calls it—is very funny.

Tiefer opposes that quest for a slew of reasons: Because she thinks it is motivated more by money than medicine. Because it uses shaky evidence to dismiss the interpersonal causes of ED. Because it reduces the mystery of sex to universal standards of nerve sensitivity, smooth-muscle relaxation, and blood flow. Because it proceeds from the idea that creating an erection is the same as creating sexual enlightenment. And because it is not a giant step forward in the eternal march of scientific progress, as urologists claim, but a social construction of the late twentieth century—a reaction against feminism, bolstered by the belief of male Baby Boomers that they are entitled to be erect forever.

"Erections are presented not only as the 'goal,'" she says, "but as knowable in and of themselves, unattached to a person or relationship." Tiefer is not a huge fan of Masters and Johnson, least of all for the way they defined intercourse in *Human Sexual Inadequacy* as "a matter of vascocongestion and myotonia" (that is, the engorgement of tissue with blood and involuntary muscle contractions). But at least Masters and Johnson were smart enough to realize the patient in sexual-dysfunction cases is the couple. "Now," Tiefer says, "the only patient is the penis."

In her view, this has transformed women from participants in intercourse to an audience. "Of course I know many women like harder and longer-lasting erections. But some of these women will be forced to deal with those chemically induced erections whether they're in the mood or not. And the medical establishment doesn't even ponder that possibility." That same establishment, she says, also absolves men from responsibility for their sexual performance. "Urologists are men. They know men don't want to talk about their relationships, or make any embarrassing disclosures. So the urologist tells his patient: 'You don't have to, because your sexual problem isn't your fault. You don't have a technique problem or a relationship problem. You have a vascular problem in your penis. And I can fix that.'" This medical view of ED is based on a misunderstanding of what sex is—and what it is not, Tiefer says. "Sex isn't a natural act, like breathing. It's not a universal, either. Sex in Peru is not the same as sex in Peoria. Sex is a talent, like dancing. Some people are good at it, some aren't. But most people can learn how to get better. That's how sex therapy can help in a way drugs can never help."

These are provocative opinions, but not ones you are likely to hear at the Society for the Study of Impotence, or any other group dominated by urologists. Tiefer's assertion that those specialists have achieved a hostile takeover, winning preeminence in ED based on weak epidemiological evidence, has some merit. The survey usually cited by urologists to support their hegemony is the Massachusetts Male Aging Study, coauthored by the ubiquitous Dr. Goldstein and a staff from the New England Research Institutes. Between 1987 and 1989, the MMAS gave medical checkups to 1,290 men between forty and seventy years of age. The men were also given psychological tests and assayed for lifestyle issues such as smoking, diet, and exercise. Then a self-administered sexual activity questionnaire was used to rate erectile potency. The final report not only confirmed the vascular etiology of nearly all cases of ED but made some startling conclusions about the prevalence of that disease. According to the MMAS the incidence of total impotence in men tripled, from 5 to 15 percent, between ages forty to seventy. That got a lot of press. But even more newsworthy was the assertion that a *majority* of men over forty had some form of impotence. This led the National Institutes of Health to project that 30 million

Americans have erectile dysfunction, three times higher than any previous number.

Those numbers were shaped by the questions. One posed by the MMAS was, "How satisfied are you with your sex life?"—in effect, rating anyone who did not answer "totally" as having minimal erectile dysfunction. Before, ED was defined as "the *persistent* failure to develop and maintain erections of sufficient rigidity for penetrative sexual intercourse." (Italics added.) After the MMAS even a rare visit from Mr. Softee was deemed a disease state. "Why the obsession with rigidity?" Tiefer asks. "A rock-hard erection isn't even necessary for satisfying sex."

Comments like that lead urologists to say Tiefer knows less about men and sex than she thinks she does. One who knows Tiefer's views extremely well is Arnold Melman, who hired her to screen ED patients at Montefiore Medical Center in the Bronx, New York, where he is chief of urology. "I brought her in because I have great respect for her intelligence and skills as a psychologist," Melman says. "Plus, I liked having her as a counterweight." For a while, anyway. In the late 1990s, Melman and Tiefer went their separate ways: he stayed, she left.

"Anyone who doesn't think a man needs a firm erection doesn't understand men," says Melman. "I see a lot of municipal workers in my practice. We have a contract with a [New York] city health plan. These are tough, physical guys—bus drivers, subway motormen, laborers, etcetera. I've gotten used to seeing them cry in my office. They cry twice, in fact: first, when they tell me they can't get an erection. And second, after we treat them, when they tell me they *can*. And, no matter what Leonore says, I haven't met one wife who was unhappy with that change.

"Where I agree with Leonore is that there are men with relationship issues, and just giving them an erection isn't going to make those issues go away. That's why we screen patients psychologically and make appropriate referrals. But I have my doubts about sex therapy. I've checked on the results for the people we sent there. Basically, one person in forty had a good result. Once I was asked to guest-edit the *Journal of Sex and Marital Therapy*. I wanted to analyze the outcomes of all the ED therapies, medical and otherwise. I asked several sex therapists to present data, including Helen Singer Kaplan, who had the largest practice in the world.* They all refused. I'm not saying they're charlatans. But they're not willing to publish their data. Urologists are, because our approach works. Patients want results—an erection—and they want it fast. That's human nature. If not human nature, it's certainly male nature."

And now it is even easier for doctors to respond to that nature. (Or at least quicker.) The sex questionnaire in the MMAS had nine questions. Now Pfizer salesmen are leaving a questionnaire they call the "Sexual Health Inventory for Men" in doctors' waiting rooms that has only *five* questions. Anyone whose answers total less than twenty-two out of twenty-five gets the message, "You may want to speak to your doctor." In Pfizer's vision of ED any score lower than the 88th percentile is a failing grade and grounds for a Viagra prescription. Even some urologists blanch at this. "There is a difference between erectile dysfunction, which is a real disease, and erectile dysphoria, which is vague sense of dissatisfaction," says James H. Barada. "I worry the line is getting blurred." Tiefer could not agree more.

But one of Tiefer's admirers, Kinsey Institute director John Bancroft, a British psychiatrist with forty years' experience in sexual medicine, would remind her there was no hard evidence to back the claim of psychotherapists that ED was almost entirely psychogenic, either. "We've gone from one myth to another," Bancroft told me at the 2000 SSI meeting. "Scientists aren't supposed to deal with myths, and they try not to, but they occasionally accept ones that are convenient. When urologists

*Kaplan, now dead, was the founding director of the Human Sexuality Program at Cornell University Medical Center in New York. Among her many books are *The New Sex Therapy* and *Disorders of Sexual Desire*.

had no treatments for erectile dysfunction, they were ready to believe it was always a psychological problem. Once they had treatments, they were ready to believe the 'it's always vascular' myth. This does not make urologists evil," Bancroft said. "Practical maybe, but not evil."

If urologists are practical, drug companies are the black belts of practicality. As this is written, Pfizer is testing a Viagra inhaler on animals, hoping to deliver this faster delivery system to humans later on. (A Viagra pill can take an hour to work.) After the bad press that followed Viagra's links to fatal coronaries, Pfizer pumped more than $50 million into consumer outreach, sponsoring a car on the NASCAR auto-racing circuit, and creating a new marketing campaign aimed at a younger clientele. In Fall 2000, American TV watchers began to see advertisements featuring a handsome male in his forties seemingly preening for a date as a bluesy voiceover growled, "I'm ready—ready as anybody can be." The man then ran down the stairs, hopped into his car, and drove to a doctor for a free sample of Viagra. These promotions are expensive, but worth it: In February 2000, *Forbes* reported Pfizer's profit margin on Viagra at 90 percent and predicted annual sales would soon top $1 billion. The campaigns have also had an evaporating effect on the public's memory: When is the last time you heard anyone mention a Viagra death?

Pfizer's jackpot has lured others into the market. Bayer, the aspirin company, is testing its own PDE-5 inhibitor, Vardenafil. So is a partnership between Eli Lilly and ICOS for a pill called Cialis. What makes these pills potentially the most groundbreaking products yet in the erection industry is that the half-life—the time it takes for a drug to lose half its potency—for each is about four times greater than that of Viagra, which is four hours. This means a man could take such a pill at noon and be fully cocked and loaded for sex for the rest of the day. A paper presented at the 2000 SSI meeting in Cleveland reported on volunteers in Europe who took Cialis once a day every day and had dramatically improved erections, without untoward side effects. This report was met with elation. Several doctors in the audience called it the urological version of putting a man on the moon.

Bancroft was intrigued by the Cialis report but questioned the drug companies' candor. "I don't think these medications are the simple erection aids their manufacturers say they are," he said. "Pfizer's position is that Viagra has no effect without sexual stimulation. They say this because their attorneys do not want the drug to be known as something that enhances sexual desire. If Viagra were an aphrodisiac, it would become an even bigger seller than it already is, but it would also create huge legal problems. A rapist could say, 'It wasn't me. It was the Viagra.' Now that companies are testing drugs that last nearly twenty-four hours, this issue could move from potential to actual. From my own clinical experience," Bancroft said, "I suspect Viagra does have certain properties of an aphrodisiac—or, more accurately, has the power to enhance one's libido without external stimulation. Mental stimulation seems to be enough."

Bancroft is not the only one wondering about such issues. Pfizer hired Arthur Caplan, a bioethicist at the University of Pennsylvania and frequent talking head on *Nightline,* to grill them with hypotheticals. How will Pfizer respond when a rapist uses Viagra? "It's out of Pfizer's control," Caplan counseled them to say. The company also discussed the drug with the Vatican, assuring the Pope's science advisers that Viagra is *not* an aphrodisiac. Whether that is true or not, one thing is certain: Some heavy hitters are betting the financial future for drugs like Viagra, Cialis, and Vardenafil is bright indeed. One guy who knows a little about grabbing market share—Bill Gates—bought a 13 percent stake in ICOS, the company that created Cialis in its Bothell, Washington laboratory.

Before Gates starts counting his next billion, however, he should know this: Another rich nonurologist, Ross Perot, was an early investor in a Texas erection-industry firm, Zonagen, which partnered up with Schering-Plough to bring oral phento-lamine (trade name: Vasomax) to market as a pill competing with Viagra. Unfortunately for Zonagen's investors, the FDA sent Zonagen a nonapproval letter in May 1999, because of "brown fat proliferations" found in rats who were given the drug. Later, an amended application was put on "clinical hold" because of the same concerns. In October 2000, the firm finally agreed to finance a new study to address those issues. Zonagen's stock, which was selling at $40 per share in late 1997, was at less than $4 when the firm made that announcement.

Another, even larger, erection-industry player got burned in 2000. After an investment of many millions of dollars, TAP, a joint venture of Abbott Laboratories in Illinois and Takeda In-dustries of Japan, withdrew its new-drug application for U-prima, a lozenge of apomorphine placed under the tongue. (Apomorphine is not related to morphine.) Rather than affect-ing the penis directly, as PDE-5 inhibitors and injectable drugs do, Uprima works on the brain, where it mimics dopamine, one of the chemicals nerve cells use to communicate with one an-other. Essentially, Uprima empowers the brain to send stronger signals down through the spinal cord and into the penis, where those signals help build an erection.

Because it dissolves under the tongue, Uprima can work in twenty minutes or less. This produced upbeat press coverage and major interest from investors; both expected Uprima to take a major chunk out of Viagra's market share. Unfortunately for TAP, Uprima also produced side effects, ranging from nau-sea to loss of consciousness. In fact, nausea was once considered one of apomorphine's beneficial side effects. According to neu-roscientist Simon LeVay, the drug was used thirty years ago in aversion therapy aimed at "curing" male homosexuals. The pa-tient was injected with 5 mg of apomorphine, then shown pho-tos of attractive naked men. "With repeated treatments," LeVay wrote in *Nerve.com*, "the patient was supposed to develop an unconscious link between naked men and nausea, and same-sex desires would be extinguished."

It's not certain whether TAP or the FDA knew about Uprima's "secret history," as LeVay calls it. But it appears the chemical's tendency to cause fainting was enough to doom the drug in the United States. When the FDA learned that one patient in TAP's trial, after taking Uprima, fainted while driving his car, and another passed out in his doctor's office, fracturing his skull on the floor, TAP withdrew its application, fearing a rejection.

Uprima's rise and fall sheds some light on the dark side of the cozy relationship between doctors and drug companies. According to one urologist who accepted a fee from TAP to take part in a mock approval hearing for the drug before it was submitted to the FDA, the company should have seen there was trouble ahead. Several doctors at that "practice" event were not impressed with Uprima's efficacy rate which, at 54 percent, was significantly lower than that of Viagra (approaching 80 percent). "A few panelists said, 'This is a lousy drug, with annoying side effects, we shouldn't approve it,'" said the urologist, who asked not to be identified. "But, in the end, the panel voted to 'approve' it anyway, basically saying, 'Why not?'" The fact that TAP had been spreading quite a bit of money around for research costs and consulting fees may have had something to do with that decision—which was not legally binding. Or maybe not. One would like to think such things have nothing to do with the process at all.

Urologists welcome pharmaceutical breakthroughs that do get FDA approval—even pills you do not need a urologist to get, like Viagra—because they know each advance brings in patients for services you *do* need a urologist to get. Viagra does not work for everyone. One well-listened-to paper at the recent SSI meeting was titled "Viagra Failures." Treating such patients has become something of a specialty for the paper's author, Dr. Gregory A. Broderick, who reported that most of those nonresponders were men over sixty with severe arterial insufficiency.

Nearly all of them, he said, chose injection therapy, revascularization, or implant surgery, monitored or performed by him at his Mayo Clinic office in Jacksonville, Florida. Broderick did not mention, nor did he have to, that the Baby Boom generation—the largest in history—will turn sixty later this decade. To assess the suitability of patients for such urological treatments, Broderick urged his peers to resume the diagnostic tests most of them abandoned post-Viagra. Interestingly, Broderick's research costs for his paper were partially covered by the manufacturer of one of those diagnostic devices.

---

This return to the operating room will be profitable for urologists, but what about patients? While there is no doubt that many men with ED have been helped by surgical interventions, it is also undeniable that some have been harmed, and not just in the distant past. In the 1980s, many reputable urologists performed a procedure known as venous ligation, which impeded the blood flow out of the patient's corpora cavernosa by tying off certain veins. The theory was that the patient was losing his erection because of venous leakage, a failure to store blood rather than a failure to fill with it. There was an 80 percent success rate—at first. Then the bad news started coming in. Erectile problems almost invariably returned. Even worse, the procedure often left the patient with a numbed penis. Forever.

Those and other surgical misadventures prompted John Bancroft to sound an alarm. In 1989 he voiced his concern as a question which doubled as the title of his essay: "Man and His Penis—A Relationship Under Threat?" As a psychiatrist (a physician trained in anatomy and physiology), Bancroft was less likely than, say, psychologist Leonore Tiefer, who did not get such medical training, to reject the urological approach completely. Even so, he was troubled by the willingness of urologists to ignore the mental aspects of impotence, whether as cause or effect. Treatments such as revascularization, inflatable silicone implants, and penile injections, he said, do not address the problem as much as they "overwhelm and obscure" it with drugs and surgery.

"I have entitled this paper 'Man and His Penis—A Relationship Under Threat?'" Bancroft wrote, "because I have concluded that the essence of male sexuality rests in the relationship, and associated misunderstandings, that exist between man and this component of his sexual anatomy. . . .

> The size of a penis is as much a function of psychological processes as it is anatomy. Often erection endows a situation with a sexuality the owner may not have recognized or be prepared to acknowledge. And how often does the penis resolutely refuse to support its owner in a sexual endeavor, as if to say, "you have no business doing this— count me out of it?"

Either way, the penis is the most honest organ on a man's body. It tells the truth, Bancroft was reminding his readers, whether its "owner" wants to hear it or not. (The identical conclusion was reached by Gay Talese in *Thy Neighbor's Wife*, the best-selling book in which Talese did some extremely personal reporting on the Sexual Revolution of the 1960s and '70s.) "Late in my career," Bancroft wrote, "and, it should be added, in my personal life, I have come to recognize the importance of this understanding between a man and his penis, ironically at a time when developments in medical care appear to be rejecting it."

Eleven years after writing those words, Bancroft said he would not retract them, though he wasn't quite as worried as he used to be. "The easy availability of oral medications has pushed surgeons aside for the moment. We're still in the early stages of all this, however, and I certainly do not think urological surgery is about to become obsolete. Most urologists still say, 'Let's concentrate on the penis. No need to think about the man attached to it.' As if you could separate them."

It just might be, however, that the erection industry and the urologists who created it understand the relationship between man and his penis far better than their critics realize. Sure, they are confident in the superiority of their approach. But this arrogance is neither new nor unjustified. It is part of a process that began more than five centuries ago with Leonardo da Vinci and Regnier de Graaf, men who used science and the spirit of experimentation to address difficult questions about sex and masculinity. What once seemed divine or demonic became neither. This process created a new relationship between man and his defining organ. Now the penis is seen as a complex but knowable organic machine. Man is capable of not only understanding Nature, but his own nature—and altering it. And most men are happy about that.

This is why the urologists who compared Cialis, the once-a-day erection pill now in clinical trials, to putting a man on the moon have not lost their sense of proportion, despite their mixed metaphor. Ending impotence by bringing a small pill to your lips—my apologies, Commander Armstrong—*is* a giant leap for mankind. With it the idea of the penis has made its most dramatic evolution yet, becoming a daily reinflatable tire, with every man just a prescription away from owning the proper pump. And even a urologist can grasp the psychological impact of that.

One ED specialist, Dr. J. Francois Eid of New York, says his practice made him realize that losing potency is like losing a part of one's mind. "I don't mean the patient goes insane," Eid says. "But he definitely loses a part of his identity." It is precisely because a man *can* hold his manhood in his hand that he needs it to feel strong and capable—and some would argue this need is now more urgent than ever. This is because technology has rendered nearly all the previous definitions of masculinity obsolete. A man is no longer measured by his physical strength—his ability to build shelter for his family, fight in hand-to-hand combat, or draw water from a well. Machines do that for him. Muscles are more symbolic than useful. So the erect penis has become the most powerfully symbolic "muscle" of them all.

One of Eid's patients told him his impotence robbed him of everything he valued most: his self-respect, the intimate part of his marriage, his patience with his children, even his sense of humor. "Every time he heard a joke about sex his head would sink into his shoulders," Eid says. "It was like he had cancer of the ego." This phallocentrism, Tiefer and like-minded critics would argue, is less a biological fact than something men learn—and therefore something they can and should *un*learn. It is a social construction, they say, part of a male-centered sexual script written by the culture at large and reinforced by the first sexual act that most males experience: masturbation. The importance of that act in writing an individual's "sexual script," say John H. Gagnon and William Simon, the coiners of that term, cannot be overestimated.

Masturbation "proclaims the male's independence," they wrote in *Sexual Conduct*. It "focuses male sexual desire in the penis, giving the genitals centrality in the physical and symbolic domains. . . . The capacity for erection is an important sign"—most men would say the most important sign—"of masculinity and control."

This concept of sexual script suggests another cinematic metaphor with which to view the erection industry and the ways it has changed man's bond with his penis. The history of that relationship has all the elements of an epic Hollywood film: sex, conflict, mystery, religion, heroes, villains, piles of money, high-tech machinery—even death. And now, thanks to the erection industry, that relationship has something every film epic needs. An ending.

For that is what you get when you answer the control question. Prior efforts to deal with the "who's in charge?" issue have created the numerous lenses that man has used to examine the most enduring mystery in his life. The history of the penis is the history of its evolution as an idea. Over time the penis has been deified, demonized, secularized, racialized, psychoanalyzed, politicized, and, finally, medicalized by the modern erection industry. Each of these lenses has been an attempt to make intellectual and emotional sense of man's relationship with his defining organ; clearly, some lenses were sharper than others. There is no denying the weighty influence of Augustine and Freud, but it appears the medicalized lens may have the heaviest impact of them all.

We have an ending to our story, but not *the* end. The bond between man and his penis, fundamentally altered as it is, continues. And while much of its central mystery has been solved, other mysteries remain. The medicalized penis is only two decades old, the era of the erection pill younger still. Both have answered huge questions but raise others. Science has helped men with erectile dysfunction, and a medicalized penis is certainly better than a demonized one, but the long-term effects of PDE-5 inhibitors on the penis have yet to be determined. Might not regular exposure to them cause the body to produce an abnormally high level of PDE-5? (Such a reaction would not be unprecedented, or even unexpected.) And what effect would that have on a man's internal chemistry? Or behavior? The answers will be known later—maybe too late for some.

On another front, admittedly more metaphysical than medical, some critics worry that the erection industry has replaced an idea of the penis with an anti-idea, a body part with a thing, a symbol of manhood with a punctureproof balloon. Whether today's erection entrepreneurs truly grasp the psychological aspects of man's relationship with his penis or not, their treatment breakthroughs have permanently altered that mental bond— chemically dissolving its most puzzling part. That, of course, is the control issue, a question that has shaped that relationship, for better and worse, for all of history. Now man can hold his manhood in his hand, confident in knowing who is in charge. When a man uses the products of the erection industry, his penis works for him.

This is more than a temporary jolt in the balance of power. It is a paradigm shift and a revolutionary restructuring of the masculine mystique. That mystique—and the psychic vault of attitudes, aptitudes, and anxieties which give it so much confusing urgency—compels man to impose his will on the world. Yet man has not always been able to impose his will on his penis, the flesh-and-blood symbol of that mystique. The penis used to have a mind of its own. Not anymore. The erection industry has reconfigured the organ, replacing the finicky original with a more reliable model. But the price tag for this new power tool is hidden. Eventually, we'll learn if we can afford it.

# ACKNOWLEDGMENTS

My editor, Chad Conway, immediately understood what I wanted this book to be and was a constant source of insight and encouragement. I am forever indebted to him. Heartfelt thanks also to Elizabeth Maguire, who acquired the book for The Free Press. My agent, David Black, was extraordinarily helpful in whipping my proposal into shape. Thanks to Bill Tonelli, then of *Esquire*, who was smart enough in 1996—two years before Viagra—to agree that an investigation of the burgeoning erection industry would be worth pursuing. That *Esquire* piece, subsequently edited by Peter Griffin, David Granger, and Andrew Ward, was the genesis of the idea that led to this book. A special thanks is owed Leonore Tiefer—psychologist, sexologist, social critic, and one of the most provocative thinkers I've ever met—for making me realize that the erection industry is more than a health story. A similar debt is owed J. François Eid, the New York urologist who agreed to oversee my personal experimentation with the drugs that have changed man's relationship with his penis forever.

Many urologists, physiologists, epidemiologists, psychiatrists, psychologists, sociologists, sexologists, and sex therapists were kind enough to answer questions. In alphabetical order they include: John Bancroft, James H. Barada, Giles Brindley, Gerald D. Brock, Gregory A. Broderick, Arthur L. Burnett, John H. Gagnon, Joshua Golden, Irwin Goldstein, Joyce A. Joseph, Sandra R. Leiblum, Eli F. Lizza, Tom F. Lue, Barry McCarthy,

Andrew R. McCullough, John C. McKinlay, Arnold Melman, Ronald F. Moglia, John Money, Abraham Morgentaler, Ajay Nehra, Harin Padma-Nathan, Michael A. Perelman, Domeena Renshaw, Leslie R. Schover, R. T. Segraves, Ridwan Shabsigh, Ira D. Sharlip, William D. Steers, Carol Tavris, Ronald Virag, Gorm Wagner, Claire C. Yang, and Bernie Zilbergeld.

Librarians at New York University's Bobst Library were consistently helpful, as were those at the New York Public Library's Center for the Humanities (including those at the Jewish Division, the Oriental Division, and the Rare Books & Manuscripts room). Staff members at the New York Academy of Medicine were always eager to assist, as were their counterparts at the College of Physicians of Philadelphia. The director of the latter institution's Mutter Museum, Gretchen Worden, deserves a special thanks for her unwavering enthusiasm. Other scholars were helpful with their time as well, including professors Ogden Goelet Jr. and Larissa Bonfante of New York University, and Helen Rodnite Lemay of SUNY–Stony Brook. Thanks to Jay Blotcher for sending me countless newspaper and magazine stories of interest. Picture researcher Natalie Goldstein did a wonderfully thorough job.

Several friends were kind enough to read early drafts of this manuscript. Ben Yagoda was, as always, a fount of good advice, as were John Capouya and Matthew Flamm.

Thanks most of all to Marion Ettlinger, who reminded me—by deed and word—of the enduring value of hard work, commitment to the task at hand, and aiming high.

# NOTES

## Chapter I

1: "Unlike her life": The death of Anna Pappenheimer is described in excruciating detail in Michael Kunze, *Highroad to the Stake* (Chicago: University of Chicago Press, 1987).

2: On Angela de la Barthe, Anna Pappenheimer's "education," and descriptions of the Devil's penis: Many books make reference to each. Among the best are Henry Charles Lea, *Materials Toward a History of Witchcraft* (Philadelphia: University of Pennsylvania Press, 1939); Rossell Hope Robbins, *The Encyclopedia of Witchcraft and Demonology* (New York: Crown, 1959); Robert E. L. Masters, *Eros and Evil* (New York: Julian Press, 1962); Ann Llewellyn Barstow, *Witchcraze* (San Francisco: Harper-Collins, 1994); Joseph Klaits, *Servants of Satan* (Bloomington, Ind.: Indiana University Press, 1985); and Brian P. Levack, *The Witch-Hunt in Early Modern Europe* (New York: Longman, 1987). Some witches burned at the stake were men; the Devil's penis was not always the "star" of their confession narratives.

3: "*The Malleus Maleficarum*": Montague Summers, ed., *The Malleus Maleficarum of Heinrich Kramer and James Sprenger* (New York: Dover, 1971), p. 121.

3: On codpieces: Lyndal Roper, *Oedipus & the Devil* (New York: Routledge, 1994), pp. 117–20; Grace Q. Vicary, "Visual Art as Social Data: The Renaissance Codpiece," *Cultural Anthropology* 4 (1989): 3–25; Lois Banner, "The Fashionable Sex, 1100–1600," *History Today*, April 1992, pp. 37–44.

4: "The priests and politicians": Roper, *Oedipus & the Devil*, pp. 23–27.

6: "Whoever could make Man": Michel de Montaigne, "On Some Lines of Virgil," *The Essays of Michel de Montaigne*, vol. III, 5, trans., M. A. Screech (London: Allen Lane, 1991), p. 1005.

7: "After Father Enki lifted his eyes": Gwendolyn Leick, *Sex & Eroti-*

*cism in Mesopotamian Literature* (New York: Routledge, 1994), pp. 24–25. Also good on Enki myths: Samuel Noah Kramer and John Maier, *Myths of Enki, the Crafty God* (New York: Oxford University Press, 1989); Jerrold S. Cooper, "Enki's Member: Eros and Irrigation in Sumerian Literature," *Dumu-e2-dub-ba-a: Studies in Honor of Ake W. Sjoberg,* eds., Hermann Behrens, Darlene Loding, and Martha T. Roth (Philadelphia: University of Pennsylvania Museum Press, 1989), pp. 87–89; Jeremy Black and Anthony Green, *Gods, Demons and Symbols of Ancient Mesopotamia* (Austin, Tex.: University of Texas Press, 1992).

7: An outstanding resource for anyone interested in the art and culture of ancient Egypt is the Wilbour Library of Egyptology at the Brooklyn Museum of Art. Professor Ogden Goelet Jr. of New York University was also very generous with his time and expertise.

Among the many helpful books and articles that deal with the Egyptian creation myths and Egyptian sexuality are Stephen Quirke, *Ancient Egyptian Religion* (London: British Museum Press, 1992); Lewis Spence, *Egyptian Myths and Legends* (New York: Dover, 1990); R. T. Rundle Clark, *Myth and Symbol in Ancient Egypt* (London: Thames & Hudson, 1959); George Hart, *A Dictionary of Egyptian Gods and Goddesses* (London and New York: Routledge, 1986); George Hart, *Egyptian Myths* (Austin, Tex.: University of Texas Press, 1995); Henri Frankfurt, *Ancient Egyptian Religion* (New York: Harper & Row, 1949); Lisa Manniche, *Sexual Life in Ancient Egypt* (New York: Kegan Paul International, 1997); David P. Silverman, ed., *Ancient Egypt* (New York: Oxford University Press, 1997); Gay Robins, *The Art of Ancient Egypt* (Cambridge, Mass.: Harvard University Press, 1997); Dominic Montserrat, *Sex and Society in Graeco-Roman Egypt* (New York: Kegan Paul International, 1996); Natalie Boymel Kampen, ed., *Sexuality in Ancient Art* (New York: Cambridge University Press, 1996); Jonathan Cott, *Isis and Osiris* (New York: Doubleday, 1994); and J. Ogdon, "Some Notes on the Iconography of the God Min," *Bulletin of the Egyptological Seminar* 7 (1986): 29–41.

9: "I am Osiris . . . stiff of penis": Spells 39, 69, and 110, in Raymond O. Faulkner, trans., *The Ancient Egyptian Book of the Dead* (London: British Museum Press, 1985), pp. 60–61, 70, 104.

9: "Penises of Libyan generals": Richard Zacks, *History Laid Bare* (New York: HarperPerennial, 1994), p. 3. The spelling of Merneptah is from David P. Silverman, ed., *Ancient Egypt* (New York: Oxford University Press, 1997).

9: "Three thousand years later": Cited in Sean Wilentz, "Lone Star Setting," *New York Times Book Review,* April 12, 1998, p. 5 (review of Robert Dallek's *Flawed Giant*).

10: "Hold him, that he might not faint": Blair O. Rogers, "History of

External Genital Surgery," *Plastic and Reconstructive Surgery of the Genital Area,* ed., Charles E. Horton (Boston: Little, Brown, 1973), p. 7.

10: Many have weighed in on the history of circumcision. Among the best are David L. Gollaher, *Circumcision* ((New York: Basic Books, 2000); W. D. Dunsmuir and E. M. Gordon, "The History of Circumcision," *British Journal of Urology International* 83, suppl. 1 (1999): 1–12; James Hastings, ed., *Encyclopaedia of Religion and Ethics* (New York: Scribner, 1951); David Bleich, *Judaism and Healing* (New York: Ktav, 1981); J. M. Glass, "Religious Circumcision: A Jewish View," *British Journal of Urology International* 83, suppl. 1 (1999): 17–21; Mark Strage, *The Durable Fig Leaf* (New York: Morrow Quill, 1980); Howard Eilberg-Schwartz, *The Savage in Judaism* (Bloomington, Ind.: Indiana University Press, 1990); and Lawrence A. Hoffmann, *Covenant of Blood* (Chicago: University of Chicago Press, 1996). This is a short list and does not include the many psychoanalytic interpretations of the rite.

10: "One healer": Gollaher, *Circumcision,* p. 5.

11: "Shall a child be born": All Bible quotations are from Herbert G. May and Bruce M. Metzger, eds., *The Oxford Annotated Bible with the Apocrypha,* Revised Standard Version (New York: Oxford University Press, 1965).

13: "What is more logical": Gerda Lerner, *The Creation of Patriarchy* (New York: Oxford University Press, 1986), p. 192.

14: "Most of them probably tried the *Pondus Judaeus*": S. B. Brandes and J. W. McAninch, "Surgical Methods of Restoring the Prepuce: A Critical Review," *British Journal of Urology International* 83, suppl. 1 (1999): 109–13. On *epipasmos:* Jody P. Rubin, "Celsus's Decircumcision Operation," *Urology* 16 (1980): 121–24; T. Schneider, "Circumcision and 'Uncircumcision,'" *South African Medical Journal* 50 (1976): 556–58; Gollaher, *Circumcision,* pp. 16–17.

14: "Roman soldiers 'would cut off'": Gollaher, *Circumcision,* p. 15.

15: "On the 11th August, 1492": Quoted by J. B. Hanna, *Christianity* (London: F. Griffiths, 1913), p. 218.

15: "The final test": Peter Stanford, *The She-Pope* (London: Heileman, 1998), p. 11.

16: "It felt like a desecration": Stanford, *The She-Pope,* p. 12.

16: "Among these other tribes": Sarah Dening, *The Mythology of Sex* (New York: Macmillan, 1996), p. 133.

17: "This is puzzling language": S. H. Smith, "'Heel' and 'Thigh': The Concept of Sexuality in the Jacob-Esau Narratives," *Vetus Testamentum* 40 (1990): 464–73.

17:: "Well, this is a fine state of affairs": Quoted in Reay Tannahill, *Sex in History* (New York: Scarborough House, 1992), p. 89.

18: On Greek nudity, *gymnasia, hermae,* views on conception, etc.: Andrew Stewart, *Art, Desire, and the Body in Ancient Greece* (New York: Cambridge University Press, 1997); Eva Keuls, *The Reign of the Phallus* (Berkeley, Cal.: University of California Press, 1993); John J. Winkler, "Phallos Politikos: The Body Politic in Athens," *Differences* 2, (1990): 29–45; Larissa Bonfante, "Nudity as a Costume in Classical Art," *American Journal of Archaeology* 93 (1989): 543–70; Larissa Bonfante, "Introduction: Essays on Nudity in Antiquity," *Source: Notes in the History of Art* 12 (1993): 7–11; Timothy J. McNiven, "The Unheroic Penis: Otherness Exposed," *Source: Notes in the History of Art* 15 (1995): 10–16; Robin Osborne, "Men Without Clothes: Heroic Nakedness," *Gender & History* 9 (1997): 504–28; Clarence A. Forbes, "Expanded Uses of the Greek Gymnasium," *Classical Philology* 40 (1945): 32–42; Richard Sennett, *Flesh and Stone* (New York: Norton, 1994); R. E. Wycherley, *The Stones of Athens* (Princeton, N.J.: Princeton University Press, 1978); Robin Osborne, "The Erection and Mutilation of the Hermae," *Proceedings of the Cambridge Philological Society* 23 (1985): 47–73; Brian M. Lavelle, "Hipparchos' Herms," *Classical Views* 29 (1985): 411–20; Maryanne Cline Horowitz, "Aristotle and Woman," *Journal of the History of Biology* 9 (1976): 183–213.

19: "The Greek link": E. E. Rice, *The Grand Procession of Ptolemy Philadelphus* (London: Oxford University Press, 1983).

20: "Dionysus was honored": H. W. Parke, *Festivals of the Athenians* (Ithaca, N.Y.: Cornell University Press, 1977); Giulia Sissa and Marcel Detienne, *The Daily Life of the Greek Gods* (Stanford, Cal.: Stanford University Press, 2000); Carl Kerenyi, *Dionysos* (Princeton, N.J.: Princeton University Press, 1976); Eric Csapo, "Riding the Phallus for Dionysus," *Phoenix* 51 (1997): 253–95; R. J. Hoffman, "Ritual License and the Cult of Dionysus," *Athenaeum* 67 (1989): 91–115.

21: "To a Greek, classicist Albert Henrichs writes"; and "a vital impulse to gush forth": Each quoted in Csapo, "Riding the Phallus," p. 260.

22: "Greeks favored a small thin penis:" K. J. Dover, *Greek Homosexuality* (Cambridge, Mass.: Harvard University Press, 1989); McNiven, "The Unheroic Penis," pp. 10–16.

22: "If you do what I say": This translation is in Winkler, "Phallos Politikos," p. 29.

22: There are many excellent sources on Greek pederasty. Among them: Dover, *Greek Homosexuality;* William Armstrong Percy III, *Pederasty and Pedagogy in Archaic Greece* (Urbana, Ill.: University of Illinois Press, 1996); David M. Halperin, *One Hundred Years of Homosexuality and Other Essays on Greek Love* (New York: Routledge, 1990); Thorkil Vanggaard, *Phallos* (New York: International Universities Press, 1972);

Robert Flaceliere, *Love in Ancient Greece* (New York: Crown, 1962); T. K. Hubbard, "Popular Perceptions of Elite Homosexuality in Classical Athens," *Arion* 6 (1998): 48–78; Bernard Sergent, "Paederasty and Political Life in Archaic Greek Cities," *Journal of Homosexuality* 25 (1993): 147–64.

24: "'In Greece,' Michel Foucault wrote": Michel Foucault, *The History of Sexuality: An Introduction* (New York: Vintage Books, 1990), p. 61.

24: On Aristophanes' homophobia: Dover, *Greek Homosexuality,* pp. 141–43.

24: First-rate sources for Roman sexuality, and sexual attitudes, abound as well. Some of the most helpful are Judith P. Hallett and Marilyn B. Skinner, eds., *Roman Sexualities* (Princeton, N.J.: Princeton University Press, 1997); Otto Kiefer, *Sexual Life in Ancient Rome* (London: Routledge & Kegan Paul, 1934); J. P. Toner, *Leisure and Ancient Rome* (Cambridge: Polity Press, 1995); Amy Richlin, *The Garden of Priapus* (New York: Oxford University Press, 1992); Michael Grant, *Eros in Pompeii* (New York: Stewart, Tabori & Chang, 1975); Catherine Johns, *Sex or Symbol* (Austin, Tex.: University of Texas Press, 1982); J. N. Adams, *The Latin Sexual Vocabulary* (Baltimore: Johns Hopkins University Press, 1982); J. P. Sullivan, "Martial's Sexual Attitudes," *Philologus* 123 (1978): 288–302.

24: "A Roman penetrated others": Jonathan Walters, "Invading the Roman Body," *Roman Sexualities,* eds., Hallett and Skinner, pp. 29–43.

25: "At the siege of Perusia": Judith P. Hallett, "*Perusinae Glandes* and the Changing Image of Augustus," *American Journal of Ancient History* 2 (1977): 151–71.

25: "The *bulla* marked him off-limits": Barbara Kellum, "The Phallus as Signifier," *Sexuality in Ancient Art,* ed., Natalie Boymel Kampen, pp. 170–83.

25: "So enduring": George Ryley Scott, *Phallic Worship* (London: Senate, 1996), p. xviii.

26: On Priapus, the god and "poet": Richlin, *The Garden of Priapus;* Richard Payne Knight, *A Discourse on the Worship of Priapus* (London: Privately printed, 1865); James Wyly, *The Phallic Quest* (Toronto: Inner City Books, 1989); Scott, *Phallic Worship;* Peter Stewart, "Fine Art and Coarse Art: The Image of Roman Priapus," *Art History* 20, (1997): 575–88; Eugene Michael O'Connor, *Symbolum Salacitatis* (New York: Lang, 1989); W. H. Parker, *Priapea: Poems for a Phallic God* (London: Croom Helm, 1988); H. D. Rankin, "Petronius, Priapus and Priapeum LXVIII," *Classica et Mediaevalia* 27 (1966): 225–42; Craig Williams, *Roman Homosexuality* (New York: Oxford University Press, 1999); Ilias Papadopoulos and Alpay Kelami, "Priapus and Priapism," *Urology* 32 (1988): 385–86; Sissa and Detienne, *The Daily Life of the Greek Gods.*

28: "Emperor Commodus elevated"; and "That was *mentula*": Adams, *The Latin Sexual Vocabulary,* pp. 9–12, 78.

28: "If from the baths you hear": Cited in Toner, *Leisure and Ancient Rome,* p. 58.

28: "The naked truth was": John Clarke, "Hypersexual Black Men in Augustan Baths," *Sexuality in Ancient Art,* pp. 184–98.

28: "The penis was so much the symbol": Kellum, "The Phallus as Signifier," *Sexuality in Ancient Art,* p. 173.

29: On phallic art in Pompeii: Grant, *Eros in Pompeii;* Johns, *Sex or Symbol.*

30: "These priests ran": Maarten J. Vermaseren, *Cybele and Attis* (London: Thames & Hudson, 1997); Lynn E. Roller, *In Search of God the Mother* (Berkeley, Cal.: University of California Press, 1999); Walter Stevenson, "The Rise of Eunuchs in Greco-Roman Antiquity," *Journal of the History of Sexuality* 5 (1995): 485–511.

30: "If you have a eunuch, kill him": Cited in Gary Taylor, *Castration* (New York: Routledge, 2001), p. 140.

31: "There are those who in soft eunuchs": Juvenal, *Saturae* 6.366–75, trans., in Victor T. Cheney, *A Brief History of Castration* (Edison, N.J.: American Focus, 1996), pp. 6–7.

31: "O fairies, O buggers": Petronius, *The Satyricon,* trans., William Arrowsmith (New York: Meridian, 1994), p. 36.

32: "Nero 'tried to turn the boy Sporus into a girl'": Gaius Suetonius Tranquillus, *The Twelve Caesars,* trans., Robert Graves (London: The Folio Society, 1964), pp. 224–25.

32: More on eunuchs, castration, and etymology of each: Taylor, *Castration;* Theodore James, "Eunuchs and Eunuchism—An Historical Discourse," Parts I and II, *Adler Museum Journal* 7 and 8 (1981): 2–7, 3–7; Vincent J. Derbes, "The Keepers of the Bed," *Journal of the American Medical Association* 212 (1970): 97–100; Tannahill, *Sex in History;* Dening, *The Mythology of Sex.*

33: "In *The Golden Bough*": Cited in Kit Schwartz, *The Male Member* (New York: St. Martin's Press, 1985), pp. 94–95.

33 "In her 1938 paper": Edith Weigert-Vowinkel, "The Cult and Mythology of the Magna Mater from the Standpoint of Psychoanalysis," *Psychiatry* 3 (1938): 347–78.

33: "Carl Jung was so moved": Eugene Monick, *Castration and Male Rage* (Toronto: Inner City Books, 1991), p. 8.

34: "Romans celebrated": Peter Brown, *The Body and Society* (New York: Columbia University Press, 1988), p. 28.

34: "Not the Christian penis": Brown, *The Body and Society;* Elaine Pagels, *Adam, Eve, and the Serpent* (New York: Vintage, 1989); Uta

Ranke-Heinemann, *Eunuchs for the Kingdom of Heaven* (New York: Penguin, 1991); Aline Rousselle, *Porneia* (Cambridge: Blackwell, 1993); Daniel F. Caner, "The Practice and Prohibition of Self-Castration in Early Christianity," *Virgilia Christianae* 51 (1997): 396–415.

34: "Jesus would not have chosen birth": Ranke-Heinemann, *Eunuchs for the Kingdom of Heaven*, p. 5.

35: "As Professor Gary Taylor": Taylor, *Castration*, p. 15.

35: "Basil the Great, later canonized": Taylor, *Castration*, p. 142.

36: "The key to the abyss": Laura Engelstein, *Castration and the Heavenly Kingdom* (Ithaca, N.Y.: Cornell University Press, 1999), p. 17.

36: "Males in the cult": Engelstein, *Castration and the Heavenly Kingdom*, p. 13.

37: The "true eunuch is": Clement of Alexandria, *Paidogogus*, III, 4, 26.

37: On the life and teachings of Augustine, and his debate with Julian of Eclanum, I have relied heavily on two experts on the subject: Brown, *The Body and Society*; and Pagels, *Adam, Eve, and the Serpent*.

39: "That is the penalty of sin": Augustine, *On Marriage and Concupiscence*, II, 22, 291.

39: "At times the urge intrudes uninvited": Cited in Pagels, *Adam, Eve, and the Serpent*, p. 111.

40: "God made bodies": Pagels, *Adam, Eve, and the Serpent*, p. 132.

41: "The English language": Kenneth Clark, *The Nude* (New York: Anchor, 1959): p. 23.

41: "Now the body": Michael Camille, *The Gothic Idol* (New York: Cambridge University Press, 1989), p. 92.

42: "Their [Adam's and Eve's] bodies were to be pure": Quoted in Leo Steinberg, *The Sexuality of Christ in Renaissance Art and in Modern Oblivion*, second edition (Chicago: University of Chicago Press, 1996), p. 249.

42: "This rejection of the body": Camille, *The Gothic Idol*, p. 94.

43: On penitentials, "Member not granted for this": James A. Brundage, *Law, Sex, and Christian Society in Medieval Europe* (Chicago: University of Chicago Press, 1990); Vern L. Bullough and James A. Brundage, *Sexual Practices & the Medieval Church* (Buffalo: Prometheus, 1982); Pierre Payer, *Sex and the Penitentials* (Toronto: University of Toronto Press, 1984).

43: "Those who put semen": Brundage, *Law, Sex, and Christian Society in Medieval Europe*, p. 167.

43: Abelard and Héloïse: Peter Abelard, *Historia calamitatum*, trans., Betty Radice (London: Folio Society, 1997); M. T. Clanchy, *Abelard: A Medieval Life* (Oxford,: Blackwell, 1998); Leif Crane, *Peter Abelard* (New York: Harcourt, Brace & World, 1970); Betty Radice, trans., *The Letters of*

*Abelard and Heloise* (New York: Penguin, 1974); J. T. Muckle, *The Story of Abelard's Adversities* (Toronto: Pontifical Institute of Mediaeval Studies, 1992); Tannahill, *Sex in History.*

43: "No natural pleasure": Ranke-Heinemann, *Eunuchs for the Kingdom of Heaven,* p. 169.

45: "'Yes,' said theologian Pierre de La Palude": Brundage, *Law, Sex, and Christian Society in Medieval Europe,* p. 456.

46: "Is it any wonder": Danielle Jacquart and Claude Thomasset, *Sexuality and Medicine in the Middle Ages* (Princeton, N.J.: Princeton University Press, 1988), p. 171.

46: On the "honest woman" and the "congress": Thomas G. Benedek and Janet Kubinec, "The Evaluation of Impotence by Sexual Congress and Alternatives Thereto in Divorce Proceedings," *Transactions and Studies of the College of Physicians of Philadelphia* 4 (1982): 1333–53; Jacquart and Thomasset, *Sexuality and Medicine in the Middle Ages,* pp. 169–73; Brundage, *Law, Sex, and Christian Society in Medieval Europe,* p. 457.

47: On Constantinus Africanus: Monica H. Green, "Constantinus Africanus and the Conflict between Religion and Science," *The Human Embryo,* ed., G. R. Dunstan (Exeter, U.K.: University of Exeter Press, 1990), pp. 47–69; Joan Cadden, *Meanings of Sex Difference in the Middle Ages* (New York: Cambridge University Press, 1995); Jacquart and Thomasset, *Sexuality and Medicine in the Middle Ages.*

47: Constantinus Africanus and Chaucer: M. Bassan, "Chaucer's Accursed Monk, Constantinus Africanus," *Medieval Studies* 24 (1962): 1127–40; Paul Delany, "Constantinus Africanus and Chaucer's 'Merchant's Tale,'" *Philological Quarterly* 46 (1967): 560–66.

48: "Who experiences greater pleasure": Mary Frances Wack, "The Measure of Pleasure: Peter of Spain on Men, Women, and Lovesickness," *Viator* 17 (1986): 174–96; L. M. De Rijk, "The Life of Peter of Spain (Pope John XXI)," *Vivarium* 8 (1970): 123–53.

48: "This is the sign": Albert the Great, *Quaestiones super de animalibus* XV, q. 14, quoted in Ranke-Heinemann, *Eunuchs for the Kingdom of Heaven,* p. 182.

48: "This is because": Ranke-Heinemann, *Eunuchs for the Kingdom of Heaven,* p. 182.

50: "With his teachings on demonized semen": Ranke-Heinemann, *Eunuchs for the Kingdom of Heaven,* p. 236.

51: The paintings by Maerten van Heemskerck are in Steinberg, *The Sexuality of Christ in Renaissance Art and in Modern Oblivion,* pp. 87–88.

52: On Holy Foreskin relics: Marc Shell, "The Holy Foreskin; or, Money, Relics, and Judeo-Christianity," *Jews and Other Differences,* eds., Jonathan and Daniel Boyarin (Minneapolis: University of Minnesota Press,

1997), pp. 345–59; Felix Bryk, *Circumcision in Man and Woman* (New York: American Ethnological Press, 1934); Lee Alexander Stone, *The Power of a Symbol* (Chicago: Pascal Covici, 1925).

## Chapter II

55: There are many excellent sources for Leonardo's secret career as an anatomist. Among the best are Kenneth D. Keele, *Leonardo da Vinci's Elements of the Science of Man* (New York: Academic Press, 1983); and Charles D. O'Malley and J. B. de C. M. Saunders, *Leonardo da Vinci on the Human Body* (New York: Greenwich House, 1982). Both books have strong biographical sections on da Vinci as well. (They do not always agree on dates, however.) Also: J. Playfair McMurrich, *Leonardo da Vinci the Anatomist* (Washington, D.C.: Carnegie Institution, 1929); Antonina Vallentin, *Leonardo da Vinci* (New York: Viking Press, 1938); Edward McCurdy, *The Mind of Leonardo da Vinci* (London: Jonathan Cape, 1928); and Sherwin B. Nuland, *Leonardo da Vinci* (New York: Lipper/Viking, 2000). A fascinating psychoanalytic and cultural-studies perspective on Leonardo's life and work can be found in Sander L. Gilman, *Sexuality: An Illustrated History* (New York: John Wiley & Sons, 1989). Taking a similar approach are Stanley J. Pacion, "Leonardo da Vinci: A Psychosexual Enigma," *Medical Aspects of Human Sexuality,* Dec. 1971, pp. 35–41; and Gilman, "Leonardo Sees Him-Self: Reading Leonardo's First Representation of Human Sexuality," *Social Research* 54 (1987): 141–70. Sigmund Freud himself weighed in on da Vinci in *Leonardo Da Vinci and a Memory of His Childhood,* in vol. XI of *The Standard Edition of the Complete Psychological Works of Sigmund Freud,* ed., James Strachey (London: Hogarth Press, 1974), pp. 59–138.

Other relevant journal articles and essays include John Herman Randall Jr., "The Place of Leonardo da Vinci in the Emergence of Modern Science," *Journal of the History of Ideas* 14 (1955): 191–202; Kenneth D. Keele, "Leonardo da Vinci's Influence on Renaissance Anatomy," *Medical History* 8 (1964): 360–70; Elmer Belt, "Leonardo the Florentine (1452–1519)," *Investigative Urology* 3 (1965): 99–109; H. Hopstock, "Leonardo as Anatomist," *Studies in the History and Method of Science,* ed., Charles Singer (Oxford: Clarendon Press, 1921); and Henri Zerner, "The Vision of Leonardo," *New York Review of Books,* Sept. 25, 1997, pp. 61–64.

There are many sources for Leonardo's diaries themselves. The standard version on the anatomical work is Leonardo da Vinci, *Corpus of the Anatomical Studies in the Collection of Her Majesty the Queen at Windsor Castle* (New York: Harcourt Brace Jovanovich, 1979). A helpful text arranged by subject is Edward McCurdy, *The Notebooks of Leonardo da Vinci* (New York: Reynal & Hitchcock, 1939).

55: "Sometime around 1503": O'Malley and Saunders, *Leonardo da Vinci on the Human Body,* p. 22.

55: "I destroyed all the [dissected] organs": Cited in Keele, *Leonardo da Vinci's Elements of the Science of Man,* p. 197.

57: "The woman likes the penis as large as possible": Keele, *Leonardo da Vinci's Elements of the Science of Man,* p. 351.

57: "The penis would enter more into the body": Keele, *Leonardo da Vinci's Elements of the Science of Man,* p. 354.

57: "I have seen . . . dead men": Keele, *Leonardo da Vinci's Elements of the Science of Man,* p. 350.

57: "In 1585 Ambroise Paré": Rainer M. Engel et al., *Impotence: A Historic Review,* a pamphlet published by the American Urological Association, Baltimore, Md. (undated).

59: "Often a man is asleep and it is awake": Cited in Gilman, *Sexuality,* p. 94.

63: "Hunter expected": Cited in Nuland, *Leonardo da Vinci,* p. 120.

64: "No one before him": Nuland, *Leonardo da Vinci,* pp. 165–66.

64: "A man who is ashamed": Keele, *Leonardo da Vinci's Elements of the Science of Man,* p. 350.

65: For biographical information on Vesalius: Charles D. O'Malley, *Andreas Vesalius of Brussels* (London: Cambridge University Press, 1964); L. R. Lind, "The Life and Work of Andreas Vesalius," introduction to *The Epitome of Andreas Vesalius,* trans., L. R. Lind (New York, Macmillan, 1949); Charles Singer, *A Short History of Anatomy from the Greeks to Harvey* (New York: Dover, 1957); F. J. Cole, *A History of Comparative Anatomy from Aristotle to the Eighteenth Century* (London: Macmillan, 1944); Meyer Friedman and Gerald W. Friedland, *Medicine's Ten Greatest Discoveries* (New Haven, Conn.: Yale University Press, 1998); Frank N. Magill, ed., *The Great Scientists* (Danbury, Conn.: Grolier, 1989); Charles Coulston Gillispie, ed., *Dictionary of Scientific Biography* (New York: Scribner, 1970–80); Daniel J. Boorstin, *The Discoverers* (New York: Vintage, 1985); J. B. de C. M. Saunders and Charles D. O'Malley, "Biographical Introduction," *The Illustrations from the Works of Andreas Vesalius of Brussels* (New York: Dover, 1973).

A good short history of human dissection exists in Bernard Knight, *Discovering the Human Body* (New York: Lippincott & Crowell, 1980). A longer treatment with broader cultural perspective can be found in Jonathan Sawday, *The Body Emblazoned* (New York: Routledge, 1996). Other interesting sources include Giovanni Ferrari, "Public Anatomy Lessons and the Carnival," *Past and Present* 17 (1987): 50–106; Jan C.

Rupp, "Matters of Life and Death," *History of Science* 28 (1990): 263–87; Mary Niven Alston, "The Attitude of the Church Towards Dissection Before 1500," *Bulletin of the History of Medicine* 16 (1944): 221–33.

65: "The testicles . . . are formed of": George W. Corner, *Anatomical Texts of the Earlier Middle Ages* (Washington, D.C.: Carnegie Institution, 1927), pp. 63–64.

66: "Vesalius showed them": Baldasar Heseler, *Andreas Vesalius's First Public Anatomy at Bologna, 1540,* trans., Ruben Eriksson (Upsala, Sweden: Almqvist & Wiksells, 1959), pp. 227–28.

67: "The truth about the penis": "Concerning the Organs Which Minister to the Propagation of the Species," *The Epitome of Andreas Vesalius,* trans., L. R. Lind, pp. 83–85.

68: A clear depiction of Vesalius's drawing of the vagina/penis exists in Saunders and O'Malley, *The Illustrations from the Works of Andreas Vesalius,* p. 171.

68: The standard source on the "one-sex" model is Thomas Laqueur, *Making Sex* (Cambridge, Mass.: Harvard University Press, 1990).

69: The poem from *Aristotle's Master-Piece* is quoted by Clara Pinto-Correia, *The Ovary of Eve* (Chicago: University of Chicago Press, 1997), p. 261.

69: On Marie, the girl who "developed a male rod": Ambroise Paré, *On Monsters and Marvels* (Chicago: University of Chicago Press, 1982), pp. 31–32. On Montaigne's visit: Stephen Greenblatt, *Shakespearean Negotiations* (Berkeley, Cal.: University of California Press, 1988), p. 81.

70: Buck's fascia, Lecat's gulf, etc.: Knight, *Discovering the Human Body,* p. 134.

70: Fallopio's advice to "prime the pump": Pinto-Correia, *The Ovary of Eve,* p. 86.

71: "If a penis dissected in the sixteenth century": Boorstin, *The Discoverers,* p. 348.

72: "Prepare the penis in the following way": Regnier de Graaf, *A Treatise Concerning the Generative Organs of Men,* in H. D. Jocelyn and B. P. Setchell, "Regnier de Graaf on the Human Reproductive Organs," *Journal of Reproduction and Fertility,* suppl. 17 (1972): 47.

72: "We have sometimes dissected": De Graaf, *A Treatise,* p. 48.

72: "There are families which excel mightily": De Graaf, *A Treatise,* p. 46.

73: De Graaf's other medical findings: B. P. Setchell, "The Contributions of Regnier de Graaf to Reproductive Biology," *European Journal of Gynecology and Reproductive Biology* 4 (1974): 1–13; Hubert R. Catchpole, "Regnier de Graaf, 1641–1673," *Bulletin of the History of Medicine* 8 (1940): 1261–89; Ruth J. Mann, "Regnier de Graaf, 1641–1673, Investigator," *Fertility and Sterility* 27 (1976): 466–68.

75: "What I describe here" (and all subsequent Leeuwenhoek quotes): Edward G. Reustow, "Images and Ideas: Leeuwenhoek's Perception of the Spermatozoa," *Journal of the History of Biology* 16 (1983): 185–224.

76: Other sources for Leeuwenhoek, preformationism, and Father Spallanzani include Carlo Castellani, "Spermatozoan Biology from Leeuwenhoek to Spallanzani," *Journal of the History of Biology* 6 (1973): 37–68; and Peter J. Bowler, "Preformation and Pre-existence in the Seventeenth Century," *Journal of the History of Biology* 4 (1971): 221–44. Also: Pinto-Correia, *The Ovary of Eve;* F. C. Cole, *Early Theories of Sexual Generation* (London: Oxford University Press, 1930); Joseph Needham, *A History of Embryology* (New York: Abelard-Schuman, 1959); and Elizabeth Gasking, *Investigations into Generation: 1651–1828* (Baltimore: Johns Hopkins University Press, 1966).

78: "Let the sperm of a man": Pinto-Correia, *The Ovary of Eve*, p. 22.

78: "The Sumerians said it came from bones": Jacquart and Thomasset, *Sexuality and Medicine in the Middle Ages*, p. 53; Giulia Sissa, "Subtle Bodies," *Fragments for a History of the Human Body*, Part Three, ed., Michael Feher with Ramona Naddaff and Nadia Tazi (New York: Zone, 1989), pp. 132–57; Françoise Héritier-Augé, "Semen and Blood: Some Ancient Theories Concerning Their Genesis and Relationship," *Fragments for a History of the Human Body*, Part Three, pp. 158–75.

79: Drawings of homunculi: Pinto-Correia, *The Ovary of Eve*, pp. 101, 212, 231.

82: On castrati: J. S. Jenkins, "The Voice of the Castrato," *Lancet* 351 (1998): 1877–84; Meyer M. Melicow and Stanford Pulrang, "Castrati Choir and Opera Singers," *Urology* 3 (1974): 663–70; Angus Heriot, *The Castrati in Opera* (London: Secker & Warburg, 1956); John Rosselli, "The Castrati as a Professional Group and a Social Phenomenon, 1550–1850," *Acta Musicologica* 60 (1988): 143–79; Brian P. Setchell, "Introduction," *Male Reproduction* (New York: Van Nostrand Reinhold, 1984), pp. 1–8; Taylor, *Castration*, pp. 214–15.

86: A number of excellent articles and books deal with Tissot and the resulting masturbation phobia in Europe. They include: Robert H. MacDonald, "The Frightful Consequences of Onanism," *Journal of the History of Ideas* 28 (1967): 423–31; E. H. Hare, "Masturbatory Insanity," *Journal of Mental Science* 108 (1962): 1–25; Ludmilla Jordanova, "The Popularization of Medicine: Tissot on Onanism," *Textual Practice* 1 (1987): 68–79; H. Tristram Engelhardt Jr., "The Disease of Masturbation," *Bulletin of the History of Medicine* 48 (1974): 234–48; Rene A. Spitz, "Authority and Masturbation," *The Psychoanalytic Quarterly* 21 (1952): 490–527; Peter L. Allen, *The Wages of Sin* (Chicago: University of Chicago Press, 2000).

87: On Rousseau, Diderot, and Tissot: Vernon A. Rosario II, "Phantastical Pollutions," *Solitary Pleasures,* eds., Paula Bennett and Vernon A. Rosario II (New York: Routledge, 1995), pp. 101–32; Vernon A. Rosario II, *The Erotic Imagination* (London: Oxford University Press, 1997), pp. 13–43.

89: "This (at first) shallow incision": Rosario, *The Erotic Imagination,* p. 31.

90n: "Galien's activities did not die": Richard D. Kenney, "Adolescent Males Who Insert Genitourinary Foreign Bodies," *Urology* 32 (1988): 127–29.

91: On American masturbation mania: G. J. Barker-Benfield, "The Spermatic Economy," *Feminist Studies* 1 (1972): 45–74; John S. Haller Jr. and Robin M. Haller, *The Physician and Sexuality in Victorian America* (Urbana, Ill.: University of Illinois Press, 1974); John D'Emilio and Estelle B. Freedman, *Intimate Matters* (New York: Harper & Row, 1988).

91: "'What's the matter?' asked Gautier": Quoted by Haller and Haller, *The Physician and Sexuality in Victorian America,* pp. 219–20.

92: Circumcision as an anti-masturbation treatment: David L. Gollaher, "From Ritual to Science," *Journal of Social History* 28 (1994): 5–36.

94: Dr. Bostwick's medical treatment and the journal of his patient: Christopher Looby, "The Roots of the Orchis, the Iuli of Chestnuts: the Odor of Male Solitude," in Bennett and Rosario, *Solitary Pleasures,* pp. 212–20.

95: "In vain we scan": R. N. Barr, M.D., *Ohio Medical and Surgical Journal* 7 (1855): 174–75.

96: "Caesar, in his *Commentaries,* said": Mark Twain, "Some Thoughts on the Science of Onanism," *Mark Twain: Collected Tales, Sketches, Speeches & Essays* (New York: The Library of America, 1992), pp. 722–24; Arthur Wrobel, "Mark Twain Baits the Masters," *Journal of Popular Culture* 15 (1982): 53–59.

97: "It was our business to squeeze these lumps": Herman Melville, *Moby-Dick, or The Whale* (New York: Random House, 1930), pp. 600–601.

98: "Would that I could keep squeezing that sperm": Melville, *Moby-Dick,* pp. 601–2.

99: The passages from Whitman's "Song of Myself" and "Spontaneous Me" are from *Walt Whitman: Complete Poetry and Collected Prose* (New York: The Library of America, 1982).

99: Whitman's synonyms for penis: Gary Schmidgall, *Walt Whitman: A Gay Life* (New York: Dutton, 1997).

99: "America's greatest 'spermatic poet'": Harold Aspiz, "Walt Whitman: The Spermatic Imagination," *American Literature* 56, (1984):

379–95. Also helpful on the phallic/spermatic nature of Whitman's work is Michael Moon, *Disseminating Whitman* (Cambridge, Mass.: Harvard University Press, 1991).

100: "It is as if the beasts spoke"; and Whitman's "disgusting Priapism": Schmidgall, *Walt Whitman*, p. 81.

101: "My verse strains its every nerve": Schmidgall, *Walt Whitman*, p. 77.

101: "The chief of an asylum": Haller and Haller, *The Physician and Sexuality in Victorian America*, p. 203.

102: Dr. Marshall's castration cure: J. H. Marshall, "Insanity Cured by Castration," *Medical & Surgical Reporter* 13 (1865): 363–64. A similar case history is presented in R. D. Potts, "Castration for Masturbation, with Report of a Case," *Texas Medical Practitioner* 11 (1898): 8–9.

## Chapter III

103: Macrophallic travel quotes from Jobson and Ogilby: Winthrop D. Jordan, *White Over Black* (Chapel Hill, N.C.: University of North Carolina Press, 1969), pp. 34–35.

104: "Richard Burton, who personally measured": William Lee Howard, "The Negro as a Distinct Ethnic Factor in Civilization," *Medicine* 9 (1903): 423–26. Also, J. A. Rogers, *Sex and Race*, vol. III (St. Petersburg, Fla.: Helga M. Rogers, 1972), p. 147.

104: "It was among the Sudanese": Allen Edwardes and R. E. L. Masters, *The Cradle of Erotica* (New York: Julian Press, 1963), p. 55.

104: "One of his predecessors": Jordan, *White Over Black*, p. 35.

104: "And entering in a river, we see": Jordan, *White Over Black*, p. 4.

105: "That the PENIS of an African": Charles White, *An Account of the Regular Gradation in Man and in Different Animals and Vegetables; and from the Former to the Latter* (London: C. Dilly, 1799), p. 61.

105: "It is said that": Johann Friedrich Blumenbach, *On the Natural Varieties of Mankind* (New York: Bergman Publishers, 1969), p. 249.

106: "'Every peculiarity of the body'": John S. Haller Jr., *Outcasts from Evolution* (Urbana, Ill.: University of Illinois Press, 1971), p. 4.

106: "I am apt to suspect": David Hume, quoted in Richard H. Popkin, "The Philosophical Basis of Eighteenth-Century Racism," *Racism in the Eighteenth Century*, ed., Harold E. Pagliaro (Cleveland: Case Western Reserve University Press, 1973), p. 245.

107: "It was thought extreme temperatures": J. W. Johnson, "Of Differing Ages and Climes," *Journal of the History of Ideas* 21 (1960): 465–80. Also, William B. Cohen, *The French Encounter with Africans* (Bloomington, Ind.: Indiana University Press, 1980), pp. 1–3.; Katherine George, "The Civilized West Looks at Primitive Africa: 1400–1800," *Isis* 49 (1958): 62–72.

107: "Galen's ten traits": David Brion Davis, *Slavery and Human Progress* (New York: Oxford University Press, 1984), p. 42.

108: "Quite a number of women": James Cleugh, *A History of Oriental Orgies* (New York: Crown, 1966), pp. 23–63; Bernard Braxton, *Women, Sex, and Race* (Washington, D.C.: Verta Press, 1973), p. 61.

108: "But there is no denying": John Clarke, "Hypersexual Black Men in Augustan Baths," *Sexuality in Ancient Art*, ed., Natalie Boymel Kampen (New York: Cambridge University Press, 1996), pp. 184–98; and Katherine M. Dunbabin, "*Baiarum Grata Voluptas:* Pleasures and Dangers of the Baths," *Papers of the British School at Rome* 57 (1989): 33–43.

108: "According to Pliny the Elder": Braxton, *Women, Sex, and Race*, p. 63.

108: "The fact that the macrophallic black": Lloyd A. Thompson, *Romans and Blacks* (Norman, Okla.: University of Oklahoma Press, 1989), p. 107.

109: "The sons of Noah who went forth": May and Metzger, eds., *The Oxford Annotated Bible with the Apocrypha*, pp. 11–12.

110: "And since you have disabled me": Robert Graves and Raphael Patai, *Hebrew Myths: The Book of Genesis* (Garden City, N.Y.: Doubleday, 1963), p. 121. Other writers who have written with insight on this passage include Joseph R. Washington Jr., *Anti-Blackness in English Religion, 1500–1800* (New York: Edwin Mellen Press, 1984); Benjamin Braude, "The Sons of Noah and the Construction of Ethnic and Geographical Identities in the Medieval and Early Modern Periods," *The William and Mary Quarterly* 54 (1997): 103–42; Edith R. Sanders, "The Hamitic Hypothesis," *Journal of African History* 10 (1969): 521–32; David M. Goldenberg, "The Curse of Ham: A Case of Rabbinic Racism," *Struggles in the Promised Land,* eds., Jack Salzman and Cornel West (New York: Oxford University Press, 1997), pp. 21–51; John Skinner, *A Critical and Exegetical Commentary on Genesis* (New York: Charles Scribner's Sons, 1925); Ephraim Isaac, "Genesis, Judaism and the 'Sons of Ham,'" *Slavery and Abolition* 1 (1980): 3–17.

111: "Scripture testifieth": Richard Jobson, *The Golden Trade* (London: Printed by Nicholas Okes, 1623), p. 66.

112: "I do not think that": Edward Long, *The History of Jamaica, or General Survey of the Ancient and Modern State of that Island,* vol. II (London: Frank Cass & Co., 1975; reprint of 1774 edition), p. 364; Robyn Wiegman, *American Anatomies* (Durham, N.C.: Duke University Press, 1995), p. 57; Philip D. Curtin, *The Image of Africa* (Madison, Wis.: University of Wisconsin Press, 1964), pp. 43–45.

112: "What do the Scriptures mean": Josiah Priest, *Slavery, as it relates to the Negro, or African race, Examined in the Light of Circumstances, History and the Holy Scriptures* (Albany, N.Y.: C. Van Benthuysen, 1843), p. 181, reprinted as *Bible Defense of Slavery* (Glasgow, Ky.: W. S. Brown, 1853).

113: "Priest, who also believed": Josiah Priest, *American Antiquities, and Discoveries in the West; being an exhibition of evidence that an ancient population of partially civilized nations, differing entirely from the present Indians, peopled America centuries before its discovery by Columbus* (Albany, N.Y.: Hoffman & White, 1834). More on Priest: George M. Fredrickson, *The Black Image in the White Mind* (Middletown, Conn.: Wesleyan University Press, 1987), p. 276.

113: "Since that despicable act": Priest, *Slavery, as it relates to the Negro*, p. 150.

113: "This made Negroes": John David Smith, ed., *The Biblical and "Scientific" Defense of Slavery: Religion and "The Negro Problem,"* Part II (New York: Garland Publishing, 1993), p. xxv; Forrest G. Wood, *The Arrogance of Faith* (New York: Knopf, 1990), pp. 105, 240.

113: "Eve's seducer in Paradise": Charles Carroll, *The Negro a Beast* (St. Louis: American Book and Bible House, 1900); Carroll, *The Tempter of Eve* (St. Louis: Adamic Publishing Company, 1902); Wood, *The Arrogance of Faith*, pp. 240–41; Fredrickson, *The Black Image in the White Mind*, p. 277.

114: "Few Europeans objected": Fredrickson, *The Black Image in the White Mind*; Jordan, *White Over Black*; Washington, *Anti-Blackness in English Religion*; Curtin, *The Image of Africa*; St. Clair Drake, *Black Folk Here and There*, vol. 2 (Los Angeles: Center for Afro-American Studies, University of California, Los Angeles, 1990); Alexander Burchart, *The Anatomy of Power* (London: Zed Books, 1998).

114: "My mother bore me in the southern wild": William Blake, quoted in Curtin, *The Image of Africa*, p. 50.

114: "When Lady Alice Kyteler": Norman Cohn, *Europe's Inner Demons* (London: Sussex University Press, 1975), pp. 198–200.

115: "Those crucial bits": Cohen, *The French Encounter with Africans*, p. 11.

115: "White did not believe": White, *An Account of the Regular Gradation in Man*, pp. 41–85.

116: "In 1607": Jordan, *White Over Black*, p. 29.

116: "In *Daemonologie*": Jordan, *White Over Black*, p. 30.

117: "The sexual union of apes and Negroes": Jordan, *White Over Black*, p. 238.

118: "I am suprized this does not hurt": Jordan, *White Over Black*, p. 159.

118: "Itanoko lacked 'pudicity'"; and Selico "penetrating" the harem: John Saillant, "The Black Body Erotic and the Republican Body Politic, 1790–1820," *Journal of the History of Sexuality* 5 (1995): 403–28.

119: "That a repected": Eric Lott, *Love and Theft* (New York: Oxford University Press, 1993), p. 121.

119: "I am informed": Quoted in Rogers, *Sex and Race*, vol. III, p. 148.

120: "Jack Johnson's padded": Susan Bordo, *The Male Body* (New York: Farrar, Straus & Giroux, 1999), p. 76.

120: "An editorial titled": Unsigned, "Genital Peculiarities of the Negro," *Atlanta Journal-Record of Medicine* 4 (1903): 842–44.

120: "Howard used the size of the Negro's penis": William Lee Howard, "The Negro as a Distinct Ethnic Factor in Civilization," *Medicine* 9 (1903): 423–26. For more on Howard and other medical racists: I. A. Newby, *Jim Crow's Defense* (Baton Rouge, La.: Louisiana State University Press, 1965); John S. Haller Jr., *Outcasts from Evolution*.

121: "Many years ago"; and "Shufeldt also claimed to observe": R. W. Shufeldt, *The Negro* (Boston: R. G. Badger, 1907), pp. 34–38.

122: "So much has been written": W. Montague Cobb, "Physical Anthropology of the American Negro," *American Journal of Physical Anthropology* 29 (1942): 113–224.

123: "Dr. Schonfeld measured": Lieutenant William A. Schonfeld, "Primary and Secondary Sexual Characteristics: A Study of Their Development in Males from Birth Through Maturity, with Biometric Study of Penis and Testes," *American Journal of Diseases of Children* 65 (1943): 535–49.

123: "The same glaring omission": Robert Latou Dickinson, *Human Sex Anatomy*, second edition (Baltimore: Williams & Wilkins Company, 1949).

123: "Frantz Fanon cited two studies": Frantz Fanon, *Black Skin, White Masks* (New York: Grove Press, 1967), p. 170.

123: "From self-administered measurements": Paul H. Gebhard and Alan B. Johnson, *The Kinsey Data* (Philadelphia: W. B. Saunders, 1979), tables 69–73, pp. 116–20; quoted in J. Philippe Rushton and Anthony F. Bogaert, "Race Differences in Sexual Behavior," *Journal of Research in Personality* 21 (1987): 529–51.

123: "The longer and thicker the organ": Rushton and Bogaert, "Race Differences in Sexual Behavior."

124: "Medical researcher Richard Edwards": Richard Edwards, "The Definitive Penis Size Survey Results," sixth edition, from Internet.

124: "*Hercule* . . . was endowed with a member": Marquis de Sade, *The 120 Days of Sodom and Other Writings* (New York: Grove Press, 1987), pp. 231–32.

125: "Like basketball": McLean Greaves, "The Penis Thing: Measuring Up," *Essence* 27 (Nov. 1996): 90–91.

126: "One of the great mysteries"; and "The black brother with a white chick": Cited in Charles Herbert Stember, *Sexual Racism* (New York: Elsevier, 1976), pp. 110–11.

126: "New York neurologist George M. Beard": George M. Beard, *American Nervousness* (New York: G. P. Putnam, 1881); George M. Beard, *Sexual Neurasthenia*, ed., A. D. Rockwell (New York: Treat, 1884).

127: "Beard believed": Kevin J. Mumford, "Lost Manhood Found: Male Sexual Impotence and Victorian Culture in the United States," *Journal of the History of Sexuality* 3 (1992): 33–57; Darwin on races: John David Smith, ed., *The Biblical and "Scientific" Defense of Slavery:* Part II, p. xxvii.

127: "This consideration, published in 1893": Hunter McGuire and G. Frank Lydston, "Sexual Crimes Among the Southern Negroes—Scientifically Considered," *Virginia Medical Monthly* 20 (1893): 105–25.

128: "According to Frank Shay": Frank Shay, *Judge Lynch, His First Hundred Years* (New York: Ives Washburn, 1938), p. 8.

129: "These images": Jacquelyn Dowd Hall, "The Mind That Burns In Each Body," *Powers of Desire,* eds., Ann Snitow, Christine Stansell, and Sharon Thompson (New York: Monthly Review Press, 1983), p. 335.

129: "When white vigilantes": Allen W. Trelease, *White Terror* (Baton Rouge, La.: Louisiana State University, 1971), p. 324.

129: "Another black accused": C. Vann Woodward, "Dangerous Liaisons," *New York Review of Books*, Feb. 19, 1998, p. 16, review of Martha Hodes, *White Women, Black Men* (New Haven, Conn.: Yale University Press, 1997).

129: For more on historical, literary, and psychoanalytic background of lynchings: Trudier Harris, *Exorcising Blackness* (Bloomington, Ind.: Indiana University Press, 1984); Joel Williamson, *The Crucible of Race* (New York: Oxford University Press, 1984); Joel Williamson, "Wounds Not Scars: Lynching, the National Conscience, and the American Historian," *The Journal of American History,* March 1997, pp. 1221–53; Joel Kovel, *White Racism* (New York: Pantheon, 1970); Paul Hoch, *White Hero, Black Beast* (London: Pluto Press, 1979); Coramae Richey Mann and Lance H. Selva, "The Sexualization of Racism," *Western Journal of Black Studies* 3 (1979): 168–77; Phyllis R. Klotman, "Tearing a Hole in History," *Black American Literature Forum* 19 (1985): 55–63; Louis Jolyon West, "The Psychobiology of Racial Violence," *Archives of General Psychiatry* 16 (1967): 645–51; Trelease, *White Terror*.

129: "It is a disguised form of worship": Calvin C. Hernton, *Sex and Racism in America* (New York: Grove Press, 1965), p. 115.

129: "On The Birth of a Nation": Michael Rogin, "The Sword Became a Flashing Vision: D. W. Griffith's *The Birth of a Nation*," *Representations* 9 (1985): 150–94; John Hope Franklin, "*Birth of a Nation*—Propa-

ganda as History," *Massachusetts Review* 20 (1979): 417–34; Donald
Bogle, *Toms, Coons, Mulattoes, Mammies, and Bucks* (New York: Continuum, 1994); Peter Noble, *The Negro in Films* (New York: Arno Press, 1970).

130: "It is like writing history with lightning": Rogin, "The Sword Became a Flashing Vision," p. 151.

131: "I was a member of the Klan, sir": Franklin, "*Birth of a Nation*—Propaganda as History," p. 425.

131: More on Faulkner and blacks and/or lynching: Harold Bloom, *William Faulkner's Light in August* (New York: Chelsea House, 1988); John B. Vickery and Olga W. Vickery, *Light in August and the Critical Spectrum* (Belmont, Cal.: Wadsworth Publishing, 1971).

132: "When the others reached the kitchen": William Faulkner, *Light in August* (New York: Harrison Smith & Robert Haas, 1932), p. 439.

132: "When the mob": John B. Cullen, *Old Times in the Faulkner Country* (Chapel Hill, N.C.: University of North Carolina Press, 1961), pp. 91–92.

133: Historical and literary background for Baldwin's "Going to Meet the Man": Peter Bruck, *The Black American Short Story in the 20th Century* (Amsterdam: B. R. Gruner, 1977); Trudier Harris, *Exorcising Blackness*.

133: "[Jesse] turned his head": James Baldwin, *Going to Meet the Man* (New York: Laurel, 1988), p. 216.

134: "In 1932 a black laborer": James R. McGovern, *Anatomy of a Lynching* (Baton Rouge, La.: Louisiana State University Press, 1992).

135: "They cut off his penis": McGovern, *Anatomy of a Lynching*, p. 80.

135: "From my standpoint as a black American": Quoted in "Anatomy of a Debacle," *Newsweek,* Oct. 21, 1991, p. 26.

136: More on Hill-Thomas hearings: Emma Coleman Jordan, "The Power of False Racial Memory and the Metaphor of Lynching," *Race, Gender and Power in America,* eds., Anita Faye Hill and Emma Coleman Jordan (New York: Oxford University Press, 1995), pp. 37–55; Anna Deveare Smith, "The Most Riveting Television," *Race, Gender and Power in America,* pp. 248–70; Jane Mayer and Jill Abramson, *Strange Justice* (Boston: Houghton Mifflin, 1994); Toni Morrison, ed., *Race-ing Justice, En-gendering Power* (New York, Pantheon, 1992).

137: "Hill testified": Anita Miller, ed., *The Complete Transcripts of the Clarence Thomas–Anita Hill Hearings* (Chicago: Academy Chicago Publishers, 1994), pp. 33–35.

138: "There was a moment": Smith, "The Most Riveting Television," pp. 264–65.

138: "Any charge that he bragged": Miller, *The Complete Transcripts*, p. 156.

138: "Language 'about the sex organs of black men'": Miller, *The Complete Transcripts*, p. 160.

139: "When Senator Hatch left": Mayer and Abramson, *Strange Justice*, p. 300.

139: On Robert Mapplethorpe and Milton Moore: Patricia Morrisroe, *Mapplethorpe: A Biography* (New York: Random House, 1995); Jack Fritscher, *Mapplethorpe: Assault with a Deadly Camera* (Mamaroneck, N.Y.: Hastings House, 1994); Robert Mapplethorpe, *Black Book* (New York: St. Martin's Press, 1986); Arthur C. Danto, *Playing with the Edge* (Berkeley, Cal.: University of California Press, 1996); Germano Celant, "Robert Mapplethorpe: Man in Polyester Suit," *Artforum*, Sept. 1993, pp. 155, 204–6; David Marriott, "Bordering On: The Black Penis," *Textual Practice* 10 (1996): 9–28; Kobena Mercer, "Reading Racial Fetishism: The Photographs of Robert Mapplethorpe," *Fetishism as Cultural Discourse*, eds., Emily Apter and William Pietz (Ithaca, N.Y.: Cornell University Press, 1993), pp. 307–39; Kobena Mercer, "Just Looking for Trouble: Robert Mapplethorpe and Fantasies of Race," *Sex Exposed*, eds., Lynne Segal and Mary McIntosh (London: Virago Press, 1992), pp. 92–111.

142: "An erection on Rodin's *Thinker*": Fanon, *Black Skin, White Masks*, p. 165.

142: "But not on a black man": Fanon, *Black Skin, White Masks*, p. 170.

143: On Saartjie Baartmann, the "Hottentot Venus," and her autopsy: Londa Schiebinger, *Nature's Body* (Boston: Beacon Press, 1993); Sander L. Gilman, *Sexuality*; Robyn Wiegman, *American Anatomies* (Durham, N.C.: Duke University Press, 1995); Siobhan Somerville, "Scientific Racism and the Emergence of the Homosexual Body," *Journal of the History of Sexuality* 5 (1994): 243–66.

144: "According to Edey": Morrisroe, *Mapplethorpe*, p. 234.

146: "Now you know": Morrisroe, *Mapplethorpe*, p. 249.

146: "We never had a real relationship": Morrisroe, *Mapplethorpe*, p. 261.

## Chapter IV

149: "His most animated 'hysterics'": Thomas T. Lewis, "French Influences on the Thought of Sigmund Freud," *Proceedings of the Tenth Annual Meeting of the Western Society for French History* (Lawrence, Kans.: University Press of Kansas, 1984), John F. Sweets, ed., pp. 449–60.

149: "My attention was siezed": Sigmund Freud, "On the History of the Psycho-Analytic Movement," *Standard Edition of the Complete Psycho-*

logical *Works of Sigmund Freud* (hereafter known as *SE*), trans., James Strachey et al., vol. XIV, p. 15. Charcot's quote was originally given in French by Freud. I have translated *"la chose génitale"* as "genital matter," rather than "a question of the genitals," as was done in the original text.

149: On Freud's use of cocaine: Ernst L. Freud, ed., *Letters of Sigmund Freud* (New York: Basic Books, 1960), Letter 92, to Martha Bernays, pp. 193–97.

150: "In such a case, Chrobak warned": Freud, "On the History," pp. 14–15. I have taken the liberty of translating *"dosim repetatur!"* into "repeated dose."

150: "No twentieth-century writer": Harold Bloom, "Freud: The Greatest Modern Writer," *New York Times Book Review,* March 26, 1986, pp. 1, 26–27.

150: "With his bedrock concepts": Freud, "Analysis Terminable and Interminable," in *SE* XXII, quoted by Jay Geller, in "The Godfather of Psychoanalysis," *Journal of the American Academy of Religion,* June 1999, p. 359.

151: "In doing this, he became": Cynthia Ozick, "The Buried Life," *New Yorker,* Oct. 2, 2000, p. 117.

151: "Psychoanalysis 'proclaims the breakthrough'": Quoted by L. J. Rather, "Disraeli, Freud, and Conspiracy Theories," *Journal of the History of Ideas* 47 (1986): 111–31.

151: "This is what happens": Freud, "On the History," *SE* XIV, p. 22.

152: "Freud's father made the identical threat": Marianne Krull, *Freud and His Father* (New York, W. W. Norton, 1986), pp. 142–43.

154: Freud on creation and consequences of penis envy: "Some Psychical Consequences of the Anatomical Distinction Between the Sexes," *SE* XIX; "Female Sexuality," *SE* XXI; "The Taboo of Virginity," *SE* XI; "The Disposition to Obsessional Neurosis," *SE* XII; "Femininity," *SE* XXII.

155: "The real consequence": Karen Horney, "The Dread of Woman," *International Journal of Psycho-Analysis* 13 (1932): 348–60.

156: "Among the core concepts": Stephen Kern, "The Prehistory of Freud's Theory of Castration Anxiety," *The Psychoanalytic Review* 62 (1975): 309–14; Kern, "Freud and the Discovery of Childhood Sexuality," *History of Childhood Quarterly* 1 (1973): 117–41.

156: "Sometimes a cigar": The phrase is attributed to Freud, though its origin is uncertain. Many historians have dealt with Freud's smoking, among them: Peter Gay, *Freud: A Life for Our Time* (New York: Anchor, 1989); and Patrick J. Mahony, "Freud's World of Work," in *Freud: Conflict and Culture,* ed., Michael S. Roth (New York: Knopf, 1998).

158: "In Imperial Rome": William Johnson, "The Myth of Jewish Male Menses," *Journal of Medical History* 24 (1998): 273–95.

158: "In Augustine's *Tractatus adversus Judaeos*": Quoted in Taylor, *Castration*, p. 164.

158: "Another Father of the Church": Peter Stanford, *The Devil: A Biography* (London: Heinemann, 1996), p. 122.

159: "First you must make a sacrifice to Satan": Joshua Trachtenberg, *The Devil and the Jews* (New York: Harper Torchbooks, 1943), p. 213; John F. Benton, ed., *Self and Society in Medieval France: The Memoirs of Abbot Guibert of Nogent* (New York: Harper Torchbooks, 1970), pp. 114–15.

159: "It was even believed": Johnson, "The Myth of Jewish Male Menses," p. 293.

159: "Hartmann Schedel's *Nuremberg Chronicles*": Gollaher, *Circumcision*, p. 39.

160: "That circumcision was often equated": James Shapiro, *Shakespeare and the Jews* (New York: Columbia University Press, 1996), p. 114.

160: "When mighty Roast Pork": Quoted by Roy S. Wolper, "Circumcision as Polemic in the Jew Bill of 1753," *Eighteenth Century Life* 7 (1982): 25–36.

160: "As soon as the glans is uncovered": Montaigne, *Complete Works*, trans., Donald Frame (Stanford, Cal.: Stanford University Press, 1994), pp. 945–46; Montaigne's Jewish ancestry: Montaigne, *Complete Works*, p. vii.

161: On Kafka's journal: Sander L. Gilman, *Freud, Race, and Gender* (Princeton, N.J.: Princeton University Press, 1993), p. 68. On Thomas Mann: Gilman, "Jews and Mental Illness," *Journal of the History of the Behavioral Sciences* 20 (1984): 150–59.

162: "Morton had mated a chestnut mare": Richard W. Burkhardt Jr., "Closing the Door on Lord Morton's Mare," *Studies in the History of Biology* 3 (1979): 1–21; Marvin Carlson, "Ibsen, Strindberg, and Telegony," *Publications of the Modern Language Association* 100 (1985): 774–82.

162: "Jews with massive syphilis-spreading erections": Frank Kingdon, "Race and Sex," *The Encyclopedia of Sexual Behavior*, vol. 2, Albert Ellis and Albert Abarbanel, eds. (New York: Hawthorn Books, 1964), p. 899.

162: Sander L. Gilman's "universalization" theme is presented in many of his fascinating books. Among them: *The Jew's Body* (New York: Routledge, 1991); *Freud, Race, and Gender;* and *The Case of Sigmund Freud* (Baltimore: Johns Hopkins University Press, 1993).

163: Many authors have described Fliess's bizarre theories. Three of the best summaries can be found in Frank Sulloway, *Freud, Biologist of the Mind* (Cambridge, Mass.: Harvard University Press, 1992); Walter A. Stewart, *Psychoanalysis: The First Ten Years, 1888–1898* (London: George Allen & Unwin, 1969); and Ernst Kris, "Wilhelm Fliess's Scientific Interests," *The Origins of Psycho-Analysis,* Marie Bonaparte, Anna Freud, and Ernst Kris, eds., (New York: Basic Books, 1954), pp. 3–13.

164: "Freud was merely": Gay, *Freud*, p. 89.

165: "Breuer abandoned this technique": Stewart, *Psychoanalysis: The First Ten Years*, p. 9.

165: All quotations from the Freud-Fliess letters are from Jeffrey Moussaieff Masson, ed., *The Complete Letters of Sigmund Freud to Wilhelm Fliess, 1887–1904* (Cambridge, Mass.: Belknap Press, 1985); and/or *The Origins of Psychoanalysis*.

166: "The first session with Freud began": David J. Lynn, "Sigmund Freud's Psychoanalysis of Albert Hirst," *Bulletin of the History of Medicine* 71 (1997): 69–93.

166: "It is not our business": Gay, *Freud*, p. 121.

167: "Rapist-murderer Vincenz Verzeni": Richard von Kraft-Ebing, *Psychopathia Sexualis*, trans., Franklin S. Klaf (New York: Stein & Day, 1965), pp. 63–65.

168: "Like the archaeologist": Ernest S. Wolf, "Saxa Loquuntur," *The Psychoanalytic Study of the Child* 26 (1971): 535–54.

169: On Freud's self-analysis: Ernest Jones, *The Life and Work of Sigmund Freud* (New York: Basic Books, 1953–57), vol. 1, pp. 318–27; Didier Anzieu, *Freud's Self-Analysis* (Madison, Conn.: International Universities Press, 1986); Masson, *The Complete Letters of Sigmund Freud*; Stewart, *Psychoanalysis: The First Ten Years*; Alexander Grinstein, *On Sigmund Freud's Dreams* (Detroit: Wayne State University Press, 1968); Gay, *Freud: A Life for Our Time*, pp. 87–103; Michael Roth, ed., *Freud: Conflict and Culture*; John M. Hartke, "Castrating the Phallic Mother," *The Psychoanalytic Review* 81 (1994): 641–57; Arnold Bernstein, "Freud and Oedipus," *The Psychoanalytic Review* 63 (1976): 393–407; Lawrence Birken, "From Seduction Theory to Oedipus Complex," *New German Critique* 43 (1988): 83–96; Roy C. Calogeras and Fabian X. Schupper, "Origins and Early Formulations of the Oedipus Complex," *Journal of the American Psychoanalytic Association* 20 (1972): 751–75.

169: "His self-analysis, one analyst has written": Harry Trosman, "Freud's Self-Analysis and His Scientific Ideas," in *Freud, the Fusion of Science and Humanism*, John E. Gedo and George H. Pollock, eds., (New York: International Universities Press, 1976).

172: "The tremendous advance": Simone de Beauvoir, quoted in Lynne Segal, *Straight Sex* (Berkeley, Cal.: University of California Press, 1994), p. 117.

174-: All quotes from the Dora case: Freud, "Fragment of an Analysis of a Case of Hysteria," *SE* VII.

174: "Freud's impressive skill": Steven Marcus, *Freud and the Culture of Psychoanalysis* (Boston: George Allen & Unwin, 1984), pp. 42–86.

174: Many other writers have weighed in on the Dora case. Among the most insightful: Hanna Decker, *Freud, Dora, and Vienna 1900* (New York: The Free Press, 1991); Charles Bernheimer and Claire Kahane, eds., *In Dora's Case* (New York: Columbia University Press, 1985); Patrick Mahony, *Freud's Dora* (New Haven, Conn.: Yale University Press, 1996); Mark Kanzer and Jules Glenn, eds., *Freud and His Patients* (New York: Aronson, 1980); Sander L. Gilman, "Freud's Dora," *Freud Under Analysis*, ed., Todd Dufresne (Northvale, N.J.: Aronson, 1997), pp. 3–21; Alan Krohn and Janis Krohn, "The Nature of the Oedipus Complex in the Dora Case," *Journal of the American Psychoanalytic Association* 30 (1982): 555–78.

175: "If they have not read": Gay, *Freud*, pp. 3–4.

178: "(Freud often seems bored)": Even Freud's supporters have had difficulty defending his summary of the case or his callous treatment of his analysand. Janet Malcolm compared Dora's experience to surgery "performed on a fully awake patient." Analyst Erik Erikson called the case "one of the great psychotherapeutic disasters; . . . Dora had been traumatized, and Freud retraumatized her." Freud's critics are even less charitable. For Frederick Crews, the case is "the story of how Freud attempted to bully a virginal and potentially suicidal teenager into agreeing that she yearned to kiss [her] cigar-breathed therapist, suck her father's penis, and have sex with her father's mistress."

181: "Even a psycho-analyst may": Freud, "Analysis of a Phobia in a Five-Year-Old Boy," *SE* X, p. 6. All quotes from the Little Hans case are also from this source. Other authors who have written on the Little Hans case include Peter L. Rudnytsky, "Does the Professor Talk to God?" *Psychoanalysis and History* 1 (1999): 175–93; John Munder Ross, "The Riddle of Little Hans," in *Fathers and Their Families*, Stanley H. Cath, Alan Gurwitt, and Linda Gunsberg, eds. (Hillsdale, N.J.: The Analytic Press, 1989), pp. 267–83; Martin A. Silverman, "A Fresh Look at the Case of Little Hans," in *Freud and His Patients*, pp. 95–120; Erich Fromm, "The Oedipus Complex: Comments on the Case of Little Hans," in Fromm, *The Crisis of Psychoanalysis* (New York: Henry Holt, 1991), pp. 90–100.

182: "When Louis XIII was one year old": Philippe Ariès, *Centuries of Childhood* (New York: Knopf, 1962), pp. 100–103.

182: Freud and Grafs; goings-on at Wednesday-night group: Gay, *Freud*, pp. 174–77; Max Graf, "Reminiscences of Professor Sigmund Freud," *Psychoanalytic Quarterly* 11 (1942): 465–76.

183: "I never got a finer insight": Gay, *Freud*, pp. 255–56.

183: "Actually, Little Hans had been aiding": James Strachey, "Editor's Note" to "Analysis of a Phobia," *SE* X, pp. 3–4.

186: Several writers have addressed Freud's views on circumcision. Among them: Daniel Boyarin, "What Does a Jew Want?" *The Psychoanalysis of*

*Race,* ed., Christopher Lane (New York: Columbia University Press, 1998), pp. 211–40; Jay Geller, "A Paleontological View of Freud's Study of Religion," *Modern Judaism* 13 (1993): 49–70; Sander L. Gilman, "The Indelibility of Circumcision," *Koroth* 9 (1991): 806–17; Gilman, *The Jew's Body;* Gilman, *Freud, Race, and Gender;* Gilman, *The Case of Sigmund Freud.*

188: "So Freud started": Edwin R. Wallace IV, *Freud and Anthropology* (New York: International Universities Press, 1983).

189: On Freud and Darwin: Lucille B. Ritvo, "The Impact of Darwin on Freud," *Psychoanalytic Quarterly* 43 (1974): 177–91; Ritvo, "Darwin as the Source of Freud's Neo-Lamarckism," *Journal of the American Psychoanalytic Association* 13 (1965): 499–517; Alex Comfort, *Darwin and the Naked Lady* (London: Routledge & Kegan Paul, 1961), pp. 23–42.

190: All quotes from *Totem and Taboo* are from *SE* XIII. Many historians and analysts have written valuable essays on *Totem* and Freud the historian. Among them: Philip Rieff, "The Meaning of History and Religion in Freud's Thought," *Journal of Religion* 31 (1951): 114–31; Philip Pomper, *The Structure of Mind in History* (New York: Columbia University Press, 1985); Bruce Mazlish, *The Riddle of History* (New York: Harper & Row, 1966); Michael S. Roth, *Psycho-Analysis as History* (Ithaca, N.Y.: Cornell University Press, 1887); Robin Ostow, "Autobiographical Sources of Freud's Social Theory," *The Psychiatric Journal of the University of Ottawa* 2 (1977): 169–80.

192: "Clinton's real crime": Jonathan Lear's essay appeared in *The New Republic,* Sept. 28, 1998.

193: Freud on "psychical impotence": "On the Universal Tendency to Debasement in the Sphere of Love," *SE* XI, pp. 184–85.

195: "I myself have made": Gay, *Freud,* p. 163.

195: Peter J. Swales's self-published articles include "Freud, Cocaine, and Sexual Chemistry" (1983); "Freud, Martha Bernays, and the Language of Flowers" (1983); and "Freud, Fliess, and Fratricide" (1982).

## Chapter V

199: "Spread semen on your face": Quoted in David Plotz, "Helen Gurley Brown: The *Cosmo* Girl at 78," *Slate.com,* April 7, 2000.

202: "The anarchist and free-love advocate": Mari Jo Buhle, *Feminism and Its Discontents* (Cambridge, Mass.: Harvard University Press, 1998), pp. 1–2.

202: Freud on vaginal orgasms: Cynthia Jayne, "The Dark Continent Revisited," *Psychoanalysis and Contemporary Thought* (1980): 545–68.

203: "In analysis, Lorand wrote": Sandor Lorand, "Contribution to the Problem of Vaginal Orgasm," *International Journal of Psychoanalysis* 20 (1939): 432–38.

203: On Helene Deutsch: Buhle, *Feminism and Its Discontents,* pp. 80–81; Lisa Appignanese and John Forrester, *Freud's Women* (London: Weidenfeld & Nicholson, 1992), pp. 307–28; Susan Brownmiller, *Against Our Will* (New York: Simon & Schuster, 1975), p. 317; Helene Deutsch, *The Psychology of Women* (New York: Grune & Stratton, 1944–45).

204: "Then, in 1927": Angus McLaren, *Twentieth-Century Sexuality: A History,* (Oxford: Blackwell, 1999), p. 110; Appignanese and Forester, *Freud's Women,* pp. 329–48; Princess Marie Bonaparte, *Female Sexuality* (New York: International Universities Press, 1953), p. 87.

205: On National Women's Liberation Conference: Susan Brownmiller, *In Our Time* (New York: Dial Press, 1999), pp. 52–55.

205: "The Myth of the Vaginal Orgasm": The full text is published in Anne Koedt, Ellen Levine, and Anita Rapone, eds., *Radical Feminism* (New York: Quadrangle, 1973), pp. 198–207.

206: "The coronation took place": Christopher Lehmann-Haupt, "He and She—1," "He and She—2," *New York Times,* Aug. 5–6, 1970.

207: "'My cock,' Armand once said": Quoted by Kate Millett, *Sexual Politics* (New York: Doubleday, 1970), p. 20. Other Genet quotes: pp. 18–19.

207: "Her college-girl snobbery": "The Time of Her Time," reprinted in Norman Mailer, *The Time of Our Time* (New York: Random House, 1998), pp. 318–42.

208: Millett on Mailer: Millet, *Sexual Politics,* pp. 325–30.

209: *Time* cover story on feminism, Millett: "Who's Come a Long Way, Baby?" *Time,* Aug. 31, 1970.

210: "A 1974 piece": Edward Kelly, "A New Image for the Naughty Dildo," *Journal of Popular Culture* 7 (1974): 804–9.

211: "According to one biography": D. T. Max, "The Twilight of the Old Goats," *Salon.com,* May 16, 1997.

211: "Dr. B. Lyman Stewart blamed": "Is Impotence Increasing?" *Medical Aspects of Human Sexuality,* Oct. 1971, pp. 34–44.

211: Millett outing herself: Brownmiller, *In Our Time,* pp. 148–51.

212: "We're expected to serve men their orgasms": Shere Hite, *Women as Revolutionary Agents of Change: The Hite Reports and Beyond* (Madison, Wis.: University of Wisconsin Press, 1994).

212n: "In 1992 British scientists placed": Alan J. Riley, W. R. Lees, and Elizabeth J. Riley, "An Ultrasound Study of Human Coitus," *Sex Matters* (1982): 29–32.

213: Brownmiller on Hite: Brownmiller, *In Our Time,* p. 253.

214: "Man's discovery": Brownmiller, *Against Our Will*, pp. 14–15.

215: "Reported rapes in the United States": Lynne Segal, *Slow Motion* (New Brunswick, N.J.: Rutgers University Press, 1990), p. 237.

216: "The studio audience": Brownmiller, *In Our Time*, pp. 251–52.

219: "In the 1963 study": Detlev W. Ploog and Paul D. MacLean, "Display of Penile Erection in the Squirrel Monkey," *Animal Behavior* 11 (1963): 32.

219: "Jane Goodall saw": Nicholas Wade, "Battle of the Sexes Is Discerned in Sperm," *New York Times*, Feb. 22, 2000, p. F-1.

220: "The Greeks certainly did": Otto F. Ehrentheil, "A Case of Premature Ejaculation in Greek Mythology," *Journal of Sex Research* 10 (1974): 128–31.

220n: "Humans, with an average time of four minutes": Jared Diamond, quoted in Deborah Blum, *Sex on the Brain* (New York: Viking, 1997), p. 4; other animals: Lawrence K. Hong, "Survival of the Fastest," *Journal of Sex Research* 20 (1984): 109–22.

221: "In several controversial papers": Randy Thornhill and Craig T. Palmer, *A Natural History of Rape* (Cambridge, Mass.: The MIT Press, 2000), pp. 238–40.

222: "The result, Thornhill says": Quoted by Blum, *Sex on the Brain*, p. 225.

222: "Pornography is the theory": Brownmiller, *In Our Time*, p. 319.

222: "A 1971 piece in the *New York Times*"; and Arthur Knight on *Deep Throat*: David Allyn, *Make Love, Not War* (Boston: Little, Brown, 2000), pp. 233–34.

223: "*Snuff* was a crass attempt": Linda Williams, "Power, Pleasure, and Perversion," *Representations* 27 (1989): 37–65.

224: "In 1983 Dworkin and MacKinnon": Catharine A. MacKinnon and Andrea Dworkin, *In Harm's Way* (Cambridge, Mass.: Harvard University Press, 1997); Brownmiller, *In Our Time*, pp. 316–25.

226: "I suggest to you": Andrea Dworkin, *Our Blood* (New York: Harper & Row, 1976), p. 13.

226: "The penis conquers and possesses": Andrea Dworkin, *Letters from a War Zone* (New York: E. P. Dutton, 1989), p. 241.

226: "Violence is male; the male is the penis": Andrea Dworkin, *Pornography* (New York: Putnam, 1981), p. 55.

226: "In some pornography and in some sex murders": Andrea Dworkin, *Intercourse* (New York: Free Press Paperbacks, 1997), pp. 187–89.

228: "'I remember many things,' Bobbitt told the jury": Quoted in Linda Pershing, "His Wife Seized His Prize and Cut It to Size," *NWSA Journal* 8, via Internet.

229: Dworkin as prostitute: Interview with Dworkin, April 2000; and Andrea Dworkin, "My Life as a Writer," in *Life and Death* (New York: The Free Press, 1997), pp. 3–38.

230: "I believe it is more true than untrue": Interview with Dworkin, April 2000.

231: "The availability of an objective method": K. Freund, F. Sedlacek, and K. Knob, "A Simple Transducer for Mechanical Plethysmography of the Male Genital," *Journal of the Experimental Analysis of Behavior* 8 (1965): 169–70.

231: "A stiff prick has no conscience": Mailer, *The Time of Our Time*, p. 337.

232: "As a psychiatrist told": Karen Freeman, "Kurt Freund Dies at 82; Studied Deviant Sexual Arousal," *New York Times*, Oct. 27, 1996, p. 42.

232n: Bancroft's plethysmograph: J. Bancroft, H. G. Jones, and B. R. Pullan, "A Simple Transducer for Measuring Penile Erection with Comments on Its Use in the Treatment of Sexual Disorders," *Behavioral Research and Therapy* 4 (1966): 239–41.

233: "In one controversial study": N. Malamuth, M. Heim, and S. Feshback, "Sexual Responsiveness of College Students to Rape Depictions," *Journal of Personality and Social Psychology* 38 (1990): 399–408.

234: "In a 1993 case": Stephen J. Adler, "Debatable Device," *Wall Street Journal*, Feb. 3, 1993.

235: "Professor Rice used genetic engineering": William R. Rice, "Sexually Antagonistic Male Adaptation Triggered by Experimental Arrest of Female Evolution," *Nature* 381 (1996): 232–34; Blum, *Sex on the Brain*, pp. 221–23.

236: "During copulation, the female biting midge": Tim Halliday, *Sexual Strategy* (Chicago: University of Chicago Press, 1982), p. 104.

236: "Fascinating answers to those questions": R. Robin Baker and Mark A. Bellis, *Human Sperm Competition* (London: Chapman & Hall, 1995).

237: "The idea of sperm competition was conceived by": G. A. Parker, "Sperm Competition and Its Evolutionary Consequences in Insects," *Biological Reviews of the Cambridge Philosophical Society* 45 (1970): 525–67.

237n: "The organization reported": Tamar Lewin, "In Genetic Testing for Paternity, Law Often Lags Behind Science," *New York Times*, March 11, 2001, via Internet.

241: "An important part of scientific progress": T. R. Birkhead, "Sex, Science and Sensationalism," *Trends in Ecology and Evolution* 12 (1997): 121–22.

241: "For Sullivan, testosterone shots were": Andrew Sullivan, "Why Men Are Different," *New York Times Magazine*, April 2, 2000.

242: "Adolf Hitler was a huge believer": Gail Vines, *Raging Hormones* (London: Virago, 1993), p. 78.

242: "The first step in this process": Gerhard J. Newerla, "The History of the Discovery and Isolation of the Male Hormone," *New England Journal of Medicine.* 228 (1943): 39–46; John H. Hoberman and Charles E. Yesalis, "The History of Synthetic Testosterone," *Scientific American,* Feb. 1995, pp. 76–81; David France, "Testosterone: The Rogue Hormone Is Getting a Makeover," *New York Times,* Feb. 17, 1999.

243: "A typical man has about sixty millionths": Blum, *Sex on the Brain,* p. 166; and "begins a steady decline after age forty": Blum, *Sex on the Brain,* p. 160.

243: "In a series of odd, gender-bending experiments": Anne Fausto-Sterling, *Sexing the Body* (New York: Basic Books, 2000), pp. 158–63.

245: "Men exercise seemingly absolute power": Ben Greenstein, *The Fragile Male* (Secaucus, N.J.: Carol Publishing Group, 1994), pp. 27–28.

245: "Professor Dabbs is to testosterone": David France, "Testosterone: The Rogue Hormone Is Getting a Makeover," *New York Times,* Feb. 17, 1999.

246: "Dabbs and his coauthors found": James M. Dabbs Jr. et al., "Testosterone, Crime and Misbehavior Among 692 Male Prison Inmates," *Journal of Personal and Individual Differences* 18 (1995): 627–33.

246: "Robert Prentky received a grant": Robert Prentky, "The Neurochemistry and Neuroendocrinology of Sexual Aggression," in D. P. Farrington and J. Gunn, eds., *Aggression and Dangerousness* (New York: John Wiley & Sons, 1985), pp. 7–55.

246: "Days after Sullivan's piece": Judith Shulevitz, "Rethinking Testosterone," *Slate.com,* April 7, 2000.

247: "Suppose you note a correlation": Robert M. Sapolsky, *The Trouble with Testosterone* (New York: Scribner, 1997), pp. 151–52.

248: On human embryology: Blum, *Sex on the Brain.*

248n: "Reimer's story is told": John Colapinto, *As Nature Made Him* (New York: HarperCollins, 2000).

249: On female hyenas: Robert Pool, *Eve's Rib* (New York: Crown, 1994).

250: "His name was Charles Brown-Sequard": Charles Brown-Sequard, "The Effects Produced on Man by Subcutaneous Injections of a Liquid Obtained from the Testicles of Animals," *Lancet,* July 20, 1889, pp. 105–6, reprinted in Carol Sue Carter, *Hormones and Sexual Behavior* (Stroudsburg, Pa.: Dowden, Hutchinson & Ross, 1974), pp. 21–24; D. Schultheiss, J. Denil, and U. Jonas, "Rejuvenation in the Early 20th Century," *Andrologia* 29 (1997): 351–55; John R. Herman, "Rejuvenation: Brown-Sequard to Brinkley," *New York State Journal of Medicine,* Nov. 1982, pp.

1731–39; Merriley Borell, "Brown-Sequard's Organotherapy and Its Appearance in America at the End of the Nineteenth Century," *Bulletin of the History of Medicine* 50 (1976): 309–20.

## Chapter VI

253: "The person on stage": This story—obviously a favorite among urologists—was told to me by two who were there, Dr. Irwin Goldstein and Dr. Arnold Melman.

253: "In 1964 Brindley invented": Phone interview with Dr. Brindley, Jan. 1997; also, interview with Dr. Arnold Melman, Nov. 1996.

256: Financial success of Viagra: Numbers are from Pfizer, Inc., and Jack Hitt, "The Second Sexual Revolution," *New York Times Magazine,* Feb. 20, 2000.

257: "Ancient medical texts reveal": Lisa Manniche, *Sexual Life in Ancient Egypt* (London: Kegan Paul International, 1997), p. 103; Mels F. Van Driel, Harry B. M. van de Wiel, and Hans J. A. Mensink, "Some Mythologic, Religious, and Cultural Aspects of Impotence Before the Present Modern Era," *International Journal of Impotence Research* 6 (1994): 163–69.

258: "The sixteenth-century anatomist": William F. Gee, "A History of Surgical Treatment of Impotence," *Urology* 5 (1975): 401–5; W. D. Dunsmuir, "History of Erectile Dysfunction," in Culley C. Carson III, Roger S. Kirby, and Irwin Goldstein, *Textbook of Erectile Dysfunction* (Oxford: Isis Medical Media, 1999), pp. 3–13.

258: "That there is a neurological aspect": Interview with Dr. Arthur L. Burnett, Aug. 1998.

259: "Case XIII. A mechanic": Samuel W. Gross, *A Practical Treatise on Impotence, Sterility and Allied Disorders of the Male Sexual Organs* (Philadelphia: Henry C. Lea's Son & Co., 1881), p. 34.

260: "In Emperor Nero's day" and *Salmon's Dispensatory* recipes: David Hamilton, *The Monkey Gland Affair* (London: Chatto & Windus, 1986), pp. 14–15. On Johannes Mesue the Elder: Gerhard J. Newerla, "The History of the Discovery and Isolation of the Male Hormone," *New England Journal of Medicine* 228 (1943): 39–47.

261: "An understanding of the true androgenic role": Brian P. Setchel, "The Testis and Tissue Transplantation," *Journal of Reproductive Biology* 18 (1990): 1–8.

262: "The patient seen by": Thomas N. Haviland and Lawrence Charles Parrish, "An Early 20th-Century Testicular Transplant," *Transactions and Studies of the College of Physicians of Philadelphia* 38 (1970–71): 231–34.

262: "A man, aged 38": Victor D. Lespinasse, "Transplantation of the Testicle," *Chicago Medical Reporter* 36 (1914): 401–3.

264: "SECRET OPERATION": *New York Times,* June 18, 1922.

264: "Under the spreading chestnut tree": John A. Grant, "Victor Darwin Lespinasse: A Biographical Sketch," *Neurosurgery* 39 (1996): 1232–33.

264: "In 1920 Dr. G. Frank Lydston": "America Was First in Gland Grafting," *New York Times,* Aug. 15, 1920, p. 8.

264: "Case 9—": G. Frank Lydston, "Further Observations on Sex Gland Implementation," *Journal of the American Medical Association* 72 (1919): 396–98.

265n: "Stanley's concern": Maria Russo, "Psycho Factories," *Salon.com,* March 29, 2001.

266: "In all [but one case]": Serge Voronoff, *Rejuvenation by Grafting* (New York: Adelphia Company, 1925), p. 9.

266: "Grafting can only be done": Hamilton, *The Monkey Gland Affair,* p. 57.

266: "Voronoff had become interested": Voronoff, *Rejuvenation by Grafting,* pp. 13–14.

267: "Retterer mistook the invading cells": Hamilton, *The Monkey Gland Affair,* p. 22.

268: "One shutter of the trapdoor": Voronoff, *Rejuvenation by Grafting,* pp. 57–58.

268: Gland-grafting operation described: Voronoff, *Rejuvenation by Grafting,* pp. 57–67.

269: "Professor, please": Quoted in D. Schultheiss, J. Denil, and U. Jonas, "Rejuvenation in the Early 20th Century," p. 352.

269: "Thorek declined to describe": Hamilton, *The Monkey Gland Affair,* p. 62.

270: "He acquires a gorilla,": Hamilton, *The Monkey Gland Affair,* p. 68.

270: "In this case": Schultheiss et al., "Rejuvenation in the Early 20th Century," p. 353.

270: "He charged $5,000": Hamilton, *The Monkey Gland Affair,* p. 62.

270: "Julian Huxley did": Hamilton, *The Monkey Gland Affair,* p. 29.

271: "Testicle grafts, Velu wrote": Hamilton, *The Monkey Gland Affair,* pp. 125–28.

271: "There are conflicting reports": Robert M. Youngson and Ian Schott, *Medical Blunders* (New York: New York University Press, 1996), pp. 164–70; Patrick McGrady, *The Youth Doctors* (New York: Ace, 1968), pp. 43–59.

272: "In *Impotence in the Male*": Wilhelm Stekel, *Impotence in the Male* (New York: Liveright, 1927), pp. 39–72. Stekel's impotence cured by Freud: Gay, *Freud,* p. 173.

272: "Freud came to despise Stekel": Gay, *Freud*, pp. 213–14.

272: "Mr. X., thirty years of age": B. S. Talmey, "Impotence in the Male," *New York Medical Journal* 116 (1922): 499–505.

274: "The patient thinks": Karl A. Menninger, "Impotence and Frigidity from the Standpoint of Psychoanalysis," *Journal of Urology* 34 (1935): 166–83.

274: "Dr. Huhner responded": Max Huhner, "Masturbation and Impotence from a Urologic Standpoint," *Journal of Urology* 36 (1936): 770–85.

276: "The use of new weapons": A. P. Frumkin, "Reconstruction of the Male Genitalia," *American Review of Soviet Medicine* 2 (1944): 14–21. As Frumkin points out, another surgeon, N. A. Bogoras, tried this operation before him, publishing his results in a German medical journal in 1936.

277: "British zoologist": W. R. Bett, "The Os Penis in Man and Beast," *Proceedings of the Royal Society of Medicine* 44 (1951): 433–34.

277: On the history of penile implants: Arnold Melman, "Development of Contemporary Surgical Management for Erectile Impotence," *Sexuality and Disability* 1 (1978): 272–81; Peter N. Bretan Jr., "History of the Prosthetic Treatment of Impotence," *Urologic Clinics of North America* 16 (1989): 1–5; William F. Gee, "A History of Surgical Treatment of Impotence," *Urology* 5 (1975): 401–5; F. Brantley Scott, William E. Bradley, and Gerald W. Timm, "Management of Erectile Impotence: Use of Implantable Inflatable Prosthesis," *Urology* 2 (1973): 80–82; Michael P. Small, Hernan M. Carrion, and Julian A. Gordon, "Small-Carrion Penile Prosthesis: New Implant for Management of Impotence," *Urology* 5 (1975): 479–86; Willard E. Goodwin and William Wallace Scott, "Phalloplasty," *Journal of Urology* 68 (1952): 903–8.

278: "Pearman defined ED": Robert O. Pearman, "Treatment of Organic Impotence by Implantation of a Penile Prosthesis," *Journal of Urology* 97 (1967): 716–19.

278: "Anyone doing implants": Interview with Dr. Arnold Melman, Nov. 1996.

279: "Finally we had a therapy": Interview with Dr. Irwin Goldstein, Sept. 1996.

279: "Michal asserted that ED": Vaclav Michal, "Arterial Disease as a Cause of Impotence," *Clinics in Endocrinology and Metabolism* 11 (1982): 725–48.

280: "While doing a routine surgical procedure": R. Virag, "Intercavernous Injection of Papaverine for Erectile Failure," *Lancet*, Oct. 23, 1982, p. 938.

280: "Later Brindley would publish": G. S. Brindley, "Pilot Experiments on the Actions of Drugs Injected into the Human Corpus Cavernosum Penis," *British Journal of Pharmacology* 87 (1986): 495–500.

281: "Papaverine, which Virag used": Gorm Wagner and Helen Singer Kaplan, *The New Injection Treatment for Impotence* (New York: Brunner/Mazel, 1993), pp. 53–54.

281: "We learned that": Interview with Dr. Arthur L. Burnett, Aug. 1998.

281: "In 1900 a German anatomist": Herbert F. Newman and Jane D. Northrup, "Mechanism of Human Penile Erection," *Urology* 17 (1981): 399–408.

282: "It doesn't take much blood": Interview with Dr. James H. Barada, Aug. 1988.

283: "Brindley said that he suffered": Interview with Dr. Giles Brindley, Nov. 1996.

284: "One patient was having an affair": Interview with Dr. Irwin Goldstein, Sept. 1996.

285: Details of DICC test: Irwin Goldstein and Larry Rothstein, *The Potent Male* (Los Angeles: The Body Press, 1990), p. 102.

286: Mortality problems with Viagra: Food and Drug Administration, "Summary of Reports of Death in Viagra Users," Nov. 3, 1998; FDA website: www.fda.gov. Also, Kenneth Paul Rosenberg, "Sildenafil," *Journal of Sex and Marital Therapy* 25 (1999): 271–79. And, World Health Organization, Alert No. 76: "Sildenafil (Viagra)—Revised Labeling: Serious Adverse Effects," Dec. 3, 1998.

287: "Manufacturers pay urologists": Interview with Dr. Arnold Melman, Nov. 1996.

287: "It isn't possible": Cited in David Stipp and Robert Whitaker, "The Selling of Impotence," *Fortune,* March 16, 1998, pp. 115–24.

288: "They read my skepticism": Stipp and Whitaker, "The Selling of Impotence."

288: "Several weeks after Viagra's approval": Jane E. Brody, "Sour Note in the Viagra Symphony," *New York Times,* May 19, 1998.

288: "There are striking similarities": Michael T. Risher, "Controlling Viagra-Mania," *New York Times,* July 20, 1998.

289: "Feminisn has emasculated the American male": *Time,* May 4, 1998, p. 56.

290: How Viagra was discovered, how it works: Jonathan Jarow, Robert A. Kloner, Ann M. Holmes, *Viagra* (New York: M. Evans & Co., 1998), pp. 75–81, 86–87; Irwin Goldstein, Tom F. Lue et al., "Oral Sildenafil in the Treatment of Erectile Dysfunction," *New England Journal of Medicine* 338 (1998): 1397–1404; Robert D. Utiger, "A Pill for Impotence: An Editorial," *NEJM* 338: 1458–59.

291: "The beauty of Viagra": Interview with Dr. Andrew R. McCullough, Sept. 1999.

291: On the physiology of erections and the penis: Abraham Morgentaler, *The Male Body* (New York: Fireside, 1993); Carson, Kirby, Goldstein, *Textbook of Erectile Dysfunction*; John J. Mulcahey, *Diagnosis and Management of Male Sexual Dysfunction* (New York: Igaku-Shoin, 1997); Goldstein and Rothstein, *The Potent Male*; Robert L. Rowan, *Men and Their Sex* (New York: Avocation Publishers, 1979). On role of nitric oxide: Jacob Rajfer, William J. Aronson et al., "Nitric Oxide as a Mediator of Relaxation of the Corpus Cavernosum in Response to Nonadrenergic, Noncholinergic Neurotransmission," *NEJM* 326 (1992): 90–94.

291: "Sensitivity is measured": Interview with Dr. Claire C. Yang, Sept. 1999.

292: "It is about as thick": Interview with Dr. Ajay Nehra, Sept. 1999.

294: An excellent place to read Leonore Tiefer's views on this and other subjects is her book, *Sex Is Not a Natural Act & Other Essays* (Boulder, Colo.: Westview Press, 1995).

294: "Erections are presented": Interview with Leonore Tiefer, Aug. 1996.

295: On the Massachusetts Male Aging Study: Henry A. Feldman, Irwin Goldstein, John B. McKinlay et al., "Impotence and Its Medical and Psychosocial Correlates: Results of the Massachusetts Male Aging Study," *Journal of Urology* 151 (1994): 54–56; Stipp and Whitaker, "*The Selling of Impotence.*"

296: "I brought her in because": Interview with Dr. Arnold Melman, Nov. 1996.

297: "There is a difference": Interview with Dr. James H. Barada, Aug. 1998.

297: "We've gone from one myth": Interview with Dr. John Bancroft, Sept. 2000.

298: "Pfizer pumped more than $50 million": Amy Barrett, "How Viagra Revived After a Cold Shower," *Business Week,* Aug. 28, 2000, p. 220; Robert Langreth, "Hard Sell," *Forbes,* Sept. 29, 2000, via Internet.

299: "Pfizer hired Arthur Caplan, a bioethicist": Daniel McGinn, "Viagra's Hothouse," *Newsweek,* Dec. 21, 1998, pp. 44–46.

300: Zonagen's problems with Vasomax: Stipp and Whitaker, "*The Selling of Impotence.*"

300: "According to neuroscientist Simon LeVay": Simon LeVay, "Uprima's Secret History," *Nerve.com,* May 2, 2000.

301: TAP's problems with Uprima: "TAP Retracts Application for its Impotence Drug," *Wall Street Journal,* July 3, 2000; other new drugs in pipeline: Alexandra Alger, "Viagra Falls," *Forbes,* Sept. 29, 2000, via Internet.

302: "In the 1980s": Interview with Dr. Irwin Goldstein, Sept. 1996.

302: Bancroft's article: John Bancroft, "Man and His Penis—A Relationship Under Threat?" *Journal of Psychology & Human Sexuality* 2 (1989): 7–32.

303: "The identical conclusion was reached by Gay Talese": Gay Talese, *Thy Neighbor's Wife* (New York: Dell, 1980), p. 135.

304: "I don't mean the patient goes insane": Interview with Dr. J. François Eid, July 1996.

305: On "sexual script": John H. Gagnon and William Simon, *Sexual Conduct: The Social Sources of Human Sexuality* (Chicago: Aldine, 1973), pp. 19–26; Alan E. Gross, "The Male Role and Heterosexual Behavior," *Journal of Social Issues* 34 (1978): 87–107.

# INDEX